Pursuing
the American Dream

PURSUING
THE AMERICAN DREAM

*White Ethnics and
the New Populism*

RICHARD KRICKUS

Indiana University Press   Bloomington   London

Indiana University Press edition published 1976 by arrangement with Doubleday, Inc. Also available in paperback from Doubleday, Anchor books.

Published in Canada by Fitzhenry & Whiteside Limited, Don Mills, Ontario

Manufactured in the United States of America

LIBRARY OF CONGRESS CATALOGING IN PUBLICATION DATA

Krickus, Richard.
Pursuing the American dream.
Includes bibliographical references and index.
1. Minorities—United States. 2. United States—Politics and government—20th century. 3. Labor and laboring classes—United States. 4. United States—Race question. I. Title.
E184.A1K79   301.5'92'0973
ISBN 0-253-34727-0
Library of Congress Catalog Card Number: 75-21336

1   2   3   4   5   80   79   78   77   76

For Anthony Krickus and Louise Reitz Krickus

Contents

Preface

This book first occurred to me in the late 1960s when I encountered appalling ignorance about working Americans among academics, politicians, government bureaucrats, Capitol Hill aides, and radical community activists. Although the latter were among the best informed members of our society, their perception of auto workers, truck drivers, secretaries, and stock clerks was marked by half-truths, stereotypes, and misinformation. It held that the white worker was economically secure, an unrepentant racist, and the principal source of support for American military adventures abroad. When I protested that most working people were not entrenched in the middle class, that it was unfair to single them out as racists or war hawks, and that much of their discontent was attributable to the left's failure to pay attention to their problems, I encountered disbelief, indifference, and at times hostility. It was apparent that many middle-class liberal reformers and radical commentators who took such a dim view of working people were engaging in the same kind of half-truths and stereotypes that caused some of their less affluent countrymen to perceive them as dangerous "radicals," dope-smoking "hippies," or liberal "elitists." But, unlike Mr. and Mrs. Middle America, they possessed the educational background, experience, and information to overcome such a parochial view. Their distorted perception of the common man and their resistance to ideas or facts that challenged that bias stemmed from looking at the world through the prism of the affluent middle class. Living and working in large cities, on college campuses, or in cosmo-

politan oases in the country's hinterland, very few of them had
resided among working people. Their knowledge on this score
was derived from books, magazines, television programs, and
movies produced by people like themselves. In contrast to the
1930s, when left-wing intellectuals depicted the workingman
as a "proletarian hero," in the 1960s he was often portrayed as
a "hard hat," a code word used to describe workers who reputedly were the mass base for reaction. Even left-wing commentators who understood that it was politically suicidal to ignore
the white worker often thought of him in these terms. They
also were inclined to speak of his problems from an economic
perspective. Noneconomic values and beliefs that gave purpose
to his life were generally ignored, denigrated, or assessed
almost exclusively from the perspective of social class. The
prevailing ignorance among liberal political reformers toward
industrial workers in the North and the propensity to ignore
ethnic related values, ties, and experiences in particular contributed to the fragmentation of the Democratic coalition in
the aftermath of the Second World War. This schism was not
new, for the failure of reformers and democratic radicals to
come to grips with the ethnic factor explains why there has
not been closer cooperation between them and working-class
ethnics throughout the twentieth century.

A product of a working-class community in Newark, New
Jersey, I knew that most of the problems my neighbors had to
cope with were common to working people throughout the
United States, but that there was an ethnic dimension to their
lives which accounted for their looking at the world differently
than working people elsewhere in the country. A majority of
them were descendants of Eastern and Southern European immigrants who emigrated over a span of forty years, from the
1880s to the 1920s. Historians called these members of the
second wave of European immigration the New Immigrants,
differentiating them from the Old Immigrants—the largely
Protestant Northern and Western Europeans who settled in
the New World prior to the 1880s. Today the New Immigrants' descendants have become known as the white ethnics. There is a dispute as to whether or not the Irish and the
Jews belong to this group; I believe they do. Those who arrived
at the turn of the century, along with the Poles, Greeks, Ital-

ians, and Lithuanians, became part of an immigrant working-class subculture which developed in the urban North. It was a fusion of values, beliefs, and social patterns transplanted from the Old World and those existing in the new one. It was shaped by the trauma of immigration and nativistic discrimination, working-class status, and ethnic family, religious, and communal life developing in an urban setting. Urban political machines and the labor movement were especially important, for they both molded and, in turn, were influenced by the white ethnic subculture. Despite religious, ethnic, and cultural differences, as well as changing circumstances, millions of white ethnics perceive the world through the prism of this subculture today.

The question of precisely how many white ethnics there are is a difficult one to answer. The Census Bureau records the nationality of foreign-born Americans and their children, but not third- or fourth-generation Italians, Poles, Lithuanians, etc. There are approximately 55 million Catholics, Jews, and Eastern Orthodox Americans, however, and a large majority of them come under the rubric of white ethnic—except most Hispanics, the post-World War II displaced persons, and those Irish, Jewish, and other non-Protestants whose ancestors arrived prior to the 1880s. Some scholars like Robert Wood estimate that there are 40 million white ethnics; that figure may not be precise but it is in the ball park.

Because my neighbors in the Clinton Hill section of Newark and my co-workers at American Can and Ballantine Brewery were part of a white ethnic subculture, they related to the political universe somewhat differently than steelworkers in Alabama or brewery workers in Colorado. Their compulsion to prove they were "good Americans" testified to the prejudice their forefathers had suffered when they first arrived in this country, and their political habits were shaped by their ethnic and religious affiliations as well as by their income, education, and social status. Older members of the white ethnic community gave FDR most of their votes because he made appeals to them both as working people and as members of ethnic minority groups. Since the New Deal the white ethnics have given the bulk of their votes to the Democratic Party and have supported legislation vital to the welfare of needy Americans. So without their support the progressive coalition necessary to come to grips with our nation's most pressing problems—racism, poverty among plenty, and the concentration of economic and political power—is doomed to failure.

As a consequence of articles I wrote to this effect, I met Geno Baroni, a Catholic priest who had been active in the Civil Rights Movement and the war on poverty. The son of an Italian-born coal miner, he had grown up in Johnstown, Pennsylvania, and felt, as I did, that it was unjust to ignore the people who lived in our old neighborhoods and politically foolish to view them as "part of the problem" rather than "part of the solution." For the next year and a half, we toured white working-class neighborhoods in the East and Midwest. As expected we found that although most of the residents were earning more than they had in the past, few were free of economic concerns. Many complained about conditions at work, the treatment they received at the hands of the boss, inadequate protection against sickness and old age, and some about the indifference of their unions. Frequently their children attended inferior schools and some of the older residents of their communities lived on the edge of economic destitution. Just about everybody of all ages in the inner-city neighborhoods was fearful of street crime and worried about racial turmoil, and many expressed displeasure with the Catholic church and with their politicians for not paying attention to them. Government agencies conducting a range of urban programs either ignored their neighborhoods or adopted policies which, along with business practices, were destroying them. Yet such residential communities were, and are, vital to the restoration of urban America and to bulldoze them makes as much sense as the remark of the American company commander in Vietnam who said that "we had to destroy the village to save it." To make matters even worse, since most of the urban programs were designed to meet the needs of black urbanites and not needy whites, they were exacerbating racial tensions dividing the people who were the principal victims of urban "benign neglect."

Our first priority was to sensitize middle-class urban experts, journalists, government bureaucrats, and progressive politicians to the unmet needs of residents of white working-class communities. Toward this end, we made good use of Baroni's extensive connections in Washington and inundated government agencies, the media, and politicians with pertinent information. We often collaborated with Irving Levine and Judy Herman of the American Jewish Committee and Ralph Perrotta, then of the National Urban Coalition, conducting workshops, conferences, and seminars. Paul Asciolla, Andrew Greeley, and Michael Novak contributed to the growing interest in the New Ethnicity by writing a steady stream of articles and books about the white ethnics. As a consequence of these efforts, a small coterie of about twenty people gave birth to what was called the "ethnic movement."

To speak of our activities in terms of a Movement was a gross exaggeration, but it prompted journalists, scholars, and free-lance intellectuals to produce articles about the "blue-collar ethnics" and "forgotten Americans." Furthermore, we were articulating grievances and needs that were of keen interest to millions of white ethnics and we were part of a new generation that was coming to grips with our ethnic heritage even though we perceived that legacy from a host of different and sometimes conflicting perspectives. The media's interest gave our efforts needed publicity and legitimacy. The misperception that the white ethnics were "backlashers" flocking to George Wallace's side helped us gain the attention of foundations. They eventually provided grants enabling us to organize in working-class neighborhoods in numerous Northern cities.

At long last academics have begun to explore territory uncharted by historians—the social, economic, and political evolution of the second- and third-generation descendants of the New Immigrants. This is a welcome change since our schools have been remiss in treating this vital part of American history, relevant not only to white ethnics but to every member of our society. Today it has become fashionable to write about the New Ethnicity—that is, rising ethnic self-awareness among Catholics and Jews. Television drama, movies, and novels depicting white ethnic life have begun to appear in increasing numbers. In the years ahead books about Italians, Poles, and other Catholic ethnic groups may become as popular as the Jewish novel was in the 1960s.

But despite the growing volume of information, there is a

host of questions pertaining to the white ethnics which need to be answered. This book attempts to answer many of them. It is an exploration into the origins and evolution of a white ethnic political culture. It is not a political history nor does it dwell upon the past. Nevertheless, to talk intelligently about the present and speculate with some confidence about the future, we cannot avoid touching upon a past to which most Americans are not privy.

Toward this end, the book treats the trauma of immigration and nativistic bigotry, the immigrant family and community, the plight of the immigrant worker, the role of the Catholic church, and the importance of urban political machines and unions in the white ethnics' political development. It explains why the left failed to attract immigrant workers, why the labor movement prior to the Great Depression ignored most of them, and why ethnic differences divided the industrial work force. It discusses the group-anchored white ethnic attachment to the Democratic Party and the GOP's ethnic strategy. It assesses black/white ethnic conflict and the political implications of this conflict. It treats the ethnic/cultural dimension to the regular/reformer split in the Democratic Party, culminating in a majority of white ethnic voters turning their backs on George McGovern in 1972. It explains why the private sector is as responsible for the decline of white ethnic neighborhoods as poorly designed government programs and the importance of these neighborhoods to the restoration of our declining cities. Through a discussion of machine politics and of the business unionist philosophy of the old guard in the labor movement, it shows why a political culture once functional to the immigrants no longer serves their descendants well today. It explains why we are on the brink of another era of reform and why a New Populist movement must be forged to attain the American dream of peace, prosperity, and majority rule. It concludes with an analysis of the political strategy the New Populists must adopt to reach the white ethnic electorate.

There are many people who, directly and indirectly, have contributed to the writing of this book. Among them are Steve Adubato, Jack Albertine, Geno Baroni, Don Eschelman, Vic Fingerhut, Gene Pasymowski, and Ralph Perrotta. I also wish to thank David Harrop of Doubleday for his encouragement and Mary Washington College for providing funds to defer typing costs. Most of all, my wife Mary Ann deserves special mention. She spent long hours conducting research for this book, provided incisive editorial comments, and frequently challenged the author's ideas and biases with enthusiasm and intelligence. If it were not for certain flaws in the author's character, her name would accompany his on the title page.

Pursuing
the American Dream

CHAPTER I

Introduction

A. The White Ethnics and Electoral Politics: *Since the New Deal, the Single Largest Bloc in the Electorate Openly Aligned with the Democratic Party*

On the eve of Richard Nixon's 1968 victory, Kevin Phillips, a young aide to John Mitchell, strung together voting data covering several decades and dropped a bombshell. According to his calculations, Catholic ethnic voters, displeased with the party of their parents, were moving en masse into the waiting arms of the GOP. Phillips predicted that this drift toward the right was the basis for party realignment; the last time a realignment in the American party system had occurred was in the 1930s when the coalition FDR midwifed relegated the GOP to minority party status. His superiors, though skeptical, were overjoyed by young Phillips' prediction. In 1970 there were approximately 40 million Catholic, Jewish, and Eastern Orthodox white ethnics, most of whom had loyally voted for Democratic candidates since the New Deal. They resided in a strategic bloc of Midwestern and East Coast states. By winning the electoral votes of these states plus the District of Columbia, Delaware, and West Virginia—what Scammon and Wattenberg have dubbed "Quadcali"—the Democrats could lose what was formerly the "solid South" and still nail down the Presidency. On the other hand, were the Democrats to lose favor with the ethnics—the single largest bloc in the electorate openly aligned with the Democratic Party—the results would be disastrous for them. In states like

New York, Illinois, New Jersey, and Pennsylvania, the Democrats needed white ethnic voting margins of 60, 70, and 80 per
cent to countervail the votes the Republicans customarily
gleaned from Wasp districts. The failure of Democratic candidates to secure such large white ethnic voting margins often
meant defeat.

While Phillips was sanguine about the GOP making great
gains among the Catholics, he was less optimistic about the
party's Jewish prospects, although he observed that low-income
Jews in New York were becoming more conservative in their
voting habits. In 1968 the Jews gave Hubert Humphrey 83
per cent of their votes, but soon afterward there were strong
indications in local races that Jewish discontent with liberal
Democrats was growing. Jews turned against John Lindsay in
New York and voted for Frank Rizzo in Philadelphia and
Sam Yorty in Los Angeles. Here was evidence that a significant
segment of the Jewish community had become disenchanted
with liberal candidates.

1. The Republicans' Ethnic Strategy

After World War II, many Republican old-timers refused
to acknowledge that if their party was to regain majority
status, reaching out to the Catholics—who comprised approximately one fourth of the nation's population—was a categorical imperative. Old guard Republicans who would curse FDR
on their deathbeds for opening the doors of political power to
the Catholics and Jews were unprepared to flirt with such an
obnoxious notion. But younger, pragmatic Republicans were
not; they urged the GOP to discard its Wasp image and get
out there and eat kielbaza and quaff "dago red" with the
"Polaks and Wops." These pragmatists became convinced of
the soundness of their position when General Eisenhower cut
deeply into the Catholic vote in 1952 and did even better four
years later when he received 49 per cent of the Catholic vote.
The Republicans were especially pleased that Ike won 40 per
cent of the Jewish vote in 1956 also. Good news, meanwhile,
was delivered to the GOP by social critics who proclaimed
that as more Catholics entered college, the professions, and
the corporate world, and moved out to suburbia, the

Republican Party could well expect to secure their votes. On making it into the middle class, they, like their Wasp neighbors, would embrace the party of the status quo. Living among Republicans, they would quickly adopt the conservative political attitudes of the older residents.

John F. Kennedy halted the GOP assault but Republican analysts were not disheartened; after all, it was predictable that many Catholics who had deserted Stevenson for Eisenhower would cast their ballots for one of their co-religionists. With anti-Catholicism bubbling to the surface, it would have defied human psychology for a Catholic not to respond to the bigots who made Kennedy's religion an issue. Goldwater's defeat—well, what could you expect? Barry made the mistake of stating publicly what many Republican politicians believed: that the New Deal represented a dramatic move toward the left, jeopardizing the prerogatives of those who deserved to rule by virtue of their demonstrated ability to acquire wealth. Most Americans did not perceive the welfare state in this light and they would not tolerate any candidate who talked about scrapping social security and other such welfare schemes. Richard Nixon would not make the same mistake, for he was gathering around him young men who clung neither to the ideological verities which impassioned the Goldwaterites nor to the noblesse oblige of the Eastern establishment—the Rockefellers, Lodges, et al. No, his lieutenants were recruited from the "go-go" ranks of the business world—the lean, hungry panthers who stalked the corporate jungle and ruthlessly disposed of their prey without a trace of authentic passion or principle. Like their boss, they were moral zombies whose only interest was power; they were indeed the living embodiment of the dark side of the American soul.

After being trounced by Pat Brown for the governorship of California, it looked as if Nixon's political career had ended; but his prospects brightened when disagreement over Vietnam reopened the regular/reformer schism in the Democratic Party —which the Goldwater candidacy had temporarily healed—and forced Lyndon Johnson to bow out of the 1968 race. Nixon's victory that year seemed to confirm Phillips' prognosis, and in *The Emerging Republican Majority* he made public what he had told Nixon's strategists prior to the election—the Catholic

ethnics were up for grabs. There were, he argued, two catalysts
contributing to further GOP gains among the white ethnics.
"The Negro problem . . . having become a national rather
than a local one, is the principal cause of the breakup of the
New Deal Coalition . . . Some Northern cities are nearly half
Negro, and new suburbia is turning into a bastion of white
conservatism." The growing influence of black votes in the
North "prompted civil rights measures obnoxious to the
South" and "social legislation and programs anathema to the
sons and daughters of Northern immigrants."

The second source of discord in the Democratic Party involved the appearance of an affluent, well-educated liberal elite
which had emerged during the New Deal and grown rapidly in
the postwar years. "By 1968, there was a very real Northeast-
ern Establishment centered on the profits of social and welfare spending, the knowledge industry, conglomerate cor-
poratism, dollar internationalism, and an interlocking
directorate with the like-concerned power structure of political
liberalism."[1] According to Phillips the establishment liberals
who championed various radical causes—the Black Power
Movement, the counterculture, student militancy, etc.—were
rapidly taking shape as the principal enemy of the white ethnic workingman. The growth of the Conservative Party in
New York, which had a mass base among Irish and Italian
Catholics, testified to the restiveness of these traditional Democratic voters. He predicted Catholic ethnics elsewhere would
follow the example of their compatriots in New York where
there was an ethnic dimension to the reformer/regular schism.
Jews, together with blacks, Puerto Ricans, and liberal Wasps,
were driving Catholic ethnics out of the Democratic Party.
Phillips observed that one could find more or less the same
protagonists at odds in other areas of the metropolitan North.

Having secured a beachhead in Dixie four years earlier via
his "Southern strategy," Nixon developed an "ethnic strategy"
for 1972 which he considered pivotal to his re-election.
Because most white ethnics considered themselves Democrats,
the President did not use the term New Republican Majority,
preferring instead to talk about a "new majority." The name
was not important; his re-election was. And he was not only
thinking about himself; if the white ethnics got used to voting

for a Republican Presidential candidate, they might find it easier over time to vote for Republican governors and congressmen too. The results of the 1972 election seemed to confirm Nixon's fondest expectations as well as the Democrats' worst fears—a majority of the white ethnic Catholics rejected the senator from South Dakota; here was concrete proof that a major bloc of traditional Democratic votes was moving toward the GOP. But conservative ideologues like Phillips were guarded in their optimism; Nixon had secured a larger percentage of white ethnic votes than even Eisenhower had, yet dreams of a New Republican Majority were dashed in statewide races and contests for congressional seats. White House advisers dismissed this assessment of the elections; Nixon's ability to attract white ethnic voters was proof that the GOP had good reason to be encouraged and to look expectantly toward the future. Jeb Stuart Magruder, second in command at the Committee to Re-Elect the President, told a Harvard seminar in January 1973: "I think everybody in our party realizes that we have an opportunity, not necessarily to turn the Republican Party into a majority party, but at least to turn more voters into independent voters and ticket splitters." He indicated that most people in the White House felt that "we should try to develop a broader-based effort" which would include "blue-collar workers, the Jewish constituency, the Mexican-American constituency—the groups that we did very well with last time. Some of these people have already made their initial effort at voting Republican, and we think it will be easier next time."[2] Six months later, however, the American people began to read about the true Watergate story and the Republicans' political fortunes took a turn for the worse.

The GOP cannot expect in this decade to secure white ethnic support in fielding a majority party, but most perceptive Republicans never thought this was possible—at least not in the 1970s. It was as nonsensical as New Left predictions that the two-party system was dead and the claims of the McGovernites that they would lead a new electoral coalition to victory in 1972. Even though Watergate, galloping inflation, and severe recession may jeopardize the GOP's electoral prospects in the waning years of the 1970s, many Republicans still look expectantly toward the white ethnics. They reason that the

Catholic ethnics in particular are most susceptible to GOP advances. In this connection, they continue to place great stock in Phillips' two-edged strategy based on the reformer/regular schism in the Democratic Party and black/white ethnic conflict.

The Republicans hope to compete with the Democrats for white ethnic votes where the old Democratic machines are faltering; where reform Democrats are battling the regulars; where prosperity has encouraged Catholic and Jewish voters to look kindly upon conservative candidates; or where, fearful of social change, low-income urban Catholics and Jews seek help from Republicans because such assistance is not forthcoming from the Democrats. The Republicans welcome the decline of the old machine pols and the "liberal take-over" of local party organizations, believing that a number of persons who customarily vote for regular Democrats, faced with the prospect of casting their ballots for reformers, will stay at home or vote for Republicans.

Also, few will admit it publicly, but many Republicans believe that racial conflict represents their best hope of winning white ethnic votes. The era of "long hot summers" which marked the 1960s may be a thing of the past but racial tensions have not abated. In the foreseeable future, racial conflict will be a persistent fact of life in cities where blacks and lower-middle-class whites share the same neighborhoods, work settings, or schools, and it is quite possible that busing schemes carrying inner-city ghetto students to the suburbs (or whites to the inner city) will foster racial strife in suburbia. President Ford, when asked about the busing-inspired racial conflict which wracked Boston in October 1974, was not speaking off the cuff when he answered, "The court decision in that case . . . was not the best solution to quality education in Boston. I have consistently opposed forced busing to achieve racial balance as a solution to quality education and, therefore, I respectfully disagree with the judge's order."[3] Now there are many pro-integrationists who take a dim view of busing; but Ford's statement was bound to rub salt in the raw wounds of Boston's school crisis and it would be naïve to dismiss the political implications of his remarks.

Even where racial conflict is confined to inner city, it will continue to influence race relations throughout these metropolitan areas, in some places setting the tone for entire states, and possibly determining the course of race relations in the United States itself. Via television, racial discord becomes "nationalized" whatever its source or locale. Consequently, in spite of the nation's preoccupation with the economy, conservatives still write and talk about racial conflict as the basis for recruiting white ethnic votes. In his most recent book, *Mediacracy*, Kevin Phillips states forthrightly that in the foreseeable future "race itself is likely to be a central denominator—if not an overt theme—of U.S. political division."[4]

Another facet of the GOP white ethnic strategy is to deny the Democrats total labor support—which, since the New Deal, has given the lion's share of its votes, money, and organizational expertise to Democratic candidates. (While approximately 25 per cent of the nonagricultural labor force belongs to unions, four out of every ten Polish and Italian workers are unionized.) There is an ideological fault line which divides the labor movement; exponents of business unionism—"unions are economic organizations formed to treat the work-related needs of the membership only"—occupy one side, and social unionists—"in treating rank and file demands organized labor must also mobilize power to foster change in society at large"—the other. In the past they have set aside their ideological differences and joined hands to elect—with some exceptions—Democrats. Since the New Deal the labor movement has increasingly operated as an integral part of the Democratic Party, providing it with the only real national electoral network it had. In any forecast attending the nation's political future, the labor movement must be closely scrutinized not only as an appendage of the Democratic Party but as the most powerful working-class institution in the United States. For some inexplicable reason, however, political commentators restrict their analysis to the labor vote and union involvement in electoral politics and ignore developments within the movement itself which are relevant to labor's capacity to operate effectively within the political system.

Soon after he entered the White House, Richard Nixon took steps to further divide the conservative business unionists and the progressive social unionists in the labor movement. He romanced Frank Fitzsimmons, the Teamsters' president who had filled Jimmy Hoffa's shoes after Hoffa was imprisoned, and invited powerful construction union leaders to the White House to demonstrate that he was their friend. This led eventually to the appointment of Peter Brennan, the head of New York City's muscle-bound Building Trade Council, as his Secretary of Labor. The nation's economic problems have made it more difficult for President Ford to pursue Nixon's labor strategy, but the doctrinal fissure running deep through the labor movement is equivalent to the regular/reformer struggle in the Democratic Party and the Republicans still hope that by massaging it they can deny the Democrats the full strength which a unified labor movement can bring to bear during elections.

2. The Reform Democrats and the Ethnics

The enmity of reform-minded Democrats toward the Catholic white ethnics which prompted Phillips' optimism grew in the wake of the 1968 election, when blame for Nixon's victory was placed at the door of the party's regulars and their labor allies. Supporters of Senators Kennedy, McCarthy, and McGovern claimed that Hubert Humphrey's nomination was calculated to end in disaster. In their view the selection of a man who had been discredited by his blatant support of Lyndon Johnson's disastrous war policies was an affront to all thinking Americans. The young, the black, the poor, and the liberal middle class had demonstrated their displeasure with the party's choice by providing tepid support for Humphrey or by staying away from the polls altogether. Because the old pols and labor bosses had forced an unpopular candidate on the electorate, they had no one to blame but themselves for the election's outcome.

The reformers accepted the alleged dissolution of the FDR coalition with little remorse or deep concern. On the contrary, they implied that they welcomed this development because it represented the first step toward a readjustment in the party which was pivotal to electoral victory and a reordering of national priorities. Liberal gurus like John Kenneth Galbraith criticized the geriatric labor leadership, the regulars who placed party above principle, and the Southern Democrats who used their leverage through committee chairmanships to extort federal monies for their states and districts. The "hacks and labor politicos" in the party, however, were not the only targets of the reformers; so were the low-income whites who supported them. Immediately after the 1968 election Arthur Schlesinger, Jr., stated that ". . . in a way the New Deal killed itself by success. By using affirmative government to assure social security and economic growth, it changed the despairing job seekers of the thirties into the prosperous suburbanites of the sixties." Apparently writing off the newly "affluent" Democrats, Schlesinger glanced toward the future. "The nation in the 1970s will divide not on the basis of income but education." Workers, who had energized a progressive coalition for change in the 1930s, henceforth would support the forces of the status quo. The historian, former Kennedy braintruster, and champion of George McGovern in 1972, noted ". . . it is the poor, uneducated who tend to be the most emotional and primitive champions of conservatism . . . who fear the niggers, despise the long-haired college kids, and can't understand why we don't drop a nuclear bomb on Hanoi." On the other hand, ". . . the affluent and better educated . . . tend to care about identity, reform, and progress."⁵ This contemptuous attitude toward working Americans had surfaced during the 1968 Oregon primary when Gene McCarthy commented before a university audience that Robert Kennedy was running best "among the less intelligent and less educated people in America. I don't mean to fault them for voting for him, but I think you ought to bear that in mind as you go to the polls."⁶ Though such feelings were usually couched in less offensive language, they were frequently articulated by McCarthy's supporters in private conversation.

Fred Dutton, former adviser to John and Robert Kennedy, and the influential exponent of the youth blitz in the 1972 McGovern campaign, wrote in his *Changing Sources of Power* that ". . . the strength of the (Democratic) coalition dropped very perceptibly from the high point reached in the mid-thirties to the bare but tenacious holding on by Harry Truman in 1948."⁷ After Truman the fissures in the coalition became even more visible; they receded with John Kennedy's narrow election in 1960 and all but disappeared with Johnson's victory in 1964, but reopened soon after LBJ took office.

Humphrey's defeat was just another example of the party's declining attraction to the electorate. In this connection, Dutton paid special attention to the rightward drift of the urban Catholics. This largely lower-middle-class group in 1960 ". . . rallied to JFK by a better than two to one margin, and in 1964 the ratio rose still higher in the Johnson landslide." Two years later, "with inflamed racial tensions breaking into the open, the Democratic vote in this group dropped precipitously in state after state. In California, it fell from over 70% in 1964 to barely above 50% in 1966. In Michigan, it plummeted from 75% to just over 40%." In 1968, nationwide, the Catholic electorate "divided almost evenly between the two parties as its historic tie to the Democratic Party in Presidential elections again reasserted itself to some extent." Nonetheless it "contributed significantly to the Wallace vote in the industrial northern states." According to the Harris poll:

> Wallace got over 20% of the so-called Italian vote and almost the same portion of the Slavic American vote. In New Jersey and Ohio . . . the defection to Wallace among these two blocs more than provided the margin by which Nixon beat Humphrey there. In the 1970 off-year elections, Gallup reported Catholics shifted to Republican candidates and the right.[8]

Having acknowledged this Catholic disaffection, the next logical step was to determine how they might be won back. The reformers did not take it. Until George McGovern was nominated at Miami in June 1972, few of his lieutenants gave much thought to this matter. Practicing what has been appropriately labeled the "politics of conscience," McGovern's supporters embraced issues, employed rhetoric, and adopted tactics which were an affront to the voter of modest means and education. Beguiled by the prospects of a new majority—an illusion manufactured by privileged New Politics activists in the Democratic Party—the cosmopolitan reformers ignored the discontent percolating in the white ethnic community. The complaints of Italian homeowners in Corona whose property had been condemned by the Lindsay Administration, the fears of Jewish storekeepers in Philadelphia about street crime and the frustration of Polish factory workers in Chicago that they were bearing too large a share of the tax burden—all were neatly filed in the pigeonhole labeled backlash.

During the 1950s left-wing intellectuals began to reassess the role of the working class in American society. Daniel Bell coined the term "end of ideology," proclaiming that working-class grievances, once the driving force for social change, had abated to the point where the revolutionary could no longer count on the proletariat to join him at the barricades.

Galbraith noted appropriately enough in *The Affluent Society* that there was a great discontinuity between private and public wealth in America. Americans individually were enjoying unprecedented affluence, but as a nation we were poor, as manifested in our miserly outlay for public programs. Like most liberals at that time, Galbraith devoted only a few lines to the persistence of widespread poverty in the richest society in the history of mankind and, by omission, contributed to the myth that the American worker was rapidly riding the escalator of socioeconomic mobility, thus impregnating the bulging American middle class. The workers' standard of living was rising and amenities denied them in the 1930s were becoming more readily available, but in many instances this was accounted for by wives joining the labor force and husbands working overtime and at a second job. Meanwhile, the problems that plagued them at work—hazardous conditions, dead-end jobs, etc.—serious, legitimate problems—no longer interested left-wing intellectuals; and only a handful of socialist old-timers wrote anymore about industrial democracy or the political powerlessness of ordinary Americans. The plight of working-class youngsters and senior citizens who could not depend on the strong right arm of a union to call society's attention to their problems was well hidden from view.

As a culmination of social science research conducted since the end of the Second World War, liberal academics and radical intellectuals identified a new specter—working-class authoritarianism. Seymour Martin Lipset, in *Political Man*, which was required reading for several generations of college students, "demonstrated" that the working class was the principal threat to our democratic institutions, the rule of law, and civil liberties. Lipset attributed this to the workingman's socialization, for as a child "he is likely to have been exposed to punishment, lack of love, and a general atmosphere of tension and aggression" contributing to "deep-rooted hostilities expressed by ethnic prejudices" and "political authoritarianism."[9] Political scientists henceforth provided even more devastating evidence lending support to Lipset's findings, so that by the mid-1960s it became commonplace among students of politics that the elites and not the masses were the most steadfast supporters of our democratic institutions. Traditional notions about democracy like popular sovereignty were scrapped for the new popular wisdom articulated by "pluralists" that mass participation in the political process was not a preferred condition at all; indeed, just the opposite was true. This conclusion was a logical extension of the belief that the ordinary citizen was most likely to restrict the civil liberties of political dissenters, to deny minorities equal opportunity, and to oppose those progressive elements which championed change.

The prominent historian Richard Hofstadter, meanwhile, revealed in *The Age of Reform* that the Catholic ethnics were adherents of a narrow, self-serving political ethos which clashed with the public-spirited, democratic Wasp ethos. Two Harvard professors, Edward Banfield and James Q. Wilson, published a book, *City Politics*, widely read by college students in the 1960s, which "proved" that the ethnics were "private regarding" citizens who turned their backs on public welfare programs while Wasps were "public regarding" citizens who supported such enlightened legislation.[10]

These findings strengthened the conviction of New Leftists that the white worker had become a class collaborator and they introduced a radical reformulation of the liberals' theory of working-class authoritarianism. Two of the most important figures here were Herbert Marcuse, the godfather of the New Left, and Frantz Fanon, the black psychiatrist who, writing from Algeria, established the framework for a Third World Movement. Marcusians proclaimed that the white proletariat sellout was neither unexpected nor disquieting and chided those Old Leftists who clung to the myth that the workingman represented a positive force for change in post-industrial

America. That naïve perspective did not conform with the objective conditions of an imperialist United States. It was crystal clear that the urban Catholics were the very racists, cultural yahoos, and war hawks who were steadfast supporters of the forces of reaction. The offspring of the New Deal proletariat—those Polish, Italian, and Slavic workers who had helped forge the Congress of Industrial Organizations that the "CPers" glorified in the 1930s—were now more than likely to accept Bill Buckley's view of the world.

Their antipathy toward welfare, poverty, and other progressive programs was cited as proof positive of their reactionary cast of mind. They were apologists for capitalism and the myths that nourished the liberal corporate state. Their law and order posture and indifference to first amendment rights reflected their blatant disregard for civil liberties. As the Civil Rights Movement redirected its focus from the rural South to the urban North, Movement people began to talk about "the real locus of white racism"—namely those Italian, Polish, and Hunkie neighborhoods that bordered the ghettos of the black and Puerto Rican underclass. Even the liberal Kerner Commission Report implied that outside the South the bedrock racists were white ethnics; and labor bosses in the North who refused to accept nonwhite apprentices and journeymen—they were Irish, Italian, and Polish Catholics. The police who cracked the hairy heads of students and hippies in Chicago, New York, and Philadelphia were usually Irishmen, Italians, and Poles. So too were the people who were most uptight about drugs, long hair, abortion, and other accouterments of the counterculture. The most zealous supporters of the Vietnam war came from the same neighborhoods the policemen who suppressed blacks, hippies, and students did. It was their "hard hat" neighbors with names like Murphy, Covello, and Burkowski who beat up on peace marchers in Times Square and in St. Louis in the wake of the 1970 Cambodian invasion. During the 1960s the parishioners of Cardinal Spellman, who said that he would support his country's involvement in Vietnam right or wrong, were the ones who filled the American Legion Halls and disseminated patriotic regalia and literary gore on the Fourth of July. It was their menfolk who killed and maimed the peasant masses of Southeast Asia.

The New Left's indictment of the white proletariat could
be explained in terms of a revisionist-Marxist analysis of advanced industrial society, which Lenin first wrote about in
1916. Imperialism, Lenin proclaimed, was an advanced state
of capitalism enabling the capitalists to exploit the colored
masses of the world and "buy off" the white workers of Europe
and North America. In other words twentieth-century American and West European capitalists overcame the contra-
dictions which Marx predicted would spell their doom because
they dumped their surplus goods on the peasant poor of
Africa, Asia, and Latin America and dominated the economies
of the Third World by manipulating finance capital. Workers
in the Occident enjoyed sleek automobiles and suburban
homes filled with furniture and labor-saving devices at the expense of the "colored peoples of the developing countries."

Mesmerized by the glut of goods made available to them,
they eschewed their revolutionary consciousness and eagerly
embraced the mores of capitalism and the myths of bourgeoisie democracy. This explained why George Meany and his
colleagues in the AFL-CIO were staunch supporters of Western imperialism and why the rank and file of their unions
represented the shock troops whom American capitalists were
counting on to achieve their imperialist objectives. Contrary to
the warnings of Marx, the New Left theorists, under the spell
of Frantz Fanon, proclaimed that the new source of revolution
resided in the underclass of America and the lumpenproletar-
iat of the Third World. Exponents of black separatism have
drunk deep from this ideological trough; and thus many nationalists in the black community have adorned their racial
chauvinism with a socialist gloss.

The New Left's enmity toward the white worker played
into Nixon's hands in 1968 since many liberal Democrats par-
roted the New Left line that the "working-class whites are part
of the problem." Richard Nixon skillfully manipulated the
middle American's fear of the New Left during his first term
in office and he hoped McGovern would be his opponent in
1972 precisely because many traditional Democrats associated
the senator from South Dakota with the "radical" left.

McGovern's defeat brought into relief a clash between two

conflicting political cultures. The South Dakota senator was trounced by a man few loved and many hated because McGovern was perceived by the electorate as the candidate of a cultural elite which denigrated the ordinary American's belief in hard work, love of country, and values which have been part of our society since the nation's founding. The failure of his braintrusters to properly assess the mind of middle America is a testament to the hubris corroding the critical faculties of people who believe they are the best and brightest in American life. Several months before the election, some of McGovern's advisers began to realize that their perception of the electorate had been wrenched out of focus and that the advertising men who conducted Mr. Nixon's campaign were simply better political analysts than they were, but by then it was too late. After the 1972 debacle, New Politics Democrats in the cosmopolitan centers of the United States, though hesitant, were beginning to come to grips with this unthinkable notion when the Watergate story broke, causing the McGovernites to forget about their own recent unpleasantness.

Nixon's resignation and the Ford Administration's inability to deal with our prevailing economic difficulties may have deepened the reformers' amnesia on this score. That would be a mistake because it is still uncertain who the Democrats will nominate for the Presidency in 1976. And in spite of the nation's economic troubles under two Republican administrations, the contest for the White House in 1976 is likely to be a closely fought one. Of larger importance is whether the person who takes office is prepared to fight for fundamental changes which are needed if the United States is going to come to grips with its problems, domestic and foreign.

3. The Regular Democrats and the Ethnics

The day after Richard Nixon trounced George McGovern, machine Democrats were found beaming. For although the reformers had outclassed them in bitter primary contests that year, their fears about pervasive party realignment were put to rest. By electing Democratic governors and state legislators, as well as senators and congressmen, the regulars demonstrated that their constituents had not deserted them and that they still wielded power which enemies and friends alike had to respect.

The regulars' spirits soared in the wake of the 1974 Democratic gains in Congress and in state houses across the land, for they claimed that the results had supported their centrist position. Ben Wattenberg, a senior adviser to Washington's Senator Henry Jackson and founder of the anti-New Politics Coalition for a Democratic Majority (CDM), cited the election of Gary Hart as United States senator for Colorado as an example. Hart, who was McGovern's campaign manager in 1972, defeated the conservative Republican incumbent, Peter Dominic, because Hart veered to the right of the issues McGovern had championed two years earlier. Ramsey Clark's resounding defeat in his race against "Jake" Javits—who many pundits claimed was beatable in 1974—clearly demonstrated that any unrepentant New Politics candidate was anathema to traditional Democratic voters. But James Hugh Carey's victory over incumbent Governor Malcolm Wilson was proof positive that a centrist candidate can draw together those groups which traditionally have been the basis for the Democratic coalition —the Jewish and Catholic ethnics, the blacks, and middle-class liberals.

This interpretation is in dispute and regular Democrats are remiss if they ignore the fact that millions of Americans voted for Democratic candidates in 1974 because the Republican Party had discredited itself, not because they were infatuated with the Democrats. Indeed, polls show that the American people do not have a great deal of faith in either party and many voted for Democrats in 1974 as the lesser of two evils.

Barring unforeseen circumstances, the white ethnics will give most of their votes to the Democratic Presidential nominee in 1976, although the size of the majority they produce is crucial. But for the rest of this decade there is a larger question which must be answered: will the white ethnics support a candidate who is prepared to fight for a more equitable distribution of our national wealth and wider citizen access to the political process? The regular Democrats generally have opposed fundamental changes in our society, believing that we can deal with our problems, domestic and foreign, through incremental reforms or through our present economic and political institutions. The New Politics Democrats in turn welcome the reformist label, yet they have not demonstrated a great deal of sensitivity toward the problems of working Americans and they have by no means won the confidence of millions of Democratic voters who deserted the party in 1972.

At present, neither the Democratic regulars nor the reformers are prepared or able to provide leadership and to build a political coalition enabling the United States to come to grips with its problems. The Republican Party offers little hope; many of its members are demoralized and some conservatives like Phillips are prepared to desert the GOP to form a new party. Significantly, in his blueprint for building a new right-wing party, he asserts that the Catholic ethnic vote is imperative to achieve this objective. Whether the Republican Party is destroyed or superseded in this fashion or not, the American right is even less prepared to face our national problems than their opponents on the left. Where does this leave us, then? Well, there is only one direction to move. Since a left-wing third party is not a viable option, progressives committed to change must work within the Democratic Party to make a mass-based populist coalition a reality in the years ahead.

In this connection, there is a bright spot to an otherwise dismal picture; the Watergate "horrors" and our present economic difficulties have compelled Americans from all walks of life to challenge the present distribution of economic and political power in the United States. This is the basis for the much discussed proposition that the electorate is prepared to support a New Populist movement.

B. The Basis for a New Populism: *Our Public Policy Fosters Socialism for the Rich*

Historians at the turn of this decade will write that 1973 was a critical year in the nation's history. Aspiring Ph.D.s will have a field day debating what single incident among many was the most crucial to our society. Most will select the Watergate revelations, for there is no historical precedent to match the Nixon Administration's blatant attempt to subvert our Constitution, destroying a two-century-old separation of powers tradition to establish what Arthur Schlesinger has called the "imperial Presidency," and more forthright critics have labeled "friendly fascism." It was this incident which led to the resignation of Richard Nixon a year later. Others will trace the rise and fall of a man who, within a few short years, moved from the bush leagues of Baltimore County politics to the second highest office in the land only to resign when several young prosecutors gathered evidence which clearly demonstrated the man was a crook. That Spiro Agnew did not go to jail for committing crimes that would have meant prison for 99 per cent of the population will inspire students of American jurisprudence to write long treatises about the failings of our legal system. But while scholars are busily at work assessing these matters, other writers will note that 1973 marked the first year when a significant number of Americans began to pay proper attention to what radicals have called the liberal corporate state. This was prompted by the disconcerting realization that the unprecedented prosperity Americans had enjoyed for a quarter of a century after World War II had come to an end; rates of inflation and unemployment previously considered troublesome would become a normal part of our economic life.

In October of 1973 the Arabs were harbingers of a message to which the average American had been deaf: the United States would no longer enjoy the envious position it had held since the end of the Second World War—near-absolute control of the international market. The energy crisis which overnight made the large, gas-guzzling cars Americans have always taken for granted obsolete, awakened us to the grim truth that some rather fundamental readjustments in our life-style were about to begin. It was not a question of millions of Americans being pitched into the abyss of squalor—although the poor and those on fixed incomes experienced an acute decline in their income and inflation outpaced the salary increases of production workers. Rather, many economists prophesied that the decline in the average American's living standards would be slow but unrelenting—this meant a smaller car, a more modest home, less fuel consumption, fewer steaks, and higher prices for just about everything. Others asserted that talk about a major recession was nonsense, as were predictions that the American standard of living was under assault. Indeed, the reason for such speculation was that we had come so far and expected so much that even a slight setback drove the prophets of doom to their typewriters. While economists are still debating whether the dislocations we are suffering are "temporary" or "long-term," there is a consensus that we can no longer remain immune from structural changes on the world market.

Years prior to the energy crisis, our former World War II enemies, Germany and Japan, proved to be stiff competitors for markets which the United States had dominated—automobiles, steel, electrical appliances, and other industrial products. Electrical workers in New York and New Jersey were among the first to recognize the implications of this development, for they lost their jobs to men and women who lived in industrial centers like Osaka and Tokyo where millions of transistor radios, televisions, and other electrical appliances were being produced. Auto- and steelworkers would feel the pressure too, but the large domestic market for the products they made enabled them to better weather the storm.

As the sales competition between the industrial nations became more intense, they found themselves also vying for the less developed world's raw materials—metal ores and lumber as well as oil. Growing affluence in Europe, North America, and Japan exacerbated this competition and produced an unexpected result: a profound change in the competitive advantages which the advanced countries have always enjoyed at the expense of the less developed nations. The oil-producing countries in particular have set a precedent for raw material-exporting nations—selling their commodities, through cartels, to the industrial nations at monopolistic prices. Political differences and market forces may prevent the formation of effective coffee, copper, and bauxite cartels but, given the scarcity of raw materials, the prices of all of them will be driven up.

Meanwhile, the flow of petrodollars to the oil-producing countries threatens the stability of the international monetary system and poses a threat to the economic security of the leading industrial countries. It is too soon to make precise predictions about the economic future of the United States, but most economists believe that even after the economy picks up once again, the steady increase in real income the American people enjoyed in the 1950s and 1960s will grow at a much slower pace in the 1970s. One of the most disconcerting aspects of our economic troubles is the failure of conservative or liberal economists to provide viable solutions. The contemporary disciples of Adam Smith will not be of much help; few people any longer seriously believe we can return to a truly free market—a myth of classical economists. Liberal economists meanwhile are no longer quite sure that the New Economics can stave off economic disaster and they are scared. Radical economists who claim that the nation's economic problems are not transitory but are structural ones which bode ill for the future of our economy can no longer be ignored. Nor can we dismiss their fear that in a desperate effort to deal with economic dislocation, the corporate elite, in collusion with frightened labor leaders and anxious liberals, will adopt greater planning—but under the umbrella of a corporate state and not democratic socialism.

Liberals may ignore those who predict that our present economic difficulties presage the adoption of "corporativism"—the division of society into corporate entities which, allied with government and organized labor, regulate the economy—but they cannot ignore corporate power and the devastating impact the abuse of that power has had on our society. Unfortunately they have. One of the principal preoccupations of liberal intellectuals after Nixon entered the White House was to reassess the Great Society legislation LBJ championed in the 1960s to rid the nation of some of its most persistent social ills —poverty, racism, and urban blight. Irving Kristol, Daniel Patrick Moynihan, and Norman Podhoretz have suggested that the "poverty warriors" overestimated the capacity of government to intervene in the social and economic systems. In the pages of *The Public Interest* and *Commentary*, the New Conservatives have written that Johnson's social engineers did not adequately assess the sources of our domestic malaise; consequently many urban programs were poorly designed and implemented. Others became vehicles for irresponsible "radicals" who, in the name of community control, misled the poor into believing that "people power" was a quick solution to their problems.

The early despondency of the liberal community attending the performance of Great Society social programs has given way to a more balanced appraisal of them. Ben Wattenberg, proffering census data to support his case, argues in *The Real America* that poverty and social inequality have been reduced in the last decade and Great Society legislation, in part, is responsible for this good news; he counsels his liberal friends not to despair but to persevere—liberalism is not dead and buried in Scarsdale but alive and well, waiting in the wings for the election of a Democratic administration in 1976.[11] His view is a fairer estimate of the performance of the welfare state than that found in *Human Events* or *The National Review*. But it is overly optimistic; the implication is that it is only a matter of time before we eliminate our most pressing domestic problems and it suggests that we can do this without taking "drastic steps" like redistributing our nation's wealth.

Moreover, in debating the pros and cons of the Great Society, liberals have blithely ignored one of the most trenchant facts about the failure of our public policy to eliminate poverty, racism, and urban blight—the pivotal role the private sector plays in shaping public policy. Consider for example that billions have been spent to restore our older cities but the results have been modest at best. Why? The stark truth is that the destruction of our cities and the failure to restore them is the logical outcome of government programs often judged sound or not by powerful forces in the private sector and not by officials elected to promote the public interest. The lending institutions, insurance companies, and developers possess a virtual veto over urban public policy because without their "cooperation" urban developmental projects remain paper plans. In the process of making it worthwhile for the private sector to join government in such programs, the business community demands a profit ratio and control over decision-making, usually resulting in tokenism or a sheer waste of public funds. At the same time, the private sector has adopted independent actions like blockbusting and withholding mortgage money and insurance coverage to homeowners and businessmen in "high risk" areas, resulting in the devastation of urban residential neighborhoods.

Meanwhile, business executives who talk passionately about

the sanctity of free enterprise have manipulated state power to eliminate risk-taking and competition, which are the guiding principles of the free enterprise system. Soon after the Washington *Post* broke the Watergate story, investigative reporters began to uncover numerous examples of collusion between the Administration and the business community. In exchange for a campaign donation amounting to several hundred thousand dollars, the milk industry was allowed to raise prices, representing a windfall of an estimated 500 to 700 million dollars. Then there was the Soviet wheat deal, masterminded by several large grain dealers with the help of the Department of Agriculture, resulting in massive profits for the exporters at the expense of the consumer, taxpayer, and farmer. It was also alleged that the Justice Department made a favorable ruling for ITT when that conglomerate was ordered to divest itself of an insurance subsidiary and let Robert Vesco, the renegade financier, off the hook for his misdeeds. It was only after these and other examples of collusion between the Nixon Administration and the corporate community were widely publicized and the energy crisis wracked the country, that liberal congressmen began to talk about corporate power. The liberals' hesitancy to talk about the incestuous marriage of public and private power stems from the knowledge that, while the Nixon Administration outdistanced its predecessors in serving corporate interests, Democratic administrations have turned their backs on the abuse of corporate power too.

Such avid exponents of the free market as conservative economist Milton Friedman have warned us about the ominous political implications of economic concentrations. Friedman's remarks are principally directed at the concentration of economic power in the hands of the state, and socialists who scoff at widespread fear about the concentration of state power are seriously mistaken; but under prevailing circumstances, Friedman's warning is even more relevant to the so-called "private sector." By virtue of their economic power, the large corporations and the rich have "bought" elected officials to gain advantages they were unable to secure through the free market. Lending institutions, utilities, insurance companies, and large manufacturers play a pivotal role in writing legislation pertinent to their commercial activities—the level of inter-

est and utility rates, manufacturing standards, safety regulations, etc. On the local level real estate speculators, developers,
and lending institutions customarily control zoning boards and
planning commissions and thereby protect their interests at
the expense of the community and the taxpayers. Anyone who
devotes passing attention to local government knows that the
elected officials and business community enjoy a symbiotic relationship which violates the public trust if not the law. Thus,
liberal reformers who proffer such bromides as public campaign financing are sorely missing the point—namely, that the
ability of private interests to dominate public policy is rooted
in our "pluralistic political system." State power generated to
promote the public interest in the 1930s often has been co-
opted by private interests to circumvent the common good.
College textbooks assert that our elected officials closely guard
against the abuse of corporate power, but the truth is that
government often colludes with business at the public's expense.

The romance between government and business is reflected
in the propensity of bright young men to enter public service—
via the ABC regulatory agencies, the Defense Department, or
Department of Agriculture—with the explicit purpose in mind
of making contacts in the corporate world and, after a several-
year stint in Washington, selling their experience and government contacts to industry at double or triple their salary. People who know how to work around government regulations or
to use them to advantage are a distinct asset to the business
community. Thus the "idealistic" whiz kids that John F. Kennedy brought to Washington discarded their public servant's
apparel for the rich garb of the corporate world soon after JFK
was assassinated; speechwriter Theodore Sorensen became a
counsel to Pepsi-Cola, Najeeb Halaby left the Federal Avia-
tion Commission to become president of Pan American
World Airways, and Pierre Salinger became an international
businessman. In most prestigious Washington law firms a
prerequisite to employment is government experience. So lawyers at HEW, HUD, or the Defense Department who guard
the public interest vis-à-vis the pharmaceutical firms, the housing industry, or the military industrial complex typically leave

government for the private sector after "learning the ropes" to
serve as advocates for the people they previously regulated.

That the regulated often "regulate the regulators" is a
clumsy aphorism but an accurate description of what is going
on. The results, of course, have been pernicious. Consider the
failure of government agencies charged with the duty of overseeing industrial safety regulations to enforce laws written to
protect miners against cave-ins and noxious gases, chemical
workers against lethal agents—outlawed elsewhere in the
civilized world—and textile workers from raw cotton wastes
which choke the lungs and slowly suffocate the victim, and
children from toys which kill or maim tots in their playpens
and schoolyards. Or consider that pharmaceutical companies
produce billions of "uppers" and "downers" for the explicit
purpose of feeding the illegal black market serving high school
pushers and adult addicts alike, sell drugs at enormous
markups, and distribute medication of little value to the user
and often of potential danger to him. Or, how about the highway lobby which jealously guards oil and gas revenues, keeping
them from the "greedy hands" of those responsible planners
who advocate rapid mass transit systems. Comprised of the
automobile, oil, steel, and rubber industries, labor unions,
and government bureaucrats—running from high-salaried
supergrade civil servants in the Department of Transportation
and top state officials right down to the "county highway en-
gineer"—the highway lobby must take much of the blame for
our energy crisis, air pollution, traffic congestion, and the destruction of residential communities severed by expressways.

The observation that our public policy fosters "socialism for
the rich" is not merely a play on words or radical propaganda.
The federal income tax, allegedly a "progressive revenue,"
pampers the affluent who accumulate wealth through stock
and bond transactions, real estate deals, dividends, profits, and
other sources of income which are protected by tax dodges and
legal loopholes. This explains why Ronald Reagan and Richard Nixon pay fewer taxes than the average workingman; it accounts for the findings of tax experts that a man earning
$8,000 a year bears the same burden as one earning an annual
salary of $50,000. In Washington and the state capitals, lob-
byists for the rich and influential wield awesome power behind

the scenes to protect their clients from public accountability, making sure Uncle Sam helps out the "needy"; thus Lockheed is bailed out of an embarrassing economic situation caused by management bungling; large agricultural conglomerates are paid massive sums not to plant food and fiber; the oil industry gets an oil depletion allowance and other favorable tax treatment; and until 1973 Washington enriched the oil companies to the tune of billions of dollars a year at the expense of the American consumer through import quotas.

Consider, in contrast, that while government continues to insure the profits of large corporations, the problems of the ordinary American, who must abide by the spartan principles of capitalism, are blithely ignored. Food and clothing are skyrocketing, as are rents; high interest rates, down payments, and monthly mortgages are pricing even middle-class Americans out of the housing market. Although medical, auto, and property insurance rates are rapidly rising, policyholders find they are not adequately protected in the event of an emergency. The fear of a major dental bill hovers over the family of modest means like a beast of prey. A protracted illness or recovery period may impoverish a family that has toiled for years to accumulate a small savings account.

In metropolitan areas where millions of working Americans live, the streets are unsafe, the air is polluted, and services are on the decline. Schools do not provide youngsters with vocational skills which adequately prepare them for employment, and the quality of the academic curricula is declining. Parents who toil and sacrifice to send their children to college despair because tuition is rising faster than their capacity to save. Lacking seniority or job skills, economic insecurity is a persistent fact of life for the young father and his family. This in turn is a major source of family discord and emotional strife among young couples whose financial obligations are most demanding at a time when their income is modest. Working Americans of all ages are badgered by a steady flow of monthly bills to pay for merchandise which is often shoddy and overpriced because consumer laws are weak or are rarely enforced. After contributing to the welfare of the nation during their prime of life, millions of workers approach retirement with well-founded anxiety. Senior citizens who attempt to live on meager savings, pension plans, or social security checks can barely meet their minimum needs for clothing, food, shelter, and medicine. The care available to old folks in nursing homes and other institutions is appalling.

The plight of the small homeowner is a graphic example of how the little guy is victimized. The single largest source of municipal tax revenues is the regressive property tax. Across the United States, municipalities are experiencing serious difficulties floating their bonds, and property taxes are escalating to meet the growing demands for classrooms, teachers' salaries, sewage systems, and other critical services. Even casual observers of municipal finance know that industry is undertaxed and the burden for financing local government is placed on the back of the small homeowner. In Lake County, Indiana, the Calumet Community Congress—a federation of neighborhood and civic organizations—charged that Inland Steel's Indiana Harbor Works in East Chicago annually is dramatically underassessed. According to CCC's evaluation of public records (that is, taxable real estate and business property) and the company's own estimates, Inland should have been assessed $20 million more than it was in 1971.[12] Of course the residents of this largely blue-collar community made up the difference.

In any responsible discussion of our nation's political future, then, we must keep two facts in mind. We have not taken care of the basic social and economic needs of millions of our citizens and we will not until we redistribute our national wealth. Equally important, until we make fundamental readjustments in our political and economic systems, ordinary voters will be denied the democratic right to hold accountable the decision-makers who keenly affect their well-being and their children's future.

To radical commentators, the shopping list of ills which have been identified above are attributable to a single cause—the liberal corporate state, involving a conspiracy of big business, big government, and big labor. They relate the following story: As long ago as the late nineteenth century, the Robber Barons who championed laissez-faire capitalism recognized that government giveaways (land grants to railroads, for example), tariffs, and even antitrust legislation which was designed to check their power enabled them to reduce risk-taking, eliminate competition, and crush labor unions. During World Wars I and II, corporate executives and their agents were brought to Washington to manage the "war effort," and in both instances they made certain that their interests were well served. But what about the New Deal? Remember how big business formed the Liberty Lobby and vowed to send FDR scurrying back to Hyde Park? The radical retort is that it was either good acting, mere rhetoric, or ignorance on the part of the mossbacks who failed to see that Roosevelt, through a program of liberal reforms, was saving what corporate propagandists labeled capitalism. Few Americans know that such liberal New Deal programs as the National Industrial Recovery Act abolished antitrust legislation, legalized cartels, and established industrial boards—which determined production quotas and prices—thus setting the stage for cooperation between business and government at the expense of the small entrepreneur, the worker, and the consumer. FDR and his brain-trusters did make certain adjustments which displeased the corporations and the rich, such as giving legal status to organized labor, but the radicals contend that after the "reds" and social unionists were expelled from the labor movement during the Cold War, the AFL-CIO willingly became a partner in the corporativist troika.

Following a long historical tradition, contemporary radicals have been ignored because they employ obnoxious rhetoric, proffer bromides distasteful to the American palate, accuse their enemies and those who challenge their analysis of immorality or complicity in evil schemes, and strike an elitist and self-righteous bearing, alienating potential allies in the process. Nonetheless, even if their conspiratorial theory is rejected, the pernicious abuse of corporate power cannot be ignored. The persistence of poverty in the richest society in the history of mankind, the plight of old folks, the cancer of racism, our failure to restore urban America and to reclaim our environment—all are related to the concentration of wealth in the hands of powerful corporations which control vital sectors of American life.

People who talk in terms of dealing with these problems have been called the New Populists. They can be found in the

Democratic Party, the labor movement, academia, and other areas of American life. Unlike the old guard in the Democratic Party and labor movement, they recognize that the concentration of economic and political power must be dealt with together and not separately. The nation's economic troubles in the 1970s have caused voters from all walks of life to ask probing questions about the distribution of economic and political power which have not been the subject of public concern since the 1930s. There is little doubt that we are entering a new era of reform, but it is not at all clear whether the New Populists can attract sufficient popular support to produce fundamental changes in prevailing power relationships. One thing is certain: without the white ethnics' support, they are bound to fail.

C. Political Culture and Political Socialization: *Linking the Past to the Present*

Anthropologists link the past to the present by studying a society's culture. Sociologists use the term socialization to refer to the process whereby members of a culture acquire knowledge, skills, and values that make them a member of society. Through socialization a child gradually comes to approximate the prevailing attitudes of the adults in his culture—learning the proper way to treat the opposite sex, the customary way to settle disputes, the mores of commercial affairs, etc. Borrowing from their sister sciences, political scientists have developed two tools, political culture and political socialization, to determine how political values and beliefs are produced and passed on from one generation to another.[13]

A political culture involves a collective orientation toward politics; in contrast to the generic term culture, it refers to phenomena specifically relevant to political matters. A political culture is comprised of values, beliefs, experiences, myths, and symbols which shape the perception of government and the political process among members of society. Political scientists claim that there is an American political culture, but since we are a pluralistic society there are a number of political subcultures which can be found in it.

Most white ethnics have internalized the principal characteristics of the American political culture: political liberty and equality, the right to private property and to worship free of state interference, and an egalitarian value system—individualism, materialism, and achievement. Despite ethnic, religious, regional, racial, and class cleavages, an overwhelming number of Americans share a consensus about political values, beliefs, and expectations; this explains why the United States has been able to cope with social, economic, and political problems that have torn other societies apart. Nonetheless, within the American political community there are political subcommunities and the white ethnics belong to one of them. It explains differences between them and white Protestant Americans. For example, since the New Deal the white ethnics have been steadfast supporters of the welfare state and Catholic and Jewish voters are more inclined to approve of state intervention in the economy, to oppose big business, and to support liberal candidates than Wasps are.

By employing concepts developed by students of political socialization, it is possible to gain insight into the principal elements of the white ethnic political culture, enhancing our understanding of white ethnic political behavior, past, present, and future. Political socialization involves learning about politics and transmitting political values and experiences from one generation to another. In much the same fashion that we are socialized to become members of an American culture, we are socialized to an American political culture. Citizens are taught to favor certain political beliefs, institutions, and procedures and to reject others. Every political system socializes its citizens in this manner.

Political sociologists contend that there are a number of "agents" of socialization which shape a person's political orientation; among those which are the most important are the following.

The Family: The family provides a child with status, a philosophy, and an arena where he first learns about society. From the outset social status has a profound impact upon an individual's developing political orientation. The son or daughter of a brain surgeon, observing the high favor which society bestows on their parents, is more likely to possess self-esteem than the offspring of a garbage collector. This "edge" is significant since studies indicate that people who lack self-esteem are less likely to participate in politics or believe they can affect political decisions than persons who have a high opinion of themselves.

The family also is the first institution to provide children with information about politics and to inculcate specific political beliefs and values. Statistically children who have been raised in homes where politics is often discussed are more inclined to vote, join political parties, or express political opinions than those who have been reared in a household where politics is less often a topic of family interest. The power of the family to shape political attitudes and loyalties is revealed in studies demonstrating that children usually identify with their parents' party and that student militants in the 1960s were likely to come from homes where liberal views were entertained.

Explicit attempts on the part of parents to inculcate children with political attitudes involve manifest socialization. A second way political attitudes are formed in the family is through latent socialization; for example, children internalize social values or observe nonpolitical behavior which have latent political consequences. People who are taught that they can trust other persons are more likely to work with them in collective action than those who were warned by their parents that "you can't trust strangers." Then, too, the first authority figure a child comes into contact with is a parent and the parent/child authority relationship may shape the child's future perception of political authority. A child who is encouraged to participate in family decisions and to think for himself is more inclined later in life to question authority than one who is reared in a home where children are intimidated by the parents and are denied the opportunity to participate in family decision-making.

The Community and Peer Group: Every community inculcates its members with political values just as every nation does vis-à-vis its citizens. The family passes on to the child the community's values as well as information about critical developments in the community's life. The murder of six million Jews at the hands of the Nazis is an undeniable fact in the collective consciousness of Jews wherever they live in the world, whatever their age, education, income, or social status.

In exploring a group's political behavior over several generations, attitudes and beliefs held by an earlier generation may be revised over time as a result of new social, economic, and political experiences—wars, revolutions, depressions, etc. Changing economic and social circumstances may also account for conflicting political habits among several generations of the same group. Nonetheless, political values and beliefs inherited from one's parents and grandparents may persist well beyond the time the original factors responsible for them have disappeared. Whether or not the individual discards his religious, ethnic, or race-related values later on in life depends upon many things, among them whether or not the individual continues to live among people like himself and whether or not he is exposed to ideas or experiences which clash with those he previously held. If your peers are members of a social, religious, ethnic, or racial group other than your own, you may be tempted to revise your earlier political perspective in the direction theirs takes. Consider for example a man born to devout Irish Catholic parents, who view Republicans in the same dim light as Unitarians, who becomes a successful Wall Street banker, marries into an aristocratic family, and runs for the state assembly on the Republican ticket. It is possible to explain his shifting political orientation as a genuine ideological turnabout, but an equally compelling reason for this readjustment may stem from pressure exerted upon him by his colleagues, adopted family, and new friends to conform to their political beliefs.

A group which lacks status in the eyes of the majority often lacks the confidence to participate in political affairs to the same degree that the majority does. (Here, of course, we are talking about other things being equal, for a minority group member who enjoys opportunities or skills which most of the majority do not—education, for example—may possess a higher level of political acumen than a member of the majority. Thus, a child born into a black family who earns a college degree may perform more effectively in the political system than a white high school dropout.) The low turnout among poor people in model cities elections demonstrates that the political socialization of ghetto blacks may be a more effective deterrent to voting than the machinations of a bigoted registrar.

This, of course, holds true for women expressing less interest in politics than men; in childhood girls are taught to relate to family-oriented games, reading matter, and ideas while boys are socialized to acquire an interest in politics—that is, they are encouraged to read about war and great national heroes, and play games which predispose them to participate in affairs outside the home.

Education: Generally the higher the level of education a person enjoys, the more likely he is to be exposed to information relevant to a comprehension of politics. A college student, in addition to political information, acquires skills which are pertinent to political participation. And college-educated Americans believe they can more effectively participate in politics than do those without degrees and the fact that they believe this is the case contributes to a higher level of participation on their part.

In school a child may be exposed for the first time to political information and develop a grasp of political affairs. His exposure to his classmates may be politically significant too; thus a student reared in a home where a picture of John F. Kennedy hangs in the foyer may be forced to reassess his political outlook when he finds himself among peers who think Ronald Reagan is the savior of "all that's good and decent in American life."

Measuring the effect of education upon political behavior is a tricky enterprise; for example, high school graduates are more inclined to embrace the ideals of our political system than dropouts. Why? Because they have been more fully exposed to knowledge and authority (the teacher) supporting the political system than the kid who leaves school his freshman year to take a job at a pizza parlor. The individual who goes on to college, however, will be exposed to people and ideas which may induce him once again to reconsider his previous political attitudes.

It should be stressed that it is not only the content of instruction which shapes a person's political orientation but the instructional atmosphere as well; the most obvious example is the autocratic environment in which students are discouraged from asking questions, learn by rote, and are compelled to parrot the teacher's lectures.

Religious Affiliation: Individuals who participate in demo-cratic religious organizations may translate that experience to political activities. Then, too, an individual is more likely to challenge authority if he has been exposed to doctrine which promotes toleration of dissent than if he has been inculcated with the notion that the teachings of the hierarchy are infallible. The content of religious instruction, of course, has a profound shaping effect upon the issue orientation of an individual; the strong enmity among devout Catholics toward abortion is a contemporary case in point. At the same time the religious community may reflect the class composition of the faithful—for example, since the New Deal the Catholic church has supported the labor movement and bread and butter legislation critical to the well-being of working people.

Nonpolitical Associational Experiences: The person whose early socialization denied him self-esteem, knowledge, or skills pertinent to expressing himself politically may acquire them in adulthood through involvement in community, business, or labor organizations. Through participation in union activities, the steelworker acquires skills relevant to political work—conducting meetings, participating in elections, etc. In most places in the United States unions are the only institutions which enable working people to effectively articulate their demands and grievances in the public and private sectors.

Work Experiences: Membership in a certain occupational group may produce a common outlook toward the political universe due to the common bond of shared interests. Doctrinaire Marxists contend that political behavior is a reflection of an individual's place in the economic scheme of things; political conflict reflects the division in society between the class which produces wealth and that which possesses it—the proletariat and the bourgeoisie. Of course, since the capitalists control the church, schools, and other institutions which are the basis for the nation's value system, they promulgate values and beliefs reflecting the rulers' self-interest. This explains why workers may harbor silly notions about representative government and believe that the legal system operates in the interests of all people and not just those who possess wealth and power. Marx called this state of mind "false consciousness," although he believed that over time the masses would gain a proper understanding of the state; viz., that it ruled in the interests of the capitalists at the expense of everyone else. The widespread belief that social class is the only real source of politics has contributed to the failure of the American left to develop an alliance with native American and immigrant workers; today it explains why many left-wing radicals discredit political theories which pay homage to the importance of religious, cultural, or ethnic values in shaping political actions.

Although the Marxist notion about the association between occupation and political behavior is oversimplified, contemporary political sociologists have found that work experiences do often account for different patterns of political behavior. For example, an executive who daily makes important decisions, who has employees working under his direction, and who is exposed to information which enables him to better understand the political process is more inclined to participate in politics than the man or woman who keeps the rest rooms clean and neat. Here again, the status one may derive from one's job will be as important as the politically relevant information acquired.

The Mass Media: Television is the principal source of political information in the United States but group affiliations and the opinion-molders in those groups serve as screens through which the average voter watches television. This explains why television viewers are prone to interpret the news from a host of different, often conflicting, perspectives. Notwithstanding the influence of opinion-molders and group affiliations, television plays a pivotal role in defining our nation's problems, establishing priorities for change, and promoting a tone which profoundly influences millions of viewers nightly via the news, documentaries, and even low-grade drama. It is for these reasons that television programming has become an important issue in its own right.

Direct Experiences with the Political System: Early students of political socialization, perhaps because they were largely psychologists and sociologists, tended to ignore the shaping influence of government per se. In a society where political dissent, free parties and elections are prohibited, the great mass of people are likely to be politically passive. For generations poor whites and blacks in Dixie were politically apathetic because they were "taught," as a result of confrontations with political authority, that they had little power over their elected officials. The political mores of the Daley machine account for the pervasive feeling among Chicago's voters that "politics is a dirty game." The belief that politicians skim off public monies to enrich themselves explains the reluctance of many voters to vote for school bond issues or other public expenditures. "The politicians may get it no matter how we vote—but at least we'll make them work for it." This is not cynicism but a rational response to the political process with which many Americans are familiar.

The historical material treated in the next three chapters will be assessed with the aforementioned comments about political socialization in mind. They will provide the basis for a comprehensive discussion of contemporary white ethnic political activity and the problems and prospects of enlisting the support of Catholic and Jewish voters for a New Populist movement in the years ahead.

CHAPTER II

The Immigrant Legacy

A. The End of an Era: *It Signified the End of the Exalted Notion That America Was Big Enough for Everybody*

On May 26, 1924, President Calvin Coolidge signed a bill supported by such unlikely allies as Hiram Evans, the Imperial Wizard of the Ku Klux Klan; Sam Gompers, the Dutch-born Jew who presided over the American Federation of Labor; and Henry Cabot Lodge, the senator from Massachusetts. The KKK had no love for Jews, especially Jewish labor leaders; Mr. Gompers felt the same way about the Imperial Wizard and his crowd; and Senator Lodge, the Yankee patrician, neither courted the friendship of Mr. Evans nor relished the company of Mr. Gompers. What brought this unlikely threesome together then?—the Immigration Act of 1924, also known as the Johnson-Reed Act, which set such strict immigration quotas that one of its architects proclaimed it marked "the close of an epoch in the history of the United States."[1] It did indeed; for the first time since the settlers had dug furrows in the mosquito-infested marshes of Jamestown, European immigrants were denied the right to take part in one of the greatest social experiments in history.

The congressmen who voted for the bill reflected a widespread fear that the country was being inundated by a horde of "dim-witted" Polish peasants, "criminally inclined" Italians, "swarthy" Greeks, and "shifty-eyed" Jews. In 1910 the Census Bureau made a startling revelation—from 1891 to 1910,

8,000,000 of the 12,500,000 immigrants who arrived in the
United States came from Eastern and Southern Europe. In
the 1870s they had only accounted for 6.3 per cent of the European immigration; in the next decade—1881 to 1891—16 per
cent. From 1891 to 1900 47.5 per cent or 2,000,000 of the
immigrants were Eastern or Southern European; and, whereas
a paltry 22.1 per cent of the immigrants entering the United
States from 1901 to 1910 came from the "advanced" European countries, a staggering 71 per cent or 6,000,000 came
from the "backwaters of the Continent."

To Americans who sought an explanation for the widespread social unrest which wracked the country during the
closing decades of the nineteenth century, these figures
provided "answers." The Haymarket Riot of 1886, the Homestead Steel strike of 1892, the Pullman Railroad strike of
1894, labor violence in the coal fields of America—they all
were the work of foreign anarchists and socialists. The crime
and corruption that was commonplace in the cities, the growing use of alcohol, the mounting incidence of prostitution, the
marauding street gangs—all were attributed to the presence of
impoverished immigrants who practiced an alien morality.
During economic downturns bankrupt farmers, disgruntled
businessmen, and displaced workers also blamed the immigrants for their troubles.

Scapegoating—diverting mass discontent from the people
responsible for the conditions breeding unrest—is a time-
honored American tradition. Throughout our history domestic
stress has periodically given rise to nativist hostility toward foreigners and "outsiders." At the turn of the century, "Catholics
and Jews," "Wops and Polaks" bore the responsibility for the
disruption wrought by urbanization and industrialization.
More recently black Americans have been fingered as the principal architects of widespread unrest in America. In both instances the victims of change are singled out for criticism, not
those who, wielding decisive economic and political power, are
responsible for the nation's fortunes, domestic and foreign.

The Irish, the most assimilated Catholic ethnic group in
America, were the first to experience the lash of hatred at the
hands of native Protestant Americans. In the 1840s Irish im-

migrants began to enter the United States in large numbers. Unlike those who had previously arrived—the Scotch-Irish Protestants or those middle-class Catholics who neatly blended in with the mainstream populace—the newcomers were poor, uneducated Catholics. During the 1840s, 1.7 million Irishmen fled the famine that depleted Ireland's villages and filled its graveyards. Living in dirty, overcrowded hovels along the nation's East Coast cities, the "shanty Irish" became the northern "niggers." The Irish who lived in New York City and Boston worked as domestic servants, dug ditches, or labored on the docks toting cargo. Editorialists wrote that they were stupid, lazy, violent, and prone toward drunkenness and criminality. It was alleged that half of the convicted criminals in the mid-nineteenth century were foreign-born and they were ten times as likely as native Americans to live off the dole; most of these miscreants were Irish.

In search of employment, the Irish moved across the country building railroads and canals, extending the transportation network into the hinterland, pushing on to the Mississippi, then to the Rockies until they stopped at the shores of the Pacific. Irish ghettos were established in the railroad and river towns they entered—Albany, Baltimore, Cleveland, Chicago, and Omaha. Some of those who followed the rail system West dropped off to work in the mines of Butte, Denver, and Virginia City; others went clear to California.

Life was bitter and harsh; violent deaths were common among the Irishmen, who performed the risky, dangerous jobs. An Irish immigrant writing home about the drowning of a fellow countryman remarked: "How often do we see such paragraphs in the paper as an Irishman drowns—an Irishman crushed by a beam—an Irishman suffocated in a pit—an Irishman blown to atoms by a steam engine—ten, twenty Irishmen buried alive by the sinking of a bank . . ."[2] Such was the fate of the Irish-Americans until the Poles, Hungarians, Lithuanians, and Italians arrived to take their place.

In newspaper and magazine cartoons, "Paddy" usually was adorned with an old top hat, a threadbare waistcoat, and shabby trousers. An enlarged nose, distorted by years of heavy imbibing, was placed on an ugly face. It was the rule that

Paddy was habitually under the influence. A whiskey bottle jutted from his back pocket or a jug was customarily placed within close proximity to his person. Intoxicated, an Irishman was a dangerous animal who would break someone's jaw, gouge an eye, or slash off an ear just for the sheer hell of it. After the Civil War a reputed secret Irish organization, the Molly Maguires, was held accountable for much of the labor strife that punctuated the hollows of the nation's coal regions. Whether there ever was an organization of Irish miners called the Molly Maguires is still being hotly debated by historians. Some say that the organization was an invention of mine-owners bent on destroying labor activities in their industry. That Irish miners responded to their employers' cruel treatment by resorting to violence—scabs were beaten, mine foremen were shot, and collieries were dynamited—is not a subject of dispute. Prior to the coming of the New Immigrants, they and the Germans fought awesome odds to organize labor unions.

While the real and reputed exploits of the Irish attracted the enmity of native-born Americans, their Roman Catholicism was deemed an even greater threat to the nation's civil order. Nativists throughout the nineteenth century were convinced that the appearance of mounting numbers of Catholic immigrants represented a plot hatched in the Vatican to wrench control of the United States from the Wasp majority. Stories were circulated among the more racy nativists that priests and nuns, behind the protective cover of the nunneries, participated in perverse and exotic sexual practices. A woman, supposedly an ex-nun with the improbable name of Maria Monk, wrote two books, in 1836 and 1837, which revealed that nuns were raped by sex-hungry priests in the nunnery she had inhabited in Montreal. Her stories were proved false, but 300,000 copies were sold prior to the Civil War. Catholic churches, seminaries, and convents were targets of thugs who tossed bricks through stained-glass windows, spread excrement on church steps, and wrote obscenities on convent walls. In Charleston, Massachusetts, a mob burned a convent to the ground in 1831. In 1844 Irish laborers and anti-Catholic marauders clashed in the streets of the Kensington section of Philadelphia in bloody pitched battles. On one occasion several persons were killed and scores wounded and two Catholic churches and a seminary were firebombed. On another occasion anti-Catholic rioting resulted in thirteen deaths and over fifty persons wounded, and thousands of Catholics fled the city in panic. The Irish in particular seemed to be the primary targets of the anti-Catholic vigilantes for in Philadelphia in 1846 an Irish Catholic church was burned while a German Catholic church a few blocks away went untouched. Most German Catholics arrived in the United States after the Civil War but those who came with the Irish in the first half of the nineteenth century were less conspicuous than their co-religionists. They were Papists and their practice of drinking, dancing, and merrymaking on the Sabbath assaulted the Puritan sensibilities of Protestant fundamentalists. But most preferred to settle in the hinterland and not congregate in urban ghettos as the Irish did. Besides, though "black sheep," they were members of the Aryan race.

But neither violence nor economic warfare (signs were plastered on the walls of places of employment which read, "No Irish Need Apply") dissuaded Irish immigration. The men and women who fled the devastation of the potato blight which wasted their fields, destroyed their economy, and starved their kinfolk had no other choice. In 1843 several nativist organizations, displeased with the failure of the Whigs and the Democrats to take decisive measures against the Papist menace, formed the American Republican Party. A year later it elected six federal congressmen representing the cities of New York and Philadelphia, and mayors in New York and Boston. Unable to sustain its popularity by championing a single issue—anti-Catholicism—the party soon disappeared, but the "threat" did not. During a five-year period, from 1850 to 1855, Catholics from Ireland and Germany continued to enter the country in large numbers, causing the nativists to resume their political activities in earnest.

In 1854 the Know-Nothing Party was formed, garnering most of its support from the urban lower middle class which competed with the immigrants for jobs and housing. The Know-Nothing leaders were seasoned Catholic-haters and their goals were to restrict Catholic immigration and to destroy parochial schools which they deemed training grounds for subversives. The deepening crisis between North and South soon overshadowed the "Catholic menace," but during the Civil War nativist agitators charged that the bloody antidraft riots in New York City in which Irish immigrants played a principal role and the antiwar activities of Catholic clergymen testified to the persistence of the Vatican's evil designs upon America. Many Irishmen, however, joined Mr. Lincoln's army, and the "fighting 69th," whose men gained fame for their valor on the field of battle, was comprised primarily of Irishmen.

No sooner had Lee and Grant signed the peace treaty at Appomattox Court House than nativist propagandists began lashing out at the "traitors within our midst." They were not talking about die-hard confederates. A writer in *Harper's Weekly* (1872) stated:

> The unpatriotic conduct of the Romanish population in our chief cities during the late rebellion is well known. They formed a constant menace and terror to loyal citizens; they thronged the peace meetings, they strove to divide the Union; and when the war was over they placed in office their corrupt leaders . . .

This did not represent the musings of a fanatic few or those without real influence, for President Grant, three years later, commenting upon the likelihood of another civil war, said, "If we are to have another contest in the near future of our national existence, I predict that the dividing line will not be Mason and Dixon's; but between (Protestant) patriotism and intelligence on one side, and (Catholic) superstition, ambition, and ignorance on the other . . ."[3]

One of the largest contemporary anti-Catholic organizations was founded in the small town of Clinton, Iowa, by a group of disgruntled members of the Knights of Labor and several lawyers whose slate of candidates had been defeated, they alleged, because Catholic clergy had instructed Irish Catholic voters to oppose it. It was named the American Protective Association and at one time it claimed a membership of two and a half million. Every APA recruit took an oath "never to vote for a Catholic, never to employ one when a Protestant was available, and never to go out on strike with Catholics." The APA published and circulated bogus documents, one of which "uncovered a Catholic plot to overthrow the government" in the name of the Vatican. Another APA tract revealed that in 1851 Catholic prelates plotted "to concentrate Catholic immigration from Europe in large American cities and by its vote to seize them for the Catholic Church." On another occasion a document was disseminated in which Pope Leo XIII was quoted as absolving Catholics from any oaths of loyalty to the United States and encouraging them to "exterminate heretics."[4] It was not then merely a matter of contesting the Vatican for the soul of the nation, for the Pope's agents were sowing discontent among the laboring classes in a bold attempt to build a political power base to topple the government itself. A second component of the conspiratorial theory, then, suggested the importation of alien political doctrine in the person of European immigrants. To propose that the Vatican and the socialists were in league was preposterous. But the nativists were peddling fear and hatred, not logic. The "alien radicals" hated the Catholic church as much as the APA bigots did.

Among the immigrants there were some political radicals. Many German "forty-eighters" who fled political oppression in the wake of the abortive 1848 liberal revolution were vigorous exponents of socialism, as were those who fled Bismarck's antisocialist campaign in the 1880s. Wherever large numbers of them settled, labor union activity percolated and in their meeting halls they frequently mentioned the names of two countrymen who would gain a permanent place in the demonology of the American right—Karl Marx and Friedrich Engels. The Germans were the first serious exponents of Marxism in America, and after the Civil War they challenged the simple-minded notion that "foreigners" were responsible for the nation's troubles. German socialists stated that there was one overriding problem which produced many symptoms— the devastation of rural life, rapid urbanization, political corruption, and labor unrest; that problem was industrial capitalism and the subservience of elected officials to the whims of the Robber Barons who controlled all vital sectors of Americ society—the government, the press, the courts, and churches, as well as the economy. The solution to this abuse power lay in the hands of the people who were capitalism's principal victims—the industrial proletariat. Lingual and cultural differences limited the Germans in their proselytizing, but they were among the first to provide a comprehensive critique of American society.

In areas where large numbers of German socialists lived, they even achieved some electoral victories. The predominantly Teutonic city of Milwaukee was the home of the most successful socialist political machine in American history. Victor Berger, long-time mayor of the city, served in the U. S. House of Representatives, one of the handful of socialists to fill that exalted office. Many of the founding fathers of the AFL, like Adolph Strasser, were Germans who, in contrast to native American workers, were inclined to join labor unions. Thus as early as 1885 "the situation in Illinois was typical; 21 per cent (of the state's union membership) were American, 10 per cent British, 19 per cent Irish, 33 per cent German, 12 per cent Scandinavian, 5 per cent Polish, Czech, and Italian."[5] One of the first unions in the United States to organize along industrial lines was the predominantly German Brewery Workers Union. And in any discussion of the American labor movement, we cannot forget that it was the German immigrant Reuther clan which gave birth to one of our most illustrious labor families.

The German Marxists were unable to adjust their theory and actions to the American milieu and, like succeeding generations of socialists, they made the fatal error of assuming that a socialist movement could be built in America along the same lines that it was being constructed in Europe. This affliction was even truer of the anarchists—the nineteenth-century equivalent of the Yippies and Weathermen; one of the earliest exponents of anarchism in America was a German, Johann Most. A former socialist who embraced anarchism, Most emigrated to the United States after being imprisoned for inciting violence in England. He was as responsible as any man for spreading anarchist doctrine in the New World. One of his more famous literary efforts, reflecting his penchant for preaching violence, was titled "Science of Revolutionary Warfare: A Manual of Instruction in the Use and Projection of Nitroglycerine, Dynamite, Gun Cotton, Fulminating Mercury,

Bombs, Fuses, Poison, Etc." Germans were prominent in the anarchist movement which preached the destruction of all "oppressive" institutions, economic and political, and the leaders of the eight-hour-day movement in Chicago which prompted the Haymarket Riot were German, as were most of the men who were falsely accused of throwing the bomb resulting in the death and injury of a score of policemen and bystanders who gathered on that fateful May Day.

Because Irishmen were active in the trade union movement and the Germans played a pivotal role in organizing workers and preaching socialism, many Americans swallowed the nativist conspiracy theory whole. Later reports that Poles, Italians, and Hungarians fought Pinkertons, militia, and strikebreakers in pitched battles in the mines and mills of America and that Jews were organizing garment workers in New York, Baltimore, and Chicago lent credence to the nativists' "fifth column" fears. One of the principal concerns of the antilabor nativists (not all nativists were opposed to unions) was that agitators were poisoning the minds of decent American-born workers who were tricked into joining nefarious labor organizations and radical movements which were bent on destroying the foundations of Protestant America.

Writers who ingeniously wove such conspiratorial theories were not dissuaded by contradictory evidence—that the Catholic hierarchy was as hostile to political radicalism as the Protestant clergy; that relations between Jews and Catholics were hardly warm; and that the American-born worker joined labor unions to gain some control over his labor power and conditions of employment. Of course, the most sophisticated nativist thinkers did not have to "prove their theories," for they knew that prejudice—racial or ethnic—was one of the most powerful deterrents to the unification of the working class.

The term "racist doctrine" today connotes prejudice and discrimination based on skin pigmentation and other physiological attributes. But at the turn of the century, it was a common practice to talk about the Italian race, the Jewish race, or the Polish race. The late nineteenth- and early twentieth-century racial theorists juxtaposed the superior Anglo-Saxon race (Aryan, Nordic, or Teutonic—all were used as synonyms) with the inferior non-Aryan races of Eastern and Southern Europe; outside the South, racist theorists were not interested in Negroes as such. Their concern was attendant upon the steady stream of New Immigrants who were filtering through Ellis Island and it was given concrete form and "scientific" legitimacy by exponents of Anglo-Saxon superiority. In 1911 the Federal Immigration Commission published a forty-two-volume report (the Dillingham Report) contrasting the "Old Immigration" with the "new" and making some startling revelations. "The new immigration as a class is far less intelligent than the old; approximately one-third of all those over 14 years of age" were found to be illiterate.

> Racially they are for the most part essentially unlike the British, German, and other peoples who came during the period prior to 1880, and generally speaking they are actuated in coming by different ideals, for the old immigrants came to be part of the country, while the new, in a large measure, come with the intention of profiting, in a pecuniary way, by the superior advantages of the new world and then returning to the old country.[6]

The report was not conducted scientifically and it was clearly tinged with racism; to compare the performance of the "Old Immigrants" with the "new ones" without taking into account the fact that the former had lived in the United States for a longer period of time (and had a better command of English and were familiar with the American culture) was to ignore an explanation for the lower "intelligence scores" of the Eastern and Southern Europeans.

In 1915 one of President Wilson's progressive braintrusters described the non-Aryan newcomers as "low-browed, big-faced persons of obviously low mentality. Not that they suggest evil. They simply look out of place in black clothes and stiff collar, since they belong in skins, in wattled huts at the close of the Great Ice Age."[7] Wilson himself believed such nonsense. A year later Madison Grant, a Manhattan socialite, charter member of the Society of Colonial Wars, and chairman of the New York Zoological Society, wrote a book which was the culmination of his racist thought. It was widely read and Grant's conclusions were popularized in newspapers and magazines across the country. Not bothering with Negroes or Orientals, Grant focused upon the lower order of Europeans who were inundating the country. He characterized the New Immigrants as ". . . a large and increasing number of the weak, the broken and the mentally crippled of all races drawn from the lowest stratum of the Mediterranean basin and the Balkans, together with hordes of the wretched, submerged populations of the Polish ghettos." He observed that America's ". . . jails, insane asylums, and almshouses are filled with this human flotsam and the whole tone of American life, social, moral, and political, has been lowered and vulgarized by them." According to Grant, if a superior Nordic intermarried with an inferior Mediterranean spouse, the mixing of the two races "gives us a race reverting to the more ancient, generalized, and lower type." So if a Jew were to be crossed with other European races, the final product would be a Jew.[8]

During World War I, social scientists conducted studies revealing the inferiority of the New Immigrants. The president of the American Psychological Association, Robert M. Yerkes, concluded on the basis of a study of American GIs that "northern Europeans scored almost as well as native whites, whereas soldiers born in Latin and Slavic countries average significantly lower." Yerkes' research prompted the eminent social scientist William McDougall to advance a racial theory of history and Carl C. Brighman, in *A Study of American Intelligence,* concluded, "The intellectual superiority of our Nordic group to the Alpine, Mediterranean, and Negro groups has been demonstrated."[9]

Textbooks used in grade schools and colleges alike propounded the intellectual and moral superiority of the Anglo-Saxon race. Generations of American students were exposed to pseudoscientific theories which confirmed the widespread belief that the New Immigrants were indeed inferior human beings. Americans who resided in even the remotest regions of the United States were fed such notions by way of *The Saturday Evening Post* and other popular journals. Kenneth Roberts, an author of popular historical novels, warned in an article for the *Post* that immigration would inevitably produce "a hybrid race of people as worthless and futile as the

good-for-nothing mongrels of Central America and Southeast-
ern Europe."[10]

The American racial theorists claimed that the Aryan race
was responsible for the genius of Western man and that the
origins of representative government could be traced to the
Teutonic tribes that inhabited Central Europe. Moving out of
the forests of Europe, these Aryan peoples migrated to
Holland and Scandinavia and crossed the English Channel to
Great Britain. With the English colonization of North
America, representative government spread to the New
World. The Eastern and Southern Europeans then were not
only genetically inferior people, they were also, by virtue of
their genetic makeup, unable to live an ordered life under
democratic institutions. Barring them from the United States
was essential if the dominant Anglo-Saxon race was to remain
pure—the very future of democracy depended upon closing the
door to them. On the basis of "overwhelming evidence,"
spokesmen in all sectors of American life concluded on the eve
of the First World War that the capacity of the United States
to absorb these "inferior peoples" had reached its limits. To
allow more of them to enter the country was to risk
mongrelization of the Anglo-Saxon majority and perhaps to
sabotage the economic and political institutions which were a
manifestation of the genius of the Aryan race.

Senator Lodge's support of restrictive legislation then was
based on the widespread belief of discerning and thoughtful
persons that the New Immigrants were inferior people, of low
morals, and prone toward criminality and anarchism. That the
New Immigrants were largely Roman Catholics, Jews, or of
the Orthodox faith did not sit well with the Klan and other
guardians of Protestant America who knew that the "Wops"
and "Kikes" were subhuman even before the college professors
told everybody they were. To Sam Gompers, there was a pragmatic explanation to account for the AFL's support of restrictive legislation: the immigrants were a source of cheap labor,
they dampened wage scales, took jobs away from "Americans,"
meekly bowed to the demands of their bosses, and snubbed
labor organizations which were the salvation of the American
worker. These pragmatic considerations, however, were not
the only reason why the AFL was unhappy with the im-

migrants, for even foreign-born labor leaders harbored notions about the New Immigrants which were tainted by racism, and the inability of the labor movement to come to grips with its "racial problem" would prove to be one of the most important developments in American labor history.

On the eve of World War I, rising nativist pressure led to legislation barring illiterate immigrants from entering the country. During the war antipathy toward "foreigners" soared and the word "hun" was used to describe Italians, Poles, and Greeks, not just former subjects of the Kaiser. After the Armistice, nativists fingered the New Immigrants to explain the country's postwar problems. "Foreign radicals" were transporting communism to America, and "immigrant agitators" were instigating the tumultuous labor strife which erupted in 1919. Restrictionist sentiment spread as unemployment escalated, the economy sputtered, and the fear of the "red menace" sent a chill down the spines of patriotic Americans. Leaders in the American Federation of Labor, many of whom spoke with a foreign accent, disheartened by declining membership roles, abortive strikes, and the destruction of affiliate unions, were convinced that their plight was related to the resumption of European immigration. More immigrants returned to the old country immediately after the Armistice than entered the United States, but by 1920 the tide was reversed. Something had to be done.

In 1921 an emergency immigration law was passed which tightened the influx of European immigrants, but this was just a momentary measure—more comprehensive legislation was soon under consideration. Congressmen from industrial districts where the New Immigrants clustered fought the imposition of new restrictions and for a time they could count on support from the business community for, while "George Babbitt" was as concerned as any of the boys at the Rotary about keeping the race pure, the "Wops" and "Polacks" were a source of cheap labor. But the influx of even cheaper Southern Negro labor and the appearance of labor-saving machinery helped assuage fears the Babbitts had about losing the immigrant worker. Eventually even the more recalcitrant captains of industry could not ignore the groundswell of public opinion which overwhelmed the exponents of "open immigration." So the Johnson-Reed Act of 1924 was passed. It signified the end of the exalted notion that Americans had long talked about with pride—that America was "big enough for everybody."

B. Leaving Home for the Distant Magnet: *They Were Pushed and Pulled to America*

"Give me your tired, your poor,
Your huddled masses yearning to breathe free,
The wretched refuse of your teeming shore.
Send these, the homeless, tempest-tost to me,
I lift my lamp beside the golden door!"

Generations of American schoolchildren have read these stirring lines of Emma Lazarus' poem, written as part of a fund-raising campaign to build the Statue of Liberty. The notion popular at the time—that it was America's mission to provide an asylum for the "freedom-loving, poverty-stricken immigrant"—revealed our national propensity to drape practical policy with moral purpose. The American industrial engine gained momentum in the aftermath of the Civil War, and by the last quarter of the nineteenth century, the demand for strong backs and agile hands outpaced the nation's capacity to produce the labor necessary for the massive undertaking. Barring a policy of forcing rural Americans from the land, the native population could not produce the power the American industrial Leviathan needed during this takeoff stage of economic growth. The immigrants who came to fill these jobs gave as much as they got; without their skills and the low-cost labor they provided, the United States would not have industrialized as rapidly as it did. In a very real way the hardships they endured for little more than subsistence wages resulted in their subsidizing America's economic development.

The promise of jobs and prosperity was compelling to approximately 23 million immigrants who would cross the Atlantic Ocean in a forty-year period covering the 1880s to the 1920s, when the flow was checked to a trickle. The pull of America was strong but it was helped along by tumultuous changes in the heartland of Europe where rural societies were crumbling, leaving millions of people landless. The Old Immigration, comprised primarily of Anglo-Saxon, Protestant,

Northern Europeans, began to abate in the late 1880s; jobs were becoming available in the cities of the Ruhr and Rhineland, in the British Isles, and Scandinavia. The United States was compelled to turn elsewhere for the labor power it so desperately needed to mine coal, copper, and iron, to sever trees, build railroads and canals, to tote bricks, spin cloth, sew garments, and man the blast furnaces of the most rapidly developing economy in the world. Henceforth men and women from Eastern and Southern Europe began to represent a larger share of her immigration, marking the beginning of what the historians called the Second Wave of Immigration.

The New Immigrants, largely Catholics and Jews, were pushed from Europe and pulled to America for a host of reasons—economic, political, and religious. The forces which prompted their departure from the old country shaped the nature of the immigration; in some cases the immigrants, largely males, came as migrant laborers; in others entire families fled persecution and discrimination; in still others the prospect of a new future was the magnet which drew settlers to the United States. The pattern of immigration which characterized the different ethnic groups and the cultural traditions they brought with them would shape the communities they built and their social, economic, and political behavior for generations afterward. The white ethnic story began in Europe but took on new dimensions in the United States where it is still unfolding.

The Second Wave of European immigration had its origins in those areas of Europe where population growth outpaced arable land and nonagricultural job opportunities. In the 1890s the Poles had one of the highest birth rates in Europe (43.5 per 1,000) and in the last half of the century what was to become modern Poland doubled its population; in the 1880s the Hungarian population rose by two million and between 1880 and 1910 Italy's population grew by six million. In other parts of the Russian and Austro-Hungarian empires, high rates of growth produced mounting pressure on the available land.

The traditional land tenure system in the hinterland of Europe, awarding the family plot to the eldest son or dividing it among the male children, could no longer sustain the demands which were being made upon it. Large landowners, moreover, began consolidating their lands to achieve greater efficiency, driving tenant farmers and landholding peasants from soil their forefathers had worked for generations. These uprooted peasants represented a growing army of migrant workers in the late part of the nineteenth century. Italians moved north to work in France, Germany, and Austria; others roamed the Mediterranean seeking employment. Slovaks served as migrant laborers in Hungary and Poles sought employment in Prussia. The plight of the peasant villagers became grimmer when fledgling industrial enterprises eliminated cottage industry and railroads undermined local carting businesses. So by the 1880s, when prospects at home did not brighten, the peasantry of Eastern and Southern Europe began to set out for the New World. The United States was not the first choice in many cases; this was especially true of the Latins—the Portuguese, Spanish, and Italians who settled in South America. Up until the 1880s most Italian immigrants sought work in Europe, but afterward they began to emigrate to Brazil and Argentina and the United States; those who migrated to North America were largely from Italy's rural south.

As the immigration from Northern Europe slowed down and the demand for industrial labor soared, agents hired by American companies, states, and territories scoured the heartland of Europe promising jobs and high wages in the New World to the uprooted peasants. The literature which was circulated always made an economic pitch. A pamphlet published by the state of Colorado claimed: "The poor should come to Colorado because here they can, by industry and frugality, better their condition." The state of Minnesota made a special appeal: "To laboring men, who earn a livelihood by honest toil, to landless men, who aspire to the dignity and independence which comes from possession in God's free earth . . ." but also made references to noneconomic amenities. Prospects were reminded that they could exchange the "thankless toil of the old world for the freedom and independence of the new . . ."[11] And Wisconsin emphasized the political rights of newcomers, pointing out that an alien, by declaring his intention of becoming a citizen after a year's residence, could vote. While the economic magnet was a compelling force, the pamphleteers of the time also knew that the prospect of living in a society where a man could rise above the lowly station of his parents was an additional incentive for emigration.

From the aftermath of the Civil War to 1910, an estimated 9,306,370 Eastern and Southern European immigrants arrived in the United States. Between 1896 and 1917, 60 per cent of the new arrivals came from Russia, Austria-Hungary, Italy, and Greece. In an eleven-year period, from 1899 to 1919, about 2,300,000 Italians migrated; all but 400,000 came from the poverty-stricken south of Italy and Sicily; approximately eight out of ten were farm workers. In 1880 there were an estimated 900,000 Jews in the United States; during the next twenty years two million Jews arrived, most of them from Russia and Eastern Europe. Altogether from 1881 to 1925 a total of 2,650,000 "Eastern" Jews emigrated. By the turn of the century there were about two million Poles in the United States. They, like the Lithuanians, Czechs, Slovaks, Croatians, and Hungarians, boarded steamers for the New World, hungry for jobs and a new life.[12]

The first to settle wrote home and informed relatives and friends about their great adventure, the availability of jobs, and the "high wages" a simple laborer could earn. In the early 1890s an unskilled worker in Austria-Hungary earned about twenty-four cents a day compared to the "astounding" daily dollar wage which was customary in America. Such letters, some historians claim, were even more important than the embellished tales shipping agents could conjure up to recruit workers. And those who were reluctant to leave their homeland for the unknown dangers of America were often infected by the thrill of emigrating—the enthusiasm of friends and relatives who were preparing to embark on the great adventure stirred their imagination and wanderlust.

It took courage, stamina, and daring to pack one's belongings, leaving behind family and friends to cross the vast Atlantic, setting foot in a land where the language, people, and customs were alien; where disaster lurked in the mines, mills, and factories; where machines lopped off arms and cave-ins crushed the life out of men or rendered them crippled. Such tragedies were encountered at home, too, but in America who would help these unfortunate souls far from their families and friends? The thought of dying among strangers was not a happy one. Letters to the folks at home revealed that, while there were jobs in America and the pay was good, the work was long, hard, and dangerous, the natives hostile, and the risks manifold; still they came.

It's no wonder that at the outset most of the immigrants drawn by jobs were men—single or married males who left their families behind. From the post-Civil War period to World War I the percentage of male immigrants never fell below 60 per cent and the average figure was 68 per cent. Among Italians the proportion of males was generally even higher. Naturally most of them were young. From 1890 to 1920 about 85 to 90 per cent were forty years of age or under.[13] Older men, because of failing health, declining energy, or because they were less willing to leave behind the village which had been such an integral part of their lives, were less inclined to make the trip.

A large percentage of New Immigrants were migrant workers who left the old country for the explicit purpose of securing employment for several years and earning sufficient cash to return home to buy land or set themselves up in a small business. Approximately 35 to 40 per cent actually did return to Europe. From 1908 to 1931 over a million Italians, 300,000 Poles, close to 200,000 Greeks, approximately 150,000 Hungarians, and 118,129 Croatians and Slovenians did so. This included persons who returned to their native countries after they had gained their independence in the wake of World War I, those who could not adapt to an alien culture, and others who were crestfallen because reality never matched their expectations; but the largest number were migrant workers who had never intended to remain in the United States in the first place.[14]

Sociologists have labeled these migrant workers "sojourners"; their first priority was to locate a job, any job, and anywhere they could find one. As long as work was available and the pay was competitive, working conditions, hours, and other matters of profound concern to other workers were of little interest to the sojourner. To amass the wealth that drew him to the United States, he was prepared to endure all kinds of hardships. Because his stay was temporary, the sojourner had "no desire for full participation in the community life of his adopted land . . . He tend(ed) to think of himself as an outsider."[15] He had no intention of settling in the United States and cared little about long-range problems or matters which were extraneous—politics for example—to his primary purpose.

Many sojourners relied on labor agents to serve as middlemen between themselves and the American employer who needed someone to converse with the "foreigners," someone who was familiar with their customs and life-styles. Labor bosses were common among most ethnic groups, but they were most characteristic of the Italians. The relationship was paternalistic and exploitative. "The boss (usually of Italian birth or extraction, although some were Irish or American) met arriving immigrants at the docks in port cities and at railroad stations in other urban centers and promised steady work at high wages. Some immigrants did not succumb to patrone promises at once." But "a number of new arrivals, and particularly those who had no definite employment in sight, found the labor agents to be a help and even a necessity."[16] It was common for the boss to make a deal with the employer as to a flat rate for the work gang and the patrone then decided how much each worker would get. In some cases he sold them food and wine and in other instances he charged them for transportation even when the employer had paid for it. A ten-hour day, seven-day work week was common and the bone-tired men who returned from laboring dawn to dusk lived in squalid huts or railroad cars which were cold in the winter and oppressively hot in the summer. An Italian-born college student working with a railroad crew comprised of his paisans wrote that the patrone's rule of thumb was "the beasts must not be given a rest. Otherwise they will step over me."[17] Many patrones became leading figures in the Italian-American community; the first Italian daily in New York City, *Progresso Italo-*

Americano, was established in 1879 by Carlo Barsotti who, upon his arrival in the United States from Tuscany, directed squads of Italian railroad workers. He later became a successful businessman, banker, then newspaper publisher.

Newcomers were told by immigrants who had arrived before they did to beware of men, usually their own countrymen, who befriended "greenhorns," bought them drinks, or went out of their way to do them favors. Often such "friends" were confidence men who preyed upon the naïveté of recent immigrants—selling them fraudulent railroad tickets, citizenship papers, and other documents, or victimizing them by arranging work for them at shamefully low wage rates. But the patrones offered jobs and the immigrants needed them; the sojourner reasoned, moreover, that he could endure any hardship because his stay in America was temporary. Among the sojourners and bachelor immigrants, booze and violence were a customary part of existence in mining or mill towns, or working on road gangs where a knife or gun often settled disputes. Roaming bands of migrant workers contributed to the unflattering reputation the New Immigrants acquired— they were "dirty, rootless, incessant drinkers, and prone toward violence and mayhem." There was some truth to these charges, but bigots unfairly singled out the aliens and accused them of antisocial behavior which typified all "frontier American society." By the turn of the century several million migrant workers—native Americans wrenched from the farms and small towns, along with uprooted immigrant sojourners— roamed the country working in lumbercamps, laying down track, harvesting crops, building tunnels, and providing the manpower for construction gangs.

Many sojourners decided to stay in the United States and, on saving sufficient money, sent for their families; bachelors often sent a letter home alerting friends and relatives to be on the lookout for a possible spouse for them. A considerable number of Americans who trace their family line will find a grandmother or great-aunt who, as a young girl, left Europe to marry a man in America she had never seen until meeting him on the eve of their marriage. As the immigrant population grew and ethnic communities struck roots, entire families emigrated and spouses from one's own nationality residing in the United States became more readily available.

While great numbers of immigrants set out for America motivated by economic expectations, millions hastily packed their bags to escape religious or ethnic persecution. Minority peoples—Greeks and Bulgarians living under Turkish rule; Poles, Lithuanians, and Jews in the Russian Empire; and Slovaks, Croats, and Serbs in the Austro-Hungarian Empire—were vulnerable to discrimination at the hands of their majority neighbors. The age, sex, and class composition of immigrant groups "pushed" from Europe by persecution contrasted with those "pulled" to the United States by economic expectations, although in many instances both factors were at work and it is impossible to determine which was stronger.

In the last quarter of the nineteenth century, the specter of nationalism enveloped Europe and discrimination against minority groups became more intolerable. German authorities adopted a "purification policy" which threatened the Poles living in Prussia; Polish schools were closed, the use of the Polish language was frowned upon, and, when it became apparent that the Germans were bent on crushing the Polish cultural legacy which had survived German hegemony, making Poles second-class citizens, many from all social classes fled Prussia. Poles who emigrated from Prussia were generally literate, urbanized individuals who possessed industrial skills; they were better prepared than their "Russian brethren" to take advantage of the new opportunities that America promised.

In Austria-Hungary the Croats, Serbs, and Slovaks suffered discrimination at the hands of their Hungarian masters. Local languages were forbidden, newspapers were suppressed, and intellectuals and political activists were imprisoned. The chauvinism of the majority ethnic groups stirred up lingering nationalism on the part of the ethnic minorities. Polish, Slovak, and Lithuanian nationalists began to indoctrinate their own people with a new, more invigorated sense of national identity and this agitation prompted the authorities to imprison, exile, or execute them. Suffering job discrimination and denied access to institutions of higher learning, aspiring middle-class urbanites joined intellectuals and nationalist agitators in their exodus to the United States. Thousands of young men who had not previously given emigration a thought fled Europe rather than fight for their foreign masters, and there are countless Americans today who enjoy the amenities of the United States because an ancestor was a draftdodger.

The single largest group among the Eastern Europeans to flee persecution was the Jews. Prior to the 1880s most of the Jewish immigrants to America came from Germany—the Frankfurters and Lehmans—or were of Sephardic extraction like the Cardozos. They were artisans, small businessmen, but often persons of substantial means. They were an educated, cultivated group and sought the rewards of a secular "gentile" education scorned by the orthodox community in Eastern Europe. Only the disrespectful, radically inclined East European Jew sought access to the gymnasium and universities. To the German Jews, their Russian landsmen were backward people living under the rule of reactionary gentile rulers and Jewish leaders. For all intents and purposes the division between the German and East European Jews paralleled that between the first and second wave of European immigration; in both cases the division was marked by class differences, clashing religious doctrines, and divergent cultures.

The development precipitating the wholesale exodus of Eastern European Jews was the nationalist fervor and xenophobia which grew after Russia's humiliating defeat in the Crimean War. In the wake of the war Russian nationalists turned against the "decadent" West, praised the superior culture of Russia, and celebrated the humanity of the Russian Muznik. French lost favor with the educated Russians and it was considered unpatriotic not to speak and write in the mother tongue. On the eve of Tsar Alexander II's assassination, 1881, Slavophilism, formerly a relatively liberal doctrine, was corrupted by the reactionary ruling class who feared the growing discontent of the Russian masses. In an attempt to divert this discontent elsewhere, the Jews became a convenient target. Some five million lived in the lands of the Russian Empire; these "foreigners" represented a fifth column—the Jews, after all, were known to be active in the revolutionary movements and labor organizations which sought to overthrow the Tsar.

In the spring of 1881 the authorities engineered pogroms in Southern Russia, the Ukraine, and Poland. Synagogues were desecrated, Jewish businesses were destroyed, and Jews in their urban and rural enclaves were killed and assaulted by marauding bands of thugs. The next May a law was passed which restricted Jews from settling in the hinterland and quotas were placed upon Jewish admission to institutions of higher learning and entry into the professions. The economic basis of the Jewish community was sabotaged when Jewish artisans, small businessmen, and laborers were systematically excluded from plying their trades outside of the pale. Under these pressures the Jews were forced into smaller and smaller enclaves, the local economies were unable to absorb them, and poverty became widespread.[18]

From 1881 to 1920 three million Jews, young and old, orthodox and liberal, male and female, rich and poor, entered the United States. Whole families, in some cases the population of entire villages, set out for the long journey to the New World. They had no intention of ever returning to the inhospitable milieu they left behind; America would become their new home. Unlike the gentiles processed through Ellis Island, Jews from all sectors of the old community emigrated—the rabbi, the small shopkeeper, the artisan, the banker, the intellectual, the labor leader, and the political agitator—the basis for the resurrection of a viable Jewish community in the United States.

C. Urban Settlers: *The Croatians Are Coming! The Croatians Are Coming!*

The Northern Europeans arrived in America at a time when the nation was largely agricultural and land was cheap and plentiful. The average yeoman farmer produced largely to sustain his family, selling enough surplus to take care of the things he had to pay for in cash; he was not obliged to spend large sums of money for the machinery which would be needed later when farmers produced primarily cash crops. During the first wave of European immigration, large numbers of Swedes, Germans, and Norwegians bypassed the Atlantic

Coast cities and struck out for the American hinterland. They
farmed or earned their livelihood as artisans and small
businessmen; a smaller number worked as lumberjacks, laborers, or industrial workers. Those of their fellow countrymen
who later arrived with the second wave of European immigration naturally charted a course for the farms and towns where
their countrymen had sunk their roots. They relocated in established communities and were less vulnerable to the
socioeconomic problems plaguing immigrants from Eastern
and Southern Europe; because of their Teutonic birthright
they were usually spared nativistic acts of discrimination.

Though largely rural people, surprisingly few of the New
Immigrants became farmers. By the 1880s land was no longer
inexpensive and American farm families were moving into the
cities. Arriving with little money, the immigrant had to find
work soon after landing even if he wanted to farm in the New
World. Others who intended to do so were discouraged
because in addition to soaring land prices the farmer needed to
buy machinery, seed, and other expensive items to survive the
ruthless world of a monied economy. American agricultural
practices intimidated people who at home worked small plots
barely providing for the needs of the family; the farms of
America were massive, the soil strange, and the weather
unpredictable. In Europe the farm population lived in villages
close to the land the peasants tilled. American farmers, in contrast, often lived on large tracts isolated from neighbors and
relatives. This isolated existence was not very attractive to people whose harsh life at home had been ameliorated by the
comfort of the village inn and warm fireside chats mellowed by
wine or vodka after the daily chores were finished. Other immigrants were sick of the soil and viewed nonfarm labor as superior to agricultural work. To the Southern Italian, the word
"peasant" connoted social ostracism, whereas factory work
represented a step up the social ladder. To the Greek:

> Urban employment and street vending, not farming,
> offered the best opportunities to obtain ready cash. Cer-
> tainly at first, when the immigrant came "to grab a few
> riches and hurry home," the thought of engaging in a

long range operation such as farming hardly entered his
mind. Cash, mobility, and the dream of going home at
the earliest opportunity dominated his thoughts.[19]

The availability of jobs determined where the immigrant
settled and in most cases this meant the large industrial cities
or smaller mining towns and mill centers of Massachusetts,
Connecticut, New Jersey, New York, Pennsylvania, Ohio,
and Illinois, the seven states where the vast majority of
the New Immigrants sank their roots. Among the Italians,
Hungarians, and Slavs, immigrants living in cities numbered
73.2 per cent in 1900 and 86.5 per cent in 1906. The Italians
congregated in New York, New Jersey, New England, and the
industrial areas of the Midwest, although many trekked to
California, accounting for 10 per cent of that state's population by 1920. The Poles set down in the textile towns of New
England; they worked in Chicago's stockyards, the mill towns
of Akron and Youngstown, the coal mines of Illinois,
Michigan, Minnesota, and Pennsylvania. Slovaks congregated
in Pennsylvania, Lithuanians in Chicago and New England,
Serbs and Croats in Lake County, Indiana, where they were
recruited to work in the steel mills of the Calumet Region.

On the eve of the First World War, most of the nation's
major cities—New York, Chicago, Boston, and Philadelphia—
were home for a population which was largely foreign-born or
of foreign stock—offspring of one or more foreign-born parents.
More than 72 per cent of all foreign-born Americans in 1910
lived in urban areas, twice the figure for those of native-born
parentage. An even larger number of Italians lived in cities and
the figure was close to 90 per cent for Jews.[20] There was, however, a great deal of movement from city to city because of
recessions and other economic disruptions. Steady work for
both men and women was a prerequisite to the formation of
stable ethnic communities. Like the Irish before them, the
newcomers did not receive a warm welcome. In addition to
their strange customs, alien religions, and foreign tongues,
they were arresting proof that fundamental changes were
reshaping the face of American society.

Imbedded in the American psyche is enmity toward urban
life. Thomas Jefferson thought cities and representative gov-

ernments were mutually exclusive phenomena and succeeding
generations of American thinkers have reached a similar
conclusion. At the turn of the century, even after the population was rapidly becoming urbanized, the "agrarian myth"
which idealized rural life and the yeoman farmer enthralled
the American mind. Anti-urbanism would take on a new resonance as visitors to Chicago, New York, and Philadelphia observed an "alien culture" developing in the nation's largest
cities. For much of the twentieth century, urban America
would take on a foreign cast—food, entertainment, humor, and
popular speech would be shaped by immigrant Catholics and
Jews and their descendants. Today, therefore, what is considered to be urban American culture owes much of its appeal to
the white ethnics.

But not all the immigrants settled in large cities. In the
mining towns of Pennsylvania, the industrial cities of Indiana,
and the factory centers of Ohio, Michigan, and Illinois,
urban settlements largely inhabited by foreign-speaking persons mushroomed. In the textile towns of Massachusetts,
Connecticut, and Rhode Island, the New Immigrants replaced
native Americans and older immigrants who sought to put the
newcomers at arm's length by moving to the suburbs. The native Americans did not extend a welcoming hand to the newcomers. In the late 1960s, when second- and third-generation
Slavs in the Glenpark area of Gary, Indiana, were organizing a
movement to secede from the city in the wake of Richard
Hatcher's election, a Croatian priest reminded his parishioners
that when their parents first began to move into the neighborhood, the Americans panicked, proclaiming "the Croatians are coming." Throughout other areas of the United
States, native Americans fled their communities rather than
live in close proximity to the foreigners who were "taking over
the cities."

The living conditions the early immigrants endured were
wretched. Packed into overcrowded tenements in the larger
cities, several families often occupied a single cold water flat,
steaming hot in the summer and bitter cold in the winter.
Running water and toilet facilities were often located outside
the dwellings; coal and wood had to be trundled up several

flights of stairs from the cellar to provide warmth in the winter and fuel for cooking the rest of the year. A study of living conditions among Italian immigrants in Philadelphia indicated that "overcrowding per room . . . is a much more serious evil than overcrowding by number of persons to the acre. In one tenement 30 . . . families, 123 persons were living in 34 rooms."[21] Urban life was strange to these rural folks and the overcrowded conditions created horrendous sanitation problems. The thirsty peasant who had dipped a cupped hand into a nearby stream in the old country discovered that the waterways in the industrial centers of America carried lethal chemicals and living organisms which killed or crippled.

In the mine, mill, and factory towns which sprang up overnight—like Gary, Indiana—the entire working-class population was often foreign-born or foreign-bred and the local native American power structure treated them in much the same fashion that the landlords at home did. Immigrant workers often lived in a company-owned shack, bought at the company store, and received medical treatment at the company clinic—if there was one. These towns took on the aspect of frontier communities; violence, vice, booze, and lawlessness were the norm. As late as the early 1960s, such adjectives were used without exaggeration to describe the mining and mill towns of Pennsylvania, West Virginia, Ohio, Michigan, Indiana, and Illinois.

Those who lived in ethnic colonies or shared immigrant neighborhoods with other newcomers, by virtue of their numbers and isolation, were somewhat insulated from violent acts against their person on the part of the natives. But in the hinterland of the United States, the newcomers were frequent victims of bigots. Drunken thugs and vigilantes often rode through "foreign areas of town" beating up people on the streets to let off steam just like machos in Dixie got their kicks from an evening of "nigger knocking." In bloody confrontations with Americans, the immigrant was the first to be arrested and, barring unusual circumstances, was blamed for the disturbance. Local authorities generally levied stiffer sentences against aliens than Americans, while newcomers victimized by native criminals often watched helplessly as their antagonist was let off with a mild reprimand. The denial of justice to immigrants on the part of the authorities was similar to the double standard blacks experienced in the South.[22]

The lynching of immigrants by vigilantes with the complicity of law enforcement officials in the hinterland of the country became so frequent that civil libertarians on the eve of World War I conducted a campaign to pass federal legislation to put a stop to mob violence and the outrageous behavior of bloodthirsty judges and sheriffs who ignored due process in their haste to "teach the foreigners a lesson." Consider, for example, the labors of one researcher who investigated reported incidents of mob actions against Italians during the period of 1874 to 1915. He uncovered the following: four Italian workers were killed by former employees of the Armstrong Coal works in Buena Vista, Pennsylvania, in December 1874; in March of 1886 Frederick Villarosa of Vicksburg, Mississippi, was lynched on suspicion of molesting a ten-year-old girl; in April of 1891 eleven Italians were lynched by a New Orleans mob which broke into a jail where they had been incarcerated as a result of a dragnet conducted because a police officer was allegedly murdered by Italian gunmen—the police stood by while the mob dragged the victims to their death; in July 1893 an Italian was lynched in Denver, Colorado, for an undisclosed reason; in March 1894, for unknown reasons, 200 Italians were driven by an armed mob from Altoona, Pennsylvania—several were wounded and others had their homes put to the torch; in Walsenburg, Colorado, in March 1896, six Italians arrested on suspicion of murdering a saloon keeper were lynched by vigilantes. The following table tells the rest of the story:

MOB VIOLENCE AGAINST ITALIAN-AMERICANS[23]

Date	Location	Number and Condition
8/11/1896	Hahnville, La.	3 lynched
7/20/1899	Tallulah, Miss.	5 lynched
7/11/1901	Erwin, Miss.	5 lynched, 1 wounded
11/18/1901	Marian, N.C.	2 killed, 5 wounded
9/20/1910	Tampa, Fla.	2 lynched
10/12/1914	Willisville, Ill.	1 shot and killed
6/12/1915	Johnson City, Ill.	1 lynched

The quick pace of urban life, the babble of strange tongues, the fear of violating American mores, and the frightening physical compactness of urban life all contributed to the immigrants' woes. Faced with discrimination at the hands of the Americans and suffering the trauma of immigration, they sought the solace of the family and comfort of the ethnic enclave where the residents spoke the mother tongue, shared a common culture, and worshipped in a similar fashion. As more of their countrymen arrived and the population grew, a new culture was taking shape, part European and part American; it was through this new prism that the immigrants and their children looked at the world.

D. The Immigrant Family: *The Family Was the Keystone to Catholic Social Doctrine*

Social critics early in the century predicted that the traditional European peasant family system would disintegrate in the United States. "Take an individual out of his own culture and set him down suddenly in an environment sharply different from his own, with a different set of cues to react to—different conceptions of time, space, work, love, religion, sex, and everything else—then cut him off from any hope of retreat to a more familiar social landscape and the dislocation he suffers is doubly severe."[24] Alvin Toffler's definition of "future shock" is descriptive of the trauma experienced by those immigrants who decided to settle permanently in America. Since the family is a composite of individuals, wrench the individual from the milieu with which he has learned to cope and place him in one new to him and he will become disoriented—the outcome is family disintegration.

Social workers observed that in Europe the father's role was clearly defined; everyone paid deference to his authority and it was expected that he would bear up best under the pressures of immigration. But in America his confidence was dealt a cruel blow when he learned that the old cues did not work; and his inability to speak English or speak it well deepened his despair. The Americans treated him with contempt or acted as if his difficulty with a strange language and culture signified that he was dense. Over time he began to perceive himself in

these terms; he had little formal education and the folk knowledge he had acquired at home proved to be of little help to
him in the New World. Working ten or twelve hours a day for
six and often seven days a week, he was unable to watch
closely over his family. It was not long before his children had
a better command of English than he did and, as they became
better educated, they looked upon his values and beliefs as
outlandish and his behavior as quaint. He was not the model
they wished to emulate. It was a great source of embarrassment to him to have to rely upon a young son or daughter to
read English documents to him and to intervene with public
officials in his behalf. Among the reasons which had prompted
many immigrants to leave home for America was the desire to
provide their children with a better life than they had had,
including the opportunity to get an education. But the school
taught the children to reject him and his culture. As they
became more Americans than Poles or Italians, he watched
helplessly as they drifted away from him. Predictions about
the collapse of the immigrant family were exaggerated but the
trauma attending immigration drove many immigrants to
despair; some numbed their pain with alcohol, others internalized their anxiety prompting various psychic disorders,
and still others—unable to cope with the awesome responsibility of providing for a family—deserted.

The role of the immigrant wife varied from community to
community; in many places Italian women were less likely
than Polish or Jewish women to work outside the home and
Greek women almost never did unless it was to take care of
family business. Immigrant women, however, were a vital economic asset for, while wages in the United States were higher
than in Europe, few men enjoyed stable job situations or
earned sufficient money to take care of the family's needs.
Consequently it was customary for the wife and older girls to
work to supplement the family's income and this has led some
historians like Caroline Golab to conclude that "strong ethnic
communities and neighborhoods took root only in areas"
where jobs were available for both sexes. "Before they were
married, Polish women would work in textile, clothing,
tobacco, boot, shoe, and paper box factories, or they would
hire themselves out as domestics."[25] After they married and

had children it was customary for them to engage in "home work"—sewing garments, pasting together greeting cards, and finishing other goods at home to supplement the family's income. When the children grew up, many women returned to the factories, washed floors, or clerked in food markets. Jewish and Italian women were prominent in the garment industry and many worked as peddlers.

The work load of immigrant housewives was awesome; they had to feed, clothe, and care for large families on meager budgets. They washed clothes, scrubbed floors, tended gardens or canned fruits and vegetables, and kept their overcrowded flats neat and clean by dint of hard work; toiling from sunup to sundown, they made otherwise grim surroundings tolerable for their families. Many of them, of course, worked at two full-time jobs—laboring during the day in factories and returning home at night to take care of the house; or taking care of family chores during the day and doing home work at night. While immigration had something of a liberating effect upon the immigrant female—this was certainly true of the second generation—her role was still primarily oriented toward the family and the home even if she worked outside the household. Lest she forget her proper role in life, the priest and the devout among her acquaintances were at hand to remind her of woman's place in the scheme of things.

The family was the keystone to Catholic social doctrine and even where the church's influence was less manifest—among the Italians for example—traditional family systems survived the trauma of immigration. The Polish and Italian families were not altogether similar but closely knit families were vital to both groups. There were few institutions to treat personal tragedies—protracted illness, death, or the loss of one's land or job; the peasant family was the principal source of social support. The integrity of the family was central to the welfare of all its members, so individual expression which threatened family cohesion was deemed a serious offense. One of the first things a child learned was that the individual's fate was inextricably tied to the family and his first loyalty was to it. Thus he thought less in terms of his own status and future and more in terms of the family's destiny. An individual who did not have a family or who was expelled from it for committing a grievous offense was to be pitied, for he was vulnerable to the travail of a harsh world which cruelly treated the unattached. The community, the church, and the family put great pressure on single persons to marry, for bachelorhood was deemed an unnatural condition. Divorce was taboo and despondent men who considered desertion because they could not bear the crushing burden of caring for a large family were usually denied that escape because of overwhelming community pressure.

Though battered, the immigrant family did not collapse, and after World War I when the sojourners, the despondent, and the nationalists returned to Europe, the immigrant communities were comprised primarily of settlers who had established families and communities along the lines they had known at home. The immigrant family survived because there was no other replacement for it; so the "old man" was still the "boss"; the children responded with dispatch to his commands, taking care not to consort with people he disapproved of, and even after they became full-time workers many brought home their pay to him to receive their weekly allowances. The very young and the very old, the sick and the mentally despondent—the family alleviated the pain and anguish of them all.

Having survived the trauma of immigration, the traditional family contributed to the encapsulation of distinct values and social relationships in the ethnic community. Even today sociologists have found that Polish-, Jewish-, and Italian-Americans are more inclined to socialize with their family and to live closer to them than other Americans.[26] The white ethnics have made cultural readjustments to American society, but their attachment to the family remains stronger than is generally true of other groups in our society. This is a politically relevant fact because we know that early childhood socialization "stays" with those who remain close to their families. Since the immigrant Catholic families have been close-knit and the lives of second- and even third-generation white ethnics have been encapsulated by relatively closed ethnic subcultures, group-anchored political loyalties and attitudes have persisted long after the first generation has faded from the scene.

The political legacy the immigrants brought with them from Europe shaped adult and juvenile behavior alike. Passive subjects from autocratic societies, the immigrants were products of a paternalistic political culture. The political experiences and values they had acquired in the old country did not vanish rapidly in the new one. In the autocratic nineteenth-century societies of Eastern and Southern Europe, the peasant masses were politically disenfranchised. Only a small minority of the population wielded political power. Under the rule of King, Tsar, church, or aristocracy, power resided in their hands by virtue of inherited privileges—royal and clerical—the force of arms, or political intrigue. Universal suffrage, open, competing political parties, a free press, and other fixtures of representative government which began to blossom in France and Great Britain lay fallow in Eastern and Southern Europe. The Poles, Lithuanians, and Czechs suffered the added humiliation of living under the heel of foreign hegemony.

While the peasants exerted little, if any, influence upon the state or church, the authorities were free to disrupt their lives. Such intrusions as taxation and forced labor to build roads, canals, dikes, or bridges were keenly resented by the peasants. They brooded over the bishops' demands to contribute labor to the church. They feared the conscription of their sons and husbands into the military above all. "At the most crucial point of their lives, when they were ready to marry and to create families, the army took them away, interfered with the whole order of inheritance, and upset the stability of the village."[27] The peasants had good reason to distrust authority and to fear the capricious actions of the state, and few harbored notions about having any impact on government. Representative government and political freedom were mere abstractions to them and political considerations per se did not figure into their leaving home for the United States. But they did balk at being denied the opportunity to better themselves. They resented being prisoners of a closed social system marking a person's future from birth to death no matter how hard one worked or sacrificed to rise above one's predetermined station. America offered them an opportunity to achieve that which men have always dreamed of—to be reborn with the option of determining one's own destiny. Even the sojourner was

favorably impressed by the absence of tightly drawn social distinctions—they existed in the New World, but they were not
nearly as visible or as onerous as they were at home. Many
sojourners who made their "fortunes" remained in America for
this reason. The plight of the ordinary workingman was harsh
in the United States, but in contrast to the indignities the
peasant bore in Europe, America was indeed the "home of the
free and the brave." Local officials and landlords complained
that immigrants who returned to their former homelands—the
"Americans"—had a new air about them; they were disrespectful and did not pay deference to authority as they had
done previously.

The peasant "political system" did not go beyond the
boundaries of the village. The concept of nationhood did not
exist for most; few thought seriously about representative government and perhaps many did not even know what it meant.
The courageous men who talked about revolution or dissent
were dangerous fools to be avoided. The "politics" which was
of most immediate concern to the ordinary person resided in
relations with the landlord, the priest, and other local authorities and persons of importance. Obtaining justice was less a
question of gaining redress through the legal system or the
clerical equivalent than it was a matter of securing the help of
a powerful local personage—a patrone. In return for the favor
rendered, the recipient and his family were honor bound to
pay back the patrone with cash, barter, or loyalty.

Politics meant working through a network of personal contacts and family ties since there were no institutional structures affording poor folk the opportunity to gain justice. Living under foreign rule had taught the Southern Italians that
outside the family no one was to be trusted. In *Blood of My
Blood*, Richard Gambino says, ". . . the culture of the
Italian-Americans is based on a centuries-old pattern inherited
from the land of their immigrant fathers and grandfathers." It
involves a strict "code of behavior"—"centered around a
family-based small town social network."[28] With the exception of special close friends, family members are taught to
avoid outsiders and to work within the code of the family to
promote its welfare as a whole.

Within the villages of Southern Italy and Sicily, these family relationships were an inextricable part of the community and the members of the community, like the members of the individual families, were self-reliant, adhering to a strict code of behavior which discouraged interaction with outsiders, especially where the family's or community's honor was at stake. Thus, the family was responsible for the poor and indigent in its midst. Not to take care of them was to bring disgrace upon the family; the same held for the community. To admit that it was unable to deal with its own problems was to lose face.

The powerless peasant masses of Europe developed a political orientation stressing passivity and submission to authority. Even the bold ones did not think it practical to hold the church or state accountable for their actions, and they accommodated to their fate in silence, fearing change as much as they did the cavalier rule of the authorities. Resistance was foolhardy and unthinkable to most.

The distrust, fear, and awe of government which the immigrant developed in Europe ill disposed him toward political activism in America. And the shock of leaving the village of one's birth, the anxiety engendered by a perilous journey, and the trauma of coping with a foreign culture all contributed to a debilitating psychological condition. It was one which hardly fostered political participation, much less political dissent. To espouse radical political doctrine or to join a dissident political movement in a society where you were already vulnerable to the scorn of the natives was foolhardy and few immigrants did so. They avoided authority whatever form it took—immigrant official, policeman, or municipal bureaucrat. They taught their children to respect authority, to obey the law, and not to expect help from the state. Yet as we shall see, when aroused, the immigrants exhibited a militancy and combative spirit which was equal to and often greater than that displayed by native-born workers.

E. The Church: *It Is Fruitless to Oppose Authority*

Struggling to preserve something from the old country, many immigrants brought their devotion to the church intact

upon immigration. Writing over fifty years ago, the noted
Polish sociologist Florian Znaniecki observed, "The Polish-
American parish is much more than a religious association for
common worship under the leadership of a priest."[29] The
church was a source of security for the immigrants; it was part
of the Old World transplanted and a refuge from a frightening environment. In America the church among the Poles took
on an importance that was unrivaled even in Poland, where
the peasants were among the most devout Catholics on the
Continent. Even those who took their religion lightly in the
old country were attracted to the church in America because it
was the focal point of immigrant life.

In America the church enabled the immigrants to sustain
old values and beliefs and to develop new institutions in an
alien society. The anticlerical members of the immigrant community—freethinkers and socialists—represented a distinct minority. These "radicals" offered their harried countrymen little
in the way of concrete assistance other than rhetoric, a thin
gruel affording the average immigrant little sustenance. On
the contrary, people who consorted with "radicals" risked
being excluded from immigrant communities where devotion
to the church was the norm.

The church was the nexus for organizations which prolif-
erated as the immigrant community grew. After World War I
the largest Polish parish in the United States, St. Stanislaw
Kostka in Chicago, was home for 140 organizations—mutual
aid societies, women's organizations, youth groups, cultural associations, and various and sundry other organizations serving
the Polish immigrants of the parish. The priest was often the
best educated member of the community and he could perform services crucial to the welfare of his parishioners; he
found work for the unemployed, served as banker, marriage
counselor, judge, and scribe, and intervened with the authorities when one of the faithful broke the law. The church for
many years was the only institution to which the immigrant
had access which wielded power; even the American authorities respected it.

At home the Poles and Lithuanians had mixed views about
the church. Like the Irish, who had suffered the domination of

English Protestantism, the Poles throughout their history had
lived under the schismatic tyranny of the Russians, had
suffered from invading Swedish heretics, and had been
oppressed by Prussian Protestants. But while the peasantry was
devoutly Catholic, it was not altogether trusting of the clergy.
Unlike the clergy in Ireland, not many priests provided the
leadership the peasants needed to come to grips with their
varied problems. The Polish hierarchy did not encourage the
local priests to get involved in nationalist intrigues, although
some did. And many Poles believed the hierarchy favored the
old order and feared change of any kind lest it lose the
prerogatives it already enjoyed. Many clergymen, moreover,
looked down upon their people and conducted parish affairs
with an autocratic hand. In the United States the clergy and
the faithful enjoyed a better relationship because they both
needed one another.

If the East European immigrants harbored mixed feelings
about the church at home, the Southern Italians were openly
hostile toward it. The church in Italy did not minister to the
needs of the people as much as it served the rich and powerful.
In parts of southern Italy, "the Catholic church owned as
much as 75% of the local land. The figure of the priest, in
whose person Christ is presumably reflected, was thus associated with the figure of the avaricious and cruel landlord."[30]
Furthermore, the church was dominated by Northern Italians,
and it was deemed an "alien institution" in many parts of
the South; the better informed Italian immigrant also knew
that at home Catholicism and nationalism were opposing, not
mutually supportive, forces. The Vatican opposed the unification of Italy and soon after Italy became a nation the hierarchy
favored the reactionaries and conservatives, not those who
sought to better the life of the workingman. At the same time,
the church was a haven for "women," and Italian men rarely
attended church—baptisms, weddings, and wakes aside—or
paid much attention to church doctrine. In the United States,
moreover, the Italians often were tended to by Irish priests
or Italians who "took orders" from the Irish. The subservient
status of their clergy did not sit well with them nor did the
idea that they were to support an Irish-controlled institution.

La Tribuna Italiana Trans-Atlantica wrote, "Irish priests work among the Italians not to save them from sin but through fear of losing fruitful clients."[31]

At the time of the American Revolution there were about 30,000 Catholics in the country. The Catholic church was comprised of people whose perception of church government and lay/clerical relations was profoundly influenced by American Protestantism. Father John Carroll advised his superiors in Rome that it would be wise to allow the Catholic community in the United States to select its bishops. The first three ordained in America were chosen in this manner and John Carroll was ordained in 1790. The liberals in the American church who were adherents of "trusteeism" were supported by secular law since the several states had enacted legislation proclaiming that church property was to be incorporated under the names of the laity and not the clergy. It was a common practice at this time for the laity to hire and fire their own priests.

But the Catholics favoring "Presbyterianism" lost ground when conservative French bishops, in league with like-minded Irish prelates, came to power after Carroll's death. In the 1820s the liberals rallied behind the leadership of Bishop John England of Charleston, South Carolina, but the massive wave of Irish Catholic immigrants who arrived in the 1840s turned the tide in favor of conservatives like Archbishop John Hughes of New York who, on the eve of the Civil War, was the most powerful Catholic leader in the United States. Under his leadership, the church began to establish autonomous institutions separate from Protestant society—schools, hospitals, and charities. Hughes has been accused of contributing to religious polarization, but Catholic historians argue that he had no other alternative given the rising tide of nativism and the fact that the Catholic immigrant masses living in poverty were huddled in cities where there were few agencies available to serve them.

After the Civil War the Irish domination of the church was unquestioned. By 1886 thirty-five of the sixty-nine bishops in the United States were Irish-born or of Irish descent, as compared to fifteen for the German-speaking community, eleven for the French-speaking, and five for those of English heritage;

the Dutch, Scotch, and Spanish had one apiece. Congregating in urban areas, the Irish made good use of their numbers, and possessing a command of English proved to be an important asset in their quest to dominate the church. But of larger importance was the strong attachment of the Irish Catholic masses to the church. At home it was a bastion for Irish nationalism and many clergymen fought with the nationalists to rid Eire of the hated English. In the face of Protestant discrimination in the United States, the church and Irish nationalism again became inseparable in the eyes of the Irish. The priest not only provided spiritual guidance, he was also the chief defender of the Irish nation on both sides of the Atlantic. Irish domination of the Catholic church was the third side of the triad of Irish power—the other two being the urban political machines and labor unions. Control of the church bestowed great prestige upon the Irish-American community and by the time the New Immigrants arrived, the Irish were very protective of "their church."

The Irish hierarchy set out to mold the American church in the image of Irish-American Catholicism. In the seminaries and convents fledgling priests and nuns were taught to disregard the Italian and Polish view of God and to adopt Irish church doctrine. Catholic students were inculcated by the nuns with typically puritanical Irish notions about sex and marriage, while the good father preached conservative social doctrine to his "alien flock." In perusing historical accounts of the relations between the Irish and their Slavic co-religionists, one finds complaints by an American-born Polish clergyman that the nexus between things "Irish" and things "American" was so fixed in the minds of the Irish clergy that an immigrant Irish priest straight from "home" with a brogue as thick as the stout he fancied was often promoted soon after he arrived at the expense of a Pole born in the United States because the latter was a "foreigner" unfamiliar with "American ways." Even today one can find Irish nuns, priests, and laymen who, in a moment of candor, will reveal that the church is really theirs and they have been good enough to share it with the Italians and Slavs who comprise the majority of Catholics in America. At the risk of mixing ethnic metaphors, the chutzpah manifested in this assertion of ownership speaks volumes

about American Catholicism. Today "seventeen per cent of
the Catholic population, 35 per cent of the clergy, and 50 per
cent of the hierarchy are Irish."[32]

To the Eastern and Southern European immigrants who arrived in the last quarter of the nineteenth century, the Irish
were "Americans"; they looked, spoke, and acted like "Americans." Barbara Mikulski, the fiery Baltimore City councilwoman, is fond of relating how in high school she was
tempted to tell her predominantly Irish schoolmates that her
name was McCloskey to gain their acceptance. Italian, Polish,
and Lithuanian youngsters in a mixed ethnic parish observed
that the priests were Irish; so were the nuns and most prominent lay members of the parish. And in those ethnic parishes
where the pastor was a fellow countryman, it did not escape
the attention of the faithful that he took orders from "downtown"; on special occasions—confirmation day or the opening
of a new wing of the school—the parish bustled madly to take
care that it would make a good appearance for the Irish
bishop. The people who wielded power in most ethnic neighborhoods were usually Irish—the ward boss and labor leader as
well as the priest.

The New Immigrants' inability to discriminate between native Americans and those of Irish descent was pleasing to the
Irish, many of whom in the privacy of their subconscious
yearned to be Wasps. Functioning as middlemen between the
New Immigrants and the Americans, the Irish exploited this
role to great advantage. The newcomers represented money
and manpower to establish the church as a significant force in
American life; with their assistance new schools, convents,
churches, and seminaries were constructed. Later the Irish political machines would manipulate Italian and Slavic votes to
topple the Wasps from political power. Yet the Irish had
mixed emotions about the newcomers for they brought their
Catholic culture, clergy, liturgy, and doctrine with them. In
the 1890s the Irish hierarchy had successfully defeated an attempt of German Catholics to establish dioceses along ethnic
lines enjoying quasi-independence from the American hierarchy and Rome too. The Irish feared that the New Immigrants
would rekindle such notions, so they mustered all their power

to fight the formation of ethnic parishes. Poles and Italians have alleged that the Irish passion to "Americanize" their co-religionists was less a humanitarian gesture to help the Eastern and Southern Europeans acclimate to American life and prosper in their new homeland than a ploy to emasculate opposition to Irish rule. The Irish helped to destroy the integrity of the immigrant communities by compelling the Italians and Slavs to discard Mass in their languages and to adopt the "customs" of the American church. The Irish, in short, engaged in cultural genocide by denying the second generation the right to use the tongue of their parents, the keystone to any culture.

There is merit to this charge but the Irish role in Americanization aside, the sad truth is that the newcomers lacked the financial resources, the leadership, and a middle class large enough to resurrect and sustain their cultures in the United States. Moreover, those in the second generation associated a command of the English language with prosperity; it did not make sense to speak the mother tongue when you lived in a society where the dominant language was English. At the same time, in an emotional reaction to ethnic slurs—"bohunk" or "greenhorn"—the second generation often associated Italian and Polish with ignorance, poverty, and minority status. Under these circumstances, there is little reason to believe that national parishes alone would have enabled the Italians, Poles, and Lithuanians to sustain their cultures in toto in America.

Initially, the Irish attempted to absorb the newcomers in an established parish or, in those areas where one did not already exist—the mining and industrial boom towns of Pennsylvania or the Midwest—they sent English-speaking priests to establish a church for the newcomers. As the immigrant communities grew, they demanded a priest who could speak their own language and who was familiar with their culture. Since few of the New Immigrants spoke English or used it with a great deal of facility, this was a practical consideration the hierarchy could not ignore. Furthermore, the newcomers' desire to practice religion in the United States the way they did in Europe was a powerful emotion which, if ignored, could result in a serious schism in the church. It was with this fear in mind that the Irish relented and permitted the Slavs and Italians to run their own parochial schools, and adapt their liturgy, holy days, and special holidays to the American scene.

Irish liberals spoke about the Catholic church in the United States being American, but in their eyes the American church and the Irish church were synonymous. Because many Poles came to this conclusion, the Polish National Catholic Church was formed in 1895 by Father Francis Hodur. Forty years later the church indicated that it had a membership of 282,411. A smaller number of Lithuanian Catholics broke away too, but the great body of Eastern and Southern European Catholic immigrants remained in the Irish-dominated church. Their presence, however, posed another threat to the peace of mind of the Irish hierarchy, who feared the New Immigrants were carriers of political doctrines which even the liberal prelates deemed "socialistic." In a speech in 1895, Archbishop Ireland informed his audience that "criminals and paupers should be excluded from the United States" and he added, "No encouragement must be given to social or political organizations or methods which perpetuate in this country foreign ideas or customs." Baltimore's Cardinal Gibbons published an article in Ireland encouraging Irishmen to emigrate to revitalize the Catholic religion in America—which he might have added was being polluted by "foreigners" from the continent. In 1901 he was quoted in the New York *Times* as saying, "The country, it seems to me, is overrun with immigrants, and a word of caution should be spoken to them."[33]

Seeking to secure a firm place for the church in the United States, the hierarchy desired to adopt a low political profile; it had no intention of challenging the prevailing economic or political institutions. The hierarchy were clearly opposed to left-wing reformers, and reactionary prelates—whose intellectual cousins on the Continent fought Republicanism—accepted American democracy (or at least did not denounce it publicly), which had tolerated the presence of a large religious minority in its midst. Had the shoe been on the other foot, fair-minded Catholics acknowledged that a Protestant minority would have had a tough time in Catholic America.

The Irish clergy were nationalist firebrands but few were revolutionaries. The American hierarchy often viewed Continental nationalist leaders as dangerous radicals. Bishop John

Hughes warned his flock against "red Republicans" from Europe, denouncing the "Hungarian" patriot Louis Kossuth (who was an ethnic Slovak) when he made a triumphant tour of the United States. Although there were some notable exceptions, the church hierarchy was steadfastly opposed to reformers who blamed the industrial system for the long hours, hazardous conditions, and low wages the working classes endured and the squalor in which their families often lived. The American Catholic church was an immigrant church, a church comprised primarily of working people, but the Irish hierarchy throughout the nineteenth century was conservative in thought and actions. The church endorsed political democracy, but as for economic democracy, people who talked in such terms were socialists and socialists were the enemies of Holy Mother Church; neither they nor the doctrines they espoused could be tolerated.

The immigrant masses who congregated in the major East Coast cities or who lived in shacks in the coal fields of Pennsylvania and the factory towns of the Midwest were ignored by their church. The church's role was tending to the spiritual needs of the faithful; the temporal needs of the day laborers, miners, and factory hands who sustained it were determined by laws beyond the realm of the church's earthly servants. Though the need was evident, the church for years rejected the pleas of progressive Catholics that it institutionalize a welfare system and build settlement houses to help the immigrants come to grips with a plethora of social problems plaguing them. It chastized those clergy or laymen who cooperated with the "socialists" and Protestants who sought to alleviate the plight of the Catholic poor. Presumably favoring a self-help approach, the Irish hierarchy throughout the nineteenth century discouraged Catholic workingmen from forming and/or joining unions.

Yet industrialization was producing such momentous social, economic, and political tremors, even the Vatican could not ignore the havoc which was being wreaked by it. In May 1891 Pope Leo XIII's social encyclical, *Rerum Novarum*, was published. To progressive Catholics like Father John Ryan, a professor of moral theology and one of the church's leading liberals, the encyclical represented a profound readjustment in

Rome's social doctrine—legitimizing church and state actions to eliminate the evils of the industrial system and providing support for labor unions. But Ryan and his allies, who favored unions, the minimum wage, and antitrust legislation, represented a minority in the church; the dominant conservative faction was inclined to read quickly over those passages in the encyclical which acknowledged that unions might do some good, preferring passages like the following ones instead: "Let it be laid down, in the first place, that humanity must remain as it is. It is impossible to reduce human society to a level. The Socialists may do their utmost, but all striving against nature is in vain . . . unequal fortune is a necessary result of inequality in condition . . ." And the Pope warned "that many" unions "are in the hands of invisible leaders, and are managed on principles far from compatible with Christianity . . ."[34] Over time the hierarchy became more accepting of labor organizations, but its "labor policy" prior to World War I was less one of open and energetic support of unions than a reluctant defensive posture calculated to combat socialism and to influence the behavior of Catholic labor leaders.

Progressive Catholics argued that the faithful were working people and if the church ignored them and fought labor organizations, they would have nowhere else to go but to the Marxists. The church could take comfort in the fact that Irish Catholic unionists were largely loyal to their church and most of them were opponents of radical unionism. Well over half the rank and file were Catholics as were a majority of the labor movement's leaders. Samuel Gompers, who presided over the American Federation of Labor, moreover, was anathema to the socialists and sought the help of Catholic unionists to defeat socialist attempts to gain control of the Federation.

The hierarchy could also take comfort in the thought that it possessed the means to check the spread of socialist doctrine among the faithful in the Federation and the great mass of Catholic workers as well. The average Catholic immigrant was devout and greatly dependent upon the church; and through its network of institutions—newspapers and magazines, trade union associations, and of larger importance, the local parish and parochial school system—it shaped the political orientation of millions of immigrant Catholics and their children.

The church's economic and political doctrine paralleled the thinking of the exponents of laissez-faire capitalism who sanctified private property, who dismissed poverty as being part of the "natural order," and who rejected government efforts to deal with squalor and deprivation lest such humanitarian acts make matters worse. The church, via the pulpit, its literature, schools, and lay organizations, taught Catholics to obey the law spiritually and temporally; to pay deference to authority, ecclesiastical or secular; to shun "revolutionaries" who advocated that workers join in collective action against the cruel treatment of their bosses or band together politically to protest the abuse of power on the part of the privileged classes at the expense of the workingman.

But even more important than manifest attempts to imbue the faithful with values, beliefs, and attitudes which supported the status quo, the church in less direct ways socialized Catholics to be good subjects and not effective members of a democratic society. The Catholic educational system imposed knowledge upon the student; it did not stress independent thinking. Students who vigorously questioned the church's teaching were severely sanctioned. Authority was not to be challenged—that thought was burned indelibly on the mind of the Catholic, child and adult. Those who dissented were made to feel as if they had committed sacrilege—and it was just as bad to tolerate dissenters as it was to engage in the practice itself. Catholic youngsters were taught that it was unpatriotic to challenge secular authority and the Irish hierarchy, which had transferred its passionate patriotism from the "olde sod" to America, out of a keenly felt need to prove that Catholics were good Americans above all, inculcated the faithful with patriotism. ". . . the primary duty of a citizen is loyalty to country. This loyalty is manifested more by acts than by words, by solemn service rather than by empty declaration. It is exhibited by an absolute and unreserved obedience to his country's call."[35] Cardinal Gibbons was the author of these words during World War I and they were not taken lightly by American Catholics.

The layman, unless he was wealthy or well connected, had

little say in governing the affairs of the parish. Power was allocated along hierarchical lines running from the priest to the monsignor, to the bishop. The content of instruction at the school, the liturgy, the expenditure of funds—all were tightly controlled by the clergy. Church government was autocratic, plain and simple. Catholics did not learn about the fundamentals of the democratic process, majority rule, or a free exchange of ideas through their involvement in church affairs; on the contrary the church strengthened a notion which prevailed among the faithful—it is fruitless to oppose authority.

F. Ethnic Associational Life: *In America the Family Alone Was No Longer Capable of Providing for All the Individual's Needs*

"Other language groups bring to this country the cultures of peasant peoples. The Jew brings a civilization."[36] Thus Robert E. Park, the University of Chicago's grand old man of urban sociology, explained why the Jews developed a network of organizations which effectively met the needs of the community. Emigrating en masse, the Jews brought with them the basis for a total society—all ages, social classes, and political persuasions made the trip. The Jewish organizations serving the immigrant's psychic needs as well as his physical requirements were formed in America soon after they arrived. In contrast to the Catholics, religious institutions played a less prominent role in Jewish community life. Educated members of the community acted as a buffer deflecting the impact of culture shock and provided intelligent, resourceful leadership which no other immigrant group could muster.

The Jewish community on both sides of the Atlantic had developed a comprehensive network facilitating the migration. Jewish relief agencies in the heart of Russia assisted the immigrants; they received help in the ports of Europe, they found kosher kitchens aboard ship and they were met by landsmen in the United States who helped ease the trauma of immigration by providing small loans, shelter, food, and jobs. The established American Jewish community offered this help for genuine humanitarian reasons, but there was a practical aspect to their generosity as well. The Jews in America would never experience the magnitude of violent reaction to their presence that the Irish did early in the century and the Italians later would, but nativist bigots certainly did not spare them their wrath. They were an "obnoxious people, Christ-killers, members of an Eastern civilization, and carriers of alien political doctrine." Symptomatic of American enmity toward the "Semites" was an 1872 illustration published in a popular magazine entitled "Parting with the Wedding Ring." It depicted a bespectacled Jewish pawnbroker and his apprentice assessing the wedding ring of a woman clutching a baby to her breast, anxiously awaiting the judgment as to how much her precious possession would bring. Clearly, American bigots embraced the centuries-old stereotype of Jews who were "cunning, avaricious, and unprincipled." Anti-Semitism existed before the East European Jews arrived, but the largely German Jewish community which had settled in the United States as far back as the seventeenth century feared that with the appearance of a massive number of crude, ignorant, Russian Jewish immigrants a new wave of anti-Semitism would crest in the United States.

They were right! It increased in volume and intensity as the second wave of European Jews broke on our shores. Henceforth, popular cartoonists turned their attention to the "Hebrews" from Russia. An illustration in one popular magazine, for example, depicted Russian peddlers with long beards, high boots, and Russian cloaks walking down a country lane hawking their goods to local villagers. The caption read: "Our peaceful rural districts as they are liable to be invested if the Russian exodus of the persecuted Hebrews continues much longer."[37] Here we see a uniquely American dichotomy of compassion and bigotry. But the Jews individually and as a group were prepared to deal with the discrimination they would encounter. Those who fled the pogroms of Russia brought with them a psychological defense developed over centuries inuring them to American bigotry—they felt the pain but they had learned how to cope with it. In contrast to the persecution they had suffered in Europe, the American brand of anti-Semitism was tolerable. Jews on occasion were victims of physical violence; their businesses were firebombed and their synagogues and cemeteries were desecrated. But such acts were isolated and were not supported by state authority as was frequently the case in Europe. Persecution was not new to them and every Jew knew that alone he was defenseless; whatever religious, political, or social differences separated them, the Jews banded together in the face of persecution and formed organizations like the B'nai B'rith, the American Jewish Committee, and the American Jewish Congress to mobilize community power and secure the support of liberal gentiles to fight anti-Semitism. Unlike the Polish and Lithuanian intellectuals who perceived their "struggle" in terms of the old country, or the Catholic sojourners who intended to return home, the Jews had burned their bridges; they intended to remain in America and the organizations they formed reflected that fact.

The Eastern European Jews settled on the East Side of Manhattan and by the turn of the century this teeming ghetto of 150,000 persons extended from the tip of the island northward to Tenth Street and eastward from the Bowery to the East River. "Here abilities that had been pent up for centuries within the tradition-bound villages of Eastern Europe were suddenly set free."[38] The crucial element in the success of the Jewish community was the presence of large numbers of educated persons including émigré intellectuals and immigrant children who in the span of a generation rose via a college education into the professions. Together with labor leaders and political activists who had earned their spurs fighting Continental autocracy, they provided skills and talents which enabled Jewish organizations to work effectively within the American political system. They knew how to organize and mobilize the community, to maximize available resources to build coalitions, and they had the guts to persevere in a fight. Using their political acumen and legal skills, they excelled in manipulating the political and legal systems to obtain their objectives. The Jewish community was riven by factions, political, religious, economic, and social, but to a greater degree than the Catholic immigrants they had developed the capacity to overcome their differences and work toward the achievement of objectives which benefited the community at large.

Universalism—the belief in the brotherhood of man—pervaded all sectors of the Jewish community. Though it was divided along class lines, the Jewish community was much more egalitarian than European gentile society. Consequently their organizations generally were democratic, not autocratic, dissent and not consensus was the norm, and leaders were vulnerable to the members in a fashion which was uncommon among other immigrant groups. The presence of educated and talented leaders in associational life enabled a large number of Jews to acquire skills, information techniques, and a participatory mindset which today accounts for widespread political acumen in the Jewish community.

In the Catholic immigrant communities there was no comparable leadership available. The Italians, Poles, and Czechs who enjoyed social status at home—the educated professional and prosperous businessman, the privileged educated middle-class—did not leave Europe. Educated nationalists who could not tolerate living under the heel of a foreign master, political radicals who had been hounded from their homeland, and dissenters who sought religious freedom did accompany their largely ignorant peasant countrymen to the United States, but they represented a tiny slice of the Catholic immigrant community. Furthermore the émigré nationalists and radicals, who were among the best educated element in the Catholic East European community, viewed themselves as exiles. Their primary interest was in the Old World, not the new one. And other educated immigrants, like most of their countrymen, were traumatized by culture shock, too. A person's worth in the United States was measured by his monetary prowess, his ability to manipulate money and men, and not his intellectual capacity. On the European Continent, the intellectual enjoyed great social status and he was privy to prerogatives compensating for a modest economic situation. The only commodity the immigrant intellectual could sell in America was his ideas and they had been developed in a milieu far different from that which existed in the United States. Without the support of like-minded countrymen—a critical mass of intellectuals whose education, literary work, and art was grounded in a common tradition—and the opportunity to market his "wares" to a relatively large audience, the émigré Catholic intellectual was unable to take up where he had left off at home. Cut adrift from a society where he enjoyed social status and derived self-esteem from his labors, he became despondent and confined his activities to a small number of like-minded persons who, estranged from American society, often viewed their "ignorant countrymen" with distaste. Others, in a desperate attempt to preserve their cultural and intellectual heritage, built walls around their communities, concluding that the only way to persevere in America was to establish closed societies safe from outside pressures and competing values. Half a century ago a Hungarian-American writer observed that Hungarian intellectuals in Cleveland "remind . . . me of a bunch of gamblers marooned on a desert island and engaged in a desperate, endless game—each trying to live on his winnings from the rest, but nobody producing new values."[39]

There were educated Catholic immigrants who successfully adapted and quickly became productive participants in American intellectual and professional circles. But many deemed the immigrant communities as parochial and hopelessly out of step with the urban industrial society they now called home. These were the people who could have mediated between the old culture and the new one, providing their countrymen with talented, intelligent leadership and protecting them against the onslaughts of mean-spirited nativists and well-meaning Americanists who denigrated the New Immigrant's culture, robbing him of his self-esteem and self-worth, for the average immigrant lacked the intellectual weapons to fight back. Znaniecki wrote in the 1920s, "The peasant class has not participated much in the higher Polish culture which has been, and still is, chiefly the product of the upper and middle classes and those peasants who actually do participate in it seldom emigrate."[40] This was true of most Italian, Lithuanian, and Slovak immigrants; the culture they brought from home was a peasant culture—not the one the aristocrats or their educated countrymen celebrated. And the values, life-styles, and mores they brought with them were very quickly challenged by life in America. Had there been a significant number of educated middle-class persons among their ranks, they probably would have retained more of Polish and Italian culture than they did and, perhaps of larger importance, they would have adapted to the American scene much differently than they did.

In America the family alone was no longer capable of providing for all the individual's needs—problems which the government ignored; consequently self-help organizations mushroomed wherever the New Immigrants sank their roots. Every immigrant community formed burial societies, mutual health groups, and other associations which for five or ten cents a week protected members against illness and unemployment and provided for a proper burial. In some cases village societies, fraternal associations, religious groups, or nationalist organizations were the basis for these activities. Later they would become part of national federations or be superseded by larger organizations like the Polish National Alliance or the Sons of Italy, but few of these organizations had a national agenda.

In addition to their economic functions, the immigrant fraternals and village societies served much like workingmen's clubs. At the Polish Falcons or Italian lodge, members could drink beer and wine and enjoy well-cooked food among people who spoke their language, sang familiar songs and performed dances which set the blood racing just as they did at home. They also sponsored social events and cultural activities which enhanced community life; yet they did not adequately serve a large cross section of the community and this was especially true of the most needy members. Florian Znaniecki noted that the first purpose of Polish-American self-help organizations was "to prevent the individual from becoming a burden to the community, and the individual who does not choose to avail himself of the opportunities" offered "voluntarily resigns all claims to the help of the group."[41] Alcoholics, the poor, juvenile offenders, and the elderly, he charged, were ignored by the Polish self-help organizations. Progressive Italian observers were inclined to say the same thing about their organizations. An Italian priest told Robert Park:

> I should like to open the eyes of the public to the fact that very little is done here for Italians by Italian organizations; such organizations like the Sons of Italy do not

use their money as they should. They may spend it in
Italy for private needs and things. They should spend it
here for American institutions for Italians.[42]

In the 1960s, when young community organizers sought to establish community development programs in inner-city white
working-class neighborhoods, the ethnic organizations were
generally criticized for spending funds on parades, banquets,
and stained-glass windows, while ignoring the plight of the
needy in their midst. Equally disconcerting was the paternalism of the leadership, its resistance to change, and the utter
disregard for genuine membership participation in policy-
making decisions.

The immigrant associations would eventually become the
focal point of community power, providing the leadership and
organization necessary to gain access to the urban political system. They were potentially "schools" for political education,
providing members with insight into organizational
techniques—how to identify problems, organize support for a
political program, and mobilize the community to project its
demands—but they were governed along hierarchical lines
affording the membership little voice in decision-making. The
political émigrés, nationalists, and radicals, as well as the
businessmen who became leaders in the community, all
adhered to political principles which were molded in the political autocracies of Europe. Leaders gained ascendancy by dint
of their personal power; they were not selected democratically.
The notion of one man, one vote generally was not honored in
theory or practice and the membership passively accepted the
rule of "their betters." For all intents and purposes, the
peasant/patrone authority relationship which was characteristic of community life at home prevailed in the immigrant
community in the United States. The strong man or patrone's
authority was legitimized by his ability to wield power—
because he had access to jobs, money, or contacts and could do
favors for his followers—not because he was the most intelligent or enlightened member of the community or best
served the interests of the people he "represented."

The ethnic communal associations, like the ethnic parish,
enabled the immigrants to organize the group around familiar

cultural and religious values—thereby helping maintain an ethnic personality—and were the basis for the immigrants coming to grips with societal pressures. Because they did not collapse under the pressure of immigration, urbanization, and industrialization, the ethnic associations helped facilitate the integration of their members into American society. But the immigrants and their children paid a price, for the ethnic organizations perpetuated a paternalistic political culture which neither effectively met the needs of the community nor afforded the individual an opportunity to develop politically.

G. Educating the Second Generation: *If It Weren't for Them . . . I'd Be Accepted*

> I look up at him in amazement. Is this man my father? Why, look at him! Listen to him! He reads with an Italian inflection! He's wearing an Italian mustache. I have never realized it until this moment, but he looks exactly like a Wop. His suit hangs carelessly in wrinkles upon him. Why the deuce doesn't he buy a new one? And look at his tie! It's crooked. And his shoes; they need a shine. And for the Lord's sake, will you look at his pants! They're not even buttoned in front. And, oh damn, damn, damn, you can see those dirty old suspenders that he won't throw away. Say, mister, are you really my father? You there, why you're such a little guy, such a runt, such an old looking fellow! You look exactly like one of those immigrants carrying a blanket. You can't be *my* father!
>
> JOHN FANTE, "The Odyssey of a Wop"[43]

The authorities in Russia and Austria-Hungary sought to impose cultural uniformity among minority peoples by prohibiting the use of "foreign" languages, cultural practices, and religious rituals which sustained cultural autonomy. In contrast the American authorities paid little attention to the growing number of "minority persons" in the United States until the late nineteenth century. The native Americans were confident that they could absorb the foreigners who settled in the vast reaches of America. With the exception of the abrasive Germans who were convinced they gave more than they got, the peasants from Eastern and Southern Europe clung to their culture more out of habit than conviction—at least this was the conclusion many American observers of the New Immigrants had favored. Teach them English and the natal cord which nourished their foreign ways in the United States would be severed.

By the 1890s it was apparent that by virtue of the number of newcomers and their propensity to settle in compact ethnic enclaves, the problem of assimilating them no longer was to be taken lightly. Two different approaches to the disruptive presence of the New Immigrants developed. On the one hand, Jane Addams, who directed the activities of Hull House in Chicago, developed programs to treat culture shock, to integrate immigrants into the neighborhood, to provide them with instruction in English, thus enabling them to communicate with the "strangers around them." She cautioned workers in the settlement house movement to be careful, in the process of lending a helping hand, not to denigrate the immigrants' cultural legacy, for it was a source of comfort to them. She noted that great damage was wrought where the immigrants were taught that their values, ideals, and beliefs were worthless baggage from a bygone era, useful perhaps in the Old World but certainly not in the new one. Indeed, she attempted to demonstrate to immigrant youngsters that their parents possessed artistic talents and vocational skills which were useful and creative; they were to be admired for such talents, not to be objects of ridicule. Many settlement house workers concluded that the immigrant children who engaged in various forms of antisocial behavior were defenseless because they had forsaken the old ways before they learned how to cope with the New World which mesmerized so many of them.[44]

As the steamers discharged their human cargo from Europe, persons motivated out of fear and not humanitarianism began to take note of the New Immigrants' presence. The Daughters of the American Revolution, the Sons of the Revolution, the Colonial Dames, and various and sundry other "patriotic" organizations feared that the newcomers represented a threat to the American way of life. And they lobbied energetically to press educators, editors, and the public to pay proper attention to the problem. They sponsored lectures and disseminated literature to immigrant neighborhoods laced with patriotic messages. The good ladies in the DAR were guided in their work by the thought that "obedience" was "the groundwork of true citizenship." Industrialists who had little patience with do-gooders like Jane Addams—"who pamper the alien scum"—responded more positively to hardheaded "Americanizers" who warned that the immigrants were largely responsible for the rising incidence of social and labor unrest in the country. The immigrants were harbingers of alien doctrine which was poisoning the minds of native Americans. Labor unrest and the "unending demands" which the workers were making were all traced to the odious presence of the New Immigrants. The quest to Americanize them was essential to secure labor peace and it was in this vein that industrialists and business organizations sponsored adult education courses for their immigrant workers. The first English words immigrant auto workers at Henry Ford's night school learned were "I'm a good American."

The First World War gave a new sense of urgency to the campaign to Americanize the immigrants, who represented a virtual "fifth column." Thus Frances Kellor, a Cornell-educated lawyer who had written with feeling about the exploitation of the immigrant worker and had masterminded legislation to fight it, drifted toward the hucksters of hundred per cent Americanism on the eve of the war. She was instrumental in replacing the slogan which government propagandists had favored early in the war, "Many People, But One Nation," with the new one which stated cryptically, "America First." In a speech before the National Security League she spoke about the immigrants as an internal peril and left her listeners with the thought that Americanization was the civilian side of national security. Henceforth, Protestant fundamentalists, racist bigots, and political reactionaries began to play a dominant role in the crusade to Americanize the immigrants. "To a nation charged with evangelical impulses, Americanization was a mission of redemption; to a country of salesmen, it offered an adventure in high pressure salesmanship."[45]

Nativist bigots had reached the conclusion that there was no room for cultural pluralism in twentieth-century America, that dissent, whether it took the form of "alien doctrine" or "resident foreigners" who refused to conform to the American way of life, could not be tolerated. People like John Dewey, who wrote that each race could make a contribution to a cosmopolitan society in which many cultures thrived, drifted away from the Americanization movement with the termination of the war. The problem would take care of itself as the immigrants, through educational and job mobility, overcame their social and economic problems and blended in with everybody else.

As long as liberal-minded Americans participated, they served as a countervailing force to the yahoos, racists, and reactionaries in the campaign, but with the postwar red scare, the hundred percenters pressed state authorities to take action against the new peril—alien radicals. In 1919, fifteen states passed laws which legislated that English must be used in all public and private schools; in Iowa the governor proclaimed only English could be used in public gatherings, including telephone conversations. California passed a new tax law which punished alien residents; it was declared unconstitutional. The Americanization drive gave new purpose to the teachings of civics in the school system and special attention was paid to the instruction of immigrant students. As the red scare faded from the people's consciousness with the bright prospect of prosperity in the mid-1920s, the steam which had driven the engine of the crusade for Americanization evaporated. Nonetheless, the campaign had left its mark upon the immigrant and second-generation youngsters who sought to take their place in American society.

The notion that our public schools enabled the immigrant and second-generation child to rapidly transcend the ignorance of his parents and achieve economic mobility is a legend. According to Colin Greer, "The truth is that immigrant children dropped out in great numbers—to fall back on the customs and skills their families brought with them to America." He found that every study taken since they began in the late 1890s indicates that "more children have failed in

Chicago's schools than have succeeded, both in absolute and relative numbers." In all the major urban centers where the New Immigrants congregated, Greer discovered that consistently something like 40 per cent of the students were either in the "overaged" (one or two years behind) or "retarded" (three to five years behind) category. In Pittsburgh and Minneapolis, at one point in time, an even larger number of students fell into these categories. In New York City in 1938 a study indicated that one-tenth of the city's school-aged children did not get beyond elementary school and 75 per cent did not finish high school.[46]

In those instances where immigrant children gained some benefit from the schools, "it was in spite of, and not because of, compulsory public education that some eventually made their way." Scholars attribute "the outstanding rate of Jewish mobility in the cities of the Northern United States" to their "urban and small township entrepreneurial experience in East Europe." According to Moses Rischin, a greater percentage of Jewish immigrants—about 66 per cent—had "industrial" experience prior to coming to the United States than was true of other New Immigrant groups.[47] The economic stability of the group was another important prerequisite to success in schools; for example, the economic security of "storekeeping Jewish" and "farmholding Scandinavians" contributed to both groups' success in school. This was also true of commercial-minded Greek and Japanese-Americans.

Among the Catholic immigrants, many children did not attend school and others left as soon as it was feasible to place them in the labor force. In other cases the older child worked so the younger ones could secure an education. The income derived from child labor was crucial to many immigrant households. But the economic mobility the family achieved was enjoyed at the expense of children who in adulthood would not rise much above the economic or social status of their foreign-born parents. For those who were lucky enough to attend school, the experience was not an altogether gratifying one. Jane Addams complained about the failings of the schools to appreciate the special problems experienced by the immigrant students. Possessing a poor command of English, the immigrant child was thrust into a situation where his peers conversed with one another and followed the instructions of the teacher with little difficulty, while he often could not keep up with his fellow students. In his eyes the other kids were "smarter," and as he fell further behind them his self-confidence was dealt a brutal blow. He could not take much solace in predominantly "immigrant schools," where the students were taught to be contemptuous of their parents' values and language. Dr. Leonard Covello, the first Italian-American principal in New York City, reminiscing about his public school days has said, ". . . throughout my whole elementary school career, I do not recall one mention of Italy or the Italian language . . . We soon got the idea that 'Italian' meant something inferior . . . We were becoming Americans by learning how to be ashamed of our parents."[48] Robbed of his self-esteem, the immigrant child often welcomed the opportunity to leave school for work.

The schools, however, were very effective in one respect—they socialized the immigrant students to become steadfast supporters of the nation's economic and political institutions. Political rituals like pledging allegiance to the flag and singing the national anthem were given special emphasis by teachers who read books, tracts, and magazine articles warning them that their pupils were potential "carriers" of alien doctrine. American history was idealized, slavery was ignored, and the ruthlessness of the Robber Barons was euphemistically depicted as "American enterprise"; the Carnegies, Mellons, Fricks, and Rockefellers—"the people who produced the wealth and jobs which the common man enjoyed"—were proffered as models to be emulated. Little time was devoted to developing the student's critical faculties and he was force-fed middle-class Wasp values not necessarily without merit, but drummed into his head to expel those which were adhered to at home. There was an awesome gap between the idealized society the schools presented to the students and the harsh facts they observed in their neighborhoods and later experienced in the factories and mines.

Even after the ethnic political machines drove the Wasps from political power, the Americanizers continued to influence school policy through influential state and national educational associations and the Settlement House Movement. The business community wielded great influence over the schools and through them children were inculcated with the business ethos of laissez-faire capitalism. Private property and the sanctity of contracts were the basis for Western Civilization; through hard work and sacrifice everyone in America—even those who were born into the most menial families—could become rich and prosperous.

The sad truth was that education meant rejecting one's parents and culture for the dominant culture. On graduation day it was the practice in some schools to conduct a ritual which represented the rebirth of the immigrant child into an American. A large pot constructed out of wood and crepe paper stood in the center of the auditorium stage and the graduates entered the Melting Pot decked out in the apparel of the old country and came out the other side dressed resplendently in identical American clothes. This ritual represented, in fact, the growing estrangement of the second generation from their parents.

"I enter the parochial school with an awful fear that I will be called Wop," John Fante writes. Comparing names of other Italian-American children with his own he concludes, "I am pleasantly relieved . . . After all, I think, people will say I am French. Doesn't my name sound French? Sure. So thereafter, when people ask me my nationality, I tell them I am French . . . Thus I begin to loathe my heritage." As soon as the immigrant child learns that he's an outsider because his parents are greenhorns, he blames them for his condition.

> I begin to think that my grandmother is hopelessly a Wop. She's a small stocky peasant who walks with her wrists crisscrossed her belly, a simple old lady . . . When in her simple way, she confronts a friend of mine and says, her old eyes smiling, 'You lika go to the Seester scola?' my heart roars. *Mannaggia!* I'm disgraced; now they all know that I'm an Italian.

The shame that the second-generation child feels for his parents is superseded periodically by the shame he feels for rejecting them. But if it weren't for them, for their being greenhorns, "I'd be accepted."[49]

Convinced that their parents' culture represented ignorance, poverty, and social ostracism, the second generation rejected the immigrant legacy. Millions of Eastern and Southern European Americans did so without ever coming to grips with the reality that one's present orientation toward the world has been shaped by the values, experiences, dreams, and trauma of one's ancestors. To deny their existence is to deny an important part of one's self. Unable to identify with or find security in their parents' culture and having been rejected by mainstream society, the second generation was stricken by an emotional affliction akin to self-hate—accounting for the reluctance of Italian- and Slavic-Americans to participate in affairs beyond the confines of their communities.

CHAPTER III

The Working-Class Legacy

A. The Immigrant Worker and the Labor Movement: *Born in Lands of Oppression, Surrounded by Squalor, Inured to Hardship,* Samuel Gompers

In 1901 J. P. Morgan purchased Andrew Carnegie's vast iron and steel empire and merged it with his own Federal Steel Company to form United States Steel; thus the nation's first billion-dollar corporation was born. "What Carnegie and Morgan did for steel, Rockefeller did for oil, Gustavus Swift for meat packing, James Duke for tobacco, Henry Clay Frick for coal mining, James Pillsbury for grain processing, and Messrs. Ward and Roebuck for merchandising."[1] The United States at the turn of the century was the most powerful industrial nation in the world. During a period of twenty years, 1880–1900, bituminous coal production expanded from 43 million to 212 million tons, hard coal from 30 million to 57 million tons, pig iron from less than 4 million to 14 million tons, and steel from 1,250,000 to 10 million tons. At the very apex of this vast industrial and financial empire sat a small coterie of men who had gained their supreme position by violating capitalism's basic tenet—competition. The large trusts and combines they controlled had overwhelmed smaller competitors who could not amass capital or pursue profits with the verve and callousness of the Morgans, Rockefellers, and Fricks. To Marxists, here was concrete proof that Marx knew what he was talking about when he predicted that monopolization and not competition would become the ruling principle in the advanced states of capitalism.

Industrial growth produced an insatiable demand for jobs, which drew Europe's "surplus labor" to the United States. The New Immigrants replaced native American workers and older immigrants who had previously performed the most hazardous and odious tasks in the mines, factories, and mills of America—duties which henceforth became the province of the Pole, Italian, and Slovak. In 1910 the percentage of foreign-born white males in these industries was as follows: coal mines, 48.3 per cent; copper mines, 65.4 per cent; iron mines, 66.8 per cent; clothing manufacturing, 75.9 per cent; meat processing, 45.8 per cent; leather processing, 52.9 per cent; textiles, 48.7 per cent; rubber manufacturing, 40.3 per cent; steel, 51.0 per cent; and breweries, 49.2 per cent.[2]

The confluence of a new industrial order, dominated by a shrinking circle of capitalist barons, and the growing incidence of immigrants among the work force was a source of great concern to the burgeoning labor movement. The American Federation of Labor had tenaciously fought heavy odds in a hostile climate to become the nation's largest labor federation. And this difficult birth is one of many factors accounting for the Federation's failure to develop a viable organizing strategy vis-à-vis the New Immigrants. Having survived the industrial strife of the last quarter of the nineteenth century, the leaders in the AFL had learned to become cautious. The very nature of industrial capitalism produced economic conditions which made labor organization difficult. Periodic depressions, frequent layoffs, and subsistence income all conspired against the formation of a stable work force and the establishment of organizations which would enable workers to challenge employers for higher wages, better working conditions, and dignified treatment at the workplace.

The Robber Barons who presided over the industrialization of the United States from the late 1860s to the Great Depression of 1929 were the product of Anglo-Saxon pragmatism, Calvinist determination, and a frontier spirit unencumbered by noblesse oblige. Labor unions, which they deemed a threat to the prerogatives of their wealth and property, could not be tolerated. Consequently, industrial warfare in the United

States was unrivaled, and nowhere in Europe were workers killed and injured in such large numbers at the hands of company goons, local police, state militia, and federal troops who throughout the Gilded Age were at the beck and call of the captains of industry. State power from the very founding of the Republic was used to crush labor unions through legislative and executive actions. In most places local authorities provided legal cover for anti-union activities. Until the 1930s courts restricted unions and intimidated workers by ruling that strikes involved criminal conspiracy and circumvented free trade. The 1890 Sherman Anti-Trust Act, legislation originally intended to curb the massive power of corporations, was used to emasculate labor unions because they "restrained trade" instead. In industrial disputes judges consistently ruled in favor of employers and ignored the violation of workers' rights of free speech and assembly.

Leaders in the AFL were inclined to perceive the immigrants in much the same terms that most bosses did—namely, that the newcomers were easily manipulated by employers, scabbed, served as strikebreakers, and worked for "starvation wages." Samuel Gompers, the Dutch-born Jewish cigar maker who presided over the AFL (except for one year) from 1886 to 1924, commented in 1912 that the Eastern Europeans who were inundating the steel industry were "untutored, born in lands of oppression, surrounded by squalor, inured to hardship" and reached manhood "without that full mental development which makes for independence and self-preservation."[3] It was on the basis of such observations that labor leaders began to talk about reducing the flood tide of European immigration.

When immigration restrictions were first debated in the 1880s, most labor leaders turned a deaf ear and restrictionist pressures abated after passage of the Foran Act of 1885, a law designed to deal with the abuses associated with the importation of immigrant contract labor. Many labor leaders were foreign-born (at the second convention of the AFL, more than half of the delegates were foreign-born) or offspring of foreign parents. They accepted the principle of "open immigration" and some believed that the European immigrants were more amenable to unions than the individualistic native Americans.

The immigrants they had in mind, however, were Northern Europeans. In the last quarter of the nineteenth century, the skilled workers in most industries were American-born or German, Welsh, Scottish, Irish, or English craftsmen. Many of these people had belonged to unions in Europe and at the very least were familiar with the industrial environment and favorably inclined toward labor organizations. Even after the Northern European migration slowed down perceptibly, many skilled immigrants who arrived at the turn of the century were "Northerners." These "aristocrats of the labor force" dominated the labor movement, serving both as organizers and as paid officials in the labor hierarchy. But as Eastern and Southern European immigrants began to represent a growing proportion of the labor force, union leaders claimed that the newcomers were stealing the jobs of craft unionists. Unskilled immigrants were replacing native American and Old Immigrant workers, but the basis for this change was technological; machines now performed skilled tasks which craftsmen had done previously. Nonetheless, officials in the AFL began to speak in favor of restricting immigration, so there is little doubt that bigotry, plain and simple, caused many AFL leaders to misconstrue the facts, preferring to attribute declining membership roles to the "Hunkies" and not to American technological ingenuity.

Not all elements of the labor movement supported restrictive legislation. The Jews in the garment unions, among the first of the New Immigrants to occupy leadership positions in the labor movement, were especially vocal in their opposition, but like the Irish unionists who feared that the Poles and Italians would undercut the labor market, the socialist-minded Jews lamented that they were "deficient in class consciousness."[4]

Socialists who took a dim view of the immigrant worker could cite no less an authority to bolster their suspicions than Friedrich Engels—Karl Marx's long-time benefactor and collaborator—who once said, "I am strongly inclined to believe that the fatal hour of capitalism will have struck as soon as a native American working class will have replaced a working class comprised in its majority by foreign immigrants."[5] Like the European immigrant, the native American who left his rural home for the factory suffered the pangs of "emigration," for the urban worksite was a new and alien world to him. It was a world governed by profit and the salary system where the clock and assembly line dictated the pace of one's output. There was no opportunity to derive pleasure from work; it was tedious, repetitious, and unending. Under these circumstances the proud American's individualism was ground down into a collective gruel upon which the industrial system fed. Some radicals argued that while the immigrant peasant had always lived on the margins of society and meekly accepted the cruelty of industrialization, the independent American, having been pitched into the abyss of the proletariat, resented his "enslavement." For capitalism violated the agrarian myth upon which he had been weaned and assaulted the human manifestation of that legend—the yeoman farmer, proud, self-sufficient, steadfast in the protection of his family, his community, and the values which sustained them. This, some historians tell us, is the basis for native American radicalism, and it explains why the most revolutionary labor organization in our history, the Industrial Workers of the World (IWW), was founded by American-born Western miners, lumberjacks, and agricultural workers.

Throughout this century the notion that the American worker was more militant than the immigrant laborer was commonplace among labor historians. But recent research indicates that just the opposite may be true, for the Eastern and Southern Europeans who constituted the "second wave" of European immigration played a decisive role in organizing workers in the garment industry and in making the United Mine Workers the largest labor organization in America by the turn of the century. When the IWW turned its attention to the East, it was among the New Immigrants that the Wobblies enjoyed the greatest success, and on numerous occasions they were the backbone of the most famous strikes in the first quarter of the twentieth century. These new findings have caused some labor historians to speculate that, while the AFL allegedly turned its back on the New Immigrants because they were "pawns of the bosses," there is reason to believe that the old guard feared the contrary was true—that the newcomers were favorably inclined toward radical unionism and, if given a chance, would follow the lead of the socialists. In other words, a successful campaign to organize the New Immigrants might have tipped the balance of power within the labor movement toward the left. But the labor radicals were as ignorant as the conservatives in the AFL about the Italians and Slavs, and they too adhered to dogma which precluded their mobilizing the newcomers into a powerful collective force for radical change.

It is conceivable that even if the AFL had made a real commitment to organizing the New Immigrants it would have failed—given the power of labor's enemies, ethnic discord which divided the rank and file, and the precarious position of the AFL at the time. But the success the UMW enjoyed organizing immigrants disproved the conventional wisdom that attempts to recruit them were a waste of time.

B. Organizing the Miners of Pennsylvania: A *Man Is a Man Even If He Is a Hungarian*: Unidentified Journalist

In 1900, 99 per cent of the hard coal produced in the United States and three fourths of the world's production was extracted from the mines of Pennsylvania. After the Civil War large railroad companies, with the resources needed to economically mine and ship coal, drove small coal mine owners out of business. While mine ownership was changing hands, the composition of the work force was undergoing a metamorphosis. By the 1880s German, Welsh, English, and native American miners were being replaced by the New Immigrants. On occasion the first ones to enter the industry were scabs or strikebreakers, gaining the "newcomers" the reputation of being anti-union and pliable pawns of the owners. A contemporary commentator claimed, "Nearly every officer of organized labor that I met expressed the fear that whenever they struck, the Poles and Hungarians and Italians were poured out to take their place." As a consequence, "the widely differing races (of Central Europe) broke down the miners' solidarity and made effective organization of the coal fields impossible."[6]

Though widespread at the time, the record shows that this view was unfounded.

In the 1880s there were two unions operating in the hard coal region—the Knights of Labor which pursued an inclusive organizational strategy involving skilled and unskilled alike, and the Amalgamated Association of Miners which was only interested in skilled workers. Both ignored the New Immigrants toward whom they were hostile. Nonetheless, when a strike was called in September 1887, most of the immigrant miners (in areas where the strike was successful) dropped their tools and joined their fellow workers in the walkout. In Slavic and Italian communities miners who refused to abide by the strike call were sought out by their own people and threatened with physical harm if they returned to the pits. On one occasion when fifty miners who refused to comply with the strike call returned home from work, a crowd of some eight hundred Poles showered them with rocks, coal, and snowballs. Police who came to clear the way for the miners were attacked and six strikers were shot in the fray. Throughout the course of the strike, the immigrants frequently spearheaded demonstrations while the English-speaking workers "kept out of trouble." Their militancy surprised fellow strikers and frightened labor leaders. One newspaper reported, "Strike leaders . . . deprecate riots and say 'twas the work of ignorant foreigners and worthless outsiders who do not belong to labor organizations."[7] With the exception of a Ukrainian, Father Wolansky, the immigrant clergy opposed the strike, but the strikers were supported by other segments of the immigrant community.

Unlike the more individualistic English-speaking miners, the Slavs and the Italians were under great pressure from their kith and kin to abide by the strike action. ". . . because of determined community sentiment, working dissenters had to pay for their transgressions. Here was the cause of the Slav-inspired beatings and riots. In this crisis the tightly knit Eastern European society could not tolerate individualists." A local reporter noted, "The striking Poles and Huns mean to stop . . . work even if it leads . . . to murdering their own kinsmen . . . They declare all Huns and Poles must stand together, live together, or fall and die together." The English-speaking miners in contrast, "whether labor leaders or only followers, seem less unified, more individualistic . . . and perhaps less determined."[8]

A split between the competing unions, the refusal of many miners to walk out, and the overwhelming force that the mine owners could muster broke the strike. Perhaps because this was the first time the Slavic and Italian communities in the anthracite region had acted as one, the labor leaders ignored their militancy, and the Americans refused to reconsider the notion that the immigrants were a "docile" lot.

As they became more visible in the mines, and ethnic enclaves spread throughout the dreary communities of the hard coal region, nativistic animosity toward the newcomers spread. Labor leaders remained convinced that the immigrants were responsible for low wages, unsafe working conditions, and management's refusal to recognize workers' organizations, and it galled the Americans that the foreigners could exist on next to nothing and stoically accept deprivation—the very qualities which enabled them to endure a long strike.

In 1894 a new mine union made its appearance in Pennsylvania's hard coal region—the fledgling United Mine Workers, which had its origins in the Midwest bituminous coal industry. Contrary to their expectations, the immigrants were receptive to the UMW organizers, and by the end of the year one of the most successful locals in Pennsylvania was a 4,000-strong Lithuanian local in Shenandoah. But after an impressive first step, the UMW effort faltered when organizational funds ran out. UMW organizers complained that the "foreigners" were disinclined to part with their hard-earned cash, and this reinforced the conviction that the New Immigrants were poor prospects for trade unionism.

However, it was not long before the immigrant miners once again demonstrated their militancy. For in 1897 they played a pivotal role in a labor protest resulting in the infamous Lattimer Massacre, the tragedy that paved the way for UMW success in Pennsylvania's anthracite coal fields. On August 12, 1897, a foreman at the Honey Brook Colliery, located south of Hazelton, adopted a new work rule which prompted immigrant workers to strike. The ethnic communities unanimously supported the Honey Brook strikers, and before that strike was settled, Slavs at the Van Wickle Company also laid down their tools and conducted protest marches. As the strike fever spread, the town of Hazelton was paralyzed. *The Wilkes-Barre Times* wrote, "Thousands of ignorant foreigners have begun a reign of terror, have closed up all the collieries, wrecked the home of the superintendent, and marched from one mine to another amid the wildest confusion, a howling mob without aim or leader."[9]

On September 3 a crowd of some 9,000, mostly Hungarians and Italians, gathered in a field in McAdoo to await management's response to their demands. About 1,000 strikers lost patience and marched down the town's main street in protest on their way to Hazelton. When they were informed that police were waiting for them, an Italian who was leading the throng paused and then responded, "I gotta the right. I am a American citizen. I have my papers. They cannot stoppa us. Forward."[10] The police contingent that stood on the outskirts of Hazelton ordered a halt, but when the marchers continued to press forward, the police wisely stepped aside.

Two days later, when another large throng of miners marched on the Pardee Company's Lattimer Mine, the outcome was much different; a contingent of sheriffs and their deputies fired upon the demonstrators, most of whom were shot in the back. "The police fired directly into the unarmed marchers, who, screaming, ran for cover. As soon as the townspeople heard the shooting, many rushed to the fallen, strewn about the field." Later it was learned that nineteen had been killed and thirty-nine were wounded. Among the victims were "twenty-six Poles, twenty Slovaks, and five Lithuanians." In the wake of the massacre, "frantic, kerchiefed women, trailing bewildered children behind" inundated the hospital and morgue searching "among the blood-spattered beds for their husbands and sons. When they found one they sought, a pitiable wailing arose."[11]

The strike fizzled, but not before the miners received wage increases. Once again the immigrant miners had demonstrated their militancy and raw courage in the face of armed police; almost singlehandedly they had kept the strike alive. Their enthusiasm and discipline caused the UMW to take heart and to return to the anthracite fields in earnest. It was at this point that the UMW hired "foreign organizers" like Paul Pulaski of Mt. Carmel, a second-generation Pole, who spoke six languages, and Cornell Pottier, a Polish-speaking Frenchman from Shenandoah. They proved invaluable in organizing the Eastern European miners.

While the UMW received a mixed reception from the American community, the immigrant community lent its full support to the union. The Polish National Catholic church, through its organization STRAZ, published the union's activities as did ethnic organizations like the Lithuanian-Polish Club of Luzerne County. In a fitting commentary on the courage and tenacity the immigrant miner exhibited, the Elmira *New York Telegraph* wrote, "Gomer (the superintendent whose work rule changes sparked the strike) has learned a lesson. He has been taught a man is a man even if he is a Hungarian."[12]

Three years after Lattimer the immigrant miners, under UMW leadership, struck again. They won a pay raise, but the mine owners would not negotiate with the union, much less recognize it as a legitimate bargaining agent for the miners; and they began to accumulate inventory, a sure sign that they were preparing to face down the UMW. The miners in the meantime pressed for higher pay and union recognition. After many months passed, they lost patience and called a strike in the spring of 1902. About 95 per cent of the miners in the anthracite region struck; at one point over 100,000 of them left the pits.

Many of the sojourners left the anthracite region for the bituminous coal fields of Virginia or relocated in New York City or Philadelphia, but most of the immigrants, especially those with families, remained behind and made preparation for a long strike. Paul Pulaski formed a food cooperative; miners and their families scavenged for coal; others picked berries for sale, while all cultivated their small gardens in earnest. These preparations and a stoical spirit enabled the immigrants to fare better throughout the strike than their English-speaking co-workers. The immigrants contended that the strike represented a cause which no miner could disavow; those who did were deemed traitors. Because they were vigilant in pursuing miners who continued to work, the immigrants skirmished with the police on several occasions. In one incident a deputy sheriff and several nonstrikers were set upon by striking immigrants and shots were fired. The names of the injured rioters were revealing: "Dolski, Lusku, Wakavage, Savinikus, Binjunas, Belliski, and Pomewicz."

The UMW disavowed the violence but the immigrant strikers refused to ignore miners who remained in the pits. Throughout the five-month strike, the immigrant community enthusiastically supported "their men." The Lithuanian band of Shenandoah, touring New Jersey and New York, sent back money to help the strikers. The National Slovak Society and the Chicago Sokols contributed over $50,000. But even more important than money, the ethnic organizations provided discipline which they sternly enforced on "their people." The ethnic press, because it was not controlled by the mine owners, provided reliable information to the strikers and lashed out at those who did not comply. Throughout the course of the strike, the owners sought to foster ethnic discord, and on one occasion a pamphlet was circulated in the Eastern European communities. Printed in German, it urged the readers to "act . . . for your countrymen and families . . . the Irish, the strike leaders, are always capable of turning against you . . . Act at once and for yourself . . ."[13] It was signed "a friend." While the leaders were Irishmen and the great mass of immigrant miners were not, the ploy failed to work. Irish leaders like the youthful John Mitchell won the trust of the immigrant strikers and, to their embarrassment, were plied with presents after the strike.

By the fall the nation's coal supply was growing short and with the onset of winter President Theodore Roosevelt called representatives from both sides to Washington to work out a settlement. Roosevelt failed but his Secretary of War, Elihu Root, convinced his friend J. P. Morgan to entreat the mine operators to agree to arbitration and on October 20 the miners returned to work. The Commission of Arbitration ended its hearings on February 5, 1903. Although the rewards were reduced and the owners refused to recognize the UMW, the miners won most of their demands and the union had gained a secure footing in the hard coal region, a condition which would eventually lead to the UMW organizing the entire anthracite region of Pennsylvania.

The immigrant miners and their communities had been steadfast in their support of the strike, and the UMW at long last gave proper recognition to the "foreigners." The vice-presidency of each of its districts was reserved for one of their leaders, men like the Pole Paul Pulaski, the Slav Andrew Matti, and the Lithuanian Adam Ryscavage. The UMW success in the anthracite region of Pennsylvania was concrete proof that the immigrant workers, under proper leadership, would join unions, stand fast in strike actions with native Americans, and endure oppression until victory was won. Here too was proof that unskilled workers could be organized. In spite of these facts, the AFL's hostility toward the immigrant worker did not abate and it continued to resist mounting pressure to organize the unskilled.

C. The Lawrence Strike of 1912: *We Want Bread and Roses Too!*

In 1912 Lawrence, Massachusetts, was a thriving textile center, the home of the world's largest textile mill, owned by the American Woolen Company. At its peak it employed 10,000 workers. Altogether the mills of Lawrence, which lined the Merrimac River, provided jobs for approximately 35,000 people, most of whom were foreign-born or second-generation Americans. By 1911 seventy-four thousand of the city's eighty-four thousand residents were of foreign stock. German, Irish, and native American workers who had previously dominated the labor force were still in evidence in the mills; most of them were skilled workers. Italians, Poles, Lithuanians, Syrians, Armenians, French-Canadians, Franco-Belgians, Greeks, Turks, and Russian Jews were in a majority by 1912. They did the dirtiest, most laborious work.

Ethnic distinctions separated the skilled from the unskilled, and managers manipulated them in a host of different ways to emasculate attempts at organizing the workers. Out of a total labor force of 35,000, only 2,800 workers were organized in the entire city. Approximately 2,500 skilled workers belonged to the AFL-affiliated United Textile Workers Union. The unskilled, with the exception of some three hundred largely Italian- and French-speaking workers who belonged to a local of the radical IWW, were non-union.

The average millworker lived in an overcrowded company tenement. The standard dwelling was four stories high, built so close to adjacent structures that housewives could build shelves on the "outside walls" next to their kitchens to store pots, pans, and canned goods. "Extra space" was at a premium. Because rents were high, more than one family often shared a flat. A sixty-hour work week was typical, with men, women, and children often working at the same grueling job. Women and children, though they often performed identical tasks as men, did not receive equivalent wages. It was estimated at that time that an average urban family was unable to live for less than $900 a year in the Commonwealth. Despite the collective labors of the immigrant families, their income was barely sufficient to provide for subsistence. The conditions which prevailed were appalling. The life expectancy of the millworker was twenty-two years less than that of management employees. Dr. Elizabeth Shapleigh of Lawrence found that "a considerable number of boys and girls die within the first year after beginning work. Thirty-six out of every 100 of all men and women who work in the mill die before or by the time they are 25 years of age."[14]

This then was Lawrence, the setting for one of the most celebrated strikes in American labor history. On January 1, 1912, the Commonwealth of Massachusetts passed a law reducing the work week for women and children. The owners retaliated. They lowered the work week for men too and sped up the machines without making pay adjustments. When a group of Polish women on Thursday, January 11, discovered shrunken paychecks, they walked out in protest. The next day an even larger number of workers discovered that their paychecks were short too. "About 9 A.M. an angry mob of Italians in the Wood Mill of the American Woolen Company . . . deserted their machinery and ran through the mill demanding that other workers march out." Moving "from one department to another, they disassembled machinery, cut wires, blew fuses, and intimidated non-cooperative workers into joining their

walkout." As they surged "out of the Wood Mill and down
Canal Street along the Merrimac River . . . the Italians
rushed from mill to mill, heaving stones and chunks of ice at
factory windows, beseeching the men and women inside to
come out."[15] By nightfall about ten thousand men, women,
and children were on strike.

On January 13 an organizer for the IWW, Joseph Ettor, arrived to provide leadership for the strikers. The local Italian
Wobblies had invited him to the strike-torn city. Twenty-six
years of age at the time, Ettor was the son of Italian immigrant parents. Born in Brooklyn, he had accompanied his
family to Chicago, where he grew up listening to stories his father related about labor history and revolutionary strife. Later
as an ironworker in San Francisco, Ettor became an IWW
organizer. He toured mining, lumber, and construction camps
spreading the radical doctrine of the IWW. In McKees Rocks
he used his command of Italian, English, Yiddish, Polish, and
Hungarian to work effectively with a polyglot work force in
strikes which erupted in this steel and coal mining region of
Pennsylvania. The youthful Ettor "infused the immigrants
with his own militancy. All night Saturday and all day Sunday,
at meeting after meeting, he urged mill workers to strike for
higher wages."[16] He so fired up the strikers that Monday they
marched on City Hall. This frightened the mayor, who alerted
the local militia to disperse the crowd.

Ettor, a skillful strike tactician, knew that the élan of the
strikers would quickly wane without leadership and coordina-
tion of strike activities. One of his first actions was to form a
strike committee comprised of two representatives from each
of the various ethnic groups. The committee drew up demands
among which were a pay increase, double time for overtime,
and no reprisals against the strikers as a basis for settlement.
The owners remained resolute and refused to deal with the
committee until the strikers went back to work. They were
convinced that the immigrant strikers would be unable to
overcome their lingual and cultural differences and without
the spirit of solidarity to fortify them, the strike would crum-
ble. The owners were so certain of this that they did not even
bring in the customary strikebreakers.

Another Italian, Arturo Giovannitti, arrived on the heels of

Ettor to set up a relief body which was of critical importance to the survival of the workers, their dependents, and the morale of the immigrant community. Born to an upper-middle-class family in Abruzzi, Italy, Giovannitti had emigrated to the United States at the age of sixteen, where he worked at a number of different jobs. At one time or another he had been a miner, a bookkeeper, and a schoolteacher. He had renounced his Roman Catholic faith in favor of Marxism and become a leader in the Italian Socialist Federation of New York. Not one to covet any dogma for long, he later discarded orthodox Marxism and became an anarchist. He spread the "word" via *Il Proletario*, an Italian syndicalist newspaper. He spoke fluent English, Italian, and French. Soliciting food, cash, and medical care, the relief task force functioned effectively throughout the life of the ten-week strike. Families, depending upon their size, were given $2.00 to $5.50 per week for food, and every second week they received $1.50 for fuel and clothing. At this time workers' poverty was the primary cause of their inability to maintain strikes and no strike was successful unless the strikers could be sure their families would receive food and other necessities.

John Golden, the head of the AFL United Textile Union which served the mill's organized workers, called the IWW leaders "revolutionaries and anarchists." He attempted but failed to wrest control of the strike from the Wobblies. Later rank and file members of the UTW and the AFL sent money to help their "brothers and sisters" in Lawrence; but most German, French-Canadian, Irish, and English millworkers were opposed to the strike. An Irish mafia, led by Mayor Scanlon, controlled City Hall. The leading Irish-American priest in Lawrence, Father O'Reilly, condemned the IWW for misleading "ignorant" immigrants. Many Irish strikers listened to him and no Irish representatives served on the strike committee. But a French priest was hooted down when he urged the strikers to go back to work—and the Poles and Lithuanians failed to pay heed to the warning of their clergy that the strike was an "antipatriotic" scheme of the "devil."

Despite a reputation for inciting violence, gained largely in defensive actions against police, management goons and vigilantes, the IWW wanted to avoid violence in Lawrence. Criti-

cal of the Italian strikers' actions on Friday, Ettor instructed
them in nonviolent protest. But when a group of strikers
marched toward the Pacific Mill to call out workers who had
not yet joined the strike, hoses projecting ice-cold water were
turned on them. When they responded by tossing chunks of
ice at their tormentors, thirty-six were arrested. They were sen-
tenced to one year in jail. No serious injuries were recorded,
yet the press called the action the "first bloody battle of
Lawrence," and some accounts reported that several workers
had been shot. These reports were all false. Nonetheless the
governor called in the militia to reinforce the local law-
enforcement personnel, who had already been mobilized by
Lawrence's mayor. The police were the first to draw blood.

On the evening of January 30, an Italian woman, Annie
LoPezzi, was shot and killed by police fire. Afterward the commander of the militia instructed his men that in the event of
trouble, "Shoot to kill. We are not looking for peace now."
Ettor and Giovannitti were arrested for inciting "the violence
which led to the woman's death." Martial law was declared,
demonstrations were outlawed, and more militia were called
in. Included among this new contingent of troopers were
students from Harvard, who thought it something of a lark to
get "in on the action."[17]

Upon learning of Ettor and Giovannitti's arrest, "Big Bill"
Haywood, the most celebrated IWW leader, cut short a
fund-raising tour and returned to Lawrence to replace the
Italian radicals. Born in Salt Lake City, Haywood had entered
the mines at the age of fifteen, where he lost an eye. He was an
organizer for the Western Federation of Miners and gained
fame when he was falsely accused of complicity in the bombing murder of an ex-governor of Idaho. One of the original
founders of the IWW, he also was a prominent member of
the Socialist Party, from which he was to be expelled for
espousing violent revolution.

Like many native American radicals, he was neither an original thinker nor a theoretician. Tough, energetic, and an effective speaker, he was a bitter foe of the powerful industrial and
financial interests which were destroying rural America.
Unlike the immigrants in the East, the American-born West-

erners attracted to the IWW had known better days and they expected more from the land of their birth than did the European immigrants of whom they took a dim view. The various "populist" parties and movements they formed identified the Catholic and Jewish "foreigners," along with the Eastern banks and railroads, as their enemies. Many, weaned on Protestant fundamentalism, feared Roman Catholicism and were inclined to buy the myth about Anglo-Saxon "racial superiority." Others thought a clique of Jewish financiers were responsible for the nation's economic troubles. Most of them were angry that they had lost status with the onset of industrial capitalism, but few of them were revolutionaries. They wanted a larger piece of the action and they were not hell-bent on destroying the free enterprise system as such.

Haywood, neither a Puritan nor a fundamentalist, but a confirmed revolutionary, believed that capitalism and social justice were mutually exclusive, and he was met by a cheering throng of immigrant strikers when he first entered Lawrence. He spoke about one of the most troublesome problems facing the strikers—ethnic discord: "There is no foreigner here except the capitalists . . . Do not let them divide you by sex, color, creed, or nationality . . . Billy Wood can lick one Pole, in fact he can lick all the Poles, but he cannot lick all the nationalities put together."[18]

The IWW organizers and other radicals who inundated Lawrence were soon followed by curious journalists. They wrote that the strike was growing through peaceful picketing and musical parading. They provided the nation with insight into the mills' appalling conditions and the workers' maltreatment at the hands of the owners. By the last week in January, some 14,000 workers were out on strike. The mills were no longer operative, but the owners refused to meet and negotiate with the strike committee. Tensions were mounting and on January 30 tragedy struck again. A sixteen-year-old Syrian boy, John Rami, was bayoneted to death by a militiaman because he refused to move on when the trooper told him to.

Although some local labor organizations and ethnic organizations provided assistance, the bulk of relief funds came from sources outside Lawrence. Every time the militia overreacted or the mill owners demonstrated their callous indifference toward the plight of their workers, the volume of donations to the cause mounted. Strike coverage by journalists from prominent newspapers and magazines now was of pivotal importance to the strikers. With this thought in mind and in an attempt to alleviate the burden of feeding and caring for the strikers' children, the Wobblies accepted the suggestion of New York Italian socialists to send youngsters from Lawrence to live with sympathetic families outside the strike-torn city. This tactic, which had been employed by strikers in Europe, proved to be crucial in forcing the owners to the negotiating table.

The first group of children sent to New York City was greeted by large crowds. Their pitiful condition vividly portrayed how bad the conditions in Lawrence were. Most suffered from malnutrition and other physical impairments. They wore tattered clothes and worn shoes. The publicity their sad presence generated excited the attention of sympathetic nonradical middle-class matrons, politicians, and church officials. The strike received continual coverage as succeeding groups of children were sent to other cities to live with "foster parents."

The tactic proved to be so successful that the millowners convinced the militia commander to bar further exportation of children from Lawrence. The strikers refused to comply, and when a group of women and children gathered at the railway station to board trains they were set upon by club-swinging policemen and dragged to waiting military trucks. This incident was the turning point in the strike. Protests from every corner of the country flooded Congress. President Taft, a bitter opponent of unions, ordered an investigation. When the Congressional hearings were held, the First Lady attended, and later traveled to Lawrence to survey the scene firsthand. This publicity prompted the owners to meet with the strike committee on March 3, fearing that a Democratic-controlled Congress might tamper with their sacred tariffs. On March 14 the management representatives agreed to all of the strikers' demands. Ettor and Giovannitti were later acquitted.

To the IWW organizers the Lawrence victory proved that immigrant workers, with proper leadership and support, could initiate and implement a strike to successful completion. It was additional evidence that, contrary to arguments of the craft unionists, unskilled workers could be organized into industrial unions. By September 1912 the Wobblies claimed a membership of 16,000 workers in the city. The strike had produced a new self-awareness among the immigrant workers and this vital spirit was first observed during the strike when a young female striker carried a sign reading, "We want bread and roses too!" This led some radicals to the conclusion that this new self-awareness was a manifest expression of growing working-class consciousness. The IWW leadership was ecstatic. Haywood, in an address to the victorious strikers, told his audience, "I want to say . . . that the strikers of Lawrence have won the most signal victory of any organized body of workers in the world. You have demonstrated, as has been shown nowhere else, the common interest of the working class in bringing all nationalities together."[19] But the Lawrence victory was short-lived. The millowners mounted a counterattack soon after the small army of Wobbly organizers left the city and Lawrence vanished from the national headlines. The mainstay of their offensive was to drive the various ethnic groups apart by selectively closing mills where the workers had been most sympathetic to the strike, while operating those mills where the Irish and other English-speaking workers had resisted the IWW strike call. By 1914 conditions in the mills worsened and the IWW called a strike; it was abortive and the demoralized millworkers drifted away from the organization.

Lawrence was perhaps the IWW's finest hour, but nine years after that victory the organization was on its knees; many of its leaders were in prison or in hiding, others were living in exile (Haywood died in the Soviet Union), and the membership had shrunk to insignificant proportions. During World War I and its aftermath the Wobblies, who opposed U.S. intervention in the "capitalist war," were the target of a government campaign; thousands of them were arrested under state antisyndicalist laws, beaten by vigilantes, and shot by militiamen or federal troops during the red scare. Their offices were closed or ransacked without due process and their newspapers were shut down in violation of the First Amendment. The IWW was a target of government oppression, but the collapse of the Wobblies was largely due to its strategy and tactics, which flowed from the IWW's commitment to the destruction of capitalism. The IWW, in contrast to the conservative craft unionists in the AFL, sought to organize unskilled immigrant workers into industrial unions; it published numerous foreign language newspapers, and recruited organizers from among the immigrant communities. But the IWW failed to gain and hold the support of the average working American, native and foreign-born, because it preached revolution and ignored the everyday bread and butter problems that preoccupied them. The IWW refused to co-operate with other labor organizations or to sign contracts with employers because they proclaimed that such "compromises" represented "class collaboration." The Wobblies were brilliant strike tacticians; they were tough, resourceful, and dogged during a fight, but they were hell bent on leading the workers in pitched battles with the "agents of capitalism," and the routine of building and maintaining a union that served the worker's daily mundane needs at the plant bored them.

The craft unionists in the AFL took great comfort in the demise of the IWW and proclaimed once again that, barring unusual circumstances, it was a mistake to organize unskilled workers; no union could long survive which strayed from a practical policy of "pure and simple unionism." Samuel Gompers, who made a deep and lasting imprint upon the doctrine of the AFL, argued that the goal of labor unions was simply to improve the lot of the worker at his place of employment. This meant organization to secure higher wages, shorter hours, and better working conditions. Gompers rejected revolutionary labor doctrine which was bent on destroying capitalism or sought to deal with societal problems because such enterprises were doomed to wither in the hostile anti-union climate prevailing in the United States.

Gompers, who had read Marx in his youth, bolted from the Socialist Labor Party because of the revolutionary pretentions of its most illustrious leader, the brilliant international lawyer and Marxist theoretician, Daniel De Leon. Gompers, who became active in the labor movement soon after he arrived in the United States, had reached the conclusion, after a brief romance with socialism, that labor had to secure gains within the context of the capitalist system. His organizational focus was upon the skilled worker, the craftsman who, unlike the common laborer, had something of value to withhold from his employer—his scarce labor skills. Because of this common bond and like-minded outlook, the skilled workers could forge and sustain labor organizations. They enjoyed job security and earned sufficient money to pay dues and build strike funds.

Some of the affiliate AFL unions were dominated by socialists—unions in the mining, garment, and brewery industries, for example—but Gompers effectively emasculated socialist attempts to define AFL policy. Gompers castigated "syndicalist IWW radicals" who sought revolution through direct economic action. He was equally critical of Fabian Socialists who acknowledged the utility of unions as instruments of reform but who believed that the primary instrument for change was the socialist party. Gompers' "voluntarist" apolitical doctrine held that the workingman could not expect much help from government, that the only way he could improve his material situation was through collective bargaining with his employer. The critical prerequisite here was the presence of a labor organization with the means to force management to the bargaining table. Higher wages, better working conditions, and a process to deal with grievances—those were the kinds of things that labor unions were meant to do. Since the New Immigrants were predominantly unskilled factory hands and "common laborers," they simply did not fit into Gompers' organizational scheme. The AFL's narrow craft-oriented doctrine excluded them by definition.

Within the AFL, however, there were industrial unions like the United Mine Workers and the Brewery Workers Union and the leaders of these unions were steadfast in the belief that unskilled workers in other sectors of the economy could be organized into industrial unions. As the First World War approached, even conservative trade unionists were beginning to toy with this idea. Machines were replacing skilled workers in many industries, leading to declining union membership, and it was apparent that where skilled and unskilled workers toiled together, management often played one off against the other, undermining worker solidarity. Changes in the industrial system, therefore, necessitated a new, more inclusive strategy—one which would bring both the skilled and unskilled workers in an industry together into a single union.

D. The 1919 Steel Strike: *It's a Slovak Strike,* Official of U. S. Steel

After the bloody 1892 Homestead Strike, the AFL-affiliated Amalgamated Association of Iron, Steel, and Tin Workers of North America, the largest union in the United States, steadily lost ground in the steel industry, a trend which was expedited by the replacement of skilled craftsmen with machines. As competition in the steel industry intensified, United States Steel's Judge Elbert H. Gary declared in 1907 that henceforth no unions would be recognized by his corporation. This was a cruel blow to the Amalgamated, which was still on the defensive and Gary's "open shop" policy forced some labor leaders in the steel industry to consider industrial unionism. The stark truth was that as mass production industries grew in size and employed new technology, it was foolish to ignore the industry's unskilled workers. Craft jobs were in jeopardy, and the massive resources of the giant corporation made it even more difficult for craft unions to maintain a toe hold in the industry and to bargain effectively with the steel trust.

"The best approach, it seemed clear . . . was . . . bringing all the workers in one industry into a single national union. This would guarantee unity of action and avert the manifold difficulties of artificially dividing a labor force made occupationally indivisible by mass production techniques."[20] But the craft-oriented unions dominated the AFL and, while they paid lip service to organizing the unskilled, they remained cool to the idea. The Amalgamated, lacking the leadership, the organizers, and the experience to organize unskilled workers, backed away from industrial organization and steadily lost membership in the steel industry until the war in Europe dramatically changed the fortunes of the American labor movement.

The war had shut off European immigration, later created

military conscription, and produced a labor shortage which dramatically improved the bargaining position of the working-man and his union. During the war, union membership increased by some two million; American industry was making large profits in meeting the demands of the "war effort" and labor organizations could be tolerated as long as the war lasted. To facilitate wartime production, the Federal Government became involved in labor/management relations to an unprecedented degree. In addition to setting prices and production quotas, Washington established a War Labor Board to facilitate harmonious labor/management relations. Under pressure from the Federal Government, the steel industry reduced working hours, provided for overtime pay, and gave tacit recognition to "labor representatives" who served as bargaining agents for the workers.

But as the war in Europe drew to a close, labor leaders began to talk about the postwar years. They nearly all agreed that management would attempt to reverse the gains organized labor had achieved during the war. With peace in Europe, corporate strategists would reduce the work force, lower wages, increase hours, and adopt a nationwide "open shop" campaign in an attempt to crush the labor movement.

The steel trust, under the leadership of Judge Gary, was likely to lead the way in this antilabor assault. Labor strategists in turn reasoned that the campaign could be sabotaged if they adopted a vigorous offensive against the steel industry. Were the steel industry to fall in the face of an AFL organizational drive, weaker links in the corporate chain would become demoralized and give way to further unionization. Since the dominoes could fall in either direction, both sides mobilized resources for the deadly contest in earnest.

In August 1918, twenty-four affiliates of the AFL formed a National Committee for Organizing the Steel Industry; John Fitzpatrick of the Chicago Federation of Labor, a liberal trade unionist, was selected to preside over the Committee. But the real sparkplug of the drive was William Z. Foster who, just prior to accepting the job of Secretary-Treasurer of the Committee, had successfully organized Chicago's stockyard workers. A product of Philadelphia's slums, Foster had worked as a sailor, lumberman, and railway hand before joining the

IWW as an organizer. He left the Wobblies because he could not accept their practice of dual unionism—of competing for workers who already belonged to unions. Secretary-treasurer of the National Committee and future leader of the Communist Party, Foster favored industrial organizing, but he was prepared to work for the craft unionists because they agreed to organize unskilled steelworkers as part of their organizational drive. They acknowledged that it was necessary to organize the industry's unskilled if the craft unions were to expand their membership in steel, but they never considered inclusive industry-wide organization. The steelworkers who signed union cards were to be placed in a host of different unions on the basis of the tasks they performed.

The steelworkers responded enthusiastically to the drive and by the summer of 1919 about 100,000 had been organized. The National Committee received reports indicating that the immigrant workers were among the first to join the new labor organization and that they did so with unrestrained enthusiasm. By the spring of 1919 the newly organized workers were pressing for a strike. Among the most compelling arguments they made were that the steel companies were firing workers who signed union cards, that the War Labor Board was no longer processing workers' grievances, and that the company was making preparations to break the imminent strike. "Why not hit them before they hit us?" The leadership in the AFL, including Gompers, however, resisted mounting rank and file pressure for a walkout, fearing the awesome power of the steel trust. But in the mill towns, the steelworkers and their families were preparing for a strike. The immigrant workers had undergone a profound psychological transformation during the war and the success of the National Committee inspired their confidence. Having enjoyed higher wages, more reasonable work days, and a modest amount of bargaining power during the war, they were acutely conscious of being exploited by Judge Gary and his minions who demeaned them as men and as "Americans." Like their American co-workers, they took to heart wartime propaganda which promised great changes for the American people after the "War for Democracy" had been won.

In July a strike vote was taken and it was overwhelmingly

approved by the rank and file. After Judge Gary refused to meet with the National Committee to discuss the workers' grievances and unionization, a strike was called for September 1919. An estimated 250,000 workers, approximately half of the work force in the steel industry, walked out. Mills in Chicago, Pittsburgh, Gary, and other steel-producing areas of the country were severely crippled. The enthusiasm of the workers was gratifying to the proponents of industrial union- ism. Here was proof that a national strike against a basic mass production industry was feasible. Never before had so many workers joined a strike action of this magnitude.

The rank and file response surprised even some of the more sanguine leaders in the National Committee. To persons who were knowledgeable about the working and living conditions of the strikers, it was less of a mystery. When the organi- zational drive first started, the work day and average work week were appallingly long. Approximately one half of the labor force still worked a twelve-hour day, and as many labored seven days a week. British steelworkers in contrast worked twenty hours a week less than the Americans. High wages at U. S. Steel were more a function of a long work week than high hourly pay. Over one third of the workers earned below the income level set by the Federal Government as the minimum subsistence standard for a family of five; 72 per cent earned less than the government's "minimum comfort level."[21]

In addition to long hours and low wages, steelworkers were engaged in heavy labor which was physically exhausting and extremely hazardous; in the mills in and around Pittsburgh, the accident rate among immigrants was twice the average. In one plant about a fourth of the immigrant workers were in- jured or killed during a five-year period.[22] After having had some voice in decisions pertinent to their employment, it galled them that they were once again defenseless in the face of management's decrees. The Interchurch Commission of Inquiry, which conducted an investigation into the strike, demolished Judge Gary's contention that the industry had taken care of the workers' housing needs. Commission inves- tigators discovered that the housing available to the average steel- and ironworker was overcrowded and substandard. "The census takers (January 1920) found in Braddock, for example, that in this steel suburb of Pittsburgh 61 families were living in 22 houses; 35 boarders were in one house where three different persons occupied each bed in the 24 hours of each day, sleeping in eight-hour shifts."[23] It was against this backdrop of long-smoldering grievances and great expectations that close to 300,000 steelworkers left the mills during the course of the strike. But by mid-November of that same year strikers were returning to work in droves. On January 8, 1920, the National Committee admitted defeat and the remaining strikers returned to the mills. It was a cruel blow to the entire labor movement and especially to workers in America's mass production industries.

The strike failed for a number of reasons: the sponsoring unions were at odds with one another; U. S. Steel was a powerful industrial giant; government and public opinion were opposed to the strike; and the rank and file were divided by ethnic discord.

Despite pledges of support the craft unions refused to give the strikers their full backing. And this held true for skilled steelworkers too. The mills could not operate without them, and many of the skilled craftsmen refused to strike and those who did were among the first to return to work. Most of them belonged to the Amalgamated which during the strike refused to remove its men from plants where it still had contracts. The inability of the unions to work effectively together was a major problem for the strikers. From the very outset of the National Committee's drive, the participating unions fought over the newly organized steelworkers. Jurisdictional battles erupted from the start—for example, the Electrical Workers and the Operating Engineers fought over the right to organize the steel mills' electrical cranemen.

The craft unions were jealous of their autonomy and it was commonly understood that in the event of conflict with member unions or the Federation itself, the individual unions were sovereign. The affiliates in the National Committee were not obligated to do anything they did not want to; this permissiveness made centralized decision-making and uniform, precise execution of policy nearly impossible. Moreover, some unions would not agree to cooperate during critical stages of the strike—for example, the railway unions would not shut down major rail interchanges which would have checked the flow of traffic to and from the mills. Other unions reneged on their promises and withheld monetary support. In a very real way then, the narrow, craft doctrine of the AFL contributed to division among the unions and set the stage for the crushing defeat the labor movement suffered.

A second factor contributing to the strike's failure was the awesome power of the steel trust. In the introduction to the best contemporary report on the steel strike, the Interchurch World Movement observers concluded, "The chief cause of the defeat of the strike was the size of the steel corporations together with the strength of its active opposition and the support accorded it by employers generally, by governmental agencies, and by organs of public opinion." The steel companies could count on the support of mayors, city councilmen, law enforcement officials, and judges, for most of them were more or less pawns of the steel trust. "The arbitrary control of the (trust) extended outside the plants, affecting the workers as citizens and the social institutions in the communities . . . In western Pennsylvania the civil rights of freedom of speech and assembly were abrogated without just cause, both for individuals and labor organizations."[24] In McKees Rocks, Pennsylvania, the mayor prohibited outdoor meetings and in other steel towns sheriff's deputies broke up legal assemblages of strikers and arrested the organizers. Since the steel companies controlled the local press, it was difficult for the workers to answer charges that the strike leaders were revolutionaries, to deny false rumors about the declining morale of the strikers, or to question assertions about the number of workers who were returning to their jobs, all of which corroded the will of the strikers.

A third factor contributing to the steel trust's victory was the failure of the strikers to gain popular support for their cause. At the outset of the strike the steel industry had a public relations problem due to Judge Gary's refusal to abide by President Wilson's request that he meet with labor representatives. After all, a steel strike then as now created economic repercussions in other sectors of the economy and many people were bound to be affected by it. If it appeared as if Judge Gary was being unreasonable, the public might turn against the steel trust, so publicists for the steel companies quickly neutralized hostile public opinion, turning it against the strikers by fanning the fears of a red scare which was gripping the United States. The steel publicists achieved this objective by focusing upon the pivotal role of the immigrant workers. They hammered away at the "foreigners" who were militant, enthusiastic supporters of the strike. Speaking before a U. S. Senate Committee, the superintendent of U. S. Steel's Homestead Mill said that "possibly all of the Slovaks are out on strike, and (that) this is a Slovak strike." The corporation's general counsel observed, "It is of account to know that in the investigation before you these men have been able to come in and organize only the foreign element. Does that not bear on the general question?"

The press linked the "Eastern European strikes" to un-American activities and violence. The New York *Journal of Commerce* wrote about the "foreigners" not having ". . . become Americanized in character or sentiment." The New York *Times* warned that they were "steeped in the doctrines of class struggle and social overthrow, ignorant and easily misled." Publicists for the steel trust circulated an Edgar Guest poem which was intended to turn the American strikers against the foreigners.

Said Dan McGann to a foreign man who worked at the self-
    same bench
Let me tell you this, and for emphasis he flourished a monkey
    wrench
Don't talk to me of this bourjoissee, don't open your mouth to
    speak
Of your socialists or your anarchists, don't mention the
    bolshevik
For I've had enough of this foreign stuff, I'm sick as a man can
    be
Of the speech of hate, and I'm telling you straight, that this
    is the land for me.[25]

In their enthusiasm, proponents of the strike failed to consider the importance of the red scare which gripped the country after the Armistice was signed. News of the Russian Revolution and of communist coups in Europe frightened the American people. A general strike in Seattle, a police strike in Boston, and domestic unrest elsewhere gave credence to rumors that communist agents were bent on sabotage in the United States itself. The media did their best to encourage these rumors and exaggerated the extent of radical agitation. Foster's association with the IWW and his authorship of an anarchist tract contributed to charges that revolutionaries were behind the strike.

Claims that the foreigners were hell-bent on revolution were nonsense; the strike was inspired by business unionists, followers of Gompers' "pure and simple" unionism who were anathema to labor radicals. The IWW, for example, publicly denounced the National Committee for rejecting industrial unionism and attempted to undermine strike activities in Pittsburgh. Press accounts depicting violence were "either false, misleading, or unrelated to the strike." Actually the strike was remarkably peaceful; "what violence there was stemmed mainly from the repressive measures of the police." But under the guise of combatting the revolution, the local authorities suppressed freedom of speech and assembly when strikers were beaten unconscious or shot for peacefully protesting. During the strike, federal authorities conducted a massive search for foreign agitators allegedly behind the strike. Attorney General Palmer, the grand strategist of the nationwide "Palmer Raids" of 1920, said in a letter to a leader of an anti-union organization in Western Pennsylvania, "It is a pity that more patriotic organizations do not take actions similar to that of your order."[26] During the raids hundreds of strikers were detained, others were arrested for revolutionary activities, and six "Bolshevik agitators" were shot to death in Sharon, Pennsylvania. Similar government-inspired witch hunts took place in other parts of the country. Radical activities unrelated to the strike were publicized as bearing on the origins and course of the steel strike. As a result of this steel-inspired campaign, the strikers were unable to mobilize public opinion on their side; this, in turn, made it politically imprudent for Washington to intervene and work for a settlement—a prospect upon which many AFL leaders had counted.

The steel trust's campaign to portray the strike as led by dangerous radicals and supported solely by alien workers succeeded to no small degree because of ethnic divisions which undermined worker solidarity. Although mutual suspicion among the foreign and American strikers was present from the very outset of the strike, the pent-up frustration of the steelworkers was so great that they momentarily overcame their differences. With five profitable years behind them, the steel companies were prepared to outwait the strikers, but steel officials were struck by their militancy and high morale. The amazing ability of the foreign workers to save and live on "next-to-nothing" strengthened their determination to hold out until the company agreed to talk with their leaders. The wartime propaganda campaign proved to be critical to the immigrants' determination. A caption under the portrait of a steelworker killed during the strike read: "Casimir Mazurek, who fought on foreign soil to make the world free for Democracy, was shot to death by the hirelings and thugs of the Lackawanna Steel Company because he fearlessly stood for industrial Democracy on American soil."[27]

The immigrant strikers, many of whom had served their adopted homeland in the war, were the backbone of the strike. Wartime propaganda had fostered an "American" consciousness among these men. Henceforth they began to think less in terms of being "Bohunks" than "Americans." As Americans they held their heads high and made demands with a firm voice. One Polish striker remarked, "For why this war? For why we buy Liberty Bonds? For mills? No, for freedom and America—for everybody. No more (work like) horse . . ."[28]

But as the red-baiting blitz gathered steam, local nativist organizations characterized the strike as a struggle between "Americanism" and "Bolshevism." American strikers were under steady pressure to go back to work and English-speaking craftsmen were vocal in venting their animosity toward the "foreigners." The following remarks are typical. Asked about the heavy labor of a co-worker, an American said, "But he was only a Hunky, and no decent American would have anything to do with him . . . for . . . we workers have our classes the same as other people." Another skilled steelworker said of the unskilled foreigners, "The Hunkies? They're only cattle."[29]

The 1919 strike disproved once again the old notion about the immigrants' aversion to labor unions and their docility, but it died hard. Even William Z. Foster, a Marxist exponent of "class solidarity," had mixed feelings about the immigrants. "So far as I can see, the foreigner wants more money. He is confronted with the immediate problem of life. His idealism stretches about as far as his shortest working day." He wants "more wages, shorter hours—the regular trade union demands are the things that count." After commenting that the foreigner quickly lost interest when the union failed to deliver material benefits, Foster added:

> "Then a peculiar thing happens. When the fight occurs, he is a splendid fighter. He has the American beaten when it comes to a fight . . . When the fight occurs the foreigner displays a wonderful amount of idealism, a wonderful amount of stick-to-it-iveness, that is altogether dissimilar to the intensely materialistic spirit he shows in his union transactions."[30]

According to David Brody, the immigrant's ability as a striker sprang from his European background. The European peasant looked on himself primarily as a member of a family and a village. "To violate the community will peculiarly disturbed the immigrant, for he identified himself, not primarily as an individual in an American manner, but as a member of a group."[31]

The collective orientation of the immigrants was a real plus; but, blinded by bigotry toward the New Immigrants and ignorant about their values and life-style, their strong points as well as their weak ones, and victims of their own narrow labor philosophy, the leaders of the AFL failed to organize immigrant workers who were the backbone of the industrial labor force.

The failure of the 1919 steel strike delayed the day when industrial unionism would become a vital and significant part of the American labor movement. The resulting momentum generated by victory might have expanded labor's outreach into other mass production industries. External factors, the

hostility of government, and the power of the industrial corporations cannot be dismissed, but the AFL must take much
of the blame for the labor movement's inability to organize
the New Immigrants and for the setbacks organized labor
suffered in the wake of the abortive steel strike. The AFL discriminated against the immigrant workers even when they
asked to become members of affiliated unions. In Newark,
New Jersey, in 1909 the International Hod Carriers and Building Laborers Union refused to accept Italians in the union and
when they asked for their own charter they were refused.
When this act of discrimination was brought to the attention
of the union's secretary general, he responded that he did not
have the power to act because the local unions had juris-
diction. Such discrimination encouraged immigrant workers to
organize their own labor organizations, but the AFL was dead
set against this practice. In 1907 the AFL denounced the
United Hebrew Trades organization "for destroying the solidarity of organized labor by functioning along 'race' lines."[32]

The AFL leadership and rank and file were trapped in the
quagmire of nativistic prejudices which precluded a proper understanding of the New Immigrants and fostered inter-ethnic
discord in the factories and mills where they worked. Granted,
lingual and cultural differences made harmonious relations
difficult. Granted, there were legitimate reasons for the Americans to hold the immigrants suspect—some did scab and break
strikes and others didn't give a damn about the collective welfare of their co-workers—but all these things held true for
many native workers as well.

Labor leaders complained that the "foreigners" were unfamiliar with American mores and living standards and that they
accepted conditions and stoically bore exploitation that the
Americans would not tolerate but often were forced to
because the immigrants did. In fact, once the newcomer
became acclimated to America's industrial climate, his expectations began to rise as did his propensity to protest. Where
labor unions made an effort to work with the immigrants,
the results were encouraging.

One of the best descriptions of how labor unions could
heighten the immigrant's consciousness was written in 1904
by Bureau of Labor Commissioner Carroll D. Wright, who

conducted a survey of labor strife in the Chicago stockyards. Reporting to President Theodore Roosevelt, he observed that the Amalgamated Meat Cutters Unions organized the immigrants out of self-defense. This defensive action produced positive side effects. ". . . the immigrant, when he learns that the union wants to raise his wages, decrease his hours, etc., begins to see the necessity of learning English, of understanding the institutions he hears talked about in the union meetings, and other matters which interest him."[33]

Language represented an acute problem since the newcomers spoke a score of tongues and this necessitated the use of translators during meetings.

> It is here that the practical utility of learning English is first brought home forcibly to the immigrant. In all other of his associations not only does his own language suffice, but, for reasons that can be well understood, shrewd leaders minimize the importance of learning any others . . . In his trade union the Slav mixes with the Lithuanian, the German, and the Irish, and this is the only place they do mix, until, by virtue of this intercourse and this mixing, clannishness is to a degree destroyed, and a social mixing along other lines comes naturally into play.[34]

While immigrant children were Americanized at school, the adults' basic introduction to American society took place at work. Only a relatively small number had the time to attend night school, and what they learned about American government and society was usually a sugar-coated distortion of the truth. What the immigrant learned at work was raw-boned reality. Among the organized, the union hall was the schoolroom and the union leaders were the teachers. The lessons their students mulled over struck at the heart of the immigrants' ignorance about American politics. In the rough and tumble of union affairs and labor strife the immigrants developed a new level of political awareness.

Even in the "conservative" unions the immigrant worker gained insight into "democratic government." Membership in a union allowed individual expression. It helped chip away at the paternalism and xenophobia which constrained the im-

migrant from participating in community and political affairs.
"It is doubtful if any organization other than a trade union
could accomplish these things, for only the bread and butter
necessity would be potent enough as an influence to bring" the
immigrant workers "out of the fixed forms and crystallizations
of life into which they have been compressed."[35]

Nitty gritty practical problems captured the attention of
the immigrants, and the unions, by raising their level of expectations, whetted their appetites for amenities that were
beyond their reach in Europe. The presumed "apathy" of the
New Immigrants stemmed in large part from their perceiving
the American environment, though certainly harsh, as being
better than the one they left behind in the old country.
Consequently,

> . . . the union must . . . produce discontent and dissat-
> isfaction with what would be otherwise satisfactory to the
> immigrants . . . The union begins by teaching him that
> his wages are not so good as another man's doing prac-
> tically the same kind of work . . . The union gets him to
> compare himself not with what he was in Lithuania, but
> with some German or Irish family and then stings him
> with the assertion that he has as much right to live that
> way as anybody.[36]

The successes that labor unions had with immigrants in the
coal mines, the garment industry, and the stockyards demonstrated that informed, sympathetic organizers could effectively
work with the European newcomers. Still the labor movement
discriminated against and ignored them until the New Deal.
Deep-seated prejudices on the part of the leadership contributed to the serious ethnic divisions among American workers.
The racist nonsense that nativist scholars, ministers, and politicians disseminated via the press and pulpit was less important than the specific acts of discrimination that the immigrants experienced at the hands of their co-workers and
union leaders. The failure of the AFL to deal with nativistic
prejudice contributed to the declining fortunes of the labor
movement in the 1920s and set back the cause of all working
Americans for a generation.

CHAPTER IV

White Ethnic Politics

A. The Political Émigrés

1. The Nationalists: *I Never Realized I Was an Albanian Until My Brother Came from America*, Albanian Immigrant

Robert Park was putting together a book about immigrant life early in the century when he made a puzzling discovery: sojourners returning to Europe displayed a patriotic zeal which was uncommon in the Old Country. The "Americans" stunned friends and relatives by lapsing into long and eloquent discourses about the glory of the "fatherland" and displayed a pronounced sense of ethnic pride customarily associated with the "upper classes." "I never realized I was an Albanian until my brother came from America in 1909," an interviewee told Park. "He belonged to an Albanian society" in the United States.[1] This experience was typical—the notion that they belonged to distinct nationalities did not dawn upon many immigrants until after they arrived in the New World. Others who were indifferent to such matters in Europe became vocal "patriots" in America. The trauma of immigration and nativism contributed to ethnic self-awareness. Americans rarely made the fine distinctions the Calabrians and Sicilians themselves did; it did not matter at all whether you were from the Italian Tyrol or Naples to the American; you were simply a "dago." It was galling to the haughty Northern Italian to be mistaken for a Sicilian, but the Americans called the immigrant from Tuscany a "wop" and treated him accordingly. Bigots in the United States created a sense of peoplehood among the Italians which was still tenuous at home; discrimination contributed to a social leveling and fostered ethnic insularity. People who would have avoided one another in Italy became "blood brothers" in America. Max Ascoli, who fled Fascist Italy, commented that his fellow Italian-Americans ". . . became Americans before they ever were Italians."[2]

Polish nationalists discouraged immigration in the nineteenth century, but to their delight they discovered that the American milieu produced a heightened Polish identity. The Polish National Alliance was founded in Philadelphia in 1880 as a result of a letter written by a Polish nationalist a year earlier. The author noted that the Polish peasant ". . . when transferred to a strange soil among foreigners develops a Polish sentiment and a consciousness of his national character"; and he urged Poles in America to gain wealth and skills to fight for the cause and one day ". . . the emigrants who have acquired training in practical lines and wealth in America will begin to return to their fatherland to be useful citizens."[3]

Among the best educated and politically most advanced members of the immigrant community, the nationalists transplanted political parties and independence movements from across the Atlantic to resume their struggle from the safe haven of the United States. The permissiveness of the American authorities toward European nationalists was a well-known fact, prompting many of them to live in exile here. In 1867 the Fenians trained and led a small force of Irish-Americans in an armed attack against Canada to strike out at the "hated British." Washington's reaction to the foray was one of indifference. European political émigrés from all corners of the Continent established bases of operation in the United States in the last half of the nineteenth century; there were the Zionists fighting for a "free Palestine" and Irish, Polish, and Lithuanian nationalists seeking national self-determination.

One of the principal deterrents to the cause in Europe was the suppression of publications in the ethnic minority's lingua franca; Lithuanians, for example, did not enjoy the opportunity to read newspapers in their mother tongue until they emigrated to the United States. Prior to the First World War the American authorities paid scant attention to the great multitude of foreign language newspapers which had a reader-ship of millions. In 1920 there were 1,043 foreign language newspapers in the United States: New York had 146; Chicago 106; Cleveland thirty-four; and Boston twenty-three. Nation-wide the Lithuanians published sixteen, the Poles seventy-six, the Slovaks twenty-eight, and the Croatians nine newspapers. Most were commercial ventures devoted to letters to the edi-tor columns, community events, advertisements, and other matters calculated to attract the attention of readers who did not enjoy a great deal of formal education.[4]

The immigrant newspapers carried "news" customarily ig-nored by the American press—engagements, marriages, "lonely hearts features," the visit of a prominent countryman, the achievements of a local boy, and other matters of interest to the immigrants. The foreign language press was over-whelmingly commercial, not political; and the nationalist papers represented a small minority of the total circulation. But the commercial and church organs published material rel-evant to the cause; there were columnists who wrote regularly about news from "home" and others who provided informa-tion about the fatherland which only a handful of people were privy to in Europe: important events in Polish history and short biographies of Lithuanian heroes were featured, and blow-by-blow accounts of the Greco-Turkish struggle prompted young Greeks to join patriotic organizations. Every immigrant community was riven by political, religious, and regional factions, but national independence was a common goal around which the "folk" could unify.

At the outset of the First World War, President Wilson saw in the nation's ethnic minorities a headache of monumen-tal proportions. At the time approximately 32 million Ameri-cans out of a population of 92 million were either foreign-born or the offspring of immigrants, and together they amounted to almost one third of the nation's population. Wilson prudently steered a naturalist course for a while, but by 1915 his Anglophilism became more apparent, causing Irish and Ger-man organizations to charge that he had "taken sides." An-gered, Wilson responded by labeling the "foreign elements"

criticizing him "hyphenates"—an awful word which depicted
the accused as a person harboring divided loyalties, someone
who clearly was not a "one hundred percent American." Wilson's pronouncement prompted the reappearance of nativists
who resurrected their organizations soon after the war started.
But concern about the "hyphenates" was not only restricted to
bigots; the nation at large was fearful that the Melting Pot
might burst at the seams, inundating the nation with warring
foreigners and alien agitators.

The national passions generated by the First World War,
some historians claim, hampered "assimilation"; perhaps that
was true of the short run, but over the long run it had just the
opposite effect. It was, for example, a benchmark for the
German-American community. The Germans were one of
the few immigrant groups which had sought to "colonize" the
United States, believing their "culture" was superior to the
one they found in the New World. Feelings of inferiority
were noticeably absent among the Germans. German noble-
men purchased large tracts of land in Texas and thousands
of German immigrants settled there with the intention of establishing a German colony in the Southwest. Some historians
believe the large German migration to Wisconsin was motivated by a similar desire. These schemes failed to materialize
but on the eve of the war Americans of German descent in
many parts of the country belonged to a Teutonic subculture
sustained by schools, churches, newspapers, and organizations
which operated independently of the mainstream culture and
society.

Once the United States entered the war, however, the
German-Americans came under heavy pressure to "assimilate";
their loyalty was held suspect and as nativist hysteria about a
"German fifth column" spread, businessmen with German
surnames were boycotted and some German language newspapers were forced to close. After American troops set sail for
Europe, citizens of German descent were under incessant pressure to demonstrate their loyalty; many responded by
relinquishing their membership in German organizations, attending churches which were distinctively "American," using
English in their meeting halls, and instructing their children
not to lapse into German outside the house. Like the

Southern Wasps after the Civil War, the German-Americans sought to protect themselves from accusations that they were antipatriotic by wrapping the Stars and Stripes tightly around themselves. Although the circumstances were somewhat different, the war had a similar effect upon the New Immigrants; they first reacted to the war as Old World nationalists but that sentiment was later superseded by New World patriotism.

The war in Europe offered the Greeks, Poles, Lithuanians, Czechs, and Slovaks great hope; what had previously been a distant dream—national independence—became a distinct possibility. The nationalists conducted drives to send needy countrymen food, clothing, and money; they formed committees to lobby in Washington to press for national self-determination. Many made preparations to return home to establish new governments in their old homelands after the United States joined the slaughter and it became clear that the Axis forces were on the verge of collapse. The famous Polish composer Paderewski served as honorary president of the Polish Central Relief Committee which carried on propaganda, collected money from American Polonians, and pressed Wilson to carry the Poles' case to the Armistice talks. In 1918 the first national convention of Polish-Americans was held in Detroit. What was to become the state of Czechoslovakia was conceived in a meeting of Czechs and Slovaks in Pittsburgh; and "South Slavs"—Slovenians, Croatians, Serbians, Macedonians, Montenegrins, and Bulgarians—made preparations which eventually contributed to the founding of Yugoslavia.

Measuring their performance against the objective which preoccupied them, national self-determination, they made a solid contribution to the cause. After the war hundreds of thousands of them returned to the "new nations" which had been carved out of the Russian and Austro-Hungarian Empires. Many became important political figures and leading governmental officials. Others contributed to the resurrection of their nation's intellectual and cultural life. Their contributions to the political development of the "American settlers," however, was less auspicious. Here there is a striking similarity between the black power activists in the 1960s and the prewar European émigré nationalists. The latter, by celebrating a shared culture and demonstrating that Poles and Lithuanians could be proud of a rich heritage, provided a positive self-image to people who were often victims of self-hate and cultural disorientation. They also contributed to the politicization of many of their countrymen. Yet their political programs were marginal to the settler community, for the power they sought to develop and wield was posed to strike at injustices which marred the lives of the folk in Europe, not America. National independence was a crusade—the sum and substance of their lives; it was inconceivable that any person of "their blood" could question their mission or deny the cause their time, sweat, and money. Intolerant of indifference or halfhearted support, they were adherents of a politics of conscience to which the average immigrant could not relate. Many counseled their countrymen not to become citizens, the prerequisite to exercising the franchise. At times they lent their talent to efforts which were designed to treat economic concerns and supported fledgling political organizations which were forming in the settler communities. But their priorities and interests were elsewhere and they denied their countrymen the leadership they so desperately needed. So it was no wonder the immigrant turned to the Irish ward heelers who possessed power relevant to residents of Chicago, Manhattan, and Newark, not Warsaw, Prague, or Kaunas.

Nationalism among the immigrants faded rapidly in the wake of the war; after all, the supreme objective, national independence, had become a reality. Henceforth one need not feel guilty about demonstrating a greater concern for more mundane matters. The founding of nation-states prompted a return to Europe, but a large percentage of the "returnees" came back to the United States in the 1920s and 1930s. Of an estimated 40,000 Lithuanians who had proudly boarded steamers and set sail for a "free Lithuania"—founded February 16, 1918—all but 10,000 returned to America.[5] The inflation and economic chaos which gripped Lithuania in the 1920s prompted this exodus, but there is no question that many Lithuanians returned for the same reason tens of thousands of Greeks, Poles, and Italians who had gone to Europe after the war did: the United States was hardly heaven on earth, but it was one of the few places in the world where the ordinary person could live free of rigid social distinctions and where, through hard work and sacrifice, they could enjoy amenities elsewhere reserved for an elite.

2. The Radicals: *The Realization of the Socialist Ideal in Poland Rather Than America,* Polish Socialist

The specter that haunted the ladies of the DAR, the fundamentalist preachers, and political reactionaries, depicting the New Immigrants as carriers of anarchism and socialism, was greatly exaggerated. The European peasant had learned to avoid such "troublemakers" at home and he observed that in America it was not prudent to associate with people who threatened the established order, whatever language they spoke. The "Bohunk" was vulnerable enough to discrimination, and consorting with radicals was an additional burden he did not wish to bear. The authorities dealt harshly with agitators, alien or American, ignoring the civil liberties of persons who held unpopular views and those in particular who acted upon them. The animosity of the American people toward foreigners was exacerbated during the war, and the word "hun" was used to describe Italians, Jews, Poles, and Lithuanians, not just former subjects of the Kaiser. In the war's aftermath nativist propagandists shifted their attention from "pro-German agents" to "Bolshevik agitators" and the immigrant community received the primary attention of the authorities and vigilantes who combed ethnic enclaves searching for "reds." On June 2, 1919, a bomb exploded in front of the house of Attorney General Palmer and a young Italian anarchist from Paterson, New Jersey, Carlo Valdioce, was blown to bits. Palmer, a reactionary Georgian who had his eye on the Presidency, made good use of this attack and began an antiradical campaign culminating in the "Palmer Raids" of January 2, 1920. Immigrants were rounded up in thirty-six cities; 6,000 were arrested and put in concentration camps and five hundred alien "communists" were deported. The raids, coordinated in conjunction with efforts on the part of the steel trust to crush the 1919 strike, were concrete proof that the state did indeed serve the interests of big business.

Many immigrants who were sympathetic to the radicals were frightened by the Palmer Raids, but the pressure to avoid

radicals was not only external, for the immigrant power structure threatened those who toyed with radical notions or consorted with known "agitators." The church, the focal point of
community life in many Catholic immigrant communities, ex-
iled persons who strayed from the fold. Such threats did not
mean much to committed anticlerical radicals, but they
influenced the behavior of ordinary people. After all, the
church controlled or sponsored many of the organizations
which enabled the immigrant to cope with the harsh facts of
American life; in the event one became sick, was fired, or was
stricken by other forms of ill fortune, who would help you out
if "your own people" turned against you? In the Italian community the anarchists spoke eloquently about a "people's revolution," but the conservative patrones controlled jobs the
Italian immigrants needed so desperately.

Yet in spite of his basic conservatism and the multitude of
forces prompting the immigrant to steer clear of radicals, he
listened to what anarchists and socialists had to say about the
plight of the proletariat because he knew firsthand about
exploitation. And he demonstrated in the coal fields of Pennsylvania, the mills of Lawrence, and the sweatshops of the garment industry that he would fight back—if properly led. On
this count the émigré radicals were wanting; many of them
were utopians who spoke about achieving a heaven on earth
which was not credible to powerless working people, and they
ignored the most immediate grievances of the immigrant
workers. Wedded to a political philosophy midwifed in
Europe, they struggled to force American conditions into a
mold which had been cast under vastly different circumstances. Some, like the Italian anarchists who believed in the
revolutionary potential of the bold deed—the assassination of a
public official or bombing of a public building—scoffed at
labor unions as bourgeois institutions which deadened
working-class consciousness. Syndicalists like Giovinnetti and
Ettor, who believed in the revolutionary potential of unions,
could not tolerate the "pure and simple business unionism" of
the AFL and were attracted to the IWW. But the IWW was
destroyed by the war; its leaders were jailed or hounded from
the country during the Palmer Raids, and the cul-
tural/ideological gap which split the IWW induced émigré

radicals to join marginal Italian radical organizations. Émigré socialists—like the nationalists—were oriented to European politics, anxious to return to their homelands to spearhead revolutionary movements there. The Alliance of Polish Socialists, predominantly comprised of intellectuals (and much smaller than the Polish National Alliance), proclaimed in 1917, "The ultimate aim has been . . . realization of the socialist ideal in Poland rather than America. When the time comes for our companions to return to Poland, may we be able to say with pride, 'These are men from the American school, trained by the Polish organizations' . . ."6

The immigrant radicals deemed their American comrades deficient in revolutionary theory and until 1912 remained aloof from the single largest socialist organization in the United States—the Socialist Party of America. That year an amendment was written into the Party's constitution providing for the inclusion of "foreign language federations." Henceforth the Russian, Lithuanian, Polish, Lettish, and Ukrainian Federations would play an important part in the party, contributing to its leftward drift. But ideological differences were not the only source of discord separating the Americans and their foreign comrades; profound cultural differences divided them too. Many native American socialists were Protestant fundamentalists who had been attracted to socialism when the populism movement began to expire. The largest socialist newspaper in the country prior to World War I, the *Appeal to Reason*, published in Girard, Kansas, with a circulation of over 700,000, was operated by J. C. Wayland. The *Appeal to Reason* carried articles which were as unflattering to the immigrant workers as they were toward "Eastern bankers." It was not merely a question of their being a source of "cheap labor" or "financial manipulators"—they were Papists and Jews whom the readership deemed a religious and cultural threat to Protestant America. Moreover, certain socialists—middle-class reformers like Margaret Sanger, who was an advocate of birth control, and her sisters, who preached prohibition—were distasteful to the immigrants. Most émigré radicals were anticlerical and were indifferent to American puritanism, but the immigrant workers the party sought to attract thought otherwise. The men who belonged to the Brewery Workers Union not only made beer, they drank it, and the thought of birth control was disconcerting to even nominal Polish, Lithuanian, and Irish Catholics.

Nonetheless, the Socialist Party under the leadership of Eugene Debs was a growing political movement prior to World War I. In 1912 it had 118,000 members, 1,200 elected officials, and published three hundred periodicals and newspapers. Soon afterward, however, the party was stricken by left/right factionalism and there was a decided ethnic dimension to the dispute. After the war socialists in Europe who had supported their governments in the prosecution of the war—most European socialists on both sides—and those who had opposed it had a falling out, contributing to the formation of communist parties on the Continent. The Socialist Party of America, however, remained steadfast and adhered to the Second Internationale declaration opposing war; nonetheless, some left-wingers contended that the "right" had supported the war effort and used this allegation as a pretext to expel the moderates from the party. Most American socialists opposed the war; many were arrested for doing so—Debs among them—and socialist candidates were denied their seats by several state legislatures and the U. S. Congress for their antipatriotic behavior. The party's antiwar posture and hostile reaction to it compelled many card-carrying socialists to leave the party.

The Russian Revolution further widened the prewar split between the moderates—predominantly native Americans and older immigrant socialists—and the "reds"—the largest number of whom were members of the Foreign Language Federations —who believed that Lenin's government and the communist uprisings erupting elsewhere on the Continent presaged a worldwide revolution which would eventually engulf the United States. Moderates like Victor Berger and Eugene Debs, while they applauded the Bolsheviks' victory, were better apprised of the prospects for revolution in the United States and their presence of mind was perceived, or intentionally misperceived, by the left-wingers in the party as a lack of commitment to revolution. In May 1919, as a result of a squabble with moderates in the party, the Foreign Language

Federations were expelled. This was a significant loss since 53 per cent of the Party's membership that year, some 57,000 people, were associated with the Federations. Approximately 26,000 Federationists then joined the newly formed Communist Party which altogether had an estimated membership of 30,000; along with some Americans, this included 6,500 Russians, 3,500 Ukrainians, 3,000 South Slavs, 6,000 Lithuanians, 1,500 Letts, 2,000 Poles, and 2,400 Hungarians. Most American Bolsheviks, in contrast, favored the Communist Labor Party. Both later realigned in a single communist organization; and after it was outlawed—resulting in a further loss in membership—the Workers Party was formed. But in a demonstration of their dogmatism, a large number of Poles, Letts, and Lithuanians refused to join the "legal arm" of the communist movement and preferred instead to operate underground. After the war many émigré radicals, like Fricis Rozins of the Lettish Federation, returned to Europe; he became head of the first revolutionary Latvian government. Others like Santeri Nuortive, who became the American representative of the short-lived People's Republic of Finland, remained in the United States as revolutionaries in exile. By the late 1920s, a small number of Bolshevik zealots maintained tiny illegal organizations, but they no longer constituted a sizable organized force in the immigrant community.

It is uncertain just how influential the Foreign Language Federations had been even prior to the war, but after the Russian Revolution they rapidly deteriorated in large part because of their narrow sectarianism. "Retaining close ties to their Eastern European homelands, and with little knowledge of the mood or traditions of American-born workers, the federations . . . accepted the slogans of the new (Russian) revolution as their own and responded eagerly to its entreaties for international action."[7] Like their more doctrinaire American comrades, they attempted to relate to the worker through political organizations which were far removed from the concerns of the immigrant community, or favored syndicalist strategies which precluded the formation of permanent labor organizations. Their messianism, revolutionary rhetoric, and distaste for reform estranged them from their less educated countrymen who opposed revolution and eagerly welcomed

small improvements in their lives—higher wages, better working conditions, and such. But like intellectuals the world over,
the radical émigrés were fascinated with theory and spent long
hours debating doctrinal fine points which had little relevance
to the plight of the miner, millwright, or railway hand.

The articles they published in their newspapers were often
incomprehensible to their uneducated subscribers. Readers of
the Russian Bolshevik paper *Novy Mir,* which Trotsky wrote
for during his stay in the United States, peppered the editors
with queries like the following: "Please send me a dictionary,
I cannot read your paper." On another occasion, a reader sent
a clipping of an article which had been underlined and attached a note which read: "Please tell me what this means
and send the paper back to me. I paid for it and I have a right
to know what it means."[8] There were a multitude of foreign
language newspapers which were published by various radical
immigrant organizations: *L'Era Nuova,* Italian Anarchist New
York City; *Dziennik Kudowy,* Polish Socialist Chicago;
Keleivis, Lithuanian Socialist Boston; and a score of IWW
foreign language papers, all of which were oriented toward the
proletariat. Some, like the Yiddish Communist *Der Kampf,*
boldly called for revolution in America.

The sheer volume of radical foreign language papers
published was impressive, except that many were "fly by
night" operations, merely newsletters published periodically,
or had small circulations and short life-spans. From 1884 to
1920, 267 Italian papers were started and 176 folded; 192
Polish papers were started, 119 folded; and while thirty-eight
Lithuanian papers were started, twenty-three disappeared during this period. It is not certain how many of the "failed
papers" were radically oriented, but the most successful ones
were "commercial," not political, and the people who ran
them were hardly revolutionaries. Before the war the foreign
language federations published over thirty newspapers but by
the early 1920s the radical press had been severely reduced.
After the war strictly political newspapers only accounted for a
small proportion of the foreign language press; for example,
among the ninety-three Italian and eighty-one Polish papers
published, only one Italian organ and three Polish ones were
strictly political. Even in the highly politicized Jewish commu-

nity, only 20 per cent of the press was "propagandistic." The political papers, especially those affiliated with action-oriented movements like the IWW, were outlawed during the war and others were forced to close during the red scare; but the radical publishers were as much victims of their own myopia as they were subject to the mailed fist of the "capitalists" they wrote about so vehemently.

In the war's aftermath the radicals lost whatever influence they had wielded in the immigrant Catholic community, largely because they could not develop programs treating the needs of their countrymen. By pursuing a politics of revolution, they lost rapport with workers who desperately needed solutions to imminent problems, who could not afford the luxury of getting intoxicated on revolutionary rhetoric and bromides no matter how appealing they might be.

The only New Immigrant group which forged a coalition of educated radicals and ordinary working people of lasting significance was the East European Jewish community. The Jews' success on this score is not merely of historical interest; it suggests a formula for an alliance between the educated middle class and the American of modest means and education in the 1970s.

The German and Sephardic Jews dominated the politics, economics, and cultural life of the American Jewish community, until well after the Russians outnumbered them. From the aftermath of the Civil War until the 1920s the Jews gave most of their votes to Republican candidates. Thus as late as 1920 ten of the eleven Jews in the U. S. Congress were Republicans—the other one was a socialist. The Russian Jews by and large were poorly educated—most of them were artisans, small businessmen, and factory workers; but in contrast to the Italians and Slavs, they were largely an urban people with some industrial experience. Many of them had been involved in politics or at the very least had been exposed to political doctrine which challenged Continental autocracy. They congregated in urban areas; many feared living outside the ghetto and others were urban-bound because they could more easily find work in larger settlements. A large number of Eastern Jews had labored in the needle trades in Europe; others sought such work because many manufacturers were German Jews, and still others—victims of economic discrimination—had no other option. Without question the needle trades employed more Jews than any other industry in America.

New York, Chicago, Philadelphia, Baltimore, and Cleveland were all leading garment centers by the close of the century when Jews, Italians, and Lithuanians began to replace native Americans and older immigrants in the industry. Working conditions were awful; men, women, and children were crowded into poorly ventilated lofts and stuffy sweatshops hot in the summer and frigid in the winter. In 1911 a fire in a New York loft (the Triangle Shirtwaist Factory) took the lives of over a hundred immigrant women who had been trapped because the exits had been barred shut to keep "labor agitators" out of the shop. Because the work was seasonal, underemployment was a serious problem and wages were low. Constant layoffs militated against a stable labor force, detracting from the prospects for unionization. The industry became decentralized on the eve of the twentieth century and many manufacturers distributed piecework to contractors who in turn subcontracted their goods out to "home workers." This further complicated matters for union organizers.

The AFL-affiliated United Garment Workers Union was controlled by conservative Irish unionists and it only served an elite among the garment workers. The Russians also found the German Jewish unionists in the industry condescending and insensitive to their needs. So soon after the New Immigrants comprised a majority in the industry, they thought about forming their own labor organizations, but the Russian Jews were badly split—socialists, anarchists, and syndicalists fought one another as bitterly as they did the old guard in the AFL and the manufacturers. The better educated radicals in the Jewish community, moreover, conducted their meetings in German or Russian which few Eastern Jews spoke well or were at all familiar with. Furthermore, some radicals like Leon Trotsky, who emigrated to the United States to escape imprisonment, evinced disinterest in the American Jewish community while others—those who belonged to the Socialist Labor Party and the IWW—were ideologically opposed to "reformist" labor organizations. Like Lenin they feared that the AFL-type unions dampened the workers' revolutionary consciousness and infused the proletariat with bourgeoisie notions about society—the most obnoxious one being that capitalism could meet the wants of working people.

There were several critical differences between the Catholic and Jewish émigré radicals and they contributed to the Jews' eventually developing a labor program attractive to their working-class landsmen: most left-wing Jews had no intention of returning to Europe; the vast majority of Jewish intellectuals, labor leaders, and political radicals were settlers, not exiles; and the Jewish masses were generally familiar with socialist doctrine. According to a settlement house worker on Manhattan's lower East Side:

> The real university of the East Side was Marx's *Capital*. Read like the Bible, with faith, like the Bible it formed the taste and molded the life of its readers. Socialism as an economic theory is one thing, as an education it is another. It is what we are excited about that educates us. What the East Side was excited about was socialism.[9]

This perhaps was an overstatement, but unionization of the "Jewish proletariat" in the United States was facilitated because a cross section of the Jewish community shared a common political philosophy. Equally important the émigré radicals achieved success among the Jewish labor force because the former overcame the suicidal scourge of sectarianism. Had they remained preoccupied with developments in the Old Country, turning their backs on "bread and butter" unionism, the two "Jewish" unions which dominated the industry—the Amalgamated Clothing Workers of America and the International Ladies Garment Workers Union (ILGWU)—certainly would have made their appearance much later than they did . . . if at all. They, however, lent their landsmen a helping hand.

In the 1890s Abraham Cahan, who was to become the editor of the *Jewish Daily Forward*, pressed his colleagues to adopt Yiddish in their public gatherings, the language most Russian Jews used, and not Russian, the lingua franca of the educated radicals. Born near Vilna in Lithuania in 1860, Cahan had fled the Tsarist police who were pursuing him for belonging to a "revolutionary" socialist organization and emigrated to the United States when he was in his early twenties. Since few Russian Jews spoke Russian, Cahan argued that radical émigrés who persisted in using it were confining their activities to a privileged few in the Russian immigrant community. Ultimately Cahan's suggestion was adopted by the Jewish intelligentsia, thereby paving the way for an alliance between them and the Yiddish-speaking masses. Perhaps the single most important institution in this respect was the *Jewish Daily Forward* which Cahan edited from 1902 to 1951. Many Jews who remained aloof from socialists in the Old World became active socialists in the new one through reading the *Forward*. It was a paper for the ordinary person, and provided useful information about the United States, covering a host of diverse Jewish community activities. Through its Bintal Briefs (which was an elaboration of the letters to the editor column), it provided sage advice to poorly educated immigrants who were wrestling with the varied problems plaguing the uprooted. In style and substance the *Forward* was a populist paper and in contrast to other strictly political journals published in the American Jewish community, it was sensitive to the masses' values and it contained material and presented it in an idiom they understood and to which they could relate.

Both the talent gleaned from the professionals in the community and the presence of a significant number of persons with labor union experience contributed to the ultimate success of the Amalgamated and the ILGWU. Many Jewish immigrants had belonged to the Bund—the secret Jewish labor organization which operated on the Continent. After the abortive 1905 Russian Revolution, a fresh wave of Jewish Bundists and political radicals arrived in the United States. Among this new group were people who by force of circumstance were compelled to make a living laboring in the garment industry cutting cloth, piecing together garments, and sweeping floors; many later became doctors, lawyers, college professors, and labor leaders. Two such men—Sidney Hillman and David Dubinsky—would become the leaders of the Amalgamated and the ILGWU.

The new wave radicals for a time sought to take up where

they had left off in Russia. Tsarist repression had convinced many of them that violent revolution was the only road to change and they rejected the notion popular among American comrades that it was possible to achieve a socialist common-wealth in the United States peacefully. At the outset then they gravitated toward the revolutionary Socialist Labor Party and the syndicalist IWW; but the pitiful condition of their landsmen in the garment industry—made resonant by the fact that some of them worked alongside the proletariat—was a convincing argument that something had to be done at once to alleviate working conditions even if it meant adopting the strategy and tactics of the AFL. It had dawned on many of them that the workers' initial attraction to political revolu-tionaries soon expired because the revolutionaries blithely ig-nored, nay riled against, measures which lightened the load the worker bore. The radical claim that liberal reforms damp-ened the workers' consciousness and prolonged the life of capitalism was not groundless, but the flip side of the coin—that only fanatics, saints, or radical middle-class bystanders could defer modest reforms for some futuristic nirvana—was an even more compelling argument.

In 1905, as a consequence of two major strikes first sparked by a walkout of young Jewish and Italian immigrant seamstresses—and with the help of people like Cahan, the so-cialist Congressman Meyer London, and the socialist attorney Morris Hillquit—the floundering ILGWU signed an agreement with the manufacturers, recognizing the union as the garment workers' labor representative. It was the ILGWU's Magna Charta. Two years later the Amalgamated would sign a similar agreement. The workers applauded the contracts but radicals attacked it and vilified the ILGWU leadership for engaging, in the words of Big Bill Haywood, in "class collaboration." The radicals' critique was founded on er-roneous presuppositions: that the American worker desired revolution; that revolution was a distinct possibility; and that the welfare of the workingman could not be vastly improved through reforms.

The garment union's success proved once again that the im-migrants were organizable and that industrial unionism was feasible. The ILGWU and the Amalgamated victories also demonstrated that pragmatic trade unionism and socialism were not mutually exclusive. On the contrary, the principal defect of radical unions was their failure to pay proper attention to the most pressing needs of working men and women, ignoring the necessity of forging effective labor unions operated on a sound financial footing. For many years the garment unions combined the best features of bread and butter unionism and social unionism; the workers' problems in the community as well as those in the workplace were deemed the proper concern of labor organizations. The garment unions developed political education programs enabling cutters, seamstresses, and pressers to participate in the American political process. The labor movement was the foundation upon which the immigrant Jews and their children built a network of political organizations in urban America, contributing to the welfare of Jews from all walks of life.

B. The Urban Political Machine

For generations political writers have portrayed urban political machines as the principal source of corruption in American politics, calling them "systems of organized bribery." The machine exists because it controls votes which citizens have surrendered for favors—a sinecure at City Hall, a paving contract, or a cash gift. This insidious exchange of ballots for material rewards represents more than a human failing, for it violates the very basis of our representative government, "which says that decisions ought to be made on the basis of reasonable discussion about what the common good requires."[10]

Early in this century municipal reformers concluded that the immigrants, along with their outlandish clothing and exotic languages, harbored notions about government which violated those prevailing in the United States. They "took for granted that the political life of the individual would arise out of family needs, interpreted political and civic relations chiefly in terms of personal obligations, and placed strong loyalties above allegiance to abstract codes of laws or morals." Here was a political ethos unique to the immigrants—and the basis for machine politics. Richard Hofstadter contrasted this system of political ethics with "one founded upon the indigenous

Yankee-Protestant political tradition, and upon middle-class life . . ." It ". . . assumed and demanded the constant, disinterested activity of the citizen in public affairs, argued that political life ought to be run, to a greater degree than it was, in accordance with general principles and abstract laws apart from and superior to personal needs."[11]

In January 1968, when Gene McCarthy and his army of young volunteers braved the chill of New Hampshire to send Lyndon Johnson a message, columnists wrote about the coming of age of a New Politics, stressing issues above electoral victory, disclaiming the sacrifice of principle to expediency, and setting a moral tone for political conduct which transformed political conflict into a war between the forces of "good and evil." Later that year in Chicago, New Politics reformers fought unsuccessfully to defeat the candidate of the "old pols," Hubert Humphrey, and watched helplessly as Mayor Daley's finest pummeled youthful demonstrators into submission. This incident brought home to them a nexus an earlier generation of reformers had observed, that ethnic politics was the basis for machine politics, the foundation upon which the Old Politics of Hubert Humphrey, Lyndon Baines Johnson, and Scoop Jackson was perched. Obliterate the ethnic machines and you destroy the cancerous growth afflicting the Democratic Party and corroding the American polity.

In the next four years, the youthful, idealistic supporters of George McGovern set out in effect to do just that without taking into account the ability of the old pols to survive onslaughts mounted against them by past generations of reformers.

1. An American Institution: *Honest Graft*

The urban political machine is a uniquely American institution; there is no precedent for it in the British political tradition. This has led many pundits to the conclusion that bossism and ethnic politics are interdependent phenomena. There is no question that the political machine was critical to the political development of the immigrants, but contrary to popular opinion, the first "bosses" were Wasps . . . not Irish Catholics! The first leader of New York City's Tammany Hall was Aaron Burr. The term boss was coined to describe the antics of William Marcy Tweed, who endowed our political lexicon with the concept "honest graft." Boss Tweed was not a mere wordsmith; he was one of the most adroit political bosses in American history and he knew what he was talking about when he discussed honest graft. By 1869, a year after he became a New York State senator, his real estate holdings had risen from zero to a total value of $12 million. Historians have written about Boss Tweed's exploits without attempting to explain why the Wasp political ethos failed to make an honest, righteous political servant out of him and his colleagues who dominated urban politics before the Irish did.

Political machines gained prominence and flourished in nineteenth-century urban America because the existing governmental institutions could not cope with rapidly unfolding social and economic developments. In 1840, out of a population of approximately 17 million, only 1.8 million Americans were urban; twenty years later the figure had grown to 6.2 million. New York City was the only urban settlement in the United States which housed 250,000 inhabitants in 1840, "but by 1920 there were twenty-one cities of this size, containing approximately twenty-one million Americans."[12] As the urban population soared, demands for better transportation, housing, and other goods and services grew apace and local institutions, including government, were profoundly shaken by the suddenness and the intensity of problems which impacted upon them.

Urbanization produced "street/railway franchises, paving contracts, construction work," and other transactions which were attractive to businessmen. "There was an increasing number of merchants, industrialists, and other businessmen, who needed—and were willing to pay for—favorable treatment from local authorities."[13] The machine performed an economic function no other legally acceptable institution did, rationalizing economic relations between government and business, while the boss served as an economic tsar who regulated the local political economy.

The new urbanites comprised a social problem of vast proportions. Their sheer numbers were staggering and their presence brought to the fore a host of uncomfortable questions: Who would take care of the poor, the unemployed, the lame, the elderly, and other needy persons who were congregating in the cities? Who would regulate the behavior of such a polyglot population? Rapid urbanization fostered a breakdown in old social controls, giving rise to crime, juvenile delinquency, and other forms of social pathology compelling government intervention in matters the state had previously ignored. The problems were not necessarily new, but collectively they posed a threat to public order on an unprecedented scale.

The task of governing rapidly growing cities was compounded by a swelling electorate challenging a power structure comprised primarily of patrician families. The men who had conducted affairs of government since the Republic had been founded were solid, honest burghers. Beginning in the mid-nineteenth century a new breed of businessmen appeared, self-made entrepreneurs whose livelihood was inextricably woven into the warp and woof of the swelling cities. Whereas the old patrician rulers they replaced were guided by noblesse oblige, the new power elite quickly perceived that political power afforded them a host of new business opportunities. Operating under the guise of "public service," private fortunes were made virtually overnight. Government contracts were especially favored because they guaranteed high profits at low risk to investors who could count on the city council, mayor, and court system to protect them against economic hazards encountered in "the free market." Whereas the patricians adhered to the Wasp "public-regarding" ethos, the new Wasp claimants for power introduced a political ethos which was shaped by the less gentle mores of the corporate world.

As the urban population grew, business activity quickened, and social problems mounted, local government proved unequal to the challenge. The founding fathers had deemed cities appendages of sovereign states, and they were not mentioned in the Constitution. Consequently as the nation advanced into the nineteenth century, institutional arrangements conceived a century earlier proved to be grossly inadequate. To make matters worse, the reforms which were adopted during the Jacksonian Era fostered a proliferation of elective offices; thus municipal executives possessed little power and the multitude of elected officials serving on numerous councils,

boards, and commissions were so jealous of their prerogatives
that decisive executive rule and legislative initiative were impossible. There was no way then that prevailing political institutions could provide the executive leadership and legislative
responsiveness necessary to meet the growing needs of urban
government. The boss provided strong executive leadership
and, through the machines and the dispersal of patronage, an
unwieldy political system became manageable.

By the time the Irish gained power—which in most places
was not until the turn of the century or afterward—the Wasp
business power structure had established political institutions
which the Irish adapted to serve their needs. What was
primarily an "American" institution then was later shaped by
Irish politicos to accommodate millions of foreigners to the
American political system.

2. The Irish and the Newcomers: *It Is Better to Know
the Judge Than to Know the Law*

In 1880 William R. Grace became the first Irish Catholic
mayor of New York City. For the next seventy-five years, most
of the major cities of the East and Midwest would be dominated by Irish-controlled machines. Irish bosses like James
Michael Curley, Tom Pendergast, Frank Hague, and Ed
Flynn have served as models for political novelists, movie
scenario writers, scholars, and other aficionados of machine
politics. With the election of FDR, Irish politicos gained national prominence—James Farley, Ed Flynn, and, of course,
the Kennedy clan come to mind. Irish dominance in urban
politics and the presence of influential Irishmen in the Democratic Party have made an indelible imprint upon the public
mind; thus even today when one thinks of the traditional political boss, one thinks Irish.

This is the basis for the misconception that the Irish rapidly
moved from the urban immigrant underclass to political prominence soon after they arrived in the United States. That was
not the case at all. Long after the Irish represented a
significant proportion of the urban electorate—in some cases
constituting a majority—the Wasp carried the day. Quick-
witted Irishmen were recruited to work the Irish wards—
saloonkeepers, officers in Irish fraternal organizations, and

those who headed church-related associations—anyone who could deliver a bloc of voters was favored with a job at city hall, special favors, or access to honest graft; but they abided by the commands of their Wasp superiors. Real power eluded the Irish until the last quarter of the nineteenth century when they began to rout the Wasps from office; in doing so they revealed a genius for machine politics unrivaled by any other ethnic group in our history.

Daniel Patrick Moynihan, who was born in Manhattan's Hell's Kitchen and has deftly survived political wars on the Potomac under four administrations—Democratic and Republican—believes the Irish brought distinctive sensibilities and experiences with them to America accounting for their political genius. They arrived in the United States with some notion about how things were done in an Anglo-Saxon society; most of them spoke English; and, living under foreign rule at home, they had acquired a special capacity to view formal institutions as illegitimate, replacing them with informal ones which better suited an "oppressed people."

In the United States the opposition was Protestant, just as it had been at home and the discrimination and acts of violence the Irish suffered fostered a keenly felt Irish-American identity. It was simply "us against them"; the field of combat had shifted but the antagonists and many of the issues were much the same. Irish machines received the blessing of the entire community in America, the priest as well as the aspiring attorney, the businessman as well as the laborer, dear Mrs. Clancy who cooked for the bishop as well as the hookers who plied their trade on streets made safe by Irish policemen.

Through the prism of a finely honed ethnic self-consciousness, America's Irish accomplished the neat psychological trick of discarding the legitimacy of Wasp institutions and establishing "Irish ones" in their place. The Irish made "readjustments," without challenging the prevailing political and economic institutions. They observed firsthand that the Wasps used political clout to secure economic advantages and they followed that example. In contrast to the German Marxists who spoke against the collusion between public and private power, the Irish accepted "the rules of the game" and set out to mobilize their countrymen, to forge effective political organizations, and "get their pound of flesh."

In routing their Wasp patrons, the Irish took advantage of another peculiarity of the American political system—universal male suffrage. A liberal franchise afforded the Irish the opportunity to exploit their growing numbers into political power. Following the practice of the Wasp bosses before them whose motto was, "It is better to know the judge than to know the law," the Irish engaged in naturalization "Tammany style." Tammany ". . . opened headquarters, many of them in saloons, in almost every ward. The alien came in and received a red ticket reading 'Please naturalize the bearer.' He signed his name to the necessary paper or it was signed for him . . ."[14] Later he was led to the courthouse with a hundred or so of his compatriots where he became a citizen of the United States.

The importance of the vote has long been exaggerated by our textbook writers but the franchise provided ethnic minorities in the United States with chips to participate in the great game of electoral politics. Had the Wasps excluded the Irish Catholics, Slavs, Italians, and Jews from the political process, the consequences would have been grim indeed. Separatist movements and dissident political factions rooted in ethnic minorities would have lent a cast to American politics akin to the stormy and bloody "communal struggles" which have torn societies asunder on the Indian subcontinent and Africa since the end of World War II. Although American schoolchildren are often fed myths and half-truths about our political system which have contributed to false notions about how power is wielded in the United States and for whose benefit, we cannot ignore the fact that the Wasp respect for the rule of law and constitutionalism is the basis for accommodating our nation's ethnic minorities, enabling Catholics and Jews to wield real power in the affairs of state. Because the Wasps honored the franchise, the Irish by dint of numbers were destined to win the game of electoral politics in the cities where they congregated. And by the late nineteenth century the Irish began to use their ace in the hole—the New Immigrants—to good advantage.

With the appearance of immigrants from Southern and Eastern Europe, the Irish received fresh troops to do battle against the Wasp politicians—who did not give up without a fight, nor did the Republican organizations they controlled rapidly collapse in the face of the Irish assault. Boston, one of the most Irish cities in the country in the last quarter of the nineteenth century, did not come under the influence of an Irish-dominated administration until the twentieth century. It was not until the 1930s that the Chicago Democratic machine dealt a coup de grâce to an especially recalcitrant Republican organization in that city, and Republicans in Philadelphia held on to the "City of Brotherly Love" as late as the 1950s.

As the Irish overwhelmed the Yankees, their opponents beat a retreat to the suburbs and small towns ringing the cities where the ethnics congregated. Defeated in the pit of the urban areas, they drew up new battle lines and lashed out at the Irish from the country courthouses and governors' mansions. Dominating the business world, the press, academia, and the intellectual community, they forestalled an expression of ethnic power nationally until the New Deal.

Soon after they replaced the Wasps, the Irish prepared to face the onslaught they knew would be forthcoming from the people who worshipped at the "dago" and "polack" churches— who, along with the "pushy Jews," could pose a real threat to Irish hegemony. Unlike the Wasps, the Irish were not prepared to move over and make room for the newcomers. The reasons were not difficult to discern; the Irish "had not fully outgrown their dependence on politics for financial and psychic security."[15] The Irish were prepared to fight bitterly to hold on to City Hall, just as they fought tooth and nail to dominate the church. They possessed an awesome arsenal; speaking English, having acclimated to America, and controlling labor organizations and the church, the Irish wielded power in all areas of urban life. Their most formidable weapon, however, was the machine; it could co-opt potential enemies with the velvet glove or smash them with a mailed fist. The Irish picked off the most ambitious members of the New Immigrant community, offering them, in exchange for their loyalty, jobs down at City Hall, a position in the "organization," contracts, or other favors that were lucrative to businessmen and those on the make. By withholding licenses, they could close down saloons or food stores, by "identifying" safety violations, the fire marshal could bankrupt a landlord in a matter of months, and when necessary the machine had goons who would cave in the skull of an especially pesky political opponent. All these tactics were employed in staving off Poles, Italians, and Jews who were attempting to horn in on Irish prerogatives.

In some places the Irish politicos were so certain of their power, they ignored the newcomers or rebuffed them, causing Poles, Jews, and Italians to lock arms with Wasp-dominated Republican organizations. The refusal of the Irish to make room for the Italians accounts for the prominence of Italians in some Republican parties in New England and the mid-Atlantic states today. The Jews in many cities, repelled by machine politics, voted for socialists and Republicans rather than support Irish Democratic candidates. But as a growing number of New Immigrants gained the right to vote, the Irish, fearing the Wasps would exploit their votes, made room for the newcomers. The Jews in New York City first demonstrated that it could be suicidal to ignore them in 1886 when voting returns indicated that Henry George, the independent Labor candidate, received a large slice of the Jewish vote. Henceforth, Tammany extended a welcoming hand to the Jews and it was not refused.

The Irish, in vying with the Wasp Republicans for Slavic and Italian votes, enjoyed the advantage of a religious bond which was sealed periodically by Protestant acts of discrimination against Catholics. Since they had emerged from the same immigrant/working-class subculture that their Italian, Polish, and Lithuanian neighbors did, the Irish enjoyed an important psychological advantage. This common legacy goes a long way in explaining the genius Irish precinct captains displayed in "servicing" their ethnic constituents.

But despite the numerous natural advantages the Irish enjoyed in vying with the Wasp Republicans for the ethnic vote, the secret of coalescing their co-religionists into a solid Democratic bloc eluded them for years in many cities. In Chicago, for example, from the turn of the century until 1928 a majority of the city's votes were cast for Republican Presidential candidates. The art of mobilizing the various ethnic groups into one solid voting bloc was not ultimately the brainstorm of an Irishman either, but of a Czech politician—Anton Cermak. Cermak came from his native Bohemia at an early age and settled with his parents in the Pilsen district of Chicago. He later moved to an Illinois coal-mining town where he became a leader of a predominantly Irish teenaged gang before he joined his father in the pits. Upon his return to Chicago, he established himself as a rising politician in the Czech community. Though uneducated, he was intelligent, tough, and possessed a brilliant political mind. It is noteworthy that one of his biographers explains the rise of Cermak —his personal attributes aside—to being a member of a small but proud ethnic group which did not suffer the self-hate which was common among other immigrant communities. Many Czechs were freethinkers or Protestants and those who were Catholic were less subservient to their clergy than was true, for example, of the Poles. The Czechs on the average were better educated than other East Europeans, and many of them were skilled artisans. An independent democratic spirit pervaded the Czech community which was not a customary facet of immigrant life; perhaps because of these special circumstances, Cermak became the first East European immigrant to gain political power in Chicago. At one point he was the most powerful white ethnic politician in the country.[16]

His first real political coup (1907) was to become the leader of a citywide antiprohibition league—funded by saloonkeepers and brewers—attracting ethnic groups which resented an attempt on the part of Protestant dries to limit the consumption of alcohol in Chicago. The pro- and antiprohibition forces there were divided along religious lines and in the minds of the Catholics and Protestants it represented more than a struggle over "booze." Prohibition was just one of many issues dividing the immigrants and the native Americans, but it became the focal point of conflict, a test of strength which neither wished to lose. Many immigrant spokesmen viewed prohibition as just another Wasp attempt to dictate to the Catholics—to impose Wasp culture upon people who did not want to adopt American "hang-ups" regarding alcohol. As the leader of the wet movement, Cermak observed that the city's Bohemians, Germans, Jews, Poles, and Lithuanians together represented a voting majority capable of defeating any political opposition in Chicago. Even the Irish could not deny these groups power if they joined together and fought under a common flag, and Cermak did just that—forging a powerful political coalition from the disparate ethnic groups which the Irish had previously manipulated to their advantage. Moving up the ranks of the machine and taking care to give proper recognition to the ethnic minorities who were the source of his power, Cermak eventually became the president of the Cook County Board and took over the party machinery. In 1931, to the displeasure of the Irish, he ran and was elected mayor of Chicago. Here was proof that the Irish were by no means invincible; but several years later Cermak was assassinated by a bullet some observers claim was aimed at President Franklin D. Roosevelt who was sharing a speaker's platform with Cermak in Miami. The machine gave Cermak one of the most elaborate funerals in Chicago's history, and it was one wake at which the Irish emptied their cups without a trace of remorse.

After his death, Irish politicos in Chicago and elsewhere began to incorporate the lessons Cermak had taught them with great acumen—every ethnic group of any size voting as a bloc was duly recognized; if it was a large group this meant ward committeemen as well as district leaders were selected from the community, and electoral slates were designed to reflect all ethnic groups of any discernible strength. The Irish, fearing Polish or Italian Cermaks, deliberately adhered to these rules and clung to power in many cities long after they became an electoral minority. Moreover, unlike the Irish, the Italians, Poles, Lithuanians, and Slovaks had to overcome a language barrier before they could develop alliances with one another. Then, too, Old World feuds—Lithuanian/Pole, Serb/Croatian, and the North/South split among the Italians —were transplanted to America and did not quickly fade as sources of intergroup discord. The Irish cleverly exploited ethnic divisions and in some places inter-ethnic feuding was so intense the Irish did not have to extend themselves at all but sat back and "picked up the pieces" after the combatants had exhausted themselves. A Chicago politician, citing the importance of this phenomenon, observed, "A Lithuanian won't vote for a Pole, and a Pole won't vote for a Lithuanian. A German won't vote for either of them—but all three will vote for a 'turkey'"—an Irishman. Consequently, "in wards where there was no one ethnic group" which "had a clear majority," the Irish "made the most acceptable compromise candidate."[17]

3. The Functions of the Machine: *Americanization . . . Welfare . . . and Status*

The urban political machine introduced the immigrants to the American political system, it ameliorated inter-ethnic discord, it served as a quasi-welfare system, and it enabled ethnic minorities to acquire wealth and gain social status.

The immigrant settlers rejected the pie-in-the-sky promises of their radical countrymen. They did not want to change the system through revolutionary upheaval; they wanted to be a part of it. The settler power structure massaged ethnic pride, perceiving it as the road to political power in America and recognizing that access to the machine was a distinct economic asset. The fraternal, self-help, and other ethnic organizations provided the infrastructure for political expression. The ethnic businessmen and leaders were pragmatists, not ideologues; the "system" had been good to them and they were opposed to the radical bromides some of their countrymen fancied.

As a larger number of the New Immigrants became citizens and registered to vote, the Irish could no longer ignore them; pragmatists themselves, they were prepared to strike a deal. The operational principles of the urban political machine paralleled those of the paternalistic white ethnic political culture. Organizationally the machine was similar to a political arrangement one might find in a feudal manor. The boss, who in the early days was customarily a leading party official and did not hold elective office, was the most powerful of the lords. He was the "boss" because he had a large personal following and had woven an alliance of other powerful personalities in the city, thus enabling him to be the first among equals. His close lieutenants and allies wielded considerable power in their own bailiwicks much like feudal underlords. They all had personal followings enabling them to veto legislation, zoning changes, or appointments which affected their district or constituents. In *Boss*, a blistering attack on Daley's machine, Mike Royko relates an incident which is symptomatic of the power which the underlords wielded. Soon after Martin Kennelly took office as mayor in 1947, Congressman William Dawson, the most powerful black in the Chicago Democratic machine, learned that Kennelly had encouraged the formation of a special police strike force which was arresting numbers runners in the city's black neighborhoods. "Kennelly had not sent in any building inspectors to lean on slum landlords, or done anything to raise the welfare limits, or opened job or housing opportunities to Negroes, but he was arresting their policy wheel operators." Kennelly refused to call off the raids even after "Dawson visited him and explained that the nickel or dime a day a black person bet on policy was a needed diversion, much like the bingo in Catholic churches" or the card games in which members of high society indulged themselves. To businessman Kennelly, Dawson was a "politician," a black one at that, and he refused to call off the raids. Three years later when Kennelly chose to run again, the organization was informed by a messenger from Dawson's office that "the candidate is not acceptable to Congressman Dawson." The congressman controlled three wards and delivered more Democratic votes than any other Democratic politician in the city. The ward committeemen who controlled the organization were first stunned and, on gaining their composure, pleaded with Dawson to change his mind. He refused but agreed to meet with Kennelly. Several days later, in a hotel conference room, the meeting took place. Kennelly, "with some of the top ward leaders on either side," sat behind a long table. "He sat a long time, blushed but silent, while Dawson limped back and forth on his artificial leg, cursing and shouting, blistering him for his coolness to the political chiefs in general, and his arrogance to Dawson in particular." The congressman, after humiliating the mayor, summed up: "Who do you think you are? I bring in the votes. I elect you. You are not needed, but the votes are needed. I deliver the votes to you, but you won't talk to me."[18] After the lecture Dawson agreed to support Kennelly, but only for one more term.

In much the same fashion that the boss could not ignore the prerogatives of his underlords, the latter could not maintain their positions in the organization if they failed to deliver the vote, which in turn depended on how well the local political underlord served his constituents. The precinct captain, who worked the neighborhoods for him, was a critical cog in the machine. He received his neighbors' votes because he delivered services and did favors for them which were critical to their well-being—a delinquent was released from jail; a senior citizen was placed in a public hospital; the poor received food baskets and coal, the temporarily unemployed cash, and a friendly businessman a lucrative contract with the city. One of the many hats the local politicos wore then was that of social worker. Until the New Deal there was no formalized welfare system serving needy persons throughout the United States. Public welfare programs were poorly funded and grossly inadequate. In many areas private agencies alone dispersed food, clothing, and coal and provided shelter, but on an ad hoc basis through settlement houses and other agencies administered by "outsiders."

The precinct captain's help was given and received in much the same fashion that the European peasant received help from his patrone at home, and on election day, for favors rendered, he and his family demonstrated their gratitude by voting for the machine slate. Because the "favor" was repaid, neither the individual's pride was wounded nor his dignity denigrated. Government was not so cold and austere as it is today. The precinct captain lived in your neighborhood and ate Polish sausage with you down at the Falcons, or drank anisette with the boys at the bocci court. Elections meant the organization conducted clambakes where massive amounts of food were consumed, washed down with an unlimited flow of beer and whiskey. Elections were a time for celebration; they were a respite from the drudgery of work, the ennui of toiling in the house, the predictability of street life, and the entire family was invited to join in the fun. This human side of the machine perhaps has been exaggerated, but it was by no means immaterial to the machine's ability to withstand the assault of reformers.

The patrone system of authority was familiar to the newcomers and the persistence of the patrone system in white ethnic neighborhoods was reinforced by the church and ethnic associations. But "bossism" would not have thrived were it not for the failure of American institutions to deal adequately with the problems of needy people. Throughout our history low income and minority Americans have been suspicious of mainstream institutions because they have worked most effectively for the affluent and well connected—the Wasps yesterday and the whites today. Residents of a black or Puerto Rican ghetto did not "take advantage" of model cities elections in the 1960s because they had little reason to believe that the system would serve them or treat them equitably. Unresponsive institutions contribute to voter apathy, and the powerlessness of the poor to compel bureaucrats to "play by the rules" accounts for the indifference of disadvantaged Americans to politicians and party rhetoric. Because many middle-class Americans have never been victims of callous bureaucrats or a fastbuck landlord, they cannot understand why many of their fellow countrymen do not vote, express interest in community affairs, or place much stock in the legal system. Thus the affluent voter is puzzled by charges that government is unresponsive or our leadership is indifferent to the ordinary citizen and is inclined to believe such expressions are unfounded or merely radical rhetoric.

Typically, on those occasions when conditions become so intolerable or the injustices so patently evident that even the apathetic rise up in protest, it will not be processed through mainstream channels or via the major parties, but through "populist" spokesmen and movements which are perceived by the oppressed as sympathetic to their plight. Demagogues like George Wallace and Anthony Imperiale can mobilize politically unsophisticated or frustrated voters because the mainstream politicians and parties have failed to meet their legitimate grievances or to take them seriously. Black youngsters applaud the "rap" of Stokely Carmichael because what middle-class whites deem irresponsible rhetoric and unjustified accusations are not totally devoid of content to people who reside in the Central Ward of Newark or Brooklyn's Bedford-Stuyvesant. There the landscape has been denuded of acres of housing and trees, junkies shoot up in school play areas, muggers terrorize the residents, and a fourteen-year-old child can find a pusher but the police cannot.

For much of this century, the working-class voter judged government on the basis of its responsiveness to his needs and cared little about abstractions like the "democratic process" and "prudent expenditure of public funds" that were allegedly of concern to the reformers. If the machine sent coal in the dead of winter to residents of chilly tenements, food to nourish their bodies, and toys to brighten the soul of a child, it was judged in a positive light. Had the immigrants and their children had access to social welfare programs which were adopted in many European countries decades prior to the New Deal, the longevity of the machines would have been shortened considerably.

The machine was a vehicle which a person of modest means and education could ride to political power, wealth, and even social status. Many contemporary Irish-American families enjoy wealth and prominence because a distant relative who favored raw whiskey, spoke with a heavy brogue, and read simple advertisements with difficulty acquired a fortune via politics. Lacking an education, capital, or proper connections, the climb from the bottom of the socioeconomic ladder to the middle class was a long and arduous journey. For much of this century, and it is still true in some areas of American life today, Americans have been shut out of the professions, the corporate world, or have been denied high office because of their ethnic affiliation.

Lacking economic power and social status, the white ethnics found a surrogate source of vertical mobility in the "person" of the machine. Richard Daley, one of the most powerful politicians in America today, got his start working for the Chicago organization and he has not forgotten that "the party" permits ordinary people to get ahead. "Without the party, I couldn't be mayor. The rich guys can get elected on their money, but somebody like me, an ordinary person, needs the party. Without the party, only the rich would be elected to office."[19] We might take issue with Daley's modesty about being "an ordinary person" but machine politics for much of this century was the principal avenue of success open to common people on the make.

Following the example of the Robber Barons who bought politicians to write legislation favorable to their enterprises or bought judges to smash labor unions, the machine politicos used their political clout to enrich themselves. They received kickbacks from people doing business with the city, sold favors, and borrowed liberally from municipal funds to acquire their fortunes. Over time they learned that they could achieve their goals through less patently criminal activities by becoming adroit at manipulating honest graft. The insurance business became one of the most convenient covers for such enterprise. For years a crony of Dick Daley, Joe Gill, operated an insurance firm which had the good fortune of negotiating insurance policies which protected city properties like the Chicago Civic Center and O'Hare Airport. Gill's firm made a yearly profit of $100,000 in this fashion. With this precedent in mind, it is no accident that two of Mayor Daley's sons are in the insurance business. One of them allegedly made $100,000 the first year he plied his trade as a return on policies he had written to protect city properties.

While really sizable ripoffs were the prerogatives of the top politicos, the average soldier in the machine benefited as well. A job with the city was a highly prized possession; the police force, fire department, and other municipal agencies offered a steady income, status, job advancements, and benefits generally not available in the private sector. The machine also contributed to the growth of the ethnic middle class, making it possible for ethnic businessmen to build legitimate enterprises as a result of public contracts. In this fashion, ethnic entrepreneurs enlarged their operations and became able competitors for the Wasps who controlled much of the commercial activity. Young Italian, Polish, and Jewish attorneys who were excluded from Wasp law firms or who could not generate enough business in private practice first worked for the city and after they became established opened up their own practices. And young people fresh out of medical school—who, fearing discrimination elsewhere, returned to their old neighborhoods to serve their countrymen—supplemented their income by working for the city health department or pulling teeth at public clinics.

Perhaps one of the most important lessons that ethnic Americans, who had been taught to fear the state, learned was that ". . . the state might also be the means of their personal advancement."[20] Offspring of working-class immigrants without education, inherited wealth, or connections, faced with the option of toiling in the mines, mills, or factories, turned to politics to succeed. Identification with an ethnic minority, otherwise a burden, proved to be a plus when the ethnics learned to exploit political power to gain the things usually denied ordinary working people.

C. The New Deal and Ethnic Power: *FDR Related to the Catholics and Jews as "Ethnics" as Well as Working People*

In 1896 William McKinley, in his race for the Presidency, repudiated the American Protective Association in an attempt to attract the Catholic electorate. His campaign advisers reasoned that the GOP had an especially good chance to win Catholic votes that year since William Jennings Bryan was McKinley's opponent. The agrarian fundamentalist Bryan championed issues far removed from the concerns of immigrant workers and his hostility toward Catholicism was not exactly a guarded secret. His Bible Belt supporters, moreover, were disinclined to lock arms with the Jews and Catholics who lived in the nation's cities where "vice, alcohol, and blasphemy" were considered a part of urban life.

Until the New Deal, the Democratic Party had to accommodate two massive voting blocs which did not see eye to eye on many things, most especially immigration, prohibition, the Klan, and religion. In the industrial North the Democratic Party had become increasingly dependent upon urban Catholic—largely Irish—votes. Below the Mason-Dixon line and in the Midwest and West, disgruntled populist-minded Protestant voters comprised another large bloc of Democratic votes. But a cultural chasm kept the small-town Protestant

and urban immigrant voter from forging a truly effective political alliance until the New Deal. Unlike the Irish, neither
Jews, Poles, nor Italians were firmly wedded to either party
and many of them supported Republican candidates. Others
who were inclined toward the Democrats were in a quandary;
the Democrats were more favorable to issues germane to working people than the Republicans, but the Democratic Party
was also home for some of the nation's most vociferous bigots.

The first Democratic President elected in the twentieth
century, Woodrow Wilson, did not assuage such fears; on the
contrary he exacerbated them. Prior to the 1912 Democratic
convention, remarks he had made earlier in the century came
back to haunt him. In *A History of the American People,* he
had written about the New Immigrants in terms of their being
"men of the lowest class from the South of Italy and men of
the meaner sort out of Hungary and Poland, men out of the
ranks where there was neither skill nor energy nor any initiative of quick intelligence . . ."[21] By 1916 Wilson made
amends with the ethnic minorities and this paid off at the
polls; the Poles in particular, pleased by his support of an independent Poland, voted overwhelmingly for him. But two of
the largest immigrant communities in the United States, the
German- and Irish-Americans, turned their backs on Wilson
because of his foreign policy.

In the war's aftermath, Wilson's popularity among ethnic
Americans declined dramatically. The Irish, who were the best
organized and most politically potent ethnic group in the
Democratic Party, were outraged because Wilson refused to
support Irish demands for self-determination. The Italians
were angered by his favoring the Yugoslavs' claim to Fiume,
and the Lithuanians, who had applauded him for supporting
their drive for national independence, later turned against him
because of his refusal to aid Lithuania, which was losing territory to the Poles. Henry Cabot Lodge, Sr., the chairman of
the Senate Committee on Foreign Relations, sought to exploit
the ethnics' displeasure with Wilson by advocating their
causes in the Senate, hoping to deny Wilson popular support
for his postwar foreign policy. On one occasion Lodge—who
had previously spoken about Italians in derogatory terms—
remarked that Fiume was "as essential to the well-being of

Italy as the mouth of the Mississippi (is) to the United States."[22] In 1920, then, many pro-Democratic ethnics voted for Harding, the Republican candidate.

Four years later New York's governor Al Smith—the tenement-born son of Irish immigrant parents—battled with William Gibbs McAdo for the Democratic Presidential nomination. He lost it in a marathon contest terminated on the 103rd ballot when the bone-tired delegates selected a compromise candidate, New York lawyer John Davis. The Smith/McAdo struggle sharply focused the growing enmity between the Protestants and Catholics in the Party; "McAdo was a dry and Smith a wet; McAdo a Protestant, and Smith a Catholic; McAdo had strong support from the Klan," and Smith of course bitterly opposed the hooded knights.[23] The Klan sent many delegates to the 1924 convention—not all of them Southerners—and it spearheaded their drive to deny Smith the party's candidacy.

The Democrats regained status in the eyes of the white ethnics in 1928 when Al Smith did receive his party's nod for the Presidency. Political scientists claim Smith's nomination was the first indication that a fundamental realignment in the party system was in the offing. In 1928 the Catholics came of age politically. For the first time in our history a Catholic was nominated by one of the major parties, but, even more important, the Catholics—who grew in size from eight million in 1891 to twenty million in 1928—began to maximize their political influence by voting in disproportionately larger numbers than the rest of the nation. Smith's candidacy had an electrifying effect upon Catholics throughout the country; those who had drifted from the Democratic fold returned and joined newly enfranchised Catholics, those who had previously ignored politics altogether, and others who had often voted for Republican candidates. From 1928 on, they and the Jews voted as a solid pro-Democratic bloc, shifting the balance of political power in the North from the GOP toward the Democrats. Smith's part in this trend is reflected in a comparison of the 1924 and 1928 elections.

In 1924 the percentage of New York's Irish Democratic vote was 63 per cent; four years later it was 82 per cent. Since Smith was a loyal son of Eire, that was to be expected, but

Smith's candidacy caught the fancy of Italian and Polish voters too. Among New York's Italians the respective figures were 48 per cent in 1924 and 77 per cent in 1928; among Poles in Chicago they were 51 per cent in 1924 and 83 per cent in 1928.[24] The groundswell of anti-Catholicism that erupted stung the consciousness of Catholics from every ethnic community. It had a similar effect upon Jews who knew that Smith's most scurrilous detractors were also anti-Semitic.

Many otherwise progressive-minded people who made Smith's religion an issue were not bigots pure and simple. They deemed their fear of the Catholic church as legitimate; after all, the church was hardly a liberal institution and numerous public statements attributed to Catholic clergymen could be trotted out to lend substance to the charges that the church did not believe in separation of church and state and that Catholics were bound to follow the dictates of the Pope. Would Al Smith dare adopt measures the Vatican disapproved of and risk excommunication? To many Protestants this question was by no means unfair. Of course, millions of voters opposed Smith because of his religious affiliation, accounting for Hoover's capturing over two hundred traditional Democratic counties, including strongholds like Oklahoma City, Birmingham, Dallas, and Houston. Smith also faired poorly in Northern Protestant districts which had traditionally voted for Democrats—districts in the Midwest, for example, populated by Scandinavian Lutherans. On the other hand, Smith mobilized millions of white ethnic voters in places which had formerly been safe GOP districts. He did especially well in the industrial cities where the white ethnics lived and worked; he received 71 per cent of the votes in Lawrence, 67 per cent in Boston, 60 per cent in New York, 57 per cent in New Haven, and 53 per cent in Milwaukee.[25]

In accounting for Smith's success, political writers tend to stress the natural attraction of a liberal Democrat to a predominantly working-class electorate and in the process play down the importance of the ethnic factor in explaining why Catholic and Jewish voters cast their ballots for him. But in addition to his reputation as an economic liberal, who concerned himself with the plight of the workingman, millions of ethnic Americans identified with Smith because he was of recent immigrant stock and was a member of a religious minority. The strength of the ethnic factor is reflected in results showing the Irish in New York and the Italians in Boston, to cite just two examples, providing fewer votes for Roosevelt in 1932, three years after the Great Depression had devastated the nation, than they gave Smith in 1928.

Roosevelt's second quest for the Presidency attracted millions of new white ethnic voters to his side, enabling him to win cities he had lost four years earlier. During his first term Roosevelt was credited for passage of welfare legislation crucial to the plight of ordinary Americans, and they flocked to him because he was the candidate of working men and women. Nonetheless, FDR secured Catholic and Jewish votes because he also massaged the ethnic pride of people who desperately wanted to be recognized and accepted as first-class citizens. FDR wisely responded to this heartfelt need.

During a twelve-year period, Harding, Coolidge, and Hoover had nominated 207 federal judges; of the 186 who acknowledged their religious affiliation, 170 were Protestant, eight Catholic, and eight Jewish. "In sharp contrast, of 197 judicial appointments made by Roosevelt, 52 were Catholic and seven were Jewish."[26] With a Democrat in the White House, ethnic politicians for the first time had access to national political power. The Irish politicians in particular were enthralled at the prospect of wielding power beyond the confines of their political strongholds. Many an Irish state legislator, congressman, and senator was elected because the New Deal had mobilized the ethnic vote into a powerful voting bloc. Meanwhile, graduates from Georgetown, Fordham, and Notre Dame were providing the Irish community with a middle class of its own—corporate executives, professionals, and young attorneys who, together, comprised a new generation of leadership. This was the basis for a new breed of Irish politician who was as wily as his "old man," but, unlike his father, could communicate with educated Wasps and Jews on their own level, secure political arrangements with people outside the ethnic strongholds, and get elected to the state legislature, the state house, and even the U. S. Congress.

FDR extended his hand to the Jews too; many of them who had previously voted for the GOP or who had favored left-

wing political parties henceforth became Democrats. Old socialists like the Amalgamated's Sidney Hillman were offered
jobs in Washington as were Jewish intellectuals like Benjamin
Cohen and scores of bright young economists and lawyers who
had cut their political teeth in left-wing politics and the labor
movement. Although FDR appointed the first Italian-
American, Matthew Abruzzo, to a federal bench and Truman
appointed the first Pole, Arthur A. Koscinski, to a similar
office, the Italians and Poles did not benefit as directly. Yet a
growing number of Italian and Polish politicians enjoyed the
power flowing from Washington to the regular Democratic organizations where they had become ensconced. The New Deal
sharpened their appetites and they began to make demands on
the Irish-dominated organizations for a larger role in party
affairs and slots on the ticket for prominent offices. This development caused some Irish politicians to perceive Roosevelt
and the New Deal as a "mixed blessing."

In New York, for example, Roosevelt slapped the Irish-
dominated Tammany Hall organization flat in the face when
he supported Fiorello La Guardia's "fusion ticket." The Little
Flower, backed by Wasp liberals, Jews, blacks, and Italians,
wrested Gracie Mansion from the Irish in 1934. La Guardia's
election demonstrated that the white ethnics would vote for
municipal reformers and oppose the machine if given a chance
to do so. La Guardia, during three terms in office, was responsible for a host of measures which improved the physical condition of the city, championed social reforms critical to its residents, set the city's finances on a secure footing, and
restructured government institutions facilitating honest and
efficient government. True to his campaign promises, he
severed the cord which had bound City Hall to the racketeers
under Tammany administrations. He did not rid the city of
the mob altogether, but he forced many racketeers to scurry to
New Jersey to escape the grasp of his crusading prosecuting attorney, Thomas Dewey, and he put a serious crimp in the
mob's money-making operations. His housing, welfare, and
health reforms were made possible as a result of New Deal
legislation, but, unlike the old-guard mayors, he energetically
pursued the funds FDR had made available, and through
honest administration he got more bang for the buck.

La Guardia was by no means a typical ethnic politician; he was unique. Born on the East Side of New York on December 11, 1882, to an Italian father and a Jewish mother, he was raised in Arizona where his father, a bandmaster in the U. S. Army, was stationed for many years. After his father was discharged from the Army because of ill health, La Guardia accompanied his family to their old home town of Trieste. In 1900, at the age of eighteen, he got a job with the U.S. consulate in Budapest, later moved to Fiume where he processed immigrants from the Balkan countries, and, after he was denied a promotion, returned to the United States. At night he attended New York University's Law School, working during the day on Ellis Island where he expanded his knowledge of foreign languages. Afterward he worked as an attorney for the garment unions and ran for Congress on the Republican ticket in 1914 because he could not stomach the crooked Tammany machine. He lost the race, but won two years later only to resign to become a pilot in the U. S. Air Service. In Italy he flew a number of combat missions and returned home a hero. He soon was back in Congress where he championed social welfare and pro-labor legislation. Restless as ever, he ran and won the race to become mayor of New York City in 1933; he remained in office for three terms, from 1934 to 1946.

This capsule history of La Guardia is revealing because, had La Guardia remained on the East Side and fought his way to the top via the route most ethnic politicians took, it is questionable whether he would have become the reformer he did. Had he come of age in the teeming streets of the East Side, the politics of Tammany Hall would have been less distasteful to his palate. Living out West, reaching adulthood in Europe, having the opportunity to transcend the closed ethnic community which would have been his fate—it is not idle to speculate that, had he remained in New York, Fiorello La Guardia would have been a different man.

During his twelve years in office, La Guardia seriously wounded the old guard. Manhattan's Tammany Hall in particular suffered grievously because he denied Tammany the patronage it needed to hold the organization together. But FDR's New Deal, the imposition of governmental reforms, and (after the war) the changing complexion of the electorate represented even more serious threats to urban political machines across the United States. Washington now was providing the kinds of "services" the machines had doled out in the past to monopolize low income voters. The welfare state formalized the quasi-welfare functions the machines had formerly performed and, in contrast to the old pols' meager resources, the federal Leviathan could dispense money, jobs, and security the machine politicians could never have matched even if they had wanted to. The patronage that flowed from Washington to the states and localities in the forms of housing, highways, and public works programs was awesome. Because FDR wielded a big stick and dangled massive federal funds before them, many old pols began to see the light; thus, to the astonishment of New York pundits, John Curry, an old Tammany powerhouse, was ousted from office by his own district leaders because he was persona non grata in Washington. Across the country, meanwhile, civil service reforms had placed many jobs beyond the pale of the old guard, robbing the machines of patronage. The old pols would learn how to come to grips with this nuisance—many of Daley's cronies have been "temporary" city and county employees for almost a generation—but it did hurt.

Perhaps an even more disquieting discovery to the machine was the changing nature of its constituency. Economic prosperity and expanding educational opportunities afforded a growing number of second-generation ethnics the opportunity to find jobs in sectors of the economy denied their parents because they lacked skills, were poorly educated, or were victims of discrimination. The children of the Melting Pot were no longer in need of the favors the machines once dangled before the immigrants; and the sinecures down at city hall they had once fought over now were low-paid substitutes for the new jobs and business opportunities available to them. In the late 1940s the flood tide of Southern blacks who had left the South to seek work in the North during the war were coming in ever larger numbers and, together with the blacks who were already in Chicago, Detroit, and Newark, they were pressing up against the old white neighborhoods causing the more mobile whites to leave center-city for the suburbs. Manhattan neighborhoods which had formerly housed Irishmen, Jews, and Italians were increasingly becoming home for blacks and Puerto Ricans. Irish politicos at Tammany Hall were rapidly losing their power base. In 1947 the Italians demonstrated their growing political prowess when Carmine De Sapio ousted the Irish from the Hall. Although they clung to power in the other boroughs—in Queens, the Bronx, Staten Island, and Brooklyn—the Irish had to make room for the Italians in the form of organizational posts, patronage, and electoral office.

Up to that point the Italians, in their competition with the Irish, had been at a distinct disadvantage; they were recent arrivals, few of them were well educated, most lacked political experience of any kind, and the Italian community was riven by factionalism. Even if an Italian politician overcame these disabilities, he could not extract money from wealthy compatriots nor could he rely on the help of middle-class paisans who possessed communications skills, vital contacts, or the self-confidence to grapple with the world outside their ethnic enclaves. The Irish financed their campaigns by milking the public trough; the Jews did likewise by squeezing their wealthy landsmen for funds. In the Italian community the only people with "big money" were mobsters and it is no wonder they often provided funds necessary for Italians to enter the political arena.

In the 1930s Frank Costello and Lucky Luciano protected their interests by supporting Tammany Hall. It was customary for the Irish pols to offer gamblers, bootleggers, and white slavers protection for a fee. After La Guardia's election, the old guard was denied patronage and so the boys at Tammany Hall became even more dependent on the mob's money. In the 1940s Costello, through judicious financing, "controlled a bloc of 'Italian' leaders in the Hall—as well as some Irish on the upper West Side and some Jewish leaders on the East Side —and was able to influence the selection of a number of Italian judges."[27]

During the war Costello expanded his political network and with the wealthy fascist sympathizer, Generoso Pope—the owner of an Italian language radio station and two Italian newspapers—set the stage for the Italians to thrust themselves into politics in the postwar years. The emergence of "Italian power" was not restricted to New York; Italians were also on the move in New Jersey, Pennsylvania, Connecticut, Rhode Island, and Massachusetts—the other five states where large numbers of Italian-Americans lived. In the aftermath of the 1948 election, Italian language newspapers proudly announced to their readers that eight Italian-Americans had been elected to the United States Congress—two of them from the city of Newark alone. Soon Italian-Americans would be elected mayors in Passaic, Hoboken, and Paterson. In 1950 John Pastore, who was the first Italian-American to be elected a governor, became a United States senator in Rhode Island. And in 1951 in the six states where the heaviest concentration of Italian-Americans lived, more than twice the number of Italians were elected to the state legislatures than had been the case fifteen years earlier.

The ethnic readjustment, however, did not foster any substantive political changes. The growing Italian business community and burgeoning middle class were conservative and cautious about change, just as their Polish counterparts in Chicago were. Upon achieving electoral success, both groups closely followed the example their Irish mentors had established generations ago. The principal function of the machine was to win elections—to provide favors, patronage, privileges, and money to the members of the organization and close friends. Widespread citizen participation was discouraged in the primaries when party posts and the selection of candidates were up for grabs. On other occasions when there was no fear that a large turnout would jeopardize the machine (during Presidential races) the old guard went to great lengths to get out the vote.

Like his fellow countrymen, the white ethnic American was not greatly interested in politics; he had just begun to taste the good life. Working long and hard and making great sacrifices, he had purchased a home, opened a business, and gathered sufficient cash to send his child to college. He aspired to middle-class life, moved to the suburbs, and vowed to give his children opportunities he had never had. Nonetheless the appearance of Italian, Polish, and Slovak names on the ballot was a deep source of satisfaction. Here was concrete proof that "we're finally making it, finally getting the recognition we deserve."

The New Deal marked the entry of the white ethnics into national politics and signified the transference of power from the first to the second generation. FDR's election helped pave the way for Italians and Poles to secure a foothold in local Democratic organizations and soon thereafter to gain national political office. But perhaps the most important change in their prospects was the resurrection of the labor movement as a powerful force in American life—a development which was pivotal to the welfare of millions of white ethnic workers and their families.

D. The CIO and the Ethnics: *Every American Had the Right to a Job, Social Security, and Decent Shelter*

1. The Depression, the White Ethnics, and the CIO

On the eve of the Depression public interest in the New Immigrants and their children faded dramatically. European immigration had slowed to a trickle not long after the 1924 Johnson-Reed Act was passed. Ties to the old country which friends and relatives from Europe had nourished slackened. Preoccupation with subversive foreigners subsided as prosperity became the national passion. The assumption that the Melting Pot was dyeing the "bohunks" and their children red, white, and blue had become commonplace among academics; scholars began to lose interest in immigrant neighborhoods and the people who resided in them. Ironically the socialist doctrine which German immigrants had first brought to the United States armed a new generation of radicals with the intellectual firepower to demolish, in theory, the importance of ethnicity as an explanation for human behavior. The Marxist notion about the primacy of social class was so persuasive even non-Marxist social scientists embraced it.

The radical aversion to ethnicity was not merely ideological, for ethnic communalism was a divisive force which undermined working-class solidarity. The 1919 steel strike was a vivid example of how ethnic resentment had divided the native American and Old Immigrant workers on the one hand and the New Immigrants on the other. Religious and ethnic

differences also drove a wedge between the Catholics and Jews
and between various Catholic ethnic groups. A YMCA
official, writing about Pittsburgh's steelworkers in 1909,
reported, "The Pole and the Lithuanian have nothing in common and each of them despise the Slovak." Upon asking a
Lithuanian worker whether any of his people were killed in a
deadly explosion, the interviewer was told, "No catch our people do such work as that: There you find the Slovak."[28]

From the outset inter-ethnic discord among the New Immigrants divided them and undermined working-class solidarity. Baseball games and other sports events between Italians
and Poles often ended in fist fights, just as they do today between blacks and whites. Jewish youngsters who had to
traverse an Irish neighborhood to get to the Yeshiva were
often set upon and beaten by their ethnic rivals. Slurs the nativists were fond of using were adopted by the ethnics to sting
one another in verbal and physical combat. Consequently,
Italian factory hands believed they had more in common with
Italians, whatever their social status or economic condition,
than with Polish or Irish co-workers. Clubs, organizations,
bars, and churches separating the New Immigrants from the
Wasps also estranged them from one another.

With the onset of the Depression, religious, racial, and ethnic cleavages became luxuries to the growing number of Americans who shared the common bond of unemployment. As the
ranks of the unemployed grew, savings vanished, and it
became clear that the Depression was going to be protracted,
the American people became restive and demanded that
Washington take decisive measures to deal with the nation's
economic malaise. Left-wing radicals in particular were heart-
ened by growing working-class solidarity and militancy; at
long last, they thought, the American proletariat was prepared
to bring capitalism crashing down.

The Depression hit the white ethnics especially hard; half
the nation's unemployed resided in New Jersey, New York,
Massachusetts, Illinois, Ohio, and California—states where a
majority of the nation's Italians, Poles, Jews, and Lithuanians
lived. The AFL's reaction to the crash was as indecisive and
misdirected as President Hoover's. Well into the Depression,
the leading labor organization in America opposed minimum

wages, unemployment benefits, and other social welfare legislation which was being considered to alleviate the plight of the Depression's victims. The tired old men who ran the Federation were fearful that this legislation constituted a direct threat to them; if the rank and file's needs were met by government, what purpose did labor unions serve any more? This reaction was a natural one in light of the business unionist philosophy pervading the AFL. The notion that unions were guilds established to meet the needs of the membership, not social movements established to treat the social ills of all working Americans, accounted for the fear that another "firm"—government—would co-opt the AFL, steal its customers, and deny it the per capita dues which were the Federation's primary source of income. Many AFL leaders were even leery of section 7a of the National Industrial Recovery Act enabling workers to join unions of their own choosing, free of management interference, so that they could bargain collectively with the boss. Like the ethnic politicians, the old guard unionists were comfortable with small organizations whose membership could be easily manipulated; a large and aroused rank and file represented a clear and present danger to "boss rule."

But John L. Lewis, the son of a Welsh miner, who presided over the United Mine Workers, was an enthusiastic supporter of 7a. A lifelong Republican who believed in free enterprise— and an autocrat with a reputation for rigging elections and red-baiting—he acted decisively after the National Industrial Recovery Act was passed. The UMW had suffered grievously in the late 1920s and the Depression further drained its membership. Upon enactment of NRA, UMW organizers were sent out to the grimy towns nestled in the nation's coal-producing regions with the message that "the President wants you to join the union." (That many miners thought the organizers were talking about FDR was precisely the impression that Lewis wanted to convey.) The patriotic Appalachian miners and ethnics who aspired to become "good Americans" responded by the tens of thousands. State power had been used to smash labor organizations in the past, but with the Depression and the election of FDR, Lewis believed the union movement could use political power to the workers' advantage.

Because the craft unionists at the 1934 AFL convention reneged on a promise to begin an organizational drive in the mass production industries, Lewis formed the Committee of Industrial Organizations, providing his talent, energy, and intellect to the most massive drive in U.S. labor history. Lewis recruited former radical opponents like John Brophy and Powers Hapgood who forgot the crusty old autocrat's past because here was the chance to organize workers—urban laborers and farm workers, ethnics and blacks, the people the AFL had ignored—into industrial unions, mobilizing them into a powerful collective force for change. To the dismay of his conservative colleagues, Lewis also extended a welcoming hand to communists, who were among the most dedicated and effective labor organizers. During the Depression they led hunger marches and formed organizations of the unemployed in many cities. They knew how to organize at the work place, conduct meetings, write and disseminate literature, mobilize workers for strikes, and take defensive actions against management-inspired violence. The workers they assisted, in turn, learned a great deal about mass action and many of them would play a vital part in forging the CIO. The "reds'" major liability was their unthinking dedication to Moscow, which had determined the American party's labor policy since the aftermath of World War I. In 1929, under Stalin's instructions, the communists discarded their "boring from within" strategy for "dual unionism" and formed the Trade Union Unity League (TUUL) as an alternative to the capitalist labor organizations. The TUUL was not very successful and it was disbanded six years later, not because Moscow thought another approach to the American worker would be more productive, but because Stalin, fearful of the Nazi threat, urged foreign communists to join socialists and democrats in a Popular Front against fascism. After the Nazis and Soviets signed a mutual defense treaty, the democratic socialists once again were labeled "social fascists" by the Stalinists and the American comrades joined American Firsters in opposing the war. The American reds changed their line after the Nazis invaded the Soviet Union and during the war they opposed strike actions—

because they interfered with the war effort—even where it was obvious that management was manipulating the war to deny their workers wage increases they justly deserved.

With passage of the Wagner Act, which had replaced the unconstitutional NRA, the CIO organized millions of workers in the manufacturing, mining, and transportation industries, primarily in the East, Midwest, and Pacific West. A disproportionate number of newly organized workers were white ethnics. C. Wright Mills found in the 1940s that whereas only 14 per cent of the AFL's leadership was descended from Eastern and Southern Europe, 23 per cent of the CIO's leadership came from the New Immigration.[29] By 1941 organized labor had a membership of 8,410,000 compared to its 1933 membership of 2,805,000. For the first time in the nation's history a significant proportion of the nonagricultural labor force—approximately 23 per cent—was organized.

Management reacted to the unionization drive as it had in the past. Company unions were formed as a ploy to pre-empt the formation of independent labor organizations and millions of dollars were spent to hire company police, spies, and scabs to intimidate workers. The political climate, however, had changed dramatically. Local authorities in many areas still violated workers' first amendment rights of free speech and assembly and incarcerated organizers on trumped-up charges; but elsewhere politicians adopted a more evenhanded posture in labor disputes. The Depression had caused the defeat of reactionaries in state, county, and municipal elections and, for the first time, strikers and labor unions enjoyed equal protection under the law. Given a free choice, the workers chose independent unions and dignity, self-esteem, and the ability to secure some control over their labor.

In many manufacturing centers like Gary, Pittsburgh, and Detroit—flash points for frequent violent clashes with the forces of reaction—white ethnic workers represented a majority of the labor force. Religious, cultural, and regional differences which had formerly fostered discord among the workers in auto plants, steel mills, and on the docks did not deflect the workers' anger. The New Deal and the campaign to organize mass production workers gave focus to discontent which had previously been diffuse and this time there were militant organizers, political radicals, and young workers who together provided tough and skillful leadership.

2. Why the White Ethnics Did Not Become the Mass Base for Revolution

According to the radical folklore the nation was ripe for revolution during the Depression but so-called labor leftists like Sidney Hillman and Walter Reuther sold out the proletariat when they rejected the formation of a radical third party and settled for New Deal liberalism instead. This interpretation accounts for the estrangement of many radicals from the labor movement today, hurting both organized labor and Democratic radicalism—and the worker most of all.

At the outset of the CIO organizational drive, radicals whose idealism had attracted them to Stalinism and Trotskyism were captives of a soaring optimism. They were ready to seize the day: the Depression was proof that Marx's prophecy about the ultimate collapse of capitalism had come true. By 1933 one fourth of the American labor force, approximately thirteen million persons, were unemployed; countless others could only find part-time employment. In 1934, 2.5 million Americans had been unemployed for two years and six million for over one year. Some polls showed that as many as one fourth of these Americans responded positively to queries about the necessity for revolution.[30] The sit-down strikes in rubber, the militancy of the auto workers at Flint, the general strike in San Francisco, the "class war" in Minneapolis which was responsible for the Teamsters' adopting industrial unionism, the horror of the Memorial Day Massacre in South Chicago, and the thousands of persons who were killed and maimed in labor strife engulfing the country during the 1930s—was this not proof positive of the American workers' authentic class consciousness?

To confuse the ideal world with the real one is to violate a time-honored political taboo. Left-wing radicals in the 1930s did that when they confused the American worker's militancy with an authentic class consciousness—the kind that Marx talked about—involving a proletariat identity, the conviction that capitalism was responsible for the travail of society, and a commitment to revolutionary change. The truth is that there is little evidence that revolutionary class consciousness existed among a significant segment of the working class, and the conservatism of American labor is better assessed in terms of conditions unique to the United States than the evil design of "labor bosses." Mention already has been made of one of these conditions—the divisiveness of ethnicity. The others are a relatively open society enabling working people to make real social and economic advances, an egalitarian value system to which an overwhelming number of Americans adhere, and a political system allowing the common man to influence government.

While the American milieu exacerbated ethnic discord, it ameliorated class differences. On arriving in America the immigrants were struck by the absence of well-defined social guidelines typical of European societies. The talented, the energetic, the lucky, and the ruthless could overcome humble beginnings and "make it" in the United States. The climb was steeper and the casualties greater than our folklore would have us believe but our bountiful resources and the relative openness of American society served as a safety valve dissipating massive lower-class protest. The workers' standard of living in the United States was higher than that of the European laborers. In every ethnic community the presence of small businessmen and workers who purchased cars and homes were living examples that material success in the United States was not beyond the reach of the common man.

The Depression caused a growing number of white ethnics to think of themselves more as workers and less as members of an ethnic minority, but they adopted a uniquely American view of society—one that differed dramatically from the class consciousness of their European counterparts. Seymour Martin Lipset, in *The First New Nation*, claims that "the worship of the dollar, the drive to make a profit, the effort to get ahead through the accumulation of wealth, all have been credited to the egalitarian character of the society, that is, to the absence of aristocracy."[31] Like his fellow American, the worker placed great emphasis upon materialism and individual achievement and because movement from the lower to the upper rungs of the social ladder was a real possibility in the United States, the quest to gain social status was vigorously pursued by all elements of society. The American dream promised that the immigrant would be judged on the basis of his performance, gaining status and wealth by the sweat of his labor, the creativity of his mind, and the dexterity of his hands. One's name, position, and inherited rights counted less in the New World than in the old one. If by chance a man overcame the burden of poverty and lower-class status and became wealthy in Europe, he still was deemed a social inferior by the upper classes. In the United States money and the respect for wealth enabled people from humble beginnings who became rich to enjoy status rewards denied their counterparts in the old country.

Lipset makes a convincing case that differences between the European and American labor movements can in large part be explained by conflicting value systems. So the rank and file in the United States does not begrudge its leaders the prerogatives of union office—high salaries and lavish expense accounts —because they believe that successful people deserve to be rewarded materially. The notion that it is the right of every American to improve his material situation also accounts for the contradiction that, while the American labor movement is philosophically conservative, it has been exceedingly more militant than the allegedly revolutionary unions in Europe. Here also is a plausible explanation for John L. Lewis's behavior; a lifelong Republican and staunch capitalist, he led the most momentous assault upon the captains of industry in our nation's history, broke with FDR when many socialists were elbowing one another to gain his attention, and initiated a coal strike during World War II when the communists were bludgeoning workers into accepting low wage rates while management was reaping enormous profits.

In addition to the attractiveness of a value system which enabled the common man to prosper, many immigrants, in a defense reaction to nativist pressure, were predisposed to accept the American way of life. Their children, who aspired to be good citizens, were even more uncritical of American society. The second generation associated their parents' culture with poverty and social ostracism, while they viewed the American culture in terms of prosperity and self-esteem. It is safe to conclude that most of them would have rejected the old culture for the new one even barring the compulsion of Americanization. The American values, after all, were functional to an industrialized, urbanized, acquisitive society.

As the pall of the Depression set upon the land, the nation despaired at the inability of government and business to put the economy back on track. People were frightened when they lost their jobs, homes, businesses, and investments; they got angry when Hoover refused to adopt dramatic countermeasures. But only a relatively small number considered revolutionary solutions and took radical actions because they believed our prevailing institutions could not cope with economic collapse. Most, out of ignorance, innocence, or conviction, neither questioned the legitimacy of our political and economic institutions nor supported revolution. An estimated two thirds of the nation in 1937 disagreed with the statement that "the Constitution should be made easier to amend." In 1940 a sample reflecting the thinking of 64.2 per cent of the American people agreed that: "Our form of government, based upon the Constitution, is as near perfect as it can be and no important changes should be made in it."[32] Workers joined labor unions in the 1930s to attain job security at the work place, to gain a voice in conditions of employment, and to get a larger piece of the economic pie, not to mobilize for mass action against capitalism.

As they expected, the immigrants observed that government catered to the wealthy and well connected, that laws were twisted to favor the boss at the expense of his workers. Yet they also noted that ordinary people at times did get justice and that the authorities did not always cavalierly dismiss them as was the custom at home. The New Deal strengthened the white ethnics' conviction that the American system was a responsive one, governed by decent people who were not at all indifferent to the problems afflicting the common man. Whatever the faults of our political and economic institutions—and there are many—the unmistakable truth is that many immigrants and most of their children rejected radical change because there was an element of truth to the American dream —it was by no means an illusion of their "false consciousness."

The seriousness with which some radicals spoke about forming a third party during the 1930s testified to their misperception of the workers' tenor and mood. Hillman, Reuther, and many other former socialists rejected the formation of a third party because they believed the prospects of its gaining power in the United States were poor; few workers favored revolution and most had become steadfast supporters of the Democratic Party. This was certainly true of most Catholic workers who were enthralled by FDR, and even among the more radical-minded Jews it was doubtful whether a significant number would have deserted him for a third party. Roosevelt captured the loyalty of many Jewish socialists because he sought their counsel and gave them the recognition that they and other immigrants wanted so badly. This was even true of intelligent, successful, self-confident men like Sidney Hillman. John L. Lewis once remarked, "Sidney often told me I could never understand what it meant to a person who was an immigrant not only to be welcome in the White House but to have the President call him by his first name."[33] The Jewish love affair with Roosevelt was not only tied to his domestic policies or sensitivity toward the aspiring Jewish population in the United States. As the scope and magnitude of the Nazi terror circulated among the Jews, FDR was perceived as the only leader in the West who had the power to defeat the hated Nazis.

In spite of the foregoing observations, the radicals would have made a greater impact upon the white ethnic industrial worker had there been a larger number of indigenous radicals among the Catholic working class. During the 1930s, Old World hatreds and stereotypes divided the Catholic white ethnic workers and the Jews who dominated many radical organizations in the North.

It was hard for Jews to forget that pogroms in Eastern and Central Europe had driven them from the Continent to the United States. Even followers of Karl Marx, who advocated working-class solidarity, could not forget the past or dismiss American anti-Semitism; many Catholics did not forget their prejudices, even some of those who preached radical doctrine. After Hitler's rise to power, Jews of all political persuasions could not ignore the fact that he had gained power in a nation whose proletariat were reputedly the most advanced on the Continent.

The Jews, however, were not free of their own biases. Many Jews believed that the Wasps were imprudent in making derogatory remarks about the Poles and Italians in public, but they spoke among themselves about the goyim in terms which were not at all flattering. And Jewish radicals, like their Wasp comrades, were unsparing in their criticism of the Catholic church. Democratic socialists, Trotskyites and Stalinists all lashed out at the church of Rome for the Vatican's friendly attitude toward fascism in Europe and the American hierarchy's animosity toward radicalism. When Catholic workers reacted to such criticism with anger, the radicals assumed that they were victims of Catholic brainwashing; but in many cases even nominal Catholics displayed hostility toward antichurch radicals because to them the "church" was perceived in terms of one's family, neighbors, and friends. Catholicism was not a religious dogma, it represented a community of people who shared the pangs of minority and working-class status.

The Catholic church deserved much of the criticism cast in its direction. Many bishops and priests bitterly opposed CIO organizers, who infused the Catholic worker with new, radical notions about trade unionism. In Jersey City Frank Hague's goons received the blessing of the local hierarchy when they ran the "reds" out of town. Reactionary prelates and old guard politicos conspired in other cities to sabotage the CIO organizational drive. The prospect of taking on or sharing power with a well-organized, tough, and dedicated group of labor radicals was not one many bosses or bishops relished. But there were a large number of pro-labor priests and members of the hierarchy who lent their support to the CIO. The American Catholic church was not formally allied with the people who controlled the state and economy as was true in many parts of Europe. Few Catholics owned or managed large corporations and not many of them enjoyed the prerogatives of the middle class. The Catholic church in the United States was the church of the common man and it recruited its priests, nuns, and brothers from the working class. It was apparent to parish priests in communities stricken by high unemployment that the faithful would not passively accept unemployment, watch their kids go hungry, or tolerate government indifference in the same fashion their parents had. A

majority of the ethnic community was now comprised of
settlers or second-generation Americans who no longer perceived themselves as Europeans. They were Americans!

During the organizational drive men like Monsignor John
Ryan and Pittsburgh's Father Charles Owen Rice supported
the new labor organizations. Ryan's progressive writing had
struck a responsive chord in the hearts and minds of many liberal Catholics and Father Rice, who was a close friend of
Philip Murray—who was soon to replace John Lewis at the
helm of the CIO—offered Murray advice about strategy, tactics, and CIO policy which Murray often followed. Had the
Catholic clergy remained indifferent to the plight of the
worker or had the hierarchy adopted a national policy of
opposing the CIO, it is likely that the radicals would have
achieved greater success with the Catholic white ethnics. The
involvement of Catholic clergy in the resurrection of the labor
movement had a modifying influence upon the CIO.

The Irish in particular took their Catholicism seriously, but
it would be a mistake to exaggerate the influence of the
Catholic church upon Irish trade unionists. Contrary to popular wisdom, the labor movement has been home for many
Irish radicals like John Fitzpatrick, William Z. Foster, and
Elizabeth Gurley Flynn. Nevertheless, while Irish workers
who were devout Catholics generally ignored antilabor priests,
they listened attentively to friendly ones and often took warnings about dangerous radicals seriously. The same was true of
most East European workers; and the Italians, though less
inclined to attend church, lived in communities where radical
activists faced a powerful entrenched group of conservative
communal leaders.

3. Gaining a New Level of Political Awareness

In spite of the conservative influences in his community
and in American society at large, the trauma of the Depression
and the CIO had a profound impact upon the Catholic
worker. Indeed, it was through his membership in the newly
formed industrial unions that he gained a more sophisticated
grasp of politics and the prospects for change. Unlike the heirs
of Gompers in the AFL, the industrial unionists viewed political action as an integral part of the labor movement. Unions,

they argued, were not merely guilds serving as agencies of collective bargaining, they were instruments allowing working people to participate as an organized force in industrial life and political affairs. And, while collective bargaining enabled the union to wrest higher wages, better working conditions, and job security from the boss, there were limits to it. The same was true of the role of the family and other private associations; in an industrial society there were matters which none of these institutions could treat properly. As things stood, only the government possessed the resources to treat widespread unemployment, provide the money for the construction of housing, and restore an economy which had been mangled by the greed of powerful business interests.

The CIO and the New Deal prompted white ethnic workers to perceive an alternative to patronage politics in the form of government programs like unemployment insurance, social security, and housing assistance—things the machines ignored. In union meetings, through labor media, and in rap sessions at the shop, the worker learned that it was the government's job to provide for the sick and needy, to compensate victims of industrial accidents, and to assist the unemployed. The New Deal programs were not handouts; every American had the right to a job, social security, and decent shelter. Although ethnic and racial discord had by no means disappeared, the radicals emphasized the common plight of all "working stiffs"—black or white, ethnic or "American." The bitter resistance of management to the CIO contributed to the workers' solidarity and militancy, prompting them to perceive change in terms of wider political, economic, and social reforms and to gain an appreciation for collective action.

The CIO's political agenda was also shaped by the nature of the low income production workers it was organizing, for they could not meet their needs through wages alone. Welfare state legislation was needed to supplement the worker's income and to protect him against the travail of a rapidly changing society. The workers the CIO organized, moreover, ". . . produced for national markets affected by government politics unlike the service and construction workers in the AFL." For all these reasons ". . . industrial-union officials

could justify an active role in national politics as directly benefiting their members . . ."[34]

While the CIO's political priority was to influence policy-
making in Washington, the appearance of militant labor organizations in urban areas throughout the industrial North
threatened the domination of the old pols. Via the CIO, the
worker learned that the district captain in his neighborhood
was not doing him and his neighbors a favor when the city put
up a stop sign at a perilous intersection; that was the government's job. Furthermore, the wise guys down at City Hall, the
same ones who drank beer with you at the local tavern and
claimed to be friends of the people—they served the big money
interests. It was, after all, the Chicago machine which controlled the policemen who shot down ten men, women, and
children (most of them in the back or side) during the 1937
Memorial Day Massacre; and the CIO organizers on the scene
claimed the massacre was premeditated.

By the end of World War II the UAW dominated the politics of Detroit where tens of thousands of auto workers living
in the metropolitan area, led by skilled organizers, shop stewards, and labor politicos, ousted party regulars from City Hall.
The UAW, through aggressive voter registration drives, also
brought blacks into the political process in large numbers, and
it was not long before the UAW represented the most powerful faction in Michigan's Democratic Party. CIO unions in
other parts of the industrial North also began to use their political influence to revise the balance of power in both city and
state politics. In St. Paul the CIO provided the muscle
enabling a liberal coalition, through the Democratic Farmers
Labor Party, to oust old guard politicos allied with the AFL
from municipal government. And even in cities like Chicago
where the AFL and the machine dominated the labor and political scene, the machine acknowledged the presence of the
new claimants to power.

While the CIO, aligned with liberal New Dealers and democratic radicals, ousted machine politicians from power in
some areas, in most cases the outcome was less clear-cut. Factionalism often precluded the formation of local political organizations housing union organizers, free-lance radicals,
Trotskyites, and Stalinists who had collaborated in the drive

to build the CIO. The more radically inclined leadership in many CIO unions rejected association with regular Democrats or New Dealers. In most instances the old guard was able to stave off attempts on the part of the CIO to push the machine aside; in others, guided by their pragmatism, the regulars reached an accommodation with labor. This involved machine support for pro-labor legislation on the state and federal levels; in other instances it involved making room for labor officials within the organization itself. By the mid-1950s, when the radicals who had resisted collaboration with the party regulars were hounded from the labor movement, it was not uncommon to find CIO officials in machine-dominated political organizations. Even Frank Hague made peace with the CIO and Joe Germano, the dominant figure in the Steel Workers Union's largest local in the Chicago area, District 31, enjoyed a comfortable relationship with the Daley machine until he retired in the early 1970s.

Through the New Deal and the CIO, the white ethnics came of age politically; henceforth they elected liberal Democrats and supported progressive legislation reducing economic and racial inequalities in the United States. But the persistent influence of their political culture, the Second World War, and the Cold War all served as deterrents to their accepting even more fundamental changes in American life.

CHAPTER V

The Cosmopolitan Left
and the Failure
of McGovern's New Populism

In 1972 Richard Nixon was the first Republican Presidential candidate in over forty years to win a majority of Catholic votes. Whereas Hubert Humphrey had received 59 per cent of the Catholic vote in 1968, McGovern only got 47 per cent in 1972. The Jews kept their faith with the Democratic Party, but McGovern's margin among the Jewish electorate slipped fifteen percentage points (from 84 to 69 per cent) below Humphrey's 1968 performance. The GOP had a long way to go before it could reasonably expect to garner a larger slice of the Jewish vote, but Nixon's appeal to the Jews in 1972 was a promising first step toward that end.

There is no enigma shrouding McGovern's failure to hold the white ethnic vote. The South Dakotan was perceived as the candidate of a cosmopolitan elite which dominated the nation's liberal institutions in the 1960s—affluent, well-educated practitioners of a New Politics whom middle America deemed responsible for a decade of turmoil and domestic unrest. The curtain rose on the first act of the McGovern tragedy in the 1950s, after a twenty-year Democratic reign in Washington.

A. The Democratic Split in New York: *The Struggle Between the Manhattan Reformers, Primarily Jews, and the Regulars, Largely Catholics, Presaged the Schism Which Would Divide the Democratic Coalition During the Johnson Administration*

Adlai Stevenson's twin attempts at the White House served as a catalyst to political reformers during the Eisenhower Administration. His intellect, wit, disdain for regular politicians, and, one is tempted to say, his breeding, attracted to his cause educated middle-class liberals who had previously remained aloof from politics. Writing in 1954, Irving Howe observed that "Stevenson was the first of the liberal candidates in the post-Wilson era who made no effort to align himself with the plebeian tradition or plebeian sentiments."[1] Nevertheless, while the American electorate opted for General Eisenhower, a majority of white ethnics spurned the World War II hero and voted for Stevenson.

After Stevenson's defeat the reformers turned to local politics with a vengeance in cosmopolitan oases in New York, California, and other large states. They set their sights on machine politicians who practiced the Old Politics, that is the politics of interest, and employed political influence for their own self-aggrandizement. They ignored real issues like poverty, racism, and militarism, and rigged elections and violated other precepts of democratic government to stay in power. The New York example is significant because there was a discernible ethnic dimension to the struggle between the Manhattan reformers, primarily Jews, and the regulars, largely Catholics; and it presaged the schism which would divide the Democratic coalition during the Johnson Administration.

"The New York story began in the late 1950s when a group of young, upper-middle-class liberals, disappointed by the New York Democratic organization's lack of enthusiasm for Adlai Stevenson, launched an all-out attack upon it under the banner of party reform." The arch villain in the piece was Carmine De Sapio, the dapper Tammany Hall boss who favored tinted glasses and sported an out-of-date pompadour. Ironically De Sapio had adopted a number of reforms which were bitterly opposed by the old guard in Tammany Hall—the election of Democratic Party district leaders by the party rank and file in open elections among others. This reform proved to be his undoing and, "beginning with a number of successful insurgent candidacies for district leadership in the 'silk-stocking' district of central Manhattan," the reformers elected "a bloc of their own Democratic county and state committee members, city councilmen, state assemblymen and senators, judges, and congressmen."[2]

Wasps were active in the reform movement—people like Marietta Tree, a member of a socially prominent family and the wife of a former British MP, who led the Lexington Democratic Club. Like previous generations of Protestant reformers, their zeal to promote "good government" was a manifestation of conflicting motives. Many believed in the democratic process and the rule of law and were repelled by the corruption which was such a visible part of the Old Politics. Others supported honest government because government efficiency served the interest of the corporate and professional communities from whence they came. Still others were motivated by a drive to even scores with the vulgar but pugnacious Catholic politicos who had wrenched the reins of power from their forefathers earlier in the century. Many were convinced that, by virtue of their breeding, education, and demonstrated excellence, it was in the best interests of the ordinary people that they return to power—as senior counselors if not political office holders themselves.

In this connection they looked approvingly toward the "liberated Catholics" who had cast off the old ethnic political ethos for the Wasp political worldview. A prerequisite to Catholic membership in the reform movement was the willingness to psychologically sever oneself from one's kith and kin in the "old neighborhood," generally located outside Manhattan in the boroughs—Brooklyn, the Bronx, Staten Island, and Queens. There was good reason for progressive Catholics to turn on the old ethnic pols who employed political power for the purpose of self-enrichment while ignoring the needs of the working people who elected them; but the reformers made the fatal error of adopting a politics of con-

science well suited for educated middle-class districts but
foreign to a working-class electorate.

The gentile contingent, however, was of secondary impor-
tance. The most prominent group in the reform movement
were "assimilated," affluent young Jewish lawyers who lived on
Manhattan Island between Greenwich Village and Harlem.
Many of them would find a place, years later, in the Lindsay
Administration—men and women who, according to Irving
Kristol, knew more about the urban problems of the Left
Bank of Paris than they did about the boroughs of New York.
They perceived machine politics with ethnically balanced tick-
ets and patronage rewards to party workers and friends as a
repugnant legacy of a bygone era. They crossed swords with
Jewish practitioners of the Old Politics, but they perceived
New York's Catholics as the real repository of reaction in the
Empire State.

According to Nathan Glazer and Daniel Patrick Moynihan,
the battle between the reformers and the regulars in New
York City has shaped up as one involving Jews and Catholics.
"Among the most notable events in New York City during
the 1960s was the decline, almost the collapse, of Catholic
power." Consequently, after the 1969 mayorality race, "the
powerful Board of Estimates, consisting of the mayor, the
comptroller, the president of the council, and the five borough
presidents, consisted of five Jews, one white Protestant, one
black Protestant, and one lonely Catholic, Robert T. Conner."
A year later Arthur Goldberg, with three co-religionists and a
black, would lead the Democratic ticket in an abortive attempt to unseat Nelson Rockefeller and his team in Albany.

"The Jews ousted the Catholics. They did this in direct toe-
to-toe encounter in a hundred areas of the city's life," and
"they carried out a brilliant outflanking maneuver involving
the black masses of the city, which combined in inextricable
detail elements of pure charity, enlightened self-interest, and
plain ethnic combativeness." The Jewish lawyers who dominated the reform clubs served as shock troops with Jewish professionals, liberal businessmen, and an army of dedicated
housewives and other landsmen bringing up the rear. The
Jews in New York "simply outclassed their competition,

which was Protestant in business, professional, and intellectual circles, and Catholic in the political ones."³

The Jews had been the first among the New Immigrants to move into the American middle class; many did it within the span of a generation. Products of a business culture, they displayed commercial acumen unrivaled by any other ethnic group in our society. Many Russian Jews first made their mark in business via the garment industry, demonstrating an ingenuity and zest for work which their Yankee and German Jewish competitors rarely matched. By the end of the Second World War, Jews were prominent in the sale of retail merchandise and, with their customary drive, they became innovators in the food industry, in department stores, and even experienced success in manufacturing—previously a Wasp preserve. Whereas Jews once were rare on Wall Street—barring a few notable exceptions—Jewish investors and stockbrokers secured a firm foothold in investment banking after the Second World War.

Offspring of immigrant seamstresses and fruit peddlers—on leaving sidewalk campuses like CCNY—attended graduate, law, and medical school in numbers disproportionate to the Jewish population in the United States. Jewish doctors and lawyers often demonstrated the capacity for hard work and ingenuity that characterized the innovative Jewish businessman, and, possessed of a keenly honed drive to achieve, they became prominent members of their professions. In academia Jews have excelled in the behavioral and natural sciences alike. Many major works in political science, economics, psychology, physics, mathematics, and biology have been penned by Jewish scholars. One can find them developing military strategy in defense-oriented think tanks (Hudson Institute and the Rand Corporation) or designing social welfare programs in policy centers (The Institute for Policy Studies) where traditional Jewish humanitarianism pervades a highly charged intellectual atmosphere.

In the United States, free of the sectarianism which had prevailed in Poland and Russia, Eastern European Jews became a pivotal force in Hollywood and on Broadway—as entrepreneurs, writers, and directors—as early as the 1920s when most of their landsmen were still working in the garment

industry or peddling fruit on the streets of the Lower East
Side. Jews would also make a rich contribution to radio and
television. At one time, Jews were heads of the three television
networks: William S. Paley, CBS; David Sarnoff, NBC; and
Leonard Goldenson, ABC. Increasingly it became customary
for prominent national newspapers to carry the bylines of Jewish journalists (David Broder, Art Buchwald, and Seymour
Hersh) and the literary and small magazines revealed the
growing presence of Jews in American letters. Publishing
houses formerly the pride of Wasp literati were bought out by
Jews and many of the most popular books and scholarly works
published were the products of Jewish labor. For much of the
1950s and throughout the 1960s Jewish authors like Bernard
Malamud, Saul Bellow, and Philip Roth produced an ava-
lanche of best sellers, causing some critics to remark that you
could no longer read the "great American novel" without a
Yiddish-English dictionary. The prominence of Jews in the literary world and publishing industry has caused gentile writers
like Truman Capote to complain about the power of a "Jewish literary mafia," and the clout Jews wield in the entertainment, publishing, and news business has been a source of concern to Jewish leaders who fear a gentile backlash attending
the dominant role Jews play in contemporary American cultural life.

The impact which the relatively small Jewish community
has had on our political life since the 1930s has been monu-
mental. Since the New Deal, Democratic and Republican administrations have sought Jews out as speech-
writers, policy-makers, and advisers. Henry Kissinger, Herbert
Stein, Casper Weinberger, Leonard Garment, and Alan
Greenspan are the most recent examples. Jews have also
played a leading role in policy-making positions in many government agencies. Moreover, they continue to be an important element in the labor movement, although the Jewish rank
and file—with the exception of white-collar unions—is small.
As international presidents, organizers, business agents, and
policy-makers, Jews continue to wield influence in the labor
movement belying their numbers—for example, Jerry Wurf,
Albert Shanker, Irving Bluestone, etc. Jewish talent, money,
sweat, and blood have been generously expended in the last

quarter century in civil rights, the war on poverty, and antiwar movements. In every city one can find Jews playing a leading role in progressive political movements and humanitarian endeavors no matter how modest the Jewish population may be.

It is indisputable that, vote for vote, no other ethnic group in America wields as much political power as the Jews do. Their political influence, of course, is not merely a function of their electoral strength which, with the exception of a few areas, is modest; the clout they wield is an extension of their economic prowess, professional talent, intellectual capability, cultural influence, and political acumen. Democratic Presidential aspirants in particular depend greatly on Jewish brain-trusters and media experts like Frank Mankiewicz, Ben Wattenberg, Max Kampelman, Charles Guggenheim, David Garth, and Daniel Yankelovich. Every major Democratic Presidential candidate in the last quarter century has relied on Jewish money from movie moguls (Arthur Krim), Wall Street investors (Meshulam Riklis), and business tycoons (Max Palevsky) as a counterpoint to the massive funding which Republicans know is forthcoming from the corporate community and Wasp rich. Given Jewish influence in the Democratic Party, one need not be a cynic to conclude that this explains in part why Democratic politicians are such staunch defenders of Israel. Jewish influence in the intellectual community and communications industry is another source of power few politicians with national aspirations dare ignore. The time and space the media devote to the state of Israel and Jewish-related matters in this country is further evidence that the Jews wield more influence per capita than any other single ethnic group in the United States.

Had Karl Marx been right, there is no way one can explain why this largely affluent segment of our population has remained at the battle lines for social justice and economic democracy. The explanation is certainly not an economic one. Rather, it lies in the centuries of persecution, the World War II holocaust, and the fact that only two generations ago many Jews were poor, ignorant, and the object of prejudice; these have burned deeply into the Jewish psyche a sensitivity toward the downtrodden and disadvantaged. Of larger importance, the Jews have acted on their convictions.

Nonetheless, in comparison with the 1930s, few younger Jews live among working people, share their problems, suffer their anxieties, or understand their fears of social change. ". . . since World War II, there is no longer a proletarian majority even among immigrant Jews, and the bulk of the Jews in America are clearly middle-class, with a large proportion of professionals and academics."[4] Most Jewish activists today are privy to amenities the affluent in our society enjoy—access to good schools, money to travel, the certainty of a college education, and the self-assurance that comes from belonging to a privileged group whose members usually succeed in the endeavors they undertake. Yet Jewish radicals who speak with feeling about society's cruel indifference to the nation's minority peoples and poor are blind to the fact that many Americans perceive them as an elite.

The reluctance of Jewish leaders to acknowledge that Jews enjoy elite status is manifested by the propensity of Jewish defense agencies to exaggerate the persistence of American anti-Semitism. Consequently, when Italian-Americans in New York complain that Jewish urban experts and social service administrators have ignored Italian neighborhoods, some overly sensitive Jewish leaders are inclined to ignore their merits and attribute such charges to anti-Semitism. But in New York City Jews are in a position of power politically, economically, and culturally, and, like others who wield power, they occasionally abuse it. Glazer and Moynihan correctly emphasize Jewish-Catholic conflict as an example of ethnic interest group rivalry exacerbated by the differential class status of the protagonists.

The Jewish community is understandably sensitive to references pertaining to Jewish economic power and their influence in other areas of American life; anti-Semites have exaggerated Jewish influence in order to "blame" the Jews for recessions, social unrest, and foreign subversion for centuries. But the inordinate influence that Jews wield in our society, especially in the cosmopolitan community, is germane to any comprehensive assessment of postwar American life.

For generations the first people many Catholic ethnics met who enjoyed the privileges of an elite were Jews not Wasps. The "rich people" most familiar to the Italian truck driver and

Polish factory hand often were the Jewish businessman, landlord, doctor, and lawyer. Oftentimes Jewish businessmen dominated the commercial activities of ethnic communities, even largely Polish, Irish, or Italian neighborhoods. "Do you know on a Jewish holiday you can't buy anything around here?" Comments like this surfaced in many ethnic neighborhoods every Rosh Hashana and Yom Kippur, and Jewish monopolization of retail merchandising was even more evident in "downtown shopping areas" where the darkened store lights and signs announced "this store is closed for the holidays." Because the Jews were among the first to enter the professions, Catholic patients were compelled to go to a Jewish M.D. to get a boil lanced, a Jewish dentist to get a tooth pulled, or to seek the advice of a Jewish attorney regarding an impending legal action. Many gentile customers ripped off by Jewish businessmen, doctors, lawyers, and accountants were inclined to attribute their misfortune to Jewish avarice rather than to the shabby business ethics of American capitalism.

In many neighborhoods and cities the Jews still are an elite, envied because of their wealth and the prerogatives of power they enjoy. Quite often they are perceived as being condescending and overbearing in their relations with the less privileged gentiles with whom they come in contact—in much the same fashion that their forebears felt they suffered Wasp indiscretions two generations ago. Some Catholic intellectuals in New York claim that the Jewish schoolteacher often unconsciously harbors ethnic stereotypes about Catholic students, deeming it natural that the Italian youngster goes to trade school while the Jewish student enrolls in a college preparatory course. Of course, one might find the Italian teacher whose relations with his Jewish students are shaped by similar unflattering stereotypes. But in many parts of the metropolitan North—and this is most especially true of the New York metropolitan area—the fact is that it is Jews who occupy positions of influence and are, therefore, more inclined to be perceived as an elite. Consequently, just as the Jews in the past have been put off by Irish political power—not because of some deeply ingrained prejudice toward the Celts—ethnic Catholics have reacted with feeling to the real or imagined instances when Jews have abused the influence they wield via the business community, academia, the mass media, or the professions.

Furthermore, there is a new dimension to Catholic/Jewish relations which has received scant publicity; that is, there is ev-idence indicating that Jews have become increasingly more in-tolerant of Catholics. Comparing poll data gathered in 1952 with survey results from 1965, Andrew Greeley observed that in 1965 Jews were "far more likely to express the feeling that Catholics do not respect Jewish beliefs, that Catholics do not want to intermarry, that Catholic clergy are not intelligent and do not promote understanding," and that "Catholic mag-azines are not fair" than the other way around. The Catholic attitudes toward Jews over the thirteen-year span became more favorable with respect to five out of seven problem areas stud-ied. "Altogether the responses suggest that the two groups have switched places: in 1952 Catholics had a more negative attitude toward Jews than Jews had toward Catholics; by 1965 the reverse seemed to be true."[5] A simple explanation for this turnabout is not available; it might stem from a rising level of self-awareness among Jews. It might have something to do with Jews adopting traditional Wasp prejudices, or it might be a by-product of Jewish security in the United States enabling Jews to articulate prejudices they previously kept to them-selves.

Jewish defense agencies, which keep a sharp eye out for even the faintest signs of anti-Semitism, have blithely ignored this phenomenon. But the Catholic ethnics have not. Among progressive Italians in New York—people who are more inclined to favor the worldview of Allard Lowenstein than Mario Biaggi—there is a great deal of resentment about the propensity of New Politics Jews to engage in anti-Italian remarks. At a Lindsay gala in November 1969, for example, comic Woody Allen speculated that the mayor's opponent, Mario Procaccino, was probably sitting at home ". . . in his undershirt, drinking beer, and watching Lawrence Welk on television."[6] This remark revealed a class bias but to most Italians it was an ethnic slur. Indeed, the election was marked by many such ethnic slurs and the butt of the humor generally was the Italian Democratic candidate. One of the jokes mak-ing the rounds alleged that if Procaccino were elected, he would remove the "rugs from Gracie Mansion and cover the bare floors with linoleum"; another gambit widely repeated in radical chic circles exclaimed, "Do you know that Mario is so confident he's going to be elected mayor that he's bought a giant plastic pink flamingo for the front lawn of City Hall!"

Italian-Americans of all political persuasions, including many of those who voted for John Lindsay, were outraged by such slurs. Indeed, educated middle-class Italians were among those most visibly angered. They knew that many of their friends and relatives still bore the scars of self-hate which was the hallmark of the second generation. And such self-hate was by no means a historical phenomenon for it was believed to account for the high dropout rate among Italian American youngsters in New York City's school system and the disproportionate rates of drug abuse found in Italian-American neighborhoods in the city—the highest of any white ethnic group. And the persistence of Italian jokes and the perpetuation of notions regarding Italian-American criminality were politically significant for they testified to the powerlessness of the Italian-Americans to put a halt to them.

The Jewish/Catholic struggle for political power in New York City testified to the growing estrangement of the largely middle-class Jewish community from the problems of the ordinary white worker. This trend was important because the Jews in this century have always demonstrated a greater sensitivity toward the plight of the white working class than other groups on the left. But in the 1960s a majority of Jewish journalists, intellectuals, political activists, and scholars perceived the world through the prism of the cosmopolitan left, which sorely needed the kind of sensitivity toward working people which Jewish leftists had displayed in the past.

While there was a definite ethnic dimension to the clash between the reformers and regulars in New York City in the 1950s, social class emerged as a key element in the struggle as the sixties matured. Unlike most other cities, New York City houses a large number of lower-middle-class Jews who drive taxis, operate Mom and Pop stores, teach school, and work as salesmen. Living in less fashionable parts of town, they, like their gentile neighbors, have clung to conservative social values and the old politics. Traditional Democrats, they have

been "more or less indifferent toward the abstract issue of
party reform raised by the reformers," but resentful of "the
reformers themselves, with their money, education, and intensity . . . Many interpreted the reformers' attacks against
'bossism' as assaults upon their own social and ethnic patterns
of behavior and traditional communal leadership."[7] This segment of the Jewish community voted overwhelmingly for Abe
Beame in 1973.

As the Civil Rights Movement gained momentum, bossism
receded as the rallying cry for party insurgents. The machine
politicians were less important than the vast white working
class which was the principal source of racism in the urban
North. In the process of redesigning their political agendas,
the Jewish reformers imputed "a good deal of wrongdoing to
working-class Catholics who weren't especially conscious of
wrongdoing at all."[8] Later, when the 1967–68 conflict over
community control set Jewish schoolteachers off against blacks
and their New Politics allies, the Jewish reformers alienated
many of their coreligionists too. And the propensity of some
black radicals to engage in anti-Semitic remarks and to equate
Jewish "colonization of black ghettos" with the Palestinian
"struggle against Israeli imperialism" had a profound emotional impact on many Jews. The political cultural chasm
separating lower-middle-class Jews from their reform-minded
brethren (in Los Angeles and Philadelphia as well as New
York) henceforth served as a divisive force in the Jewish community.

In the first edition of *Beyond the Melting Pot,* Glazer and
Moynihan predicted that, while the reformers could defeat De
Sapio (they ousted him in 1963), they could not replace
him. At the outset it did not look that way at all; the newcomers were "fresh and vital" while their opponents were
"anachronisms of the past." Following the successful formula
of the machine politicians, the reformers gained control of
party offices and dominated the primaries and selection of candidates.

Toward this end, they enlisted the support of college
students and middle-class liberals who were excited by the
smell of battle and charged by the élan the reformers

generated. They formed dissident clubs and infiltrated existing
political organizations. The regulars' initial reaction was one
of derision, but the laughter subsided when dedicated bands
of youthful middle-class activists, working long hours, knocking on doors, manning phone banks, and distributing literature, wrested the reins of power from their hands. They
watched outraged as the reformers exploited that old standby
of machine politicians—the primary; in brilliantly executed
blitzkrieg strikes, the "snotty do-gooders" won party elections
for district leaders, ward chairmanships, and important citywide posts.

The insurgents defeated the regulars in intraparty feuds but
in the process they emasculated the party. While dominating
the primaries, they could not mobilize enough votes to win
the general election. From 1958 to 1972 the New York Democratic Party only elected two Democrats to statewide office:
Robert Kennedy to the U. S. Senate and Arthur Levitt to his
perennial post as state controller. Both men received the support of the party's regulars and their white ethnic constituents. In other parts of the country where the exponents of
New Politics fought with party regulars, the outcome was similar to New York; party insurgents nominated their candidates
but often could not get them elected in the general election
because they promulgated issues and projected an image
which the average Democratic voter could not abide.

On the national level, however, the fortunes of the Democratic Party soared and the election of John F. Kennedy in
1960, the grandson of an Irish political boss, set the stage for
cosmopolitan Democrats gaining a foothold in the national
Democratic Party. It would enable Eugene McCarthy to send
Lyndon Johnson into retirement eight years later and secure
for George McGovern his party's nomination for the
Presidency in 1972.

B. The Cosmopolitan Left: *To Most Practitioners of the New Politics, a Coalition with Labor and the Old Left Was Out of the Question*

"Old Joe" Kennedy and "Honey Fitz" Fitzgerald, Rose
Kennedy's father, imbued the Kennedy brothers with an Irish

political sensibility which enabled them to talk turkey with party regulars, many of whom were Irish. The old pols did not fail the Kennedys and, because of Richard Daley's supreme effort on his behalf, John F. Kennedy became the first Catholic President of the United States. It was a great day for the Irish—one of their very own had made it to the pinnacle of political power. Kennedy's election signified the nullification of nativist fears regarding the loyalty of American Catholics and anxiety concerning whether or not they would employ political power to insinuate their religious dogma upon Protestant America. In a very real way Kennedy's election set the stage for the Republicans' ethnic strategy in 1972; for once it was established that Catholics in America were no longer second-class citizens, religious prejudice per se henceforth figured less decisively in their voting preferences.

John Kennedy, like most members of his party who had national ambitions, maintained harmonious relations with the vote-producing regulars; but in the jet age, ambitious politicians needed something the old pols could not deliver—ideas, the ability to capture the media's attention and the means to secure the votes of a growing number of issue-oriented voters. This talent could be found among the burgeoning educated middle class.

Since the end of the Second World War a phenomenal number of Americans have graduated from institutions of higher learning. To meet the demands of a post-industrial society, the knowledge industry has grown dramatically. It has produced the best educated generation of Americans in our nation's history—a new cosmopolitan elite. The men and women involved come from middle-class backgrounds, often enjoy the prerequisite of having been to one of the better universities, earn comfortable incomes in professional occupations, and live in metropolitan centers of the United States. They are well informed, articulate, and possess a cosmopolitan mindset which has fostered a common vision of American society. The more famous among them comprise an elite that hues to a liberal political orientation, while many others dabble in "radical chic." The cosmopolitans have been trend setters whose research, writing, and artistic output dominates the intellectual and cultural life of the country. Much of the work conducted by cosmopolitan academics is picked up by the mass media and is rehashed by like-minded people in the liberal professions, government, and the Movement. The cosmopolitan network is extensive and effective. In the 1960s social commentary and political strategies first articulated by a Berkeley activist or struck from the pen of intellectual gurus like Norman Mailer, Charles Reich, or John Kenneth Galbraith were quickly digested and disseminated among members of the fraternity.

Ideologically the cosmopolitans may occupy a place on a spectrum running from the moderate to the radical left, but most are sensitive to, if not always supportive of, the latest utterance fashionable in cosmopolitan circles. The principal spokesmen of the cosmopolitan community—situated in elite universities, TV network offices in Manhattan, or Washington political law firms—held sway over millions of Americans who cull their values and derive their information from the people who "think" for the nation. The cosmopolitans out in the "field"—be it Peoria or Greenwich Village—are brainy, committed, and possess the time and self-esteem to participate in community affairs and political primaries—activities the average person ignores. You will find them attending meetings of SANE, ADA, Common Cause, and ACLU, and active in other "do-gooder" causes.

A Democratic aspirant to the White House naturally is attracted to such talented and resourceful people. They can write speeches, produce scholarly position papers, and project their candidate as a thoughtful, sophisticated person who deserves the respect of discerning voters; and the contacts they have in the best universities, the media, the foundations, and the liberal professions are important assets to a man with Potomac fever.

In staffing his cabinet and other critical posts in his Administration, Kennedy recruited members of the old Eastern Establishment—Dillon, McCloy, Lovett—and brilliant new stars in the corporate/foundation/elite university complex—McNamara, Rusk, and Bundy. But many of the younger aides and lower level people he brought to Washington to fill the policy-making slots were extracted from the ranks of the New Politics community. Some of the younger ones among them were struck by Kennedy's verve and energy; but the older Stevensonians still distrusted the pragmatic Kennedy. Nonetheless they resigned themselves to the task of doing their best to nudge his Administration toward the "left."

After Lyndon Johnson moved into the White House, he forced through a string of bills earmarking funds for the war on poverty, urban development, and human resources through OEO, HUD, and HEW. Henceforth thousands of radical college professors, graduate students, pro bono lawyers, and idealistic young activists found themselves in a position to engage the problems which preoccupied them—racism, poverty, the monopolistic power of the "establishment," and indirectly the "war." While the old foreign policy establishment, aided and abetted by Cold War intellectuals, girded to confront international communism, the cosmopolitan reformers established the nation's domestic priorities and set the tone for social change. Sitting on top of federal money, they provided funds to like-minded persons on the state and local levels. Through a host of poverty and urban programs, they hired administrators, community organizers, and professional consultants who were exponents of a "new politics of conscience"—abstract principles took priority over concrete political objectives, issues over electoral victory, and ideological purity over alliances with allies who were not totally committed to the principles, issues, and objectives of the Movement. To most practitioners of the New Politics, organized labor and the old left, having "made it," had sold out the worker and the minorities; under these circumstances a coalition with labor and the old left was out of the question.

As the Civil Rights Movement gained momentum and mounting U.S. intervention in Vietnam gave impetus to the Peace Movement in universities and liberal enclaves, the cosmopolitan network grew in size and sophistication. One of the most important resources the Movement (the collective name given to civil rights, peace, and poverty activists) possessed was the sympathetic support of the national media and the preoccupation of academia and the literary community with its activities. This near-domination of the institutions which communicate news and disseminate information, however, would hurt the cosmopolitan reformers in two crucial ways. It would

produce a sense of power in terms of numbers, scope, and
commitment that was more illusory than real. And because of
the media's fascination with the activities of the more bizarre
elements in the Movement, a great many TV viewers—whose
own problems were being ignored and who were outraged that
the institutions and values they cherished were being ex-
coriated in the process—would conclude that the "radicals"
were not a tiny fringe group, but represented a large segment
of the population which was being encouraged by college
professors, writers, and, yes, prominent leaders in the Democratic Party, too.

Television is the single most important channel of political
communications; it reaches into millions of homes, defines
issues, and posits solutions in a nationally significant manner.
Approximately "65% of all voters consider TV their most reli-
able source of information for national and international
news, and especially in making up their minds how they are
going to vote." About "40 to 50 million Americans watch the
nightly news shows produced by the three major networks,
CBS, NBC, and ABC."[9] It is no wonder then that television
broadcasting has become a subject of hot debate. Coverage of
Vietnam throughout the 1960s was a source of great concern
for Lyndon Johnson and the brutality, gore, and terror of war
which television brought home to the American people encouraged the protest prompting him not to run in 1968. This
is why Richard Nixon confronted the media soon after entering the White House via his Vice-President, Spiro Agnew.
The President, who had never looked favorably upon the
press, was concerned that his conduct of the Vietnam war
would be closely scrutinized by television journalists, creating
difficulties for him. His fear of the antiwar movement as a
threat to his political fortunes was the basis for the White
House campaign to discredit Daniel Ellsberg which, in turn,
gave rise to the "plumbers." Even after the Vietnam settlement, the Administration's concern about news coverage of its
performance, domestic and foreign, did not decline.

A new phase of the struggle began soon after Richard
Nixon entered his second term. Clay T. Whitehead of the

White House Office of Telecommunications Policy charged
that TV and radio affiliates should strive to be "objective,"
lest they jeopardize their operating licenses. In spite of
Nixon's fantastic victory in November, the Administration
continued to exert pressure on the media to discredit, in particular, efforts linking the White House to Watergate and
other illegal activities launched from the Oval Office. The assault was two-pronged: exacerbate the credibility gap separating the media from middle America on the one hand, and intimidate the media on the other by directly threatening the
legal basis for its operations—for example, challenging the
licenses of stations owned by the Washington *Post* Corporation in Florida. The goal was to neutralize a free press and
emasculate those enemies in the media who would evaluate
the Nixon Administration's performance fairly and objectively.

With Nixon's resignation, the media's performance and
middle America's hostility toward it in the 1960s have been
prematurely dismissed by political pundits. Yet to gain a
proper understanding of the credibility gap which estranged
traditional Democratic voters from the McGovernites, the
media's performance during the 1960s deserves to be closely
scrutinized.

The New York *Times,* Washington *Post,* and major television networks customarily report the news objectively and do
not hew to a partisan line; yet the people who gather and
report national news are members of the cosmopolitan subculture. They determine what is and what is not news, what
stories should be covered, and what personalities are newswor-
thy. They perceive all these things through the prism of an educational experience, a value system, and a cosmopolitan
worldview which clashes with the culture of middle America.

The news covered by the national media is filtered through
a distinct mindset which, in turn, is influenced by what fellow
cosmopolitans are doing, discussing at cocktail parties, or writing about in academia and the *New Republic,* the *New York
Review of Books,* and other avant-garde journals. Even though
newscasters attempt to be objective, they may inadvertently
project a point of view which is one-dimensional. Few realize
they are an elite; indeed, this is true of most cosmopolitans.

In this connection, there is much talk among the more radical cosmopolitans about the Establishment—namely, Ford and General Motors, Wall Street banks, California agro-conglomerates, and the oil companies—a power elite that rules the United States through their agents in the Republican Party. There is no question that a small minority in the corporate world wields awesome political power and the influence they employ at all levels of government and in many sectors of American life is attributable to a concentration of wealth.

What the cosmopolitans overlook is that they themselves comprise an elite dominating the intellectual community, academia, the arts, and much of the mass media. A near monopoly of vital informational and cultural sectors of life has enabled them to generate an impressive amount of influence. The corporate elite wield power through the control of wealth and the manipulation of resources. The cosmopolitan elite wield power through the manipulation of ideas and of the nation's cultural outlets. A spokesman for the cosmopolitan left possesses status and an aura of intellectual legitimacy which commands the respect of his constituency. He uses power in his world with the same authority that the millionaire does in his. In both cases one is apt to internalize values and adopt behavioral cues within the confines of a relatively closed society which in turn fosters parochialism, elitism, and a dogmatic adherence to moral precepts and a life-style segregating the elite from the "masses."

Throughout the 1960s cosmopolitans in the Democratic Party and their peers among the Establishment left defined issues and posed solutions to our nation's political ills with little sensitivity to the concerns of the average Democratic voter. Their perception of society and the issues to which they gave priority attention conflicted with the images and priorities of Americans of modest means and education. Thus as the cosmopolitans were gearing up to capture the Democratic nomination for the Presidency, the credibility gap separating them from traditional Democratic voters was expanding. The reformers' parochialism also contributed to their adopting a strategy which exaggerated the political influence of minority voters, young people, and the liberal middle class. Since we have already treated the educated middle-class reformers, let us focus upon the cosmopolitans' perception of black power and the alleged youth revolt.

C. McGovern's New Majority: *The Blacks, Kids, and Liberal Middle Class*

After John F. Kennedy's assassination, the consciousness of white Americans who had previously ignored racial discrimination was seared by TV's portrayal of the appalling mistreatment of blacks at the hands of the "Bull Conners" who used fire houses, dogs, cattle prods, and night sticks on defenseless, peaceful demonstrators. To some white viewers the Watts, Newark, and Detroit riots prompted hostility, but to more perceptive viewers these tragedies graphically demonstrated the depth of despair and rage throbbing in American black ghettos. The media played a major, positive role in relating the truth to the American people and thus helped develop a climate supportive of the Civil Rights Movement and the plight of poor folks. But, while television developed support for the Civil Rights Movement on the one hand, it inadvertently exacerbated racial misunderstanding on the other. A typical example involved a segment of CBS's 60 *Minutes* (in the late 1960s) which dealt with racial prejudice in the armed forces.

Several black GIs were interviewed to present their case against the Army and their fellow white soldiers. The interviewees spoke about blacks receiving harsher punishments than whites for identical offenses, overt antiblack behavior on the part of noncoms, and the failure of officers to promote qualified black soldiers merely because of their race. The men interviewed were intelligent, articulate, and they discussed their problems in a reasonable and convincing fashion.

The GIs selected to "present the white soldier's point of view" were inarticulate country boys whose racial biases were poorly disguised. Juxtaposing their argument against those of the blacks, the viewer was led to believe that racial strife in the Army victimizes blacks alone. Yet this was and is not an accurate conclusion, for one can find white GIs, articulate and free of racial bias, who can cite numerous examples of attacks upon white soldiers by blacks, assaults which are motivated solely by race. This is not a new phenomenon but it was not until the 1970s, when the media began to reassess their coverage of the racial question, that this aspect of racial conflict received the attention it deserved. But by that time, the damage already had been done.

If the producers of this segment of 60 *Minutes* had done their homework, they would have found numerous examples (some officers call it a trend) of blacks attacking white soldiers merely because of their race.[10] On the basis of such black assaults and other abusive behavior, many white youngsters entering the armed forces free of racial prejudice are returning home with a profound antipathy toward blacks. The tragedy of the program in question is that many viewers who are aware of this side of the question probably concluded that the "TV people are covering things up," and had conspired to "make the whites look bad." The show in question, it should be stressed, was not an isolated example: it was one of many which could be cited to illuminate the root cause of the credibility gap which separated the national media from many middle Americans in the 1960s.

Throughout the urban East and Midwest, white ethnics who live close to, work with, or share public transportation with blacks experience black racism. This hostility may be manifested in verbal abuse, bullying, or outright physical assaults. Living in overcrowded substandard dwellings in ghettos wracked by social disorganization and poverty, the urban black poor have developed a street culture marked by violence and crime. Whites who are familiar with this segment of the black community are disinclined to empathize with this behavior, forgetting that several decades before rural blacks trekked north in search of jobs, strangers who wandered into Italian, Irish, or Polish enclaves treaded carefully. To approach one of the neighborhood girls, to stare too long at street corner youths who glared at you, or to play on a baseball diamond that was not "your own" was to court violence. It was not too long ago (it is still true in some cities) that persons who lived in better parts of town steered clear of working-class white ethnic ghettos in the same way that prudent whites keep out of Harlem, Bedford-Stuyvesant, and Roxbury today. Nonetheless, the CBS show was not credible to white viewers in Cleveland, Gary, or Newark who have experienced black racism; it probably encouraged them to question the very basis of the charges the black GIs made, and many no doubt concluded that the scope of anti-black prejudice per se had been exaggerated.

It is improbable that the show's producers purposely concealed facts which depicted black GIs in a less favorable light. In all likelihood this one-sided picture was portrayed because black racism is outside the experience of the people involved or it is deemed of small import when it is contrasted with the suffering of blacks in America. Because of pent-up frustrations and anger, "is it any wonder that some blacks strike out at whites indiscriminately?" Most knowledgeable Americans know that, despite significant progress, the plight of blacks is a national disgrace. Worse yet, the white majority possesses the means to achieve social and economic justice for all Americans. The knowledge that the will to attain these goals does not match our national resources is a source of guilt among whites with a social conscience.

Largely because of this, middle-class white liberals are inclined to view black/white incidents in terms of defenseless blacks being victimized by white aggressors, and this explains why black hostility has been neglected by cosmopolitans in the mass media, academia, and government. Consequently when blacks and whites clash in disputes over housing, schools, or jobs, the cosmopolitan community usually gives the blacks the benefit of the doubt, and often as not dismisses the possibility that whites may be on the receiving end of black hostility. The history of black/white discord in the United States after all is one characterized by KKK thugs, pot-bellied sheriffs, and drunken vigilantes brutalizing blacks. On those rare occasions when it becomes public knowledge that whites are experiencing similar treatment at the hands of blacks, it is usually dismissed as a natural reaction to centuries of white racism. As a consequence, it has been the rule that issues which are in any way related to racial discord are often misread by cosmopolitan commentators. The propensity of white liberals in 1968 and 1972 to view concern about street crime and demands for law and order as code words calculated to mask white racism is an example of this kind of thinking.

The cosmopolitans' one-dimensional racial perspective (which will be assessed in greater detail in Chapter VI) was a costly error politically, as were the McGovernites' naïve notions about "black power." During the 1960s and early 1970s the political gains of the black community were impressive. Blacks were elected as mayors in Cleveland, Newark, and Gary, and throughout the deep South blacks were elected to public office in ever-growing numbers. Because blacks were located in critical urban areas in important states, they had the potential to wield significant political power, but it was not likely that this latent power would become manifest in 1972. On the eve of the 1972 election, blacks were less inclined to be registered than whites and were less likely to vote even if they were registered. In recent elections, the turnout rate of Northern blacks in particular has plunged (fewer blacks voted in 1972 than had four years earlier). Poverty, educational deprivation, and discrimination all have contributed to this condition.

McGovern's strategists, confronted with the fact that blacks only comprised 11.2 per cent of the population, had little difficulty with this observation; blacks represented only one source of support. The educated middle class and the most significant new force in American politics—the young—also were deemed vital to McGovern's successful bid for the White House. Independently they were politically impotent, but together the blacks, kids, and liberal middle class comprised a new majority.

The youth cult which preoccupied the cosmopolitans until the myth was burst in November 1972 was a vivid example of how parochialism addled the critical faculties of many intelligent people. Youth was a persistent topic of concern throughout the 1960s. The term generation gap became a commonplace in the lexicon of the American language. The cliché that "you can't trust anyone over thirty" found a secure place in our social analysis. Academics who coveted the praise of their students were mesmerized by their idiosyncracies, and academic tomes and research papers were published detailing the scope and import of youth alienation and radical protest. Humanists who were dissatisfied with the performance of their

generation looked hopefully to the formation of a counterculture. In 1970 as the youth cult was reaching a crescendo,
Charles Reich's *The Greening of America* was published. It
became an instant best seller and for a time it was required
reading for cosmopolitan America. Reich asserted that American youth had obtained a "new consciousness" and as this revolutionary consciousness spread across the land, it would ultimately lead to a peaceful revolution sans politics or violence.
George McGovern read the book and said he liked it; Fred
Dutton treated Reich's work as that of a serious social critic.

Reich called the new state of mind infecting young people
"Consciousness III." It was diametrically opposed to Consciousness II, the mind set of the older generation which celebrated materialism, achievement, and puritanism, the things
Reich proclaimed were responsible for the "sickness of American society." He was not too precise in defining Consciousness
III, but it was powerful stuff. "Consciousness III is capable of
changing and of destroying the Corporate State, without violence, without seizure of political power, without overthrow of
any existing group of people." Reich asserted that the young,
armed with Consciousness III, would bring the old order
crashing down without political parties, platforms, or revolutionary cadres.

> . . . the way to destroy the power of the Corporate
> State is to live differently now. The plan, the program,
> the grand strategy, is this: resist the State when you
> must; avoid it when you can; but listen to music, dance,
> seek out nature, laugh, be happy, be beautiful, help
> others whenever you can, work for them as best you can,
> take them in, the old and the bitter as well as the young,
> live fully in each moment, love and cherish each other,
> love and cherish yourselves, stay together . . .

Critics who employed rational criteria to attack Reich's
musings were cut short by the master's disciples for using Consciousness II values and logic. Reich anticipated such attacks
in his book:

> To the realists, the liberals, and radicals and activists
> who are looking for a program and a plan, we say: this is

the program and the plan. When enough people have decided to live differently, the political results will follow naturally and easily, and the old political forms will simply be swept away like immovable logs when the river rises.[11]

Many cosmopolitans took Reich seriously; he reinforced others, at the very least, in their belief that American youth were prepared to reject the status quo and would lock arms with their progressive elders, the poor, and the black in a new coalition for change. Reich, perhaps, went too far, but was there any doubt that the younger generation, through its efforts in the peace and civil rights movements, had demonstrated its moral commitment and impressive political and organizational skills?

On the strength of Eugene McCarthy's showing in New Hampshire and President Johnson's decision not to seek another term, reformers began to proclaim the death of the old politics of Lyndon Johnson, Hubert Humphrey, and Richard Daley. But the assassination of Robert Kennedy demoralized the insurgents and robbed them of an attractive candidate who could have reassembled the Democratic coalition of old. At the ill-fated Chicago convention, the insurgents found the regulars and political pros in the labor movement well entrenched. Mayor Daley's tight-fisted control of the convention proved that the regulars would never relinquish power —"it has to be taken from their hands."

In an article for the New York *Times* following the election, Eugene McCarthy wrote that the growing presence of young people in the political system enhanced the prospects for a third party movement in 1972 should the regulars ignore them. With the passage of the 26th Amendment, a horde of new young voters would enter the political arena and everyone knew whose side they would be on. The media, academia, and the literary community as well as the reformers in the Democratic Party developed an unshakable belief that the youth vote in 1972 would insure the nomination and election of one of their own. Arguments which challenged this notion were cavalierly dismissed since they were so patently "absurd."

Several months prior to the 1970 off-year election Richard

Scammon and Ben Wattenberg's *The Real Majority* was published. The authors took issue with the thesis that the poor, the black, and the young would provide the votes needed to elect a New Politics candidate. Their analysis of the projected import of the youth vote was especially prescient although it was roundly rejected by the reformers. Exponents of the under-thirty strategy, argued Scammon and Wattenberg, exaggerated the size of the youth vote and the effect it would have overall on the electorate; radical college youth would be entering the political system but so would those who were inclined toward Wallace or Nixon; with the exception of 1964, the college-educated electorate always went for the Republican Presidential candidate; and young people, like their elders, would become less militant and radical as they grew older—to assume that the student activists would not mellow as they matured was to ignore a pedestrian but nonetheless cogent truism of human nature.[12]

Exponents of the youth strategy brushed aside Scammon and Wattenberg's treatment of the youth vote. After all, Scammon was close to Hubert Humphrey and Wattenberg was a White House aide during the Johnson Administration. Their book was merely an apology for the old guard regulars who were not about to make room for young people.

These views were expressed in private and in numerous magazine articles, but the brunt of the counterattack against *The Real Majority* appeared in the form of Fred Dutton's *Changing Sources of Power*. Dutton devoted the bulk of his book to the "emergent youth vote." There was no question where he stood: "In 1964 just over 10.5 million young people became eligible to vote in their first Presidential election." By "1968 the number of first-timers abruptly jumped to just over 12 million. It will increase to over 25 million in 1972 . . ." At that time "over 10 million eighteen and twenty year olds" would be eligible to vote for the first time, "plus a natural growth of roughly 2 million in those turning twenty-one since 1968." Dutton claimed that the importance of this massive wave of new voters would be heightened by an incontrovertible fact of nature—that is, approximately 5 million older voters would die. "Together, the arrivals and departures between 1968 and 1980 will result in a change of roughly one out of every three people in the eligible electorate."[13] It was with numbers like these in mind that the reformers in the Democratic Party could anticipate a progressive future for America. Dutton was also impressed with data revealing that, while the level of political participation among the electorate at large was low, college activists were demonstrating a novel propensity for political activity. Without the support of the young, the Democrats were doomed.

There were few cosmopolitans in the Democratic Party who questioned Dutton's thesis, for it was a firm part of the reformers' worldview. It did not dawn upon many cosmopolitans that they were talking about "their kids" and not the children of bus drivers, auto workers, stock clerks, and secretaries. Newspaper and magazine readers as well as TV viewers were led to believe that the average American youngster attended college, was into radical politics, or was an exponent of the counterculture. Young people who looked, spoke, or acted like they were members of this youthful avant-garde were sought out by representatives of the Fourth Estate.

Youthful "radicals" and black militants became very adept at hustling the media and manipulating it to project themselves and their idea. Thus Rap Brown, Jerry Rubin, and Mario Savio among others were able to gain national recognition without establishing a real grass-roots base of their own. Campus unrest which involved riots, the occupation of academic buildings, massive head-breaking brawls with police, raids on ROTC offices, the bombing of campus research installations, flag and draft card burnings, "smoke-ins," and "curse-outs" convinced many Americans that most college students were unpatriotic, violence-prone, foul-mouthed, dope-smoking anarchists bent upon destroying our nation's institutions and not just the universities which harbored them. This was far from the truth but chaos on the college campuses, peace demonstrations which were taken over by the crazies, the trauma of several hot summers in the nation's ghettos and the appearance of gun-toting Black Panthers who threatened to "off" honkie pigs caused TV viewers to exaggerate the potential threat this relatively small number of "radicals" represented.

The cosmopolitans' preoccupation with youth and their

belief that the average American youngster was just like "their kids" was a manifestation of their myopia and represented the failure of the liberal intellectual community to maintain its objectivity. The political behavior of noncollege youth and the problems of the young clerk typist and truck driver were ignored by people who prided themselves on their sensitive political antennae and their concern about the less advantaged in society.

There was another side to the youth picture—namely, those youngsters who did not attend college did not view the world through the same counterculture lens that students at Berkeley or Cambridge did. A growing number of working-class youngsters smoked pot, wore long hair, and favored mod clothes, but in most cases they were as straight as their parents on other matters and those who were politically discontented were probably more inclined to vote for a George Wallace or Richard Nixon than a George McGovern. In the wake of the 1968 election, the Survey Research Center of the University of Michigan conducted a study revealing that the Wallace movement in the North was largely a youth movement and that Wallace was not merely the candidate of crotchety old bigots. On the contrary, members of the older generation who liked him but who had traditionally cast their vote for Democrats could not quite bring themselves to vote for Wallace when they entered the polling booth. Their decades-old allegiance to the Democratic Party proved a stronger force than their new romance with the Alabama "populist."[14]

The SRC researchers concluded that the New Left's "confrontational politics" estranged voters from that movement, noting a heightened level of political awareness among noncollege youth inclined toward the right. By renouncing "politics of persuasion," student radicals apparently helped politicize a heretofore apathetic sector of our society. For while the Wallace voters rejected the New Left's programs, many embraced participatory politics in the sense that they no longer limited their political behavior to the voting act alone. Indeed, it could be argued that the Wallace campaign was a prototype of the New Politics: without a national political organization to speak of and nourished largely by small donations, he made his presence felt in 1968. Wallace's appeal to

young voters refuted the popular notion that a rising proportion of young people in our body politic portended a more
progressive political future for the nation.

On the basis of such evidence, how can we explain the cosmopolitans' simplistic view of the youth vote? Hubris, the
conceit which blinds any elite—it cannot be denied that this,
in part, accounts for the appalling ignorance the cosmopolitans displayed in their discussion of "America's youth."
Turned on by the counterculture, academia and other mainstream institutions paid little attention to the life-style of the
young factory worker, the problems of his wife, the fate of his
neighborhood. One searched in vain for government programs
that dealt with the young worker. During the hiatus of our national preoccupation with the young in the late 1960s, a
"youth agency" in HEW, for example, had programs for
blacks, Chicanos, and college students, but white youngsters
who were in the labor force were not included. The same
thing held true by and large for the Office of Economic Opportunity (Appalachian whites were the exception), the Office
of Education, the National Institute of Mental Health, and
foundations and other private agencies serving young people.

The mass media's treatment of young workers likewise
reflected the tunnel vision of cosmopolitan America. Coverage
was intermittent at best, usually superficial, and generally
manifested a parochial (class) bias. The truck driver, supermarket clerk, and steelworker's wife were rarely the subject
matter of TV documentaries, much less of TV drama. Sympathetic treatment of the frustrations young workers suffered
were not forthcoming from Hollywood. There was, of course,
Joe, which deserves to be mentioned only because the stereo-
typed Joe Curran represented what, in the minds of many
otherwise thoughtful people on the left, the American workingman would be like if his "natural instincts" ever rose to the
surface of his consciousness. The locale shifted in *Easy Rider*,
but it was the shotgun-toting "crackers" in the pickup truck
who murdered the youthful dope-dealing motorcyclists for no
other reason apparently than that they did not like "freaks."
On those rare occasions when working-class youths received
attention (usually a by-product of investigation into the
problems of affluent youngsters), they were depicted as racist,

superhawk, cultural Neanderthals. Yet the young men and women who were portrayed in such one-dimensional terms were grappling with the same kinds of identity problems— "Who am I?" "How should I spend my life?" "Is my work meaningful?"—which produced alienation among campus youth.

Against this backdrop of neglect and distortion, many working Americans found it difficult to sympathize with the dissident behavior of young radicals. It was especially maddening that the student demonstrators and articulate black activists who constantly broke the rules seemed to receive sympathetic support from the mass media, government, and the educational system. It was galling to the young high school dropout that if he violated the laws the college students broke, he would be arrested without much fanfare or discussion about the grievances that led to his antisocial behavior.

The alienation of black youngsters was mollified in part by the black community's invigorated sense of group identity. In the face of poverty and racial prejudice, this did not offer much consolation; yet the Negro who shared the workbench with a white youth at least felt "plugged into" the movement for social change. Like black people of all ages, he derived emotional support from the activities of leaders like Malcolm X and Martin Luther King. But the white youth next to him had no role model to help him reduce his frustration and no one seemed to be concerned about his despair.

The cosmopolitans' one-sided view of the racial crisis, "youth alienation," and the clash of deep-seated cultural values all contributed to the widening gap which separated reformers and traditional white ethnic Democrats; but the war in Vietnam opened that fissure even further. It had become commonplace among leftists that the Catholic ethnics were among the most vociferous cold warriors in the nation and the mass base for our ill-advised military ventures abroad. They were part of the problem and they were to be treated as pawns of the defense establishment and not potential allies. This conviction circumvented the peace movement's efforts to muster popular support against the war and it contributed to the election of Richard Nixon in 1968 and 1972. But as we shall see in the brief survey of the white ethnics and foreign policy which follows, they have been no more hawkish than the nation at large.

D. The White Ethnics and Foreign Policy: *The Ethnic "Hard Hat" Was Perceived as an Unregenerate Hawk by the Peace Movement*

Prior to Pearl Harbor, German Nazis and Italian fascists sought to recruit Americans of German and Italian descent to the cause. In a few German-American organizations, notably Fritz Kuhn's German-American Bund, members greeted one another with a Zieg Heil, but this tiny minority had no discernible impact on their neighbors—although FDR would lose German votes as a result of his declared support for the Allies and isolationists found a large number of German-Americans receptive to their antiwar campaign. In the Italian-American community the fascists were well financed and had access to the Italian language media. Although only a minority were practicing fascists, Mussolini's well-publicized feats were a source of pride to many Italian-Americans. They noted with approval that even prominent Americans praised Mussolini's government. FDR, therefore, lost many Italian-American votes after he characterized Italy's invasion of France as a "stab in the back." But once the war started, every ethnic group in the United States sent its men off to fight.

In the aftermath of this war, the Catholic white ethnics were spared the onslaughts of "patriots" who exploited Soviet-American discord to launch a red scare in the United States. The Catholic community gained an anticommunist reputation which was bolstered by the Vatican's well-publicized enmity for the Soviets. The rise of fascism had not sidetracked the Vatican's holy war against communism. In 1937 Pope Pius XI had issued a Papal Encyclical which declared, "Communism is intrinsically wrong, and no one who would save Christian civilization may collaborate with it in any undertaking whatsoever." Although many opponents of communism developed amnesia after Pearl Harbor, and we embraced the Russians as our allies, that affliction was not detected among the church's hierarchy. Indeed, the Catholic church's hostility toward the Soviet Union did not even melt before the heart-rending propaganda movies the Pentagon inspired, depicting Stalin as our "Uncle Joe" and the Soviets as agrarian reformers cousin to the rural progressives one might find in Wisconsin or Minnesota. The Paulist publication *Catholic World* editorialized in May 1942, "The Soviet brand of Communism is atheist, materialist, anti-God, anti-Christ, and I think anti-human . . . To me the Russian leaders seem more cruel than the Czars and the Russian people in worse plight than they were under the old regime."[15]

The Catholic church continued its struggle with communism after the war with a vengeance. Behind the Iron Curtain Catholic clergymen and nuns were imprisoned by the Soviets, church property was confiscated, and the faithful were prohibited from practicing their religion. American prelates warned their parishioners that communism was not merely a European problem. The good nuns conjured up "Soviet agents" far more frightening to Catholic grade schoolers because, in contrast to the Satanic forces serving as heavies in their Catechisms, the reds were real people occupying bodies in this world. Catholic students who attended public schools in some areas of the country were warned by the nuns to beware lest they be brainwashed by their teachers; unfortunately, in many cases, this warning masked Catholic fears about "Jewish communists" poisoning adolescent Catholic minds. The conviction and execution of the Rosenbergs lent credence to such charges, causing some Catholic parents to remove their children from public schools.

Francis Cardinal Spellman proclaimed in 1946 that the communists were "digging deep inroads into our nation," and three years later, from the pulpit of St. Patrick's, the Cardinal declared that the country was in imminent danger of "Communist conquest and annexation." The Catholic archdiocese in New York City circulated a comic strip, "Is This Tomorrow?" depicting a communist mob setting St. Patrick's aflame while the Cardinal, nailed to the Cathedral's door, watched helplessly.[16] Conservatives in the church, behind the protective shield of the great crusade, sought to even old scores too. Philip Murray, the devout Catholic who presided over the CIO, complained bitterly to clergymen friends that reactionaries in the church were circulating material charging the

CIO for being soft on the communist "rape of Eastern Europe."

East European Catholics were deeply disappointed that Washington had failed to prevent the Russians from subjugating their former homelands. The white ethnic community received firsthand reports of Soviet imperialism from Displaced Persons who had fled the Red Army. Beginning in the late 1940s, the DPs formed organizations like the Polish American Congress for the sole purpose of freeing the "captive nations" from the grip of the Red Bear. Some unrepentant Stalinists sought to discredit the DPs, pointing out that many of them had been fascists and Quislings who had fled their homelands only because the Nazi cause was hopeless. These charges were not always groundless, but the Soviets' subjugation of the satellite countries and Stalin's persecution of minority ethnic groups within the Soviet Union itself was a brutal fact. The concern of Lithuanian-, Polish-, and Ukrainian-Americans about the plight of their loved ones behind the Iron Curtain was genuine. In the 1946 elections the Republicans charged that the Democrats had sold the Poles out at Yalta and they made an effort to wrench Polish votes from their opponents. The campaign was modestly successful and the Democrats quickly responded in subsequent elections by raising the decibel count of their anticommunist rhetoric.

Under the tutelage of men like George Meany, the labor movement was another source of Cold War fervor in Catholic white ethnic communities. Meany boasted during the 1950s, when his enmity for Richard Nixon first began to fester, that Nixon was probably the only national figure who was more bitterly opposed to communism than he was. On this matter he saw eye to eye with a man whom he perceived as one of organized labor's most persistent enemies. Until the summer of 1974 Meany's foreign policy adviser was Jay Lovestone, born Jacob Liebstein in Lithuania in 1898. Lovestone was a dominant figure in the communist part in the late 1920s before he was ousted in the wake of a dispute which pitted him against Stalin's American supporters. Lovestone's politics underwent a dramatic transformation during the 1930s and by the end of

World War II he was one of the leading anticommunist theoreticians in the labor movement. Like other former communists, once having "switched sides" he "brought to the anticommunist struggle some of the Manicheanism and paranoia of Stalinism, a taste for ideological orthodoxy inherited from the Party, along with the outrage of the betrayed, and the zeal of the convert."[17]

Under the direction of Meany and Lovestone, the AFL waged a bitter struggle against communist trade unionists in Europe. Yet many students of the labor movement who credited the AFL for contributing to the stabilization of postwar Europe were less sanguine about its intervention in labor affairs in the developing world. Perhaps the most well-publicized case in point involved Guatemala where AFL-funded agents helped overthrow an allegedly "communist-leaning" regime in that country in 1954—the upshot of which was that the very trade unions the Americans sided with against the "reds" were later crushed by the right-wing junta.

During the 1972 Democratic primaries, George Meany made it clear that his thoughts on foreign policy were at variance with those of George McGovern. As early as 1954 Meany had favored American support for the French in Vietnam and later gave his blessings to Presidents Johnson and Nixon's hard-line policies in Southeast Asia. At the Democratic convention in Miami that June, AFL-CIO Cope workers circulated a White Paper revealing that the South Dakota senator had an antilabor record—voting against the repeal of section 14b of Taft-Hartley, the so-called "right to work" provision on the law—was a timid supporter of civil rights, and was hardly the progressive his supporters claimed he was. But the specific matter which turned Meany against McGovern was his opposition to the war in Vietnam, manifesting "his dangerous isolationism." McGovern's dovishness was the single most important factor in Meany's refusal to oppose Richard Nixon.[18] Although the Executive Council of the AFL-CIO endorsed Meany's proclamation that the Federation remain neutral in the Presidential contest, most of the Federation's affiliated unions supported McGovern, joining the UAW which worked mightily for McGovern's victory.

That a majority of organized labor's leadership supported McGovern did not dissuade the cosmopolitan left from their firm conviction that the rank and file worker and the working American at large wholeheartedly supported our involvement in Southeast Asia. During the Korean War, a growing number of progressives had concluded that the working class most vigorously supported American military adventures abroad and in the 1960s there was a consensus among the peace movement that the "hard hat" ethnics were the most pugnacious supporters of our involvement in Vietnam.

From 1940 to 1972 the American voter was denied the opportunity to select a President (Henry Wallace aside) whose perception of foreign policy differed dramatically from the outlook of the two major parties. Barring a tiny segment on the far left and isolationists on the right, the United States "enjoyed" bipartisanship for over thirty years. The emasculation of the left as a viable force in American politics after the Second World War contributed to this condition. Most Americans active in radical politics during the 1930s who had spoken favorably about the great experiment in the Soviet Union later felt Stalin had betrayed them. The Moscow trials, the Hitler-Stalin Pact, the Jewish doctors plot—these and other examples of Stalin's crimes which Khrushchev detailed in 1956 caused many old leftists to recoil from their youthful dreams of the Soviet Union as the harbinger of humanistic socialism. Many Jewish communists and an even larger number of radical Jewish socialists drifted away from left-wing politics because of Soviet anti-Semitism in the late 1940s. And after the formation of Israel and Moscow's pro-Arab posture in the successive Arab-Israeli wars, it became ever more difficult to find Jewish Marxists who spoke favorably about the Soviet Union. For all these reasons many leftists (from all ethnic backgrounds) offered only halfhearted resistance to the prevailing worldview of the foreign policy establishment, while others remained silent lest their careers and reputations be ruined by demagogues like Senators Joe McCarthy of Wisconsin and Richard Nixon of California.

The emasculation of the left during the early Cold War period helped set the stage for our disastrous folly in Vietnam.

But, contrary to notions popularized by revisionist historians, the Berlin crisis, the Korean War, the suppression of the East Berlin uprising, and the Soviet invasion of Hungary all gave concrete form to American fears about Soviet aggression. And just when a growing number of Kremlinologists began to write hopefully about the mellowing of the Soviet dictatorship, the Russians crushed the Dubcek government in Czechoslovakia. Peace activists during the 1960s correctly rejected arguments that we were aiding and abetting a freely elected government; that the struggle was part of a large communist design to conquer the world; and that our presence in Vietnam contributed to world peace; but they made a factual and political error when they proclaimed that the Cold War itself was merely a Frankenstein monster of the military-industrial complex and argued that the United States was solely responsible for it. Furthermore, as the war continued and casualties mounted, the certainty that they were right about the war in South Vietnam convinced them that the failure of the American people to join them in the streets testified to the moral bankruptcy of the nation and was proof positive that the ordinary working American was prepared to trade a hefty paycheck for the blood of countless Vietnamese and Americans.

George McGovern clearly did not understand the basis for the average voter's perception of foreign affairs and national security matters. To most people, foreign policy is a distant issue; unlike domestic affairs, it is outside their realm of experience. Washington can shape the thinking of the populace on nitty gritty economic issues but the working American knows when his paycheck and savings are being devastated by inflation; unemployment is an existential fact which soothing rhetoric and inflated promises cannot alter. The average citizen's understanding of foreign affairs, however, is largely shaped by the consensus among the "best and the brightest" who make and discuss foreign policy.

The liberal cold warriors John F. Kennedy invited to Washington perceived the world in bipolar terms—"communist" and "free." The Bundys, Rostows, and Rusks evaluated revolution and revolt wherever it occurred as communist-inspired. Tito's split with Stalin, Mao's clash with Khrushchev, the inevitability of political upheavals and civil wars in the less-developed countries—some of which were designed by communists and most of which were not—did not persuade the hardliners that there was no monolithic communist movement with the power to conquer the world. The Rusks and Rostows ignored arguments which challenged their cold war assumptions: that the communist world was divided; that nationalism was as potent a source of division in the communist world as it was in the free world; that the communists had limited resources; that the West had the power to devastate the Soviet Union and the People's Republic of China; and that the leaders in Moscow and Peking knew it. The national security managers Lyndon Johnson inherited from Kennedy remained adamant; even if the major communist powers were not about to confront the West in a major war, it was apparent that they were plotting, through wars of national liberation, to chip away at the free world piece by piece and eventually surround the United States and Europe with hostile communist forces. Johnson's advisers also erred in thinking that the United States possessed the means to check "communist revolts" even when the insurgents possessed greater support for their cause than the corrupt right-wing governments opposing them. Moreover, many ordinary Americans as well as cold warriors in government supported the war in Vietnam out of misplaced idealism, confident that the United States had the means to transform the world into the image of America and that it was our destiny to do so. Fidel Castro made a speech to this effect in the spring of 1972, but surprisingly it received little attention. Nonetheless the Cuban Marxist-Leninist's observation was one that the peace movement should have heeded.

By 1968 many educated Americans and prominent liberals like Arthur Schlesinger, Jr., who earlier were among the most articulate cold warriors, became vocal opponents of the war. Unlike the ordinary citizen, they were quick to perceive a change in attitude among their friends and the cosmopolitan press in the 1960s; furthermore, they were privy to information and had the background enabling them to fathom that the Johnson Administration was deluding itself and the American people as to the developments in Southeast Asia. This change of heart on the part of the educated middle class sup-

ported the notion that the "lower classes" and Catholic hard
hats were hawks while the "upper classes" were doves.

Richard Hamilton, in a comprehensive study of mass attitudes toward McCarthy and the Cold War, proffers a number
of observations which dispel the simple-minded view that the
"lower classes" since the end of the Second World War have
been consistently more hawkish than the "upper classes." He
notes also that although the Catholic community was visibly
preoccupied with communism during the Cold War, the people who allegedly worshipped Joe McCarthy on the Polish
South Side of Milwaukee were less inclined to vote for him
than Wasps who lived in more fashionable parts of town. During the first phase of McCarthy's crusade, largely confined to
an attack on Democrats, many prominent newspapers and
Americans who later became his critics supported the senator,
observing that "where there's smoke, there must be fire." They
turned against him after he lashed out at figures in the
Eisenhower Administration and the U. S. Army. By that time,
he had already served a "good purpose," having cowed many
troublesome "left-wing radicals and soft-headed liberals."
"This belated response on the part of some 'distinguished'
figures contributed to the notion of the . . . upper classes as
the protectors of civil liberties" and the working-class ethnics
as McCarthy's most steadfast supporters.[19] During the "build-
up" stage, McCarthy received the support of prominent politicians and publishers, causing ordinary Americans to follow
their lead. But the man on the street who had been told that
there was a "red threat" abroad in the country was slow to perceive the establishment's reversal; thus, during the "put-
down" stage, the senator's lower-class supporters—who had
first endorsed his witch hunt in part because their "betters"
gave the Wisconsin senator a bill of approval—became his
most visible source of support.

Yet in the only instance where working-class ethnic support
for McCarthy was measured against his appeal to affluent
voters, the evidence is definitive—the former rejected him. In
his bid for a second term for the Senate in 1954, every ward in
the city of Milwaukee but one voted for McCarthy's opponent; the ward that favored McCarthy was located on the
affluent non-ethnic North Side. Outside the city the more

fashionable suburbs gave most of their votes to McCarthy too. In the predominantly working-class ethnic South Side the vote was more than two to one against him.

> The lesson would appear to be clear. Working-class populations responded with alarm and concern over the domestic "communist threat" and felt a need for decisive action to oppose it. When, however, it came to a clearcut choice between the leading demagogue advocating the "tough" position and a liberal Democrat, they preferred the latter.[20]

Studies of mass attitudes conducted during the Korean war indicated, moreover, that manual and lower-middle-class respondents were more inclined to favor a negotiated settlement than upper-middle-class Americans. According to Hamilton the evidence ". . . does not support the image of jingoistic and warlike masses. It indicates just the opposite, that the tough, hard line is a proclivity of established, educated upper-middle-class white Protestants."[21]

Polls conducted throughout the protracted Vietnam war also refute the notion that manual workers and the ethnics in particular were more favorably inclined toward a hawkish policy than the population at large. A national poll taken in 1964 revealed that 53 per cent of college graduates favored our sending more troops to Vietnam even if we did so at the risk of war with China, and this compared with one third of those respondents who had a grade school education; moreover, three fourths of the college graduates opposed total troop withdrawal, while only 38 per cent of the less educated respondents were so inclined. A Gallup Poll in 1966 found that 44 per cent of the blue-collar workers surveyed approved of the way that President Johnson was handling the war while 39 per cent did not. The corresponding national response showed 43 per cent of the nation approving and 40 per cent disapproving. Significantly, in 1972 the Gallup organization found that, whereas 47 per cent of the blue-collar workers approved of President Nixon's handling of the war, 44 per cent disapproved. The public as a whole was more hawkish, 50 per cent approving and 39 per cent disapproving. The blue-collar worker has exhibited a "liberal stance" in reference to other war-related issues too; for example, in August 1972, 60 per cent of the blue-collar respondents asked favored conditional amnesty;[22] in November 1973, 42 per cent said we were spending too much on defense, 31 per cent just right, and 15 per cent too little; in December 1973 workers were almost unanimous in their opinion that the President should need the permission of Congress to send troops to war—83 per cent said yes, and only 13 per cent said no.

Turning to ethnic differences pertaining to the war, a 1971 survey revealed that 40 per cent of the Wasps asked favored withdrawal from Vietnam, 36 per cent victory; the results for Irish Catholics were 64 to 32 per cent, Italians 53 to 32 per cent, and Poles 41 to 30 per cent.[23] Notwithstanding such findings, the ethnic "hard hat" was perceived as an unregenerate hawk by the men and women who belonged to the predominantly white middle-class peace movement. The truth is the white ethnics were no more hawkish than the rest of the country, and some polls reveal that they were less inclined to take a hard line on this score than their fellow Americans.

The white ethnics' traditional patriotism has its origins in a legacy of poverty and oppression associated with the Old World, in a sensitivity to shrill nativist slurs suggesting that the immigrants were second-class citizens, and in gratitude for the economic opportunity, political freedom, and social advancement America offered newcomers. As early as the First World War the ethnics went off to war to demonstrate that they were loyal patriots, and during the 1960s, when avoiding the draft was condoned in middle-class youth circles, working-class ethnics were repelled by the thought. Their parents, peers, and leaders had told them that they owed a debt of gratitude to their country; thus many youngsters whose grandparents once called Poland or Italy their home, although opposed to the war, "did their duty" and fought in the jungles of Southeast Asia. Also, while Cardinal Spellman gave his blessings, journalists who bothered to talk to Poles in Hamtramck or Italians in Newark noted that, rather than blindly supporting U.S. military adventures abroad, they questioned the advisability of sending our young men off to die for a corrupt dictatorship in Asia. Television had brought home the horrors of war to working Americans, causing them to question pronouncements from the White House regarding our reasons for being in Vietnam and the progress we were making there. Still, they were not sure about what the alternatives were; and in spite of growing disbelief in LBJ's statements, they often reluctantly concluded that "the President has all the facts—he knows best. What else can the ordinary citizen do but place his faith in the nation's leadership?" And, like most Americans, they reasoned that "as long as the boys are fighting in Vietnam, we have to support them even if the generals and the White House no longer level with us."

Although a growing number of people were troubled by the Vietnam war, the manner in which elements of the peace movement protested the war was equally distressing to them. In late 1967 a national sample, by the margin of 68 to 22 per cent, indicated disapproval of LBJ's conduct of the Vietnam war, but the respondents also said they thought the antiwar demonstrations were "acts of disloyalty against the boys fighting in Vietnam." By 64 to 21 per cent they agreed that "most antiwar demonstrators are not serious, thoughtful critics of the war but are peaceniks and hippies having a ball."[24] Richard Nixon later exploited such concerns to extract support for his Vietnam policy and to muster opposition to George McGovern whom Nixon's operatives portrayed as indifferent to the plight of "our fighting men."

McGovern's statements that the war was an "immoral one" and a "frightful waste of men and money" was not bound to win him votes in those working-class communities where the young men went to Vietnam and not college or Canada. It was not easy for parents and wives whose sons and husbands had been killed to admit that their loved ones had died for nothing or that they had participated in an immoral war. Many people otherwise opposed to our intervention in Vietnam supported the effort because it was their menfolk who had been drafted into the armed forces.

During the Korean war it was revealed that "if a white man had no college and was the son of a blue collar worker, he had an 87 per cent chance of serving. Since so many fit that description, the 'common soldier' was typically white, a high

school graduate, the son of a blue collar family, and a
Northern city dweller."25 In Vietnam a disproportionate number of blacks would do the fighting, but among the white
combatants the people involved were much like the ones who
fought in Korea. On one of the few occasions when the columnist Joe Alsop wrote anything relevant about the Vietnam war,
he noted that during the entire war only one student each
from Harvard, Yale, and Princeton was killed. In the minds of
many Americans the appearance of young men protesting the
war on the nightly news during the 1960s testified to one
thing—it was the kids from working-class communities whose
lives were in danger and not the "privileged peaceniks."

For almost a decade middle America, via television, watched
outraged as young men burned their draft cards, set matches
to the flag, screamed obscenities at the police, taunted federal
troops, surrounded the Pentagon, trashed main thoroughfares
of numerous cities, and resorted to arson and bombings on
college campuses to punctuate their abhorrence of the war.
Such actions and allegations on the part of some intellectuals
and Hollywood personalities that the United States was engaging in war crimes and that "we deserve to lose the war" were
tantamount to treason in the eyes of the working American.
To those who clung to the certainties of the old culture, the
nation's institutions and the values they cherished were under
attack. As a malaise of fear and frustration shrouded the
country, a diffuse enemy became specific in the form of black
militants, college radicals, and privileged cosmopolitan liberals
who, by excusing the excesses of the "revolutionaries," endorsed their subversive thinking and treasonous actions.

E. The White Ethnic's Perception of McGovern: *The McGovern Reform Guidelines Created Quotas for Women, Youth, and Blacks, But None for Poor People, or Senior Citizens, or Ethnic Minorities,* Jack Newfeld

After McGovern's nomination white ethnic politicians bitterly complained that the McGovernites ignored them. Since
most of McGovern's campaign workers in the North were the
same local reformers who had been at odds with the party reg-

ulars, the latter's objectivity was legitimately suspect. On the other hand, student activists and white ethnic politicians who supported McGovern were concerned that the senator's workers were turning ordinary voters off too. Blanche Twadorski, a second-generation Polish-American college student from Reading, Pennsylvania, who worked for McGovern in the primaries, complained upon returning to school in the fall that "too many of the people I've met in the campaign are elitists; they won't listen to anybody who tells them that the issues they talk about don't mean much to people who live in working-class neighborhoods like the one I come from."[26] Steve Adubato, the maverick chairman of the North Ward Democratic Party in Newark, expressed his concern about the quota system to New Jersey McGovernites. Adubato, who had the courage to take on Harry Lerner, the aging boss of the Essex County Democratic Party, that summer was elected on an "uncommitted slate" in the Presidential primary. Several weeks prior to the Miami convention he announced his support for McGovern, but he was a vocal critic of the way the quota system was being implemented. "Making room for more young people, women, and blacks is long overdue, but there is no reason why some of the new youth and female delegates are not Polish, Italians, or members of other white ethnic groups." It did not make sense to ignore the white ethnics in a state where they voted in large numbers and where they were demanding a greater voice in community and political affairs. During the convention an incident occurred which enraged many Italian-American delegates. When they approached their fellow delegates with the idea of placing Congressman Peter Rodino on the ticket as Vice-President, they were greeted with derisive laughter or were rudely ignored.

What few McGovern strategists realized was that the protest emanating from white ethnic communities was being articulated not only by older party regulars, but by a small but growing number of young leaders like Steve Adubato of Newark and Councilwoman Barbara Mikulski of Baltimore. These people opposed the war and the old politics but also rejected the conceit of reformers who were long on populist rhetoric but short on concern for the "common man." If the objective

of the reformers was to make the party more reflective of the
Democratic electorate, did it make any sense to ignore social
class or ethnicity in drawing up the quotas? These educated,
younger white ethnic leaders, forceful advocates of the communities they represented, were demanding a greater voice in
the councils of the Democratic Party, but the reformers were
no more receptive to their pleas than the old guard party regulars.

Cosmopolitan elitism took forms other than ethnic slights.
Dan Gaby, who made an unsuccessful Democratic primary
bid for a U. S. Senate seat in New Jersey, was astounded when
he discovered that some reform-minded persons he had
worked with in the past harbored anti-Catholic views. Gaby,
the son of a Jewish junk dealer, was raised in the working-class
Clinton Hill section of Newark. A stalwart in the 1968
McCarthy movement, a civil rights activist, and champion of
other progressive causes, he possessed impeccable "reformist"
credentials. Gaby was shocked when he discovered that liberal
political allies whose support he had counted on were lukewarm toward his candidacy. One of the reasons given for their
attitude was even more startling. At one point in the campaign he had said he favored a constitutional method to
provide support for parochial schools. Friends later told him
that his position earned him the reputation of being "pro-
Catholic."

At the Democratic convention the diffuse complaints one
heard in white ethnic communities became specific for
members of the news media who had previously been inclined
to chalk up grumbling about quotas and elitism to "sour
grapes." Mike Royko, the author of a scathing exposé of Boss
Richard Daley, wrote an open letter to Alderman William
Singer who headed up the anti-Daley slate. Royko wrote in
one of his columns:

> I just don't see where your delegation is representative
> of Chicago's Democrats . . . about half your delegates
> are women . . . a third . . . black. Many . . . young peo-
> ple . . . There's only one Italian name there. Are you
> saying that only one of every 59 Democratic votes cast in
> a Chicago election is cast by an Italian? And only three of

your 59 have Polish names. Does that mean that only 5% of Chicago's voting Democrats are of Polish ancestry? If that were true, a Republican would be mayor of Chicago.[27]

Royko concluded, "Your reforms have disenfranchised Chicago's white ethnic Democrats, which is a strange reform." Jack Newfeld, a columnist for the *Village Voice* and delegate to the convention, later wrote a piece in which he stated that he welcomed the outcome of the convention and its platform, but was disturbed that "the new Democratic Party did not make room for the white ethnic working man. The McGovern reform guidelines created quotas for women, youth, and blacks, but none for poor people, or senior citizens, or ethnic minorities—Irish, Italian, Polish . . ."[28]

The quotas not only excluded the white ethnics, they contributed to greater class exclusiveness too. Haynes Johnson of the Washington *Post* found that the average wealth of the delegates at Miami was more than twice that of the typical American and, whereas only 4 per cent of the American people possess graduate degrees, 39 per cent of the Democratic delegates were privileged to attend a graduate school.

On the basis of this criticism, some of McGovern's supporters urged him to make a special effort to win back the white ethnics, whom the polls showed were disappointed with their party's nominee for the White House. A Yankelovich poll published in early September revealed that Nixon was beating McGovern by 66 per cent to 20 per cent and 46 per cent to 33 per cent among Irish and East European voters respectively. In mid-October a Harris poll indicated that Italian and Jewish voters, when asked if McGovern "inspired confidence as a President should," answered by 61 per cent to 21 per cent and 51 per cent to 31 per cent that he did not.[29]

Under pressure, McGovern selected two young aides, Gerry Cassidy and Ken Schlossberg, to oversee the campaign's quest for the white ethnic vote. Both knew that the senator's senior advisers were locked into a campaign strategy which for all intents and purposes ignored middle America and, although Fred Dutton paid lip service to the "ethnic effort," he really did not believe in it. Not long after they secured office space in McGovern's Washington headquarters, they complained that the people who had clout in the campaign ignored them and their activities. In private they too used the word elitism to explain why McGovern's senior advisers stuck to their "new majority" game plan and to the illusion that the youth vote would prove to be the deciding factor in McGovern's favor.

When R. Sargent Shriver was asked to replace Senator Eagleton, he asked Mike Novak to join his staff as a speech writer. Some of Novak's material, designed to attract the ethnic working-class voter, found its way into McGovern's public statements, but the senator's top advisers never really paid attention to the only people in the campaign who had some insight into the white ethnic vote for which McGovern's "new populism" was designed. To do so was to admit that McGovern's principal advisers had been wrong, that the strategy they had clung to for so long was absurd, and that out of zeal, ignorance, or self-preservation, they had badly misled McGovern and themselves.

As the election drew near, political writers were astounded that there was no sign that McGovern was closing the gap with Nixon as they had expected. In seeking an explanation for his dismal performance, they cited McGovern's inept handling of the Eagleton affair, the Salinger fiasco in Paris, the internal bickering among his campaign staff, and his inability to provide decisive leadership which had led to major revisions in his stated positions on defense spending, welfare reform, and other domestic matters. All of these missteps hurt, but his inability to project himself as the "people's candidate" was the cruelist blow McGovern suffered; this was especially true in the case of the average white ethnic voter.

When McGovern talked about Nixon's mishandling of the economy, the Administration's favorable treatment of the corporations, and socialism for the rich, he was not very convincing—not because these charges were unfounded but rather because he evidently could not get very excited about them. Vietnam was his number one passion. Whatever the substance of a McGovern speech, he invariably returned to the war, to the bombing, to the killing in Southeast Asia. He refused to believe advisers who warned him that most Americans believed Richard Nixon when he said his war policies should be judged on the reality that, when he entered the White House, somewhere around 500,000 Americans were fighting in Vietnam, while only 20,000 remained there in the fall of 1972. Ted Van Dyk, McGovern's lieutenant in charge of issues, agreed with these observations, but at the end of a conversation with this writer, he said, "You're right, but the senator believes that the war is the most important issue in the campaign, that he cannot ignore it . . . there is nothing we can do about it."

McGovern's inability to exploit the concerns of middle America and focus them politically stemmed from an inaccurate assessment of the populist impulse—which historically has been manifested in a heightened level of activity on the part of newly politicized lower-middle-class persons. Nineteenth-century populists appeared when large numbers of people living in rural America suffered from economic dislocations attributable to the growth of industrial capitalism. The populists directed their political protest toward an economic elite of railroad magnates, bankers, and industrial tycoons who were exploiting the small farmer and wreaking havoc with rural society. But running parallel to the populists' economic woes was the fear that urbanization and industrialization were producing social changes which violated their system of values and undermined a way of life they highly cherished. This was the source of the populists' exaggerated fears about the looming presence of Catholic and Jewish immigrants at the turn of the century. McGovern and his braintrusters ignored this cultural component of populism in 1972.

That year Americans of modest means and education, the potential mass base for a new populism, were also reacting to changes they feared would destroy values and life-styles which provided them with a semblance of security and moral purpose. The work ethic, love of country, conventional sexual practices, maintaining the integrity of family life, all were being challenged by social critics, scholars, and middle-class liberals, who, by virtue of their education, professional experiences, and social status, represented a cultural elite.

When McGovern talked about economic concerns, the intrigue of powerful vested interests, and government indifference toward the people, he embraced the substance of a populist campaign. He failed, however, to project a campaign that was populist in style to millions of voters who had lost faith in government and no longer trusted their elected officials. This entailed a keen understanding of the problems, fears, and dreams of the average voter and some empathy for his way of life. George Wallace demonstrated his adeptness at this sort of thing when he resorted to rhetoric and experiences which struck a responsive chord in the heart of the steelworker in Pittsburgh and the autoworker in Detroit. Spiro Agnew also projected a populist image—even though the Nixon Administration had ignored the economic problems of the workingman.

Strategists in the McGovern camp were convinced that George McGovern could do the same, but had his senior aides paid any attention to people who knew what was on the minds of the critical white ethnic voters, they would have been quickly disabused of that mistaken assumption. To many urban Catholics and Jews, his moralizing, rhetoric, and fundamentalist Protestant bearing was unappealing. According to Ralph Perrotta, the director of the New York Center for Ethnic Affairs, "Many white ethnic voters in New York are turned off by McGovern's self-righteousness. It's a cultural thing. The Italians, Poles, Jews, and Irish in New York have a sense of human imperfection, they know that every human being is flawed in some way. To imply that man is otherwise and to talk self-righteously about our nation's problems is bound to create suspicion in their minds."

In the eyes of many white ethnic voters, McGovern was a captive of those middle-class intellectuals who equated law and order with a code word for racism; who were openly hostile toward the white worker and viewed him as a "hard hat" racist pawn of the establishment; and who implied that the American voter's refusal to perceive the bombing in Vietnam in the same terms that Ramsey Clark did reflected the moral bankruptcy of the nation. Like past generations of reformers, McGovern's political ethos was ideological in tone and alien to people who, by virtue of their limited influence, practiced pragmatic politics.

The white ethnic voters' dissatisfaction with McGovern was

not unrelated to the fear that his crusade to gain national political power was bankrolled and masterminded by a cosmopolitan elite which held the ordinary American in contempt.
This writer, in a sidewalk tour of the Italian-American North
Ward (Newark, New Jersey) in early summer, asked local residents what they thought of George McGovern. Their
responses were similar to the comments made by lower-
middle-class Jews and Catholics elsewhere in the metropolitan
North soon after the Democratic convention.

A heavy-set middle-aged housewife answered, "McGovern's
okay . . . it's the people around him who scare me." Her husband, a truck driver who had lost his job when Ballantine
Brewery folded the year before, added, "He's concerned about
the blacks, the minorities . . . but he doesn't say anything
about my problems." An unemployed Vietnam veteran observed, "He yells about the war . . . but the Democrats got us
in there." The owner of a small candy store was applauded by
two of his customers when he exclaimed, "He wants to give
everybody $1,000—hey, I work for a living, why should I pay
for people who don't work?" A Port of New York Authority
policeman made an observation that should have sent chills
down the spines of McGovern's white ethnic strategists, "He's
another Lindsay."

An insurance claims adjuster, when asked why he wasn't
going to vote for McGovern, volunteered, "You know, what
bothers me about McGovern and people like Bella Abzug, the
student militants, and others like them . . . is that they know
everything . . . what to do in Vietnam, what's wrong with
America, how you should raise your kids, amnesty, abortion,
everything . . . If you don't agree with them, you're stupid.
Well, I know one thing . . . I'm not the smartest guy in the
world, but I know what's right and wrong and I know I don't
like them or anything about them."

These Newarkers, like white ethnic residents elsewhere in
the United States, perceived domestic and foreign affairs
through the prism of a value system and position in society
which conflicted with that of privileged cosmopolitan
McGovernites. They were unhappy with Vietnam, but they
were convinced that Nixon was getting the United States
out of Southeast Asia; besides, they did not believe that

McGovern could do any better. At the time, before the full story was known, they could not get excited about Watergate because politicians were expected to say and do just about anything to get votes. The crime these urban Americans were concerned about was taking place on their streets and in the hallways and rest rooms of the schools their children attended. To people who had worked hard for a living and sacrificed to make ends meet, the Senator's pronouncements on welfare reform prompted a hostile reaction. Even after McGovern had revised his domestic programs to better reflect these concerns, he was unable to bridge the credibility gap alienating him from these Democratic voters.

For all intents and purposes, George McGovern lost the 1972 election in the 1960s because, via television—news programs and talk shows—the newspapers, and popular magazines, many working-class voters had come to associate their problems and powerlessness with the growing presence of educated, middle-class liberals and radicals who, they believed, were somehow responsible for the nation's ills and their own. They were bitter that they played by the rules, worked hard, obeyed the law, and respected authority; yet their problems were ignored by the nation's mainstream institutions, which dwelt on the activities of affluent persons, many of whom cavalierly disregarded all these things. This was the basis for the irony that white ethnic discontent with McGovern's candidacy in 1972 constituted proof that a populist impulse was abroad in America, but this resentment was directed not toward Richard Nixon and the "fat cats" in the Republican Party, but toward a man and movement that espoused populism.

CHAPTER VI

Black/White Ethnic Conflict

A. Nixon's Ethnic Strategy: *Every Time I'm at an Italian-American Picnic, I Think I Have Some Italian Blood*, Richard M. Nixon

Richard Nixon stood solemnly at attention, his right hand draped over his heart as a military band played the national anthem. Some three thousand persons were gathered around the base of the Statue of Liberty to attend the opening of the American Immigration Museum. Hundreds of Catholic school children wearing their school uniforms and Jewish yeshiva youngsters sporting yarmulkes listened attentively to the President that July morning in 1972. Flagbearers decked out in the national dress of their ancestors—Lithuanian, Czech, Italian, just about every European nation which had sent its children to the New World was represented—maintained their decorum under a broiling sun. Richard Nixon was hot on the trail of the white ethnic vote; the rhetoric he used that day reflected his "game plan." (And a game plan it was, for in private conversation Nixon displayed deep-seated prejudice toward the white ethnics. One tape-recorded conversation had him speak of "Jew-boys," while in another he told John Ehrlichman, "The Italians, they're not like us . . . They smell different, act different . . . The trouble is, you can't find one who is honest.") The immigrants, he intoned, "didn't come here for handouts; they came for opportunity, and they built America." Thus he obliquely denounced the permissive welfare policy of George McGovern and struck a blow for hard work and free enterprise, making it "perfectly clear" that he cherished the old values—love of country, respect for traditional family life, and deference to authority—just as those who listened to him did.[1] Later that day, when he returned to Manhattan, the President would meet with thirty-two prominent Jewish leaders.

Nixon got a larger slice of the Jewish vote than he ever had before, over one third, which was twice the amount he had received four years earlier. Jewish intellectuals, even old socialists like Sidney Hook, publicly supported Nixon and wealthy Jews sent him checks to demonstrate where they stood. One young rabbi who campaigned diligently for Senator Hubert Humphrey in the primary volunteered his talents to the Nixon campaign after the Democratic convention. Prior to the election, commentators speculated about the source of McGovern's unpopularity among Jews: he struck many urban Jews as a rural populist, a breed that has never been popular with them; lower income Jews turned against him because they perceived him and his supporters as "Lindsayites"; rich Jews, it was proclaimed, feared his economic policies would cost them money; and Zionists were concerned that he would not equal Richard Nixon's hard-line support for Israel. Israeli officials publicly and in private expressed their preference in no uncertain terms—they favored Richard Nixon. Since the Yom Kippur War, which has given rise to fears among the American Jewish community that Israel is not militarily invincible but desperately needs the protection of the United States, many Jewish liberals have been more forthright in admitting that McGovern's reluctance to commit himself to a hard pro-Israeli line in the Middle East caused them great concern. There is no doubt that this specific "ethnic issue" accounted for many Jews voting for Nixon or withholding their votes from McGovern.

Nixon anticipated Jewish votes as a bonus, but the Catholic ballots he hoped to deny McGovern were deemed crucial to his victory and his long-term political objectives. During the course of the year, Nixon met with Catholic spokesmen in the White House, demonstrating that he cared about them and their concerns. He told a Knights of Columbus gathering that he opposed abortion and favored aid to parochial schools. He met with John Cardinal Krol, the highest-ranking Polish clergyman in the United States, and spoke with him about these matters as they enjoyed a moonlight cruise on the Potomac aboard the Presidential yacht *Sequoia*. On the return trip from his summit conference with Soviet leader Leonid Brezhnev, the President stopped off in Poland to punctuate his interest in "things Polish." He met with Mayor Frank Rizzo (a hero to Philadelphia's white ethnic voters whom the media portrayed as the "toughest cop in the United States"), who said that Mr. Nixon was "the greatest President the country ever had."

In September he visited an Italian-American picnic in Maryland; "Every time I'm at an Italian-American picnic, I think I have some Italian blood." Pat Nixon flew to Chicago to attend a Lithuanian festival and she commented that the dancers were the "best I ever saw." *Time* magazine wrote that the white ethnic workers, who had traditionally given their votes to the Democratic Party, were responding to the appeals of the Nixon Administration. Should Nixon capture a majority of their votes as the polls indicated, the New Majority that President Nixon talked about so confidently during the campaign could become a reality.[2]

Kevin Phillips cautioned that it was premature to conclude that 1972 would be the year of party realignment; ". . . the Democrats can still survive as the majority on congressional and state levels." "But," he conceded, ". . . it may be that we are just seeing a behavior lag that has happened before" during the 1930s. Republicans at that time mistakenly believed, even after FDR was elected for a second term, that his was a personal and not a party triumph. "Not until six years after Roosevelt took office did the Democrats pass the Republicans in Gallup Poll voter identification (gaining a 40–38 per cent lead in 1938)."[3] On the other hand, White House strategists, though cautious, were positively brimming over with confidence that the white ethnic vote was theirs. Americans with a sense of history, meanwhile, were asking whether it was possible that the party which had passed restrictive immigra-

tion laws was about to capture the votes of the descendants of
the targets of these laws.

In the 1930s the Republicans had formed the Republican
National Committee's Division of Nationalized Citizens to attract white ethnic votes, but the results were disappointing.
After the war GOP strategists circulated the charge among the
ethnic community that the "Democrats had sold out the captive peoples of Central Europe"; it produced modest results.
The Republican "ethnic campaign strategy" during the Cold
War—which was not dissimilar to that of many Democrats—
was to manipulate the sorrow of Americans whose relatives
lived behind the Iron Curtain. General Eisenhower, in his
back-to-back victories, received many more Catholic votes than
Dewey had, but Republican congressmen did not do as well
with the white ethnics. The Republican commitment to the
captive nations was put to the test and failed when the Soviets
brutally suppressed the Hungarians in 1956 and President
Eisenhower prudently ignored the pleas from Budapest for
U.S. troops and weapons. The tragedy, however, did not silence John Foster Dulles who, after a momentary pause,
revved up the captive nations rhetoric to which he was so
fondly attached.

The Republicans had attracted a growing number of
middle-class Catholics after World War II; but the simplistic
notion popular in the 1950s that suburbanization would
strengthen this trend did not pan out the way many political
pundits had predicted it would. The urban Catholics who
relocated in the suburbs brought their party identification
with them and improved the fortunes of the Democratic Party
in areas which had long been under GOP control. Some broke
ranks and voted for Eisenhower, but most remained loyal to
Democrats running for offices other than the Presidency.[4] Yet
the Republicans could take some comfort in the fact that
Irish, Italian, and Slavic voters who had entered the middle
class were more inclined to vote for Republicans than their
working-class friends and relatives. Expectantly the Republicans concluded that it was only a matter of time before
these middle-class Americans discarded the political habits of
their working-class parents.

But John F. Kennedy in 1960 received most white ethnic votes, including many from Catholic voters who had acquired the habit of voting for Republicans. In 1964 Barry Goldwater fared even worse than Richard Nixon had in 1960 and when Ray Bliss, the old pragmatist, replaced Dean Burch as head of the Republican National Committee, he remarked that one of the problems with the GOP was that it was too "Waspish." Bliss's campaign to attract urban Catholics and Jews to the GOP had to leap over some rather awesome barriers: most Catholic white ethnics were working people, and the GOP's record—especially on bread and butter issues so critical to the average American—was poor; the Democratic Party had made room for ethnic European voters and politicians; the Republican Party in most industrial areas was a minority party and did not offer political aspirants much of a future; and prominent Republican leaders were largely Wasps whose knowledge about white ethnics was riddled with prejudices and stereotypes.

In 1968 Richard Nixon decided to adopt a more systematic white ethnic strategy and hired a Hungarian "freedom fighter," Laszlo Pasztor, to become the Director of the Nationalities Division of the Republican National Committee. He was given a staff with a permanent budget which, according to some reports, amounted to several hundred thousand dollars; whatever the figure, the money the Republicans committed to their ethnic strategy was far larger than that which was available to the ethnic strategists in the Democratic National Committee.[5] The National Republican Heritage Groups Council was formed in 1971 in preparation for the upcoming election. The new organization's goal was to build a grass-roots network to serve as a permanent adjunct to the Republican National Committee. Pasztor toured the country contacting leaders of various ethnic organizations and newspapers to encourage them to form state councils and federations of nationalities groups. By late 1971 some twenty state councils were formed. Significantly, the leader of the Republican operation in New Jersey was an anti-Castro Cuban exile; elsewhere Chinese-Americans who supported the government on Taiwan and East European political émigrés filled many of the offices in the new federation. Many of these people had belonged to right-wing political organizations in their homelands and the Democratic Party was too liberal for most of them. The materials the state councils distributed dwelt on foreign policy, traditionally a Republican issue of special concern to the captive nation immigrants whom Pasztor recruited, but of marginal interest to the third-generation white ethnics.

Whether it was intentional or not, the GOP made a serious error (although a common one which even advocates of a New Ethnicity have made) in failing to make a distinction between the pre-World War II ethnics and those displaced persons (DPs) who have arrived here since the war's aftermath. The differences—cultural, social, economic, political, and historical—are manifold and profound.

The New Immigrants were largely poorly educated peasant people who sought employment as industrial workers and low-paid laborers; they were victims of prejudice and discrimination and, lacking leadership or self-assurance, they suffered grievously from self-hate; they were politically unsophisticated; and in most cases their offspring remained in the working class for at least two generations. The DPs in contrast have been largely urban, middle-class, fairly well-educated people; significant numbers of them from Eastern Europe and Cuba were government officials, academics, students, and professionals at home. Possessing a firm grasp of their culture and mother tongue, they often display a conceit about the superiority of the culture they left behind when emigrating to America. They and their children have prospered in the United States; few of them have been traumatized by nativistic discrimination. Many of these DP groups—the Lithuanians, Latvians, Estonians, and Cubans, for example—have established language schools and social networks which constitute closed subcultures within the larger society. Older members of these groups think of themselves as exiles and not settlers and they are prepared to make great sacrifices to preserve their cultural heritage and to discourage their young people from marrying outside the community. Having lived under fascism or communism or both systems, they display a level of political sophistication which was uncommon among the second wave of European immigrants.

To lump the white ethnics and DPs together then is to

make a grave error. Consider for a moment that a retired Lithuanian steelworker from Pittsburgh who arrived as a child prior to World War I, as well as a fifty-year-old Lithuanian-born physicist who emigrated in the 1950s, are both first-generation Americans according to our census data. Yet words and names which are meaningful to the steelworker—"Bohunk," "the Depression," "FDR," "the CIO," "John L. Lewis," and "Dick Butkus"—are not likely to figure profoundly into the consciousness of the DP physicist.

While the white ethnic subculture has its roots in Europe, it has been largely shaped by the American milieu. This of course is true of the black ethnic subculture too. The reaction of Fred Sanford (the fictional TV character portrayed by Redd Fox) to his son's newly discovered African heritage, manifested in Lamont's adorning their house with African art objects, is relevant here. Fred said to Lamont, "If you want to celebrate my heritage, put up pictures of Joe Lewis and Billy Eckstein." The third-generation Italian-American who is searching for his roots should listen attentively to Fred Sanford and dwell not only on the work of Da Vinci and Michelangelo but explore the Italian-American culture which took root when his grandparents settled in the United States and developed through the toil and trials of brave peasant people and succeeding generations of their offspring. The Italians who are most relevant to the butcher in Little Italy are not Michelangelo, Garibaldi, and Mussolini, but La Guardia, Di Maggio, Sinatra, and Pastore.

Spiro Agnew seemed to understand that, while the DPs were preoccupied with foreign affairs, the third-generation Polish blue-collar worker was even more sensitive to domestic issues. Unlike past Republican ethnic strategists, Agnew did not talk at length about the plight of the captive nations; he focused instead on matters bothering many middle Americans —law and order, the arrogance of the "effete, liberal left," the "welfare cheaters," and so on. Agnew employed the term middle American to separate the white lower middle class from the black poor and the affluent cosmopolitans in the Democratic Party. Like Wallace, Agnew recognized that, while economic problems were still of great moment to these traditional Democratic voters (historically the issue voters believed the

Democrats handled best), they were also concerned about rapid social change and the emergence of people in the Democratic Party who reviled their values, symbols, and patriotism. Agnew's goal in 1970 was to convey the idea that the Democratic Party had come under the control of radical liberals and black militants and was no longer the party of the white lower middle class; the Republican Party was. He failed that year to convince the white ethnics that their local candidates were "limousine liberals" or dangerous radicals, causing pundits to conclude that the old "The Democrats are good for the economy" defense worked well against the GOP social issue offense. Yet he clearly helped the ticket two years later when the McGovernites, in the eyes of many voters, fit Agnew's description of "effete snobs."

During the primaries White House tacticians, convinced that McGovern would be the easiest Democrat to defeat in November, rooted for him. It is an interesting footnote that Nixon's "business-minded advisers" were certain of McGovern's likely defeat, while many cosmopolitan intellectuals thought otherwise. Both groups were privy to the same polling information, electoral data, and other indices of the national temper; why the discrepancy? The answer is simple—their membership in an elitist cosmopolitan subculture distorted the McGovernites' critical faculties, while Mr. Nixon's "soap salesmen" adhered to the pragmatic business practice of "giving the customer what he wants." The election's outcome unequivocally indicated which group best understood the temper of the "masses." Nixon's gains among the white ethnics in 1972 were significant, as the table below indicates:

Category	Nixon	McGovern	Gross Nixon Gain[6] Over 1968
Catholics	53%	47%	+20%
Irish	53%	47%	+20%
Italians	58%	42%	+18%
Jews	34%	66%	+19%

The day after the election, Charles Colson and the President's less prominent ethnic strategists took great pride in their work: Hubert Humphrey had received 64 per cent of the

Irish vote in 1968; four years later Nixon got 53 per cent of that vote. For the first time Nixon won a majority of Italian-American ballots—58 per cent, a 20 per cent jump in four years, representing an eight to ten point improvement over Ike's best showing with this group in 1956. Consider also that 49 per cent was the best Eisenhower could do among the Catholic electorate, while Nixon secured 53 per cent in 1972; and, as previously noted, the Jews gave most of their votes to McGovern, but Nixon's gains with this group jumped 19 per cent. Nixon's coattails were not long enough to help most Republican congressional candidates but the white ethnic votes he attracted convinced the White House that it was only a matter of time before the Catholic electorate would switch to the GOP.

The outlook changed dramatically six months after the election when two young Washington *Post* reporters revealed that the Watergate break-in was part of an ambitious White House campaign to subvert government institutions and secure its grip on federal power to systematically eliminate its political opposition. Since then not many Republicans talk about a New Republican Majority, but when the subject comes up they frequently talk about their prospects being enhanced by the prevailing racial climate.

Beginning in 1948 with the disgruntled Dixiecrats who ran Strom Thurmond as the States Rights Party's Presidential candidate, liberal Democratic support for racial justice has caused Southern whites to turn their backs upon "national Democrats." As the Civil Rights Movement gained momentum in the 1960s, traditional Southern Democrats voted for Republican candidates in increasing numbers. With the exception of Texas in 1968, Richard Nixon carried every state of the Old Confederacy in his two successful bids for the Presidency. In the aftermath of the 1968 victory, Republicans proclaimed the success of the Southern strategy and predicted that 1972 would be the year the ethnic strategy bore fruit, carrying the GOP further along the road to majority party status. Racial turmoil in the schools, neighborhoods, and factories where the Catholic ethnics lived and worked and their growing estrangement from the cosmopolitan left would drive them into the waiting arms of the GOP.

Several weeks after Nixon's re-election, Louis Harris produced electoral data reinforcing Republican expectations that racial divisions were tearing asunder the Democratic coalition. "The sharpest division in the recent vote for President could be found according to race, with blacks giving 79% to 21% for" McGovern, "while whites went 67% to 33% for President Nixon." Harris concluded, ". . . the black and white communities have rarely been so far apart in modern times."[7]

Many Democrats, even those who are optimistic about their party's winning the Presidency in 1976, admit that one scenario which frightens them is the resumption of heightened racial tensions—breaking out into ghetto rioting on the scale of the 1960s—fostered by the despair of the black underclass living under conditions akin to Apartheid in the urban North. A larger number fear what may be an even more likely prospect, white backlash prompted by attempts to achieve racial balance in metropolitan school systems through busing schemes. Commentators may disagree about the political significance of race in the years ahead, but all agree that the focal point for black/white ethnic conflict is in the troubled metropolitan areas of the North. Here, they claim, is where the GOP's ethnic strategy will or will not bear fruit.

Before turning to the subject of racial conflict, it is necessary to explore the reasons for white ethnic discontent which surfaced in the late 1960s, for racial strife is merely one symptom of a larger problem shared by most residents of urban America—powerlessness.

B. White Ethnic Neighborhoods: *They Are Ripe for the Bulldozer Because the Residents Lack the Power to Fight Back*

In the late 1940s the movement of urban Americans to the suburbs—a trend curtailed by the Depression and the war—resumed with a new earnestness. The old ethnic neighborhood no longer appealed to many people who associated the good life with a single family dwelling surrounded by a large lawn in a setting simulating the tranquility of the rural hinterland. This new generation, by turning its back on the city, demonstrated that it had internalized what is a uniquely American bias against urban life; its attraction to suburbia testified to the growing acculturation of the European ethnics. At first residents of what were formerly immigrant enclaves had moved to "better parts of the city"; as early as the late 1930s Italians, Jews, Lithuanians, and Poles moved from the Ironbound section of Newark to Clinton Hill, Weequahic, Vailsburg, and the North Ward. Italians and Jews who had formerly resided on New York's lower East Side sought better housing in the Bronx, Brooklyn, and Queens. But after World War II, millions of white ethnic urbanites relocated in the suburbs, seeking modern dwellings and greater living space.

Along with this "voluntary" outmigration was an exodus marked by those who were pushed from their old neighborhoods by rising crime, soaring taxes, congestion, racial strife, and declining schools. Most of us are familiar with this litany of urban ills, but few realize that the very policies government adopted to give coherence to urban development expedited the decline of our cities. Indeed, the thrust of our urban policy—such as it is—has destroyed stable residential neighborhoods on the one hand while billions have been spent to build new dwellings and nourish residential communities on the other. Government programs and private actions are both responsible for this mad contradiction—the results of which are millions of abandoned dwellings, acres of blighted landscape, the destruction of bustling inner-city neighborhoods, plunging tax revenues, and a climate of despair which defeats subsequent attempts to restore urban America. Unless dramatic measures are taken to reverse this trend, a frightening prospect will become a certainty by the end of this decade—many of our cities will become urban reservations for the poor, the elderly, and the nonwhite, carrying us even closer to de facto Apartheid.

Conservatives have cited the failure of government-sponsored urban legislation to produce significant results, but they have ignored the role of the private sector in this matter. For a quarter of a century urban neighborhoods have been destroyed because the soundness of government programs has often been judged by powerful forces in the private sector and not by officials elected to promote the public interest. Actions taken by the business community have made it impossible in many areas for working people to maintain homes and neighborhoods in center-city. Working-class white ethnic neighborhoods have been deemed ripe for the bulldozer because the residents lack the power to fight back.

After World War II, the highway program and the Federal Housing Administration mortgage insurance and Veterans Administration mortgage guarantee programs stimulated suburbanization. Bankers, builders, insurance underwriters and land speculators encouraged home building in the outer reaches of the metropolis. These measures were necessary to meet the pressures of population growth and the rising demand for housing. Unfortunately, while Washington was enabling potential homeowners to relocate in the suburbs, very little was done to preserve and improve existing inner-city neighborhoods. FHA actually discouraged home-buying in the city except in those cases where the home buyer was black; so did lending institutions and insurance companies. At the same time, urban redevelopment programs bulldozed sound housing and destroyed viable neighborhoods because they were designated "gray areas." The conceptual basis for this procedure reflected the physical determinism of planners, who abhorred mixed land uses (areas where factories and commercial enterprises can be found nestled among residential neighborhoods) and who ignored their own strictures about viewing the city as a "system."

Old dwellings were often designated substandard even though they were structurally sound and conformed to housing codes and safety regulations. High density, but not overcrowded, neighborhoods and those in which mixed land uses prevailed were tagged for urban renewal. Urban experts who toured older white ethnic neighborhoods were often inclined to describe them as slums, though the defining feature of a slum is social disorganization—high unemployment, family fragmentation, crime, and other forms of social pathology—not physical decay.

Even today despite all the rhetoric one hears in planning

circles about "urban systems"—that changes in one part of a
system will affect its other components—our urban policy has
ignored the importance of residential neighborhoods in urban
restoration. It has even escaped the attention of many hard-
nosed investors. In cities across America, billions are being
spent on "downtown projects," usually involving high-rise
office buildings, apartments, hotels, shopping malls, and oc-
casional townhouses in which only the wealthy can afford to
live. As the reinforced concrete is being poured, residential
communities in proximity to downtown are being bulldozed;
the city's tax base shrinks, the business community loses customers, and the cancer of de facto Apartheid spreads.

Moreover, even lower-middle-class neighborhoods which
have escaped the bulldozer have been excluded from most federal housing programs, contributing to the demise of white
ethnic inner-city neighborhoods. The housing programs
designed to meet the needs of the poor in turn have been a
windfall for unethical businessmen and have expedited the destruction of stable working-class communities. A case in point
was the FHA-sponsored Title 235 program, which enabled
poor people to purchase homes with small down payments
and long-term mortgages. Under the program—scrapped when
it became public knowledge that real estate speculators were
exploiting it to the tune of millions of dollars—poor people
bought homes on the assumption that, since the government
had guaranteed the dwellings, they met FHA standards. But
although under FHA regulations no home with code violations was acceptable, fee appraisers, in collusion with the
seller, simply ignored them in their reports. In addition, the
applications of buyers who were financially unable to bear the
burden of the purchase were frequently falsified. After moving
in and finding violations or discovering that they could not
afford the house, many buyers defaulted on their mortgages.[8]

The program's goal was commendable but, like numerous
others, it failed because corrupt or indifferent officials permitted unprincipled businessmen to rip off the poor who desperately need shelter. It contributed to the destruction of many
working-class neighborhoods where the homes were purchased, because after the buyer defaulted and the inventory of abandoned dwellings mushroomed, long-time residents

rushed to sell their homes in the fear that the collapse of the local housing market was imminent. The people who manipulated the program profited while the poor families lost their investments and the taxpayer picked up the tab for the defaulted mortgages.

After Richard Nixon entered the White House, Washington continued to ignore white ethnic neighborhoods. As expected, the Administration was not really interested in urban America and was opposed ideologically to the kind of massive program that needed to be mounted to attack our national urban malaise. But equally significant was the continuing gap separating the cosmopolitans and the white working class, reflected in the former's resistance to the problems of needy white folks. Urban decision-making in Washington bore the stamp of the Republican Administration, but the people implementing these rulings out in the field were pretty much the same ones who had first become involved in urban affairs under the Johnson Administration.

Presently, white ethnic neighborhoods and the people residing in them are still ignored, even where they qualify under law or administrative guidelines for participation in manpower, housing, drug abuse, crime, remedial education, and senior citizens programs. Economic deprivation and racial discrimination have prompted urban administrators to respond, though modestly, to the unmet needs of urban minority groups. One can find advocates for their cause in government, the foundations, academia, and the media, as there should be; at the same time, affluent citizens possessing political influence, economic power, and social status make certain that public agencies and private interests play by the rules with them. This accounts for a youngster whose father earns an impressive salary as a corporation executive acquiring a college tuition grant while a truck driver's son, whose father does not know how to "work the system," is denied this assistance. It explains why a college woman infected by a venereal disease can receive a free shot at a clinic serving college youth while the youngster who earns eighty-five dollars a week pumping gas must pay twenty dollars for similar care. And while white activists are less visible in black communities than was true ten years ago, one can still find radicals from Upper Montclair who display a passionate concern for Newark's disadvantaged citizens but who are appallingly misinformed about needy whites in the city and the problems of their neighborhoods.

The plight of old folks who cannot make the trek to the suburbs is especially heart-rending. (In Newark, New Jersey, for example, and this is true of many other cities, a disproportionate number of senior citizens are white even though the black population is in the majority.) Neighborhoods once bustling with commerce, where residents enjoyed the security of viable community life among relatives and friends, have been transformed into alien places where elderly citizens are afraid to walk the streets, sit in the park, or spend hot evenings on the front porch. Fear, prejudice, and pride account in part for the reluctance of elderly whites to enter a community action agency to inquire about programs which might offer them assistance. But the policy-makers and people staffing these organizations have not extended themselves by conducting white "outreach" drives either. It is not customarily a matter of callous indifference or antiwhite feeling which accounts for such oversights; rather, it reflects a one-dimensional definition of the "problem." The people staffing most "urban programs" are black or middle-class whites who do not know a great deal about white working-class neighborhoods or the people who live in them.

Professor S. M. Miller, a forceful advocate of social planning, has observed that the preoccupation of social welfare workers and urban specialists with blacks is the basis for much white opposition to the war on poverty and the drive to restore urban America. The exclusion of whites from Great Society programs heightened racial tensions and fostered the mistaken notion among many whites in the 1960s that the problems of minority Americans were "being taken care of."[9]

Although Washington possesses the funds and the leverage and it therefore must accept most of the blame for the sad state of our cities, the record of local governments is a sorry one too. The Lindsay Administration, which was praised by reformers for its sensitivity to "people's problems," ignored the residential communities outside Manhattan and adopted measures which expedited their demise. In a study of New

York's ethnic neighborhoods, John Esposito and John Fiorillo of the New York Center for Ethnic Affairs found, as expected, that poor neighborhoods in New York received a larger share of city revenues than working-class ones—but surprisingly so did more affluent neighborhoods. David Garth, John Lindsay's "media consultant," said on the eve of Lindsay's re-election campaign that "we're trying to find out what is bothering them (the city's blue-collar ethnics) . . . Our problem is that we never had contact with (their) neighborhoods until last year."[10] The Lindsay Administration's ignorance on this score did not come as a surprise to the residents of Staten Island, the Bronx, Queens, or Brooklyn.

In the fall of 1972 commuters on the Brooklyn-Queens Expressway were subjected to a horrendous traffic jam when a group of protesters formed a human chain across the thoroughfare. Most of the demonstrators were women, housewives from the Williamsburg section of Brooklyn—the wives and daughters of blue-collar workers who were employed by the city or by factories in and around the New York metropolitan area. These women had never before confronted political authority and sitting down to block traffic was an "illegal act" which caused them much guilt and soul-searching. One of their leaders, Mrs. Anastasi Zawakzki McGuinnes, observed, "That was the first time we ever did anything like that in our lives. But it's amazing what you can get yourself to do if it means survival." Survival meant defeating the city's plan to condemn housing which would eventually force some eighty-six families and several businesses from the predominantly Polish-American "Northside" neighborhood. Frustrated by their powerlessness and angered by the city's refusal to meet with them, the women took to the highway to publicize their plight.[11]

City officials claimed it was unfortunate that the homes had to be destroyed, but the action was necessary to permit the S&S Corrugated Paper Machinery Company to expand and make several hundred more jobs available. In 1969 the company had been offered a low-interest federal loan contingent upon its not relocating in New Jersey; to make it more attractive, the city Economic Development Administration promised it would make land available to permit the company to expand its facilities. The City Planning Commission and Board of Estimate conducted public hearings, but it was apparent that a deal had been made, and the Northsiders did not have the influence to prompt a serious reassessment of the scheme.

Community spokesmen argued that they certainly were in favor of making jobs available, for they were working people themselves; but they questioned whether the reason for the condemnation was to provide jobs. Many concluded it was a windfall for the company. The city had not given the people proper warning about the condemnation and the hearings were rigged against them; the decision to bulldoze their homes was made before the hearings; the residents were being awarded below market prices for their homes; the city never bothered to comply with its own relocation statutes; it was withholding subsidies soon to be put into effect; and it was questionable whether it was legal to condemn property for the sake of a profit-making corporation. Had the city's planners done their job, they could have taken measures to meet the needs of both the cardboard company and the homeowners.

In the fall of 1973 the Northsiders were evicted. Because of the assistance of an energetic former civil rights worker, Jan Petersen, the help of City Councilman Fred Richmond, and the technical advice of the Pratt Institute's Center for Community and Environmental Development and other outside allies, the people got a better deal than was originally anticipated. Nonetheless, they found little comfort in the measures the city took to soften the blow. Nor can their neighbors, who fear it is only a matter of time before the city decides to remove them as well. In an interesting footnote to the episode, the New York *Times* reported after the eviction that Paul Levine, an Economic Development Administration official who played "a leading role in the controversy," had resigned his job to join the S&S Corrugated Paper Machinery Company "as a top executive."[12]

The Northside story is only a single example of how an allegedly reformist administration contributed to the destruction of New York City's residential communities. Several years prior to this incident, Italian-American residents of Corona waged a bitter, protracted struggle with the Lindsay Adminis-

tration before they saved their homes from condemnation.
Today, Chelsea in Manhattan, one of the oldest residential
areas in the city, is fading rapidly because of actions first taken
by Lindsay's planners. Liberal political pundits who take comfort in the growing "alienation" of the populace because they
attribute it to the failure of the Old Politics of a Dick Daley or
an Abe Beame must recognize that the New Politics of a John
Lindsay does not work any better. The only political movement deserving the adjective "new" is one which acknowl-
edges that as long as public policy is a captive of private interests, we cannot hope to adequately resolve many of our most
pressing problems or treat the estrangement of millions of citizens from our political system.

Until ordinary people can hold businessmen accountable
for decisions which affect the fate of their neighborhoods, we
are not going to check urban blight, much less improve the
quality of urban or suburban life. The "money people" have a
virtual veto over government housing and related urban renewal programs. Herbert Gans, in his highly acclaimed study
of a Boston Italian-American community, *The Urban Villagers,* noted over a decade ago that in the initial stages of a
West End redevelopment program, some streets in the target
community were excluded because the housing was in good
condition. Later, the lending institutions involved ordered
that they be torn down because it would be difficult to sell
cleared land "surrounded by aging if well-kept tenements."[13]
Even Harold Kaplan, who has written favorably about Newark's urban renewal program, acknowledged the central role
the private sector played in that city's housing programs in the
1950s. "The big question about any redevelopment site was
whether a private firm could make a profit on middle-income
housing in that area. If the answer was negative, no redevel-
oper would buy the site, and no FHA official would agree to
insure mortgages for construction there."[14] Kaplan's conclusion accurately characterizes joint public-private sector programs today. According to George Gross, counsel to the
House Subcommittee on Housing, there is no dark mystery
about the failure of our "low-cost" housing programs. The big
decisions are really made by private developers, who "decide
where subsidized housing will go, how much each unit will

cost within a range set by the federal government, the size of the unit, and most important, whether there will be any such housing at all."[15]

The social cost of urban blight is enormous to city dwellers, as the economic cost is troublesome to the taxpayer. But urban malaise has proven to be profitable to unethical businessmen who prey on the minority poor and their lower-middle-class white neighbors alike. Real estate speculators zero in on inner-city white ethnic communities for the purpose of blockbusting because the residents lack the power to resist. Panic peddlers exploit white fears that the presence of blacks will result in plunging property values and the wholesale exodus of whites from the neighborhood. Several years ago an investigative reporter for a Newark newspaper found, in a probe of blockbusting in the city, that certain realtors were manipulating Newark's racial tensions. For example, he spoke to a widow who was told by a real estate agent that she could "not get a nickel more than $7,500" for her home because of the "ethnic situation" in Newark. Eager to relocate her family to Southern New Jersey, she reluctantly sold for the quoted price. The reporter, tracing the real estate records, found that the house was sold later that same day for $17,000. Under such circumstances, both the white seller and black buyer are being exploited. Blockbusting continues to foster wholesale white urban flight, North and South; and to a significant degree, it is responsible for what has now become a truism of many cities—that there are no integrated neighborhoods in our cities, only changing ones.

Blockbusting has received the condemnation it so richly deserves; but an equally destructive practice of the business community, "red-lining" by insurance companies and lending institutions, is often ignored. Homeowners in many white ethnic neighborhoods are told that they live in a "riot," "disaster," "high-risk," or "gray" area; hence, they are ineligible for mortgage money or insurance coverage. Red-lining works like a self-fulfilling prophecy. Because rehabilitation money is withheld, small homeowners are unable to take proper care of their dwellings; roofs, sidings, and porches begin to decay and, as the housing in the community becomes unsightly, home-

owners and businessmen, fearful that their neighborhood is on
the decline, are reluctant to "keep up" their property. As the
neighbors' dwellings deteriorate and the more mobile residents
move, the people largely responsible for the outcome sit back
and take pride in their prophetic powers and business acumen.

C. Rediscovering the Working American: *Wallace Was the First National Political Figure to Appreciate What So Many Working Americans Were Bitching About*

Although vastly outnumbered, there were a few people in
the Johnson Administration and the Movement who urged
that needy urban whites be integrated into the Great Society
programs. Robert C. Wood, a prominent political scientist
and then Under-Secretary of Housing and Urban Development, speaking before an audience in Lincoln, Massachusetts
in December 1967, said that some twenty million working
families in the United States were bearing the burden of taxation and providing the bulk of the troops in Vietnam while
being left out of the political process. "The upper-middle-class
establishment asked the ordinary working man to make room
in his plant for the unemployed minorities; to open up his
neighborhoods; to bus slum children to his neighborhood
schools or to bus his children to downtown schools."[16] Wood
observed that the privileged Americans who were making
these demands themselves were not prepared to pay the price
to promote the welfare of the black underclass. Unfortunately,
during the eight years the Democrats controlled the White
House in the 1960s, there were few urban experts in the federal agencies, politicians on the "hill," or members of the
White House staff who demonstrated a real appreciation for
the discontent percolating in white ethnic communities. The
party regulars thought they had the white ethnic vote in the
bag, while the reform-minded element in the Democratic
Party and the Movement tended to view our urban problems
exclusively in terms of black or brown poverty.

Meanwhile, Irving Levine at the American Jewish Committee, against stiff resistance from some of his superiors, conducted seminars pertaining to white ethnicity and Father

Geno Baroni of the Urban Task Force of the United States Catholic Conference was busily at work pressing the church to expand its "urban agenda" and include millions of ethnic Catholics. As a consequence of the workshops, seminars, and conferences the AJC and Baroni's Urban Task Force conducted, the media began to send reporters to neighborhoods where the "forgotten ethnics" lived. Soon after the *Wall Street Journal*, the New York *Times*, and the Washington *Post* picked up the story, the major television networks and the weekly news magazines also got into the act. Some editors favored the label "working-class white ethnics"; others merely used the term "white ethnics" and assumed their working-class status; while still others spoke about "blue-collar workers" but dwelt primarily on the Irish construction worker, the Italian truck driver, and the Polish autoworker. The media's confusion was a by-product of a simple fact: the urban Catholic white ethnics living in center-city were largely working people, grappling with problems the left had ignored or had assumed away. At any rate, the national media's recognition of "ethnic discontent" and the "blue-collar blues" legitimized scholarly research and popular discussion of the American working class per se.

Soon thereafter the foundations Levine and Baroni had pressed for grants indicated they were prepared to be forthcoming with funds. Ford was the first to act. The American Jewish Committee received a grant primarily to conduct seminars, conferences, and consultations which would encourage white ethnic research and Baroni's newly founded National Center for Ethnic Affairs received money to explore community action strategies in white ethnic neighborhoods. Ford's project managers made it clear that they viewed both programs in terms of "racial depolarization"; this was the major focus of the AJC's activities at that time, although Baroni reminded Ford that the people in question had legitimate needs that deserved to be addressed whatever the program's related social or political implications.

The network of organizations and individuals who were principally involved in urban programming nonetheless resisted mounting pressure to enlarge their activities to include Northern white victims of poverty and urban malaise. Many black activists, but even more whites in the Movement, expressed concern that "scarce resources otherwise allotted to meet the needs of minority groups will be siphoned off should working-class whites demand a slice of the pie from Washington, local government, the foundations, the churches, and the business community."[17] They wondered whether "talk about the 'white worker' is not proof positive that conservative pressure has intimidated many old allies who are deserting the Civil Rights Movement in the face of a reactionary counterattack." Others warned: "To organize whites on the basis of self-interest is to reject racial cooperation attained through brotherhood. To pander to the claims of white ethnic groups is to further fragment a society that is already divided, black and white, rich and poor, old and young." Still others remarked, "There is no question that well-meaning persons who attempt to organize working-class whites and assist them in community programs will be co-opted by demagogues who will sabotage efforts to achieve genuine multiracial cooperation."

The ethnic activists lobbying the government and foundations to allocate funds to their neighborhoods answered that the poverty program had to be revised and expanded to meet the needs of all disadvantaged Americans. The resources devoted to the elimination of poverty and racial prejudice were grossly inadequate. To deal meaningfully with both, the constituency of support for their elimination had to be expanded. The pertinent issue was not slicing up an inadequate pie, but developing the political clout to produce an adequate response to the unmet needs of the poor and workingman in every corner of America. The most articulate advocates for the working-class white ethnics, like Geno Baroni, Irving Levine, Ralph Perrotta, Councilwoman Barbara Mikulski of South Baltimore, and the North Ward Educational and Cultural Center's Steve Adubato, were all active in the Civil Rights Movement or Poverty Program in the 1960s. Even a casual background investigation of these people and their colleagues indicated that the charge of a "sellout" to a racist backlash was groundless. And, regarding fears about organizing whites on self-interest, they responded that the only way the chasm separating the races could be bridged was to find a common bond of self-interest. They agreed that demagogues were exploiting racial fears to achieve personal gains; this was why leaders with a positive agenda who wished to combat the causes and not the symptoms of their communities' problems had to be supported.

The men and women who would be dubbed the "ethnic activists" were the first to argue that the working-class white ethnics had many legitimate problems which needed to be attended to at home and at work; that their neighborhoods were the basis for restabilizing many cities; and that there was little prospect of building a multiracial coalition for change without their support.[18] In spite of the logic of their arguments, they did not have sufficient influence to prompt policy-makers to seriously reconsider the plight of the urban ethnics. Nor were they successful in convincing Democratic politicians that the discontent which was brewing among the white ethnics was a cause for concern. The cosmopolitan left first began to turn its attention to the "revolt of the ethnics" when they realized that George Corley Wallace had become a powerful political figure who could not be easily dismissed as a racist demagogue whose appeal was restricted to "crackers" in Dixie. Wallace's appeal among the white ethnics was exaggerated, but in many places it signified the growing estrangement of traditional Democratic voters from their party.

In the 1964 Democratic Presidential primaries the "little Judge" captured 34 per cent of the vote in Wisconsin, 30 per cent in Indiana, and 43 per cent in Maryland, causing Theodore White, the chronicler of Presidential campaigns, to observe that Wallace had

> . . . demonstrated . . . for the first time the fear that white working-class Americans have of Negroes. In Wisconsin he scored heavily in the predominantly Italian, Polish, and Serb working-class neighborhoods of Milwaukee's South Side; in the mill town of Gary, Indiana he actually carried every white precinct in the city . . . and in Maryland he did better, running almost as strong among the steelworkers of Baltimore as among the hereditary racists of the Eastern Shore.[19]

In the 1968 general election Wallace lost much of the

white ethnic support he got during the primaries; in white South Philadelphia he got 12 per cent of the vote, 26 per cent in Gary, 21 per cent in the five white wards of East Baltimore, and 15 per cent in the four white wards of Chicago's West Side. In spite of growing discontent with the Democratic Party, Hubert Humphrey got a majority of white ethnic votes. In 1972, before he was cut down by a would-be assassin in a suburban Maryland shopping center, Wallace demonstrated that approximately 25 per cent of the Democratic electorate favored his candidacy. He won the Florida primary, came in second to McGovern in Wisconsin, and emerged victorious in Maryland and Michigan. But Wallace did not do as well among the white ethnics as political pundits predicted he would. With the exception of Pennsylvania, Wallace fared better among Wasps than among white ethnics. All but a small percentage of Jews rejected him; for example, he only received 9 per cent of the Jewish vote in Maryland and 2 per cent in Florida. The Catholic ethnics gave him a mixed reception. In Wisconsin he won 13 per cent of the Polish vote, while statewide he got 22 per cent of the ballots cast; the Poles gave McGovern 19 per cent, Humphrey 16 per cent, and Muskie 41 per cent respectively. The Italians in Massachusetts gave Wallace 12 per cent, Humphrey 11 per cent, and McGovern 42 per cent of their votes. Wallace in Pennsylvania captured about 22 per cent of the Italian vote, which was a point higher than his statewide showing, and he nearly split about 90 per cent of the East European vote with Humphrey there.[20]

The governor from Alabama was preferred by different segments of the white population in the North. In Michigan and Wisconsin his support came largely from blue-collar voters, while in Pennsylvania and California white-collar voters were more inclined to vote for him. In most cases his supporters were deeply concerned about busing, welfare, and other race-related issues, but many people voted for him to protest the indifference of the regular Democrats to their powerlessness in the face of decisions which keenly affected them and their loved ones.

Beginning in the 1960s, Wallace was the first national political figure to appreciate what so many working Americans were bitching about—their economic problems, their fear of rapid social change, and their inability to influence big government and the powerful private interests which controlled most aspects of their lives—and many of them perceived him as the means to mobilize their discontent and channel it politically. Millions of voters for the first time were questioning the rules by which they had always abided and the good will of the people who governed them. Many Wallace voters were not traditional Nixon conservatives; they rejected both major parties and crossed swords with Republican voters on many issues— government support of housing, medical assistance, and other bread and butter legislation that contributed to the welfare of the ordinary American.[21]

Wallace's performance jolted regular Democrats and his appeal to the ethnics reconfirmed cosmopolitan fears that the Catholic ethnics no longer represented a force for progressive change and that the left had to look elsewhere for votes.

Liberal Democrats who first began to track the white ethnics' local electoral behavior in the 1960s made an alarming discovery. The vast majority of white ethnics, when they went into the voting booth, were motivated by a single compelling thought—they would reject any candidate who was not a member of their race.

Gary: Richard Hatcher in 1967 became the first black mayor of this grimy steel town; he received virtually every black vote but only 15 per cent of those cast by whites. That three fourths of the white Democrats in the city rejected their party's nominee was proof to many that talk about a "backlash" vote was not idle chatter.

Cleveland: Carl Stokes became the first black mayor of a major American city in 1967; a handsome, articulate campaigner, Stokes received 19 per cent of the white vote in this largely working-class ethnic town and almost all of the black vote. Two years later he only received 22 per cent of the white vote; and in 1971 a Republican, Ralph Perk, a second-generation Czech, became the first Republican elected in Cleveland's history when he received 38 per cent of the votes cast in a three-man race. Resisting their past Democratic affiliation, the white ethnics voted overwhelmingly for Perk, and his re-election in 1973, at a time when his party was taking its lumps, demonstrated unequivocally that race was the single most important issue in the eyes of Cleveland's electorate.

Boston: Louise Day Hicks, a former school board member who campaigned on an antibusing platform, was elected to the U. S. Congress in 1970.

Philadelphia: Frank Rizzo, the chief of police of the "City of Brotherly Love," known as the "Cisco Kid" by friends and enemies alike for his inclination to react violently to lawbreakers (on one occasion, called from a formal affair, Rizzo stood by, a night stick in his cumberbund, as his men stripped naked a group of Black Panthers), was elected mayor in a three-way contest. Voting returns indicated that the white ethnics voted overwhelmingly for him and rejected his two opponents.[22]

Liberal politicians in private remarked that they expected as much from the Slavs in Gary and Cleveland, the Irish "hard hats" in Boston, and the Italians in Philadelphia; but that Jews were turning their backs on minority candidates and issues was unexpected and a source of deep concern. Jewish opposition to the civilian review board in New York City in 1966, black/Jewish conflict over community control of schools in 1967–68, Jewish "overreaction" to anti-Semitic statements on the part of some black leaders, growing Jewish enmity toward Mayor Lindsay, the "hysteria" of middle-class Jews in Forest Hills to low-cost housing, and the significant number of Jews who voted for Rizzo in Philadelphia (about half of them voted for the Cisco Kid) and Yorty in Los Angeles all indicated that Jews could no longer be counted on in the "struggle for racial justice."[23]

Students of race relations drew ominous conclusions from the growing saliency of race in white ethnic voting preferences. Nathan Glazer and Daniel Patrick Moynihan, in the second edition to *Beyond the Melting Pot,* reported that an obvious change had occurred in race relations in the 1960s. They perceived what they called the Southern model of race relations insinuating itself upon the North. "In the Southern model, society is divided into two segments, white and black. The line between them is rigidly drawn . . . Violence is the keynote of relations between the groups. And 'separate but equal' is an ideology if not a reality." (Many civil rights activists agreed with this analysis although they carried it a step further, refusing to acknowledge that there ever had been a Northern model of race relations.) According to Glazer and Moynihan, "The Northern model is quite different. There are many groups. They differ in wealth, power, occupation, values, but in effect an open society prevails for individuals and for groups." The nature of conflict between the groups, moreover, is nonviolent and the antagonists ultimately resolve their differences through peaceful accommodation. Unfortunately, they concluded, the "Southern style" had moved North, and with a new wrinkle to it. "The demand for a rigid line between the races is now raised again, more strongly from the black side this time." For "in the course of the 1960s . . . It became possible . . . for blacks to attack and vilify whites in a manner no ethnic group had ever really done since the period of anti-Irish feeling of the 1840s and 1850s." Moreover, "the (traditional) 'nigger' speech of the Georgia legislature (has become) the 'honky' speech of the Harlem street corner or the national television studio, complete with threats of violence. In this case, it (is) the whites who (are) required to remain silent and impotent in the face of the attack."[24] Across the Hudson River in the industrial town of Newark, Steve Adubato, the most progressive political force in the city's Italian-American community, spoke of this role reversal by informing a reporter that the white residents of his community were the "New Niggers" of Newark.

D. The "New Niggers" of Newark: *Wherever America's Cities Are Going, Newark Will Get There First,* Kenneth Gibson

The 1970 census recorded that Newark had the highest per capita crime rate . . . the greatest percentage of slum housing . . . the worst incidence of venereal disease and maternal mortality in the country. Epidemic street crime, unemployment (citywide it was about 16 per cent and one third of the city's youth could not find jobs), drug abuse, rape and murder, poverty and welfare dependence (approximately one third of the city's population was on welfare), runaway property taxes (about 9.63 dollars per hundred of assessed evaluation)—few American cities matched Newark's dismal statistics. Racial strife, school strikes, low test scores in reading and writing (only 42 per cent of Newark's population has gone beyond the eighth grade), declining services—once again Newark was right out front. Soon after Kenneth Gibson, Newark's black mayor, entered office, he told reporters, "Wherever America's cities are going, Newark will get there first."

Because of its many problems, the media have devoted considerable attention to Newark. The city's racial strife in particular has received widespread publicity, but it has been treated primarily from the black perspective. This is an unfortunate oversight, contributing to a one-dimensional analysis and approach to racial conflict there. To most whites in Newark, this "biased" view has reinforced their distrust of the "liberal" media.

Following we will consider the plight of Newark's white residents, for their problems are typical of those which white ethnics face in many cities where they live and work with a growing black population.

In the 1950s Newark's white residents viewed the invasion of Southern, rural blacks in search of jobs with the same trepidation that native Americans had when their ancestors moved into Wasp communities earlier in the century. Newark was praised for being one of the first cities to provide low cost housing for its needy residents. Whites, however, out of prejudice, but out of fear as well, fled the "projects" which gained a reputation for all kinds of violence—gang wars, knifings, and shootings—public displays of drunkenness, and a threat new to most working-class whites—drugs. As the black population spilled over from the projects into the two- and three-story timber dwellings that surrounded them, the whites who could fled. Those who remained complained about the rising incidence of street crime; residents who had previously walked the streets safely at any hour of the day were getting mugged. Many of the muggers were black. Vandalism and juvenile delinquency increased and gained a new resonance; schools, playgrounds, and other places where youngsters congregated became flash points for racial conflict. White youngsters returned home from school with stories about being beaten up by "colored kids," of having their lunch money taken from them by black toughs, and of being set upon by knife-wielding blacks in the park or playground.

To most white residents, "outsiders" from Dixie were surrounding them, denying them the fruits of decades of hard work and self-denial. They felt cheated. They had adhered to the rules: work . . . save . . . persevere in the face of bad times—work harder, two jobs if necessary . . . don't take vacations, go to the ball game, or buy the wife the new sofa . . . save . . . save to get enough money together to buy a house, to own your own home, with a garden in the back . . . save to leave something for the kids . . . save, toil, sacrifice, that's the American way. But then as the new migrants from the South move closer, your wife's afraid to walk the streets, your kids talk about frightening things happening at school, the policeman next door tells you that "the cops can't do much, those niggers aren't afraid of guns, they're not afraid to die." It is not much compensation that most blacks in the city feel much the same way you do about street crime and turmoil in the schools, nor do you recognize that, like the black man, you are a victim of decisions made by powerful people remote from your anger. As you become more anxious about your future and the safety of your children, you watch perplexed and then become outraged when self-proclaimed radicals speak about "community control" and "people power" but never apply these prescriptions to you and your neighborhood. Bureaucrats from Washington, college professors, and "progressive" businessmen also have the gall to lecture you about having to make room for the city's newcomers; yet these same humanitarians often live in communities where zoning laws protect affluent suburbanites from "riffraff," whatever their color, religion, or nationality.

Newark's population declined by 50,000 in the 1960s and by 1970, 70 per cent of its 380,000 residents were black and Puerto Rican. Newark's whites inhabit three enclaves—Ironbound, Vailsburg, and the North Ward. A large percentage of the white population in Ironbound are Italian, Polish, Portuguese, and Cuban, while in Vailsburg the Italians, Irish, and Ukrainians are dominant. The largest white section of the city is the predominantly Italian-American North Ward where approximately 70 per cent of the people, 70,000 residents, are white.

Italians first arrived in Newark at the turn of the century, seeking work in New Jersey's largest city, a manufacturing center and hub of the state's insurance and financial activities. At that time, German, Jewish, Polish, Lithuanian, and Irish immigrants all called Newark their home; the first to arrive resided in Ironbound, where factories and shops were nestled among residential two- and three-story dwellings. By the 1920s a large Italian community resided in the less attractive parts of North Newark and, working their way out of the most menial jobs, they entered the city's breweries and factories; some opened businesses and others found work at City Hall, especially after the Italians became important enough to be included on the ethnically balanced tickets characteristic of Newark's politics. In 1948, the Italian community's growing political clout became manifest when two Italian-Americans were elected to Congress. One of the young men elected was Peter Rodino; the other was Hugh Addonizio, who left Congress in 1966 to run for mayor of the city of Newark. Addonizio was popular among his Capitol Hill colleagues and most of them could not understand why he would give up his prestigious House seat to become mayor of a city that had a reputation for being one of the nation's most deplorable examples of neglect. The story, according to Newark's grapevine, was that the congressman, in debt to the "mob," was ordered to return home. Congressmen can do things, but mayors can do much more; they have large city contracts they can dispense to their friends, who are grateful for the "business." Generations of politicians in Newark have adroitly manipulated public office to enrich themselves in this fashion. Addonizio's election meant a great deal to the city's Italian-Americans; it was a source of pride that one of their own was governing Newark and, like other white Newarkers, they took comfort in the thought that their worst fear had not materialized—black control of City Hall.

During the 1960s, as white residents relocated in the suburbs and the black population rose, racial tensions mounted. The 1967 riot dramatically sharpened racial anxieties. It cost twenty-six lives, acres of burnt-out dwellings, and millions of dollars in property losses. In Ironbound, North Ward, and Vailsburg, whites armed themselves and prepared for the black rioters to surge out of the ghetto into white neighborhoods; that terrible possibility never materialized. But the riot thrust two men into prominence: Imamu Amiri Baraka (LeRoi Jones), the black nationalist playwright, and Tony Imperiale, a state senator, karate buff, and the most powerful grass-roots leader in the city's Italian community. Since the riot, when they opened a "hot line" between their respective headquarters, "LeRoi" and "Tony" have attracted widespread media attention. The symbiotic relationship they enjoy is not unique to Newark; it is detectable elsewhere where racial demagogues can manipulate the prejudice, fear, and powerlessness of the many for the benefit of the few, undermining the efforts of responsible leaders in both communities to come to grips with the desperate plight of whites and blacks alike.

Baraka is a short, slightly built man who sports a wispy beard. When talking about white people, he constantly refers to "white boys" as a takeoff on the "crackers'" predilection for calling black men "boys." A nationalist, he believes that black people, wherever they reside in the world, share a common destiny, that the defining feature of their history has been exploitation at the hands of white people. The most pivotal force in the black man's future, he proclaims, is Pan-Africanism, the mobilization of global black power to rid Africa of the remnants of white rule and to cast off the yoke of "colonialism" oppressing black Americans. Professing Third World doctrine, Baraka contends that American blacks suffer a colonial existence akin to European exploitation of Africans prior to World War II. To break this chain of oppression, blacks must secure political power, develop economic institutions, promote pride in the African heritage, and celebrate those values which shaped a tough slave people over several centuries.

During the 1970 mayoralty race, Baraka worked diligently for Kenneth Gibson's election. Addonizio's supporters circulated antiwhite passages from Baraka's literary work and

frightened white Newarkers by warning them that "Jones" was
the power behind the Gibson candidacy. The charge was unfounded but most whites were visibly frightened by the
thought that Baraka would be a power in City Hall after Gibson was elected. Most would have opposed Gibson in any
event; but even discerning whites in Newark are convinced
that Baraka is plotting to oust them from the city.

Approximately 20 per cent of the North Ward's residents
are nonwhite and the Italian residents there are demonstrably
less concerned about living with blacks than they are about
racial conflict in the ward's public schools. Baraka has said
that the school system is his priority target, and many whites
claim that he has manipulated racial strife in the schools to
frighten them into leaving Newark.[25] During the 1971 school
strike—the longest in the nation's history—Baraka said that
the strikers were "racists" who didn't give a damn about the
students and he pressed Gibson to stand firm against their
demands. He promulgated this line even though the president
of the teachers' union, Carol Graves, and a large number of
the teachers were black. On one occasion some young blacks,
wielding clubs spiked with nails, beat several strikers senseless;
some striking teachers accused Baraka of engineering the assault in an attempt to intimidate black unionists who rejected
his philosophy and white teachers whom he wished to replace
with black instructors. In the spring of 1972 Barringer High
School, situated in the North Ward, was closed down for two
weeks. The white students walked out claiming they were not
safe in Barringer, and they would not return until the administration offered them protection. The next year the predominantly white Vailsburg High School was closed over a dispute
prompted by the firing of a Negro school disciplinarian who,
blacks claimed, punished Negro students more harshly than
whites. Large crowds of students and parents milled outside
the school for several days and school authorities feared a race
riot.

Newark's whites, like residents of other predominantly
black cities, are deeply concerned about the future of the
public schools. Those that are integrated are often hotbeds of
racial strife, causing many parents (of both races) to seek a
safe alternative by enrolling their children in parochial

schools. This often means that a working-class family must make a great economic sacrifice to spare their children the turmoil of the public schools. (In Newark the parochial school tuition ranges from $400 up to $800 a year per child. For a workingman with two or three school-aged children, this is an enormous economic burden.) Throughout the industrial North, parochial schools are deemed places of refuge enabling whites and blacks who would otherwise flee to remain in center-city. Thus blacks in Newark and Detroit, primarily Protestants, have fought attempts on the part of the Catholic hierarchy to close parochial schools in center-city. Like most white families, many blacks who have the financial means to do so will leave should the urban parochial school system collapse as many observers believe is inevitable.

Because of pervasive white fear of Baraka, almost any incident associated with him is cited as evidence that he is plotting to force whites from the city. In February 1973 violence flared at the construction site of Kawaida Towers, located in the predominantly white North Ward. The apartment house was sponsored by Baraka's Pan-African Temple of Kawaida, and whites wondered why it was not being built in the Central Ward where there was ample land for construction and the predominantly black community desperately needed new shelter. Baraka, they concluded, chose the North Ward site to stir up fear in the white community. The national media played up Newark's desperate need for housing and implied that white opposition was motivated solely by white racism. Opposition to the construction of Kawaida Towers was not unrelated to racial feeling; but the media failed to consider that, on the basis of Baraka's racist rhetoric and his past behavior, whites had good reason to suspect that Kawaida represented something more than the construction of an apartment house. Baraka responded that he had made a deal with the white councilmen—that they had agreed to his plans but changed their minds later when the community became aroused as the construction workers broke ground. Astute observers in the North Ward believe Baraka told the truth, but the duplicity of the white councilmen in no way minimized charges that Baraka knew that any venture associated with him would stir up white folks. "How would the black commu-

nity react if they learned that Tony Imperiale was construct-
ing a project for Italians in one of 'their neighborhoods' and
planned to call it Garibaldi Towers?" one of the whites who
picketed the Kawaida site exclaimed.

Tony Imperiale is a one-time city councilman, two-time
candidate for mayor, and leader of the North Ward Citizens'
Committee, a paramilitary organization which first attracted
attention during the 1967 riot. Due to the media exposure he
received during the riot, he won a city council seat bran-
dishing a law and order platform. This was the start of his political career. A five-foot-six, 230-pound hulk of a man, Imperiale represents, in the eyes of most North Warders, the
most forceful leader they have in their struggle with the
Baraka-led black nationalists. In the mid-1960s he won widespread support among the community's whites for his security
activities (his men patrolled the neighborhood nightly) and
his ambulance service. During the school strike, black teachers
were overheard remarking that they were glad "Tony and his
boys are offering the teachers protection." In a city where one
often waits precious hours for desperately needed medical attention, the ambulance service—though only a part-time operation—is an attractive organizational ploy. Imperiale has a
flair for the dramatic; during the Kawaida Towers dispute he
daily led crowds in a pledge of allegiance before the site and at
one point chained himself to a gate, barring the way of construction. On another occasion he rode a horse decked out
in armor during a Columbus Day parade. He has skillfully
projected himself as the champion of Newark's white population and he is often quoted in the media. Like George
Wallace, who reputedly made him an "honorary Southern
colonel," Imperiale's popularity is a reflection of the powerlessness of the people he represents and the failure of liberals
to pay proper attention to their grievances. Like Baraka, Imperiale's future would be grim indeed should racial tensions
subside in Newark. "Tony" depends on "LeRoi's" antics to
keep the racial pot boiling. Baraka in turn depends on Imperiale for the "services" he renders the city's black nationalists. Unlike Baraka, Imperiale does not publicly resort to
racial slurs, although most blacks are convinced he is a racist;
but it is apparent that he has taken advantage of racial in-

cidents in the schools and the Kawaida Towers squabble to further his own political career. Imperiale's political philosophy is similar to that of his hero, George Wallace—it might be labeled right-wing populism. Welfare cheaters must be eliminated from the welfare rolls; the police must be given a free hand to fight crime; and the liberals, in conspiracy with black militants, are the ones to blame for most of the nation's problems. On occasion Imperiale complains about Prudential and other large firms in Newark for their support of "troublemakers," but he does not relate the abuse of private power to the plight of his white working-class constituents. Yet to many frightened, angry people of the North Ward who doubt whether they have a future in the city, who feel threatened by the blacks, and who are enraged that the suburban liberals "who live miles away from Newark blame us for the city's problems"—Imperiale is all they have.

Although Imperiale enjoys the support of the white residents of the North Ward, another leader with a different kind of political organization and agenda has also emerged—Steve Adubato.[26] The grandson of an Italian immigrant, Adubato was born in the old First Ward, North Newark's original Italian enclave. He taught school for fifteen years and gained the reputation of an oddball for his outspoken support of the Civil Rights Movement. In the mid-1960s he became involved in politics. Determined, yet unsure of his prospects, he plunged into the roughhouse politics of the North Ward's Democratic Party. At that time one congressman, four county freeholders, three councilmen, and two state assemblymen resided in the North Ward. Adubato gained access to inner-party councils after winning a minor party office as district leader and he was appalled at what he found. Intelligent, idealistic, but tough-minded, he accepted patronage as the basis for political participation, especially in a working-class community. He knew that politics in the North Ward represented a step up the economic ladder and was a source of status for Americans from immigrant/working-class backgrounds. But it disturbed him that the old pols ignored the needs of the people even when it was in their power to deal with community problems—they were too busy peddling favors and stuffing their pockets. Adubato astounded them when he suggested that the party become more responsive to community problems. He was verbally abused, publicly ridiculed, and threatened with bodily harm when he questioned the party chairman's budget.

Adubato, a man of short, broad-shouldered stature and with a rough-hewn face, thrives on conflict. Refusing to be scared off, he decided to take the offensive and run for chairman of the North Ward Democratic Party. The chairman, elected by the ward's ninety-eight district leaders, has the final word in nominating candidates for city, county, and state offices. The machine could lose one or several elected offices and still survive, but an enemy chairman would be a Trojan horse whose presence could lead to serious consequences. The old pols scoffed at Adubato's candidacy; they had firm control of the chairmanship. Few people voted in the primaries for district leaders and a slate consistently favorable to the machine had always elected a member of the "club." A small cadre of voters who held political jobs could be counted on to vote for the machine's slate, and usually that was enough.

When Adubato continued to fight the machine, he received threats on his life, but he persisted and proceeded to build his own political organization. His large family was the nucleus for it but he recruited friends and neighbors from all sectors of the community—small businessmen, blue-collar workers, and blacks whom the machine had ignored. Through his activities in the teachers' union he knew all the Italian-American teachers who lived in the area. They became his largest reservoir of political activists. Long-time residents of the community, these young men and women were sensitive to its problems. They were an indigenous cadre of dedicated people on intimate terms with the voters of the area. Having acquired political savvy in their union, and sensitive to the larger problems of the city, they rejected the machine's paternalism. While many of them were "militant Italians," they resented the crass exploitation of ethnic loyalties and petty political payoffs which robbed the people of the opportunity to take part in matters germane to the well-being of their neighborhoods. They were not exactly exponents of the New Politics, but it irked them that the machine did not bother any longer to take care of complaints about street lights, truck traffic, and demands for stop signs. Adubato's young activists discussed matters of real concern to the voters. Sons and daughters of factory workers, truck drivers, and day laborers, they had little trouble relating to the blue-collar residents who lived in the Ward. They "turned on" people who had never before considered voting in the primaries.

Adubato defeated the machine in 1969 as he has every election since. Reflecting upon his success, he has said, "We were better politicians; we beat them at their own game. We were militant. By that I mean we consistently worked hard to get out the vote." Like other "new breed ethnic activists," Adubato was involved in the civil rights struggle before realizing that he could most successfully fight racial and economic injustice by working in his own community with his own people, who had been ignored by liberal reformers. It is noteworthy that he did not receive support for his activities until the media began to write about an "ethnic movement." Today Adubato directs the North Ward Educational and Cultural Center, conducting housing, manpower, senior citizen, and youth programs which until 1970 were foreign to the North Ward. He is particularly interested in the problems of the youngsters in the community.

> You know I taught in the Newark school system for many years. I can remember on a number of occasions in the past where a black kid in my class appeared to be dull and slow. Yet outside the classroom, under other circumstances, I found the same student to be alert and bright. The problem was that at that time a black student in the school did not feel at ease. He was not involved, he did not feel he was part of the school. That's what's happening to white students at Barringer.

Although the school is in a predominantly white neighborhood, white students are a minority there. They eat their lunches out in the street or in nearby stores and not in the cafeteria, which is used predominantly by black students. Many are afraid to walk down certain corridors or use the rest rooms for fear of being assaulted or intimidated for their lunch money. Where members from both races are involved, the aggressors are usually black and the victims white. In most cases the white students' fear is genuine and it is unrealistic to think it can be reduced by explaining the deep social and historical reasons behind the hostile behavior of their black classmates. With the advent of black power (which has fostered an ideology of black racism in some areas), racial lines have become even more starkly drawn. A white student at Barringer, bright and sensitive, but with a reputation for being "good with his hands," when asked about his black classmates, exclaimed:

> You can't talk to them because then they start looking for trouble. The only way you can survive there is to become an animal because even if you keep out of their way, they'll provoke you into a fight—they make you an animal! But I don't want to live like an animal . . . I hate them, I hate Barringer, man as soon as I can, I'm going to leave Newark.

A great deal has been written about the crisis of our urban schools, but the response has largely focused upon the travail of the minority student. This is further evidence of a one-dimensional approach to our urban malaise. For the schools most urban working-class white youngsters attend are poor and the dropout rate is high. Among Italian-American youngsters who attend public high schools in Cleveland's Mayfield Murray Hill district, the dropout rate is close to 50 per cent, and in Baltimore's largely Polish-American Highlandtown-Canton area the figure is about one third. Peter Binzen, in his *Whitetown, USA*, has found that in the white ethnic Kensington section of Philadelphia the schools are generally old buildings with meager facilities, unimaginative curricula, and substandard teachers. Students often score as low here in citywide reading and writing exams as they do in the city's black ghetto schools.[27]

In many places students from blue-collar homes are placed in an educational cul-de-sac. Vocational schools serve as mere holding areas for them and rarely provide instruction geared to their vocational needs. Even those with college potential are shunted off to industrial schools or are prematurely pushed out to the job market. Administrators and faculty too often believe that their job is merely to inculcate the students with proper notions about decorum and respect for authority. The sad truth is that educators and professionals in government overseeing educational enrichment programs have ignored the white working-class student.

This explains why the proportion among black and Puerto Rican students going to college in Newark is higher than among white public school students. Adubato's Center has sought to provide white students with assistance in remedial education, counseling, and college financial support which they cannot get through the public educational system. But the Center's programs fall far short of the help they need. Here again, the stated goals of public policy and governmental actions clash; while integration is a goal of our educational policy, the thrust of our public education programs is to foster further racial segregation. Adubato fears that unless something is done about the plight of the white students in Newark, the city's schools will become all black in the near future. From 1971 to 1972 alone black enrollment in the public schools jumped 22.5 per cent.

In addition to the services the Center renders all segments of the community, one of its principal goals is to sensitize mainstream public and private institutions to the legitimate, unmet needs of Newark's white working-class residents. Adubato admits that

> the problems we face you can find throughout the city, and the blacks and Puerto Ricans as a group are worse off than we are. But there appears to be an attempt made to understand the trauma of the blacks in the city. There is no apparent concern at all about the problems of the white residents of Newark. When I listen to what I just said, I know that to people who live elsewhere in white America, my words don't ring true. That's because when you hear the word "white" being used, you automatically relate it to the general white experience in America and that has nothing to do with the problems of the whites in Newark today . . . who are the "new niggers."

Adubato does not dispute racial prejudice among the city's whites, but he argues that "everyone living in the United

States, black and white, has been afflicted by racism." The emotions which Tony Imperiale has so adroitly manipulated derive from a pervasive feeling of powerlessness among Newark's whites; they are not exclusively race-related. By ignoring the legitimate problems of the Italian-Americans in the North Ward, the reformers helped make a Tony Imperiale. "Why is it that college professors and journalists who write sympathetically about the frustration and rage which produce a Rap Brown fail to realize that they also produce a Tony Imperiale?"

Claims that the whites in Newark are discriminated against can be found in all sectors of the white community. Some of the progressive young Italian-American schoolteachers who have gathered around Adubato make a convincing case that if the white groups in Newark had been Irish, Jewish, or Wasp during the 1971 school strike, Trenton would not have washed its hands of the crisis as it did. They also feel that it is unfair to ask them to compensate for generations of white discrimination. Like many other youngsters from working-class families in the industrial North, they attended teachers college to escape from blue-collar life into the professional middle class. But after Gibson's election, white teachers and administrators whose exam scores encouraged them to think about advancement found that less qualified blacks with shorter service were being promoted before they were. They were informed that, since a majority of the city's population was black and Puerto Rican and an even larger percentage of the children in the public schools were minority youngsters, nonwhite teachers and administrators would be given special consideration in promotions. To the whites who were victimized by this policy, this was another example of Italians playing by the rules for years only to discover that when they were on the brink of benefiting from them, they were changed.

Unlike Imperiale, Adubato recognizes that the plight of Newark's residents stems from their lacking the economic resources and political power to influence those interests which control most sectors of American life. And in contrast to Baraka, he contends that the eventual elimination of the problems which afflict the city's black and white residents necessitates a multiracial coalition for change. The struggle between Newark's have-not blacks and have-little whites is not the crux of the city's malaise. "The real problem is that the people who have the power, who are in a position to do something about America's social and economic problems are not committed to bringing about changes which will eliminate poverty, racial discrimination, and urban blight."

E. Setting the Record Straight on White Ethnic Racism: *Catholics of All Backgrounds Are More Supportive of Black Demands for Equality Than Similarly Situated White Protestants*

There is a great deal of evidence disputing the widespread notion that white workers in general and Catholic ethnics in particular are demonstrably more likely to oppose black bids for racial justice than other segments of the white population.

Richard Hamilton has evaluated studies of racial attitudes conducted since the end of the Second World War and has found that outside the South there is no difference between manual and nonmanual Americans on measures of racial tolerance. Below the Mason-Dixon line manual workers are more inclined to be intolerant of blacks than nonmanual Southerners, but if questions regarding racial integration in public schools are stricken from the questionnaire, the difference between the two is statistically insignificant. And in some instances working-class Southerners prove to be more favorably inclined toward black demands for equal opportunity—for example, job equality—than middle-class respondents are.[28] The popular misconception that working-class whites are more inclined to be racists than middle-class Americans then stems in some measure from the propensity to lump together data collected from all parts of the country, and not to take regional differences into account.

Turning to the racial attitudes of Catholic ethnics per se, we also find data that run counter to popular wisdom. On August 19, 1970, the Urban League distributed the following press release:

> According to the Harris Survey conducted for the League, native Americans—white Anglo-Saxon Protes-

tants—rather than so-called "white ethnics" are more likely to: ". . . think blacks are pushing too fast for racial equality; . . . disapprove of the Supreme Court's 1954 school decision; and . . . favor separate schools for blacks and whites."

The late Whitney Young concluded, "The study suggests that some Americans may be projecting their own prejudices to minorities of recent foreign origin."[29] This survey supports Hamilton's findings that Catholics of all backgrounds are more supportive of black demands for equality than are similarly situated white Protestants.[30] But since both the League's poll and Hamilton's data reflect a national sample, it is necessary to focus upon white ethnic and Wasp attitudes on race-related matters which exclude Southern respondents lest we distort the results at the expense of white Protestants outside Dixie.

The University of Chicago's Andrew Greeley has conducted research restricted to Northern whites providing insight into this matter. His findings show that Irish Catholics are more inclined to support black demands for civil rights than Northern Protestants, with Italian Catholics slightly below the Wasps. The Slavic Catholics score the lowest, but the difference between them and the Protestant respondents is less than one half of a percentage point. The picture changes when education is held constant, for the Italians score higher than the Wasps although the Slavic respondents still score slightly below the white Protestants. Of all Catholic groups, however, Italians tend to voice most displeasure about a black family moving into their neighborhood, but they are more inclined to support open housing legislation than native Americans. Looking at the emotional issue of busing, 7 per cent of the Anglo-Saxon respondents favored it and 16 per cent of the Scandinavian Protestants; in contrast, the figure for Irish Catholics is 10 per cent, for Slavic Catholics 9 per cent, and for Italian Catholics 6 per cent.[31] Clearly, white Americans (as well as many blacks) oppose busing by a wide margin and the white ethnic response differs little from that of the population at large. This is especially significant since it is fair to conclude that most Scandinavian Protestants, for example, reside in areas where the black population is small. Finally, among Irish and Italian Catholics there have been more impressive gains in favor of racial integration than among Wasps or Jews, although of all ethnic groups Jews still score highest on Greeley's pro-integration scale.[32]

Keeping in mind that working-class Catholics reside in urban pressure cookers where racial tensions run high, there is no basis for singling them out from the population at large for their racial attitudes. On the contrary, under the circumstances the case can be made that, while middle-class liberals have bolted the city, the white ethnics who still live there hew to a more progressive racial posture than their detractors who reside in one-acre suburban tracts zoned to keep out minorities and working people alike.

To assess black/white ethnic conflict solely in terms of white prejudice is a serious mistake. There are other forces at work which cannot be ignored if we are to gain a balanced view of racial tensions in the North—competition between the two for scarce resources, differences stemming from social class and conflicting cultures, and black racism.

Earlier in this century Irish-Americans competed for jobs, neighborhoods, churches, labor unions, and political organizations with Slavic and Italian immigrants who, as their numbers grew, forced the Irish to reach an accommodation with them. The Irish bitterly resisted encroachments on their prerogatives because, unlike the Wasps they had unseated from political office, alternative opportunities for them were still scarce. Today inner-city white ethnics, especially those lacking economic mobility, are in much the same bind that the Irish once were. It is a mistake, therefore, to interpret their fear about black encroachments on their communities exclusively in terms of racial prejudice, but this view prevails and it is responsible for the adoption of measures calculated to exacerbate strife between have-little whites and have-not blacks. Take racial quotas; to cosmopolitan reformers they make a lot of sense—after all they are a simple way to redress centuries-old black grievances. Equity is not enough; minority Americans must be given a helping hand, and, yes, at our expense if need be. The problem with this observation is that the people who make it generally do not have to worry that quotas will threaten their jobs or promotions.

Nathan Glazer, commenting on the resistance of lower-middle-class New York Jewish teachers to special treatment for their black colleagues in the late 1960s, has observed:

> Wealthy Jews who lived on the East Side of New York and sent their children to private schools and never dreamed of having their children become school teachers were quite happy to give up the positions of teachers in the public schools to blacks. Poor working-class Jews in Brooklyn who hoped their children would become teachers were by no means so happy to graciously surrender these posts.[33]

The Jewish schoolteachers, like their Italian counterparts across the Hudson, have been asked to bear a load which few affluent Americans need carry.

Society must devote special attention to the needs of the poor, the elderly, the disadvantaged, and those who are unable to care for themselves or who have been denied opportunities available to the rest of us. But many forms of racial quotas place the burden on working Americans who, when they object, are singled out as being responsible for minority group deprivation. What is most reprehensible about the quota system is that it penalizes the workingman and lets privileged members of our society off scot-free. As with any other system of resource redistribution, the cost must be determined on the basis of the ability to pay.

It is noteworthy that corporate spokesmen, through organizations like the Urban Coalition, have endorsed the presupposition that racism is responsible for the plight of most nonwhite Americans, because to blame everyone is to blame no one; thus concrete solutions to racial and economic injustice—a more equitable distribution of our national wealth and a restructuring of our political institutions—escape the attention they deserve. As Bayard Rustin has observed, the solution to racial conflict is not a matter of taking a white man's job and giving it to a black, but of providing jobs, housing, educational opportunities, etc. for both. This means fundamental reforms of our political system and economic institutions.

A second aspect of black-European ethnic conflict which has been overlooked involves a clash of two life-styles, shaped in large part by social class and culture. Black novelists like Ralph Ellison, James Baldwin, and Claude Brown have written eloquently about the plight of rural blacks who migrated North during and after World War II in search of jobs and a new life of dignity, only to discover an even more hideous form of deprivation at their journey's end. The delicate institutional and social controls prevailing in the rural South were shattered in the Northern ghettos, where poverty and the hidden scars of racial prejudice fostered a street culture of violence. Poor people the world over, stripped of the psychological mechanisms enabling them to cope with poverty, are inclined to seek escape from despair through drugs and alcohol and to engage in criminal activities to obtain material things. At the same time, the moral standards of the poor and the cosmopolitan black middle class often conflict with the more puritanical mores of the upwardly mobile white working class.

From the perspective of the Polish resident of the Northwest Side of Chicago who lives in close proximity to an expanding black ghetto, the Italian truck driver who delivers Coca-Cola in the all-black Central Ward of Newark, and the Jewish storekeeper who sells produce in the Bedford-Stuyvesant section of Brooklyn, the black people they come into contact with violate those values they cherish—tightly knit families, a fastidious observance of community mores, hard work, and deference to authority. What they perceive as "black values" are often the product of poverty, racial discrimination, ignorance, and social dislocations common among uprooted people. Were the individuals who cling to these same values to be white, the reaction would be much the same; this is evident in Cleveland and other cities where poor Southern whites constitute the newest source of urban immigration. In this connection, by overwhelming percentages, the white ethnics have no problem living on the same block with blacks of the *same class*. A mere 8 per cent of the Irish object to blacks of the same class living on their block; they are almost equaled by the Italians, 12 per cent of whom object. Only among the Poles is the figure somewhat higher—20 per cent—but this is almost identical to the Anglo-Saxon sample of 19 per cent objecting. Clearly, it is not the blackness of the newcomers that upsets the Catholic ethnics; it is the perceived differences in socioeconomic status, values, and lifestyles.[34]

Richard Gambino believes conflicting cultures are the basis for black/Italian-American conflict in Newark, New York, and other Northern cities. "It is difficult to think of two groups of Americans whose ways of life differ more."[35] Although the Southern black and Southern Italian's cultures have been marked by centuries of oppression, the similarities between the two are superficial, for while the organizational focus of Italian culture is the family, the community is the keystone to African culture. Upon their arrival in the United States, the Southern Italians set up urban villages which were characterized by tight-knit families whose members adhered to strict codes of behavior. Gambino says that the black street culture is perceived by Italian-Americans as a threat to their family-centered communities.

Their respective views of government, work, and sex also conflict. For example, while the black American looks to the state to ameliorate social deprivation rooted in generations of white racism, to the Italian-American it is a disgrace to accept help from outsiders. And whereas some blacks favor confrontation politics, the Italians tend to abhor political militancy. Gambino contends that while "blacks regard the work ethic as a smoke screen used to hide economic injustice by rationalizing it . . . Italian-Americans regard it as a tried-and-true, inescapable truth." And whereas blacks adhere to a liberal code of sexual behavior, "among lower-middle-class and middle-class whites . . . Italian-Americans have the most conservative attitudes toward sex."[36] Over and above racial prejudice and differences stemming from conflicting interests then, black/Italian-American conflict involves two clashing cultures.

A third facet of interracial conflict in the industrial North which is rarely mentioned by most social critics is black racism. In contrast to the exaggerated fears of white suburbanites pertaining to pent-up black rage, white fear of blacks pervading most Northern cities is not abstract but based on concrete experience. It is dangerous for any person, white or black, to walk the ghetto streets of Newark or Bedford-Stuyvesant, but the enmity whites encounter in these areas is at best ominous. During the 1960s when black militants were nightly threatening the "honkies" and bullet-draped, rifle-toting Black Panthers marched before the TV cameras shouting revolutionary slogans, the harried white residents of most Northern inner-city neighborhoods were frightened by what they saw. The guns the Panthers flashed were not deemed symbolic props of protest but menacing weapons of violence. In assessing their rejection of decent men like Kenneth Gibson and Richard Hatcher at the polls, we should not forget that fear of black violence has burned deeply into the minds of many urban white residents.

The foregoing data clearly demonstrate that the Catholic ethnics and white workers outside the South are no less supportive of black demands for equal opportunity than white suburbanites, and in some cases they demonstrate greater tolerance toward blacks. But since inner-city working-class whites live and work with blacks, they are more likely to find themselves in a situation where they interact with blacks in a stressful environment. And despite the data we have cited, racial tensions still run high in most Northern cities.

The schools continue to be flashpoints for racial conflict and there is reason to believe that heightened racial self-awareness among white and black students will give the lie to the findings of social scientists covering the last quarter century which correlate youth with racial tolerance. This situation may be restricted to integrated school systems in selected areas, but it is nonetheless an ominous prospect. It shatters the wishful thought that as the older generation of Americans born and reared in an earlier, racially intolerant era die, so will racial strife. Overall, Americans are becoming more racially tolerant but it is naïve to assume that racial tensions will subside in the near future.

Turning to the adult population, the economic troubles of the 1970s, causing widespread concern about jobs and economic insecurity, have in many places heightened racial tensions as white and black workers compete for available jobs. And in a tight economic environment, affirmative action measures adopted to compensate for past acts of discrimination represent an additional source of black/white discord. This has been the case in those industries where court rulings or contracts challenge the seniority system, resulting in whites with as much as ten years' seniority being laid off while blacks with only a year in service are retained. To the white workers such practices are unfair and racist. To blame them for past discrimination against minority workers is to engage in a form of guilt by association which is patently unjust. It is no wonder then that there are political implications of existing black/white ethnic conflict. As blacks transform a numerical advantage into political power and take control of a growing number of cities, racial strife is bound to mar urban government and many problems will take on racial configurations; consider, for example, conflict between municipal unions dominated by whites and city halls controlled by blacks. Black mayors whose cities are on the brink of fiscal disaster are not likely to react favorably to wage demands of municipal employees. Following the examples of New York and Newark, black nationalists will portray the struggle for higher wages, fringe benefits, and improved working conditions as just another form of "white exploitation." Meanwhile, demands for greater black employment in the fire, police, and other municipal departments predictably will escalate white fears about job security and advancement determined on the basis of race and not ability or seniority.

Relations between white policemen and ghetto residents are not likely to improve dramatically either; most white youngsters who become policemen are locked into a system which is calculated to traumatize them and the people they are obliged to protect. Under the best of circumstances and even in racially homogeneous cities, policemen who daily face the reality of crime and violence become hardened cynics about their fellow man. We ask our policemen to perform functions which are the province of social agencies and to deal with problems that law enforcement agencies cannot properly treat. When race is injected, a bad situation becomes a desperate one. White cops in our major cities are afraid to enter ghettos because they know the angry, frustrated inhabitants often are not afraid to die and any confrontation, no matter how minor, may well lead to the death of a human being. Many white policemen, in turn, continue to mistreat blacks, giving impetus to black hostility and prompting otherwise responsible white cops to overreact.

As black power becomes a reality in cities across the land, white residents will become vocal exponents of community control. Soon after Richard Hatcher was elected mayor of Gary, whites in Glen Park organized to disannex from the city. White parents in Newark's Vailsburg have organized community support for the construction of a new high school to be located in the heart of Vailsburg farther from the ghettos than the present high school is. The school issue will continue to foster racial confrontations and, should the parochial school system collapse, this may heighten racial tensions; it will certainly give new impetus to a white exodus to the suburbs. The Office of Education has reported an 8.1 per cent drop in parochial school enrollment from 1961 to 1971, 17 per cent in the grade schools; this is at a time when public school enrollment grew by 22.3 per cent.[37] The closing of parochial schools and the subsequent exodus of whites will have serious repercussions for the people who remain behind and for the entire metropolitan area. The white ethnic enclaves have served as anchor points, checking the flight of white residents and businesses to the suburbs. Frequently they function as moats separating poor blacks and Puerto Ricans from middle-class residential communities. When they begin to dissolve, middle-class residents, finding that the working-class buffer zones no longer keep the poor at a "safe distance," pack their bags for the suburbs. This precipitous white exodus always creates a climate of panic; henceforth even generously funded public and private efforts fail to slow the lemming-like migration.

The economic consequences of white outmigration have been grim, and black separatists who await the day when their "brothers and sisters" gain control of City Hall have blithely ignored them. Federal revenue-sharing funds will help somewhat, although the allotments presently are inadequate and the money earmarked to "pass through" to the cities is subject to being hijacked. As de facto Apartheid becomes a reality, whites residing outside the predominantly black urban core are going to resist supporting expensive "urban programs" or favoring measures to alleviate the fiscal problems of the cities. They will fight state grants-in-aid and the passage of enabling legislation expanding the taxing powers of urban governments —for example, legislation empowering cities to tax commuters who enjoy city services but do not pay for them. Barring a multiracial coalition for change, it is inconceivable that society will adopt the measures needed to care for the disadvantaged persons who are congregating in our cities.

Although a black/white ethnic rapprochement in cities like Newark is not likely in the near future, there are some positive, though modest, signs that both groups might be ready for détente. Steve Adubato believes the days of the black "militant" and overt white "backlash" candidate in Newark are numbered. Imperiale still has widespread white support in his senatorial district, but there are few observers who believe he can obtain a more powerful political office. It is noteworthy that in his last unsuccessful bid against Ken Gibson, Imperiale tried hard to win the support of black voters and he himself has said that a candidate running on a racial platform alone cannot expect to be elected.

The prospects of Baraka and other nationalists do not look too promising either. Here a historical parallel leaps to mind, for the black nationalists remind one of the immigrant radicals earlier in the century who failed to secure protracted mass support for their activities because they adopted a political style and program which did not focus on the immediate needs of their people or take into account the political realities of the United States. Black community organizers in many ghetto areas have reported that soapbox orators who "beat up on whitey" can no longer attract large crowds. Most inner-city blacks are still angry, frustrated, or despondent because progress has been slow in coming, but it is apparent that demagogues who manipulated black rage in the 1960s have lost their appeal; their rhetoric has become stale and their inability to develop viable political organizations and to wield real power has caused blacks to turn their backs on them.

Race will continue to figure in the voting preferences of white (and black) voters in cities where blacks are politically ascendant, but white voters have begun to realize that they must reach an accommodation with black mayors and city councilmen. Furthermore, it is a mistake to assess white ethnic acceptance of black candidates by generalizing from troubled cities like Newark, Gary, and Cleveland, for elsewhere they have shown they will vote for blacks if they are not perceived as "militants" or hostile toward the white community. Basil Paterson in New York and Edward Brooke in Massachusetts have both done well among the white ethnic electorate in their states.

Black candidates in turn have begun to acknowledge that it is political suicide to turn their backs on white constituents who may no longer possess sufficient votes to elect a white man, but who wield votes enough to help end the career of an insensitive black politician. Of larger importance, it has become apparent to inner-city residents of both races that the color of the mayor's skin does not change the harsh realities of urban life. We may be talking about a minority, but it has begun to dawn upon a growing number of Americans that racial conflict is often a symptom of other, more pervasive problems.

Turning to the national political implications of black/ white ethnic strife, there is no question that its persistence poses a threat to the future of the Democratic Party. Conversely, it represents an opportunity the GOP is prepared to exploit. Conservative strategists believe they can attract white ethnic voters by opposing welfare and "expensive do-gooder" programs paid for out of the pockets of working people, small homeowners, and other persons of modest means. The GOP's opposition to busing is another race-related issue which Republicans hope to capitalize on in their quest for white votes.

The Democrats in turn are banking on the GOP's mishandling of the economy to serve as a counterforce to the Republicans' manipulation of race to gain votes. While labor leaders continue to voice concern about racial conflict among the rank and file, some have reported that white and black workers have begun to recognize they are in the same boat, sharing a multitude of problems. Racial fears and hostilities are still there, but inflation, the housing shortage, and other economic issues have begun to overshadow them. During the Depression white workers overcame their ethnic differences to build the CIO; perhaps our present economic malaise will help facilitate greater interracial cooperation among low income black and white ethnic Americans. This will not happen unless leaders in both communities commit themselves to this goal, but the common bond of "hard times" may foster opportunities for interracial cooperation which did not exist a decade ago.

It is difficult to determine the impact recession will have on race relations. It is probably true, however, that, whereas an economic decline that is relatively short in duration but long enough to create racial competition for jobs may hurt the Democrats, a protracted economic crisis that occurs under a Republican Administration will hurt the GOP. In the latter instance it can be presumed that the economic issue will become the overriding one, as was the case during the Great Depression, and other issues will decline in the minds of the worried electorate.

In the final analysis the Democrats will have something to do with whether or not the Republicans maximize their use of race to attract white ethnic votes. The propensity of New Politics Democrats, in particular, to treat our urban ills and related problems principally in terms of black deprivation and to assess racial strife primarily from the black perspective has been a serious mistake. Henceforth, the Democrats must demonstrate greater sensitivity toward the plight of white urbanites, and suburbanites facing similar problems, and develop a more balanced approach to black/white ethnic conflict.

In some places such conflict may prompt disgruntled whites to realign with the GOP or vote for conservative candidates. But an even more likely prospect is that in racially troubled cities white voters will deny black candidates most of their votes while continuing to vote for other Democratic candidates. At any rate, because of traditional voting loyalties and deep concern about other issues, the Republicans are sadly mistaken if they think they can turn the white ethnics away from the Democrats solely by manipulating racial fears.

CHAPTER VII

The Limits of the Old Politics

A. The Persistence of the White Ethnic Political Culture: *At One Time Functional to the Needs of the Immigrants and Their Children, It Has Stunted the Political Development of Succeeding Generations*

Contrary to conventional wisdom, political machines are by no means dead; there's Richard Daley's organization in Chicago, Joseph Crangle's in Buffalo, and Meade Esposito's in Brooklyn, to name only those which are best known. In other cities lesser known ward heelers dominate the politics of entire cities, congressional districts, and counties. Granted, political machines have declined in number and few rule with the confidence they once did; nevertheless the stark truth is that machine politics is very much alive. This is especially true of white ethnic communities, where "boss rule" and "patronage politics" define the style and substance of political activity, contributing to the inability of Poles in Chicago or Italians in New York to preserve their neighborhoods and to secure a fair share of public funds and services.

The failure of many unions to come to grips with workers' grievances can be traced to the limitations of a business unionist ethos not dissimilar to machine politics; for it discourages rank and file participation in union affairs and subscribes to a restricted view of the labor movement. Machine politics and business unionism have a great deal in common since they are offspring of a political culture formed generations ago when most of its members were immigrants and blue-collar workers. At one time functional to their needs, this culture has stunted the political development of succeeding generations.

1. Machine Politics: *The Very Parochialism and Bureaucracy That Enabled (the Irish) to Succeed in Politics Prevented Them from Doing Much with Government,* Daniel P. Moynihan

The ethnic machine politician today is the contemporary equivalent of the hard-driving, autocratic patrone and, like his predecessor, he rules by manipulation, intimidation, deceit, and guile. His authority is legitimized by dint of his will, physical courage, and political acumen, not necessarily by the rule of law, the consensus of his constituents, or by virtue of his sensitivity to their concerns. Because political power is a surrogate source of economic advancement or social status, he treads carefully lest he take a misstep and jeopardize his control over the organization. Since his rule is personal, loyalty takes precedence over ability; his influence is largely limited to a network of loyalists and their number depends on the patronage he can deliver. He is reluctant to engage in activities beyond the network of his loyal cronies or to enter into alliances with "outsiders." Since he uses power for the organization's self-aggrandizement and not to make fundamental social changes, coalition-building is not a critical part of his existence.

The ordinary citizen living in a machine-run city perceives political authority in terms of personal power. Strong men manipulate the political process to promote their own welfare. Because criminal elements have traditionally enjoyed intimate relations with urban machines, many white ethnic voters believe their politicians are linked to organized crime. Substantively this is less true today than thirty years ago, but the press frequently links the names of judges, councilmen, mayors, state representatives, and even United States congressmen to organized crime in areas where it flourishes. This is especially true of the New York metropolitan area, where the voters have noted that public officials who earn relatively modest salaries often live lavishly. The notion that abstract, universalistic criteria determine public policy is alien to the constituents of most machine politicians. Peter Bridge, a New Jersey journalist, claims that white ethnic voters in his state customarily oppose school bonds and other forms of government spending because they are convinced that many government programs represent the distribution of honest graft. What Harvard professors have deemed proof of selfish contempt for the public interest is one of the few ways the voter can demonstrate his displeasure with government.[1]

Given their reputation for being "crooked," politicians, whatever their labels, are distrusted. According to Michael Pesce, an Italian-born state assemblyman who led a reform movement against the James Magnano machine in South Brooklyn, middle-class reformers rarely do well in blue-collar ethnic districts because "their 'throw the rascal out' approach hardly appeals to" voters whose "historical experience is that rascals replace rascals and better our old 'padrone' whose corruption is at least a known quantity."[2]

For generations machine politicians have manipulated ethnic prejudices to achieve electoral victory; in the process they have divided working-class voters, denying them the opportunity to wield power collectively to achieve substantive political goals. Even today Irish and Italian politicos Jew-bait reformers who threaten their turf and Jewish politicians manipulate their constituents' fear of anti-Semitism to defeat "outsiders." Moreover, black politicians often secure black and white liberal votes by portraying white opponents as racists. White ethnic politicians complained during Carl Stokes's Administration that the mayor frequently deflected well deserved criticism of his Administration by spreading the word that he could not do anything about Cleveland's problems as long as "white racists" dominated the city council.[3]

Machine politics has caused many white ethnic voters to turn their backs on politics as a means to deal with their problems; it has undermined faith in collective action and has discouraged forward-looking people from running for public office. This applies to white ethnics living in middle-class communities and blue-collar suburbs, not only to those who still reside in old inner-city neighborhoods. Values and beliefs shaped during an earlier era, in a different social and geographical setting, explain why many Italian- and Polish-

Americans who fled the old neighborhood ten or twenty years ago still teach their children that "you can't fight City Hall or trust politicians and it is foolish to think you can."

Since political machines have played a critical role in the immigrants' economic and political advancement, some commentators use the terms machine politics and ethnic politics as synonyms, assuming that their goals are similar. They're not. If ethnic politics is to have any meaning, the ethnic group's welfare must be the political leaders' primary concern. Yet soon after the Jewish, Italian, and Polish politicians were integrated into the machine, most of them adhered to the precept that the welfare of the party took priority over the needs of the ethnic community. Many members of the community benefited from the jobs, city contracts, and favors which the ethnic politicians doled out, but the recipients of such rewards represented only a small number of people. Political enterprises jeopardizing the machine's ability to distribute patronage and money were rejected even if they were vital to the community. Housing, health, and employment needs were ignored, deemed beyond the purview of politics, or labeled dangerous because they involved confrontation with powerful economic interests. Such confrontations were politically foolish and economically unrewarding since the business community was the source of campaign funds, political payoffs, and honest graft which enriched the boys at City Hall. Later, after the ethnic politicians acquired interests in a host of different commercial enterprises, the relationship between business and government became even more intimate. Henceforth what was mislabeled ethnic politics involved the manipulation of ethnic ties and prejudices to elect candidates who used their power to distribute patronage to a favored few. The rest of the community had to settle for "symbolic rewards"—the appointment of an Italian to a municipal judicial post or the selection of a Pole as a city clerk or some other innocuous reward. Victims of self-hate, the second generation, in particular, meekly accepted the crumbs of "recognition" politics; today it takes the form of candidates having their pictures taken munching on a slice of pizza, a kielbasa sandwich, or a potato knish. But these harmless displays of recognition politics mask a grim truth:

> By shaping political competition so that voters' expectations center on recognition, ethnic strategies divert working-class political expectations away from substantive policy questions. If the political demands of a worker who happens to be of Italian descent are satisfied by putting an Italian on the ticket or by building a statue of Columbus, why should a party try to win his votes by promising better schools?[4]

At best the notion that the ethnic machine politicians take care of their people is a half-truth. Indeed, in many places they have adopted policies leading to the destruction of working-class neighborhoods. Perhaps Chicago is the best-run major city in the United States; nonetheless Daley has sacrificed many residential communities as a price for "rebuilding" the city. Urban development means money and many ward heelers in Chicago have gained wealth through the manipulation of public works programs; therefore neighborhoods like the one Mayor Daley brags about living in are rapidly becoming part of the city's history. The performance of ethnic politicians on the East Coast is not any better. During the Lindsay Administration regular Democrats vilified the "limousine liberals" for their indifference to New Yorkers who resided in neighborhoods outside Manhattan. But when the residents of the Northside of Brooklyn watched grief-stricken as their homes were flattened, the regular politicians were nowhere to be found. And, according to a Corona housewife, when her neighborhood was threatened by condemnation in the mid-1960s, she went to the local political club where she had been a bloc captain for twenty years. She was told there was nothing that could be done. In desperation she tried the largest church in the area and was informed that they could not help her either. "I realized," she said, "that after all those years in the political club, I didn't know anything about politics."[5] The most helpful advice she received was from a black neighbor's son who suggested several community action strategies. If it had not been for the intervention of a young law-

yer, Mario Cuomo—who at that time was not involved in politics—the residents of Corona would have been forced to leave
their neighborhood.

Ethnic machine politicians must also take much of the
blame for the exclusion of urban white working-class communities from public and private programs designed to salvage
"urban America." When Washington first began to pump
money into poverty and urban programs in the late 1960s,
many white ethnic politicians viewed it in terms of "black patronage" or as a means to keep the ghettos cool during the
long hot summers. Others, who were worried about the political implications of "organizing the poor," opposed them, and
still others ignored social and community programs because
the old lucrative sources of patronage kept them busy.

It is against this backdrop of patronage politics—favoring
the few at the expense of the many—that the reputed bread
and butter liberalism of the machine politicians must be
judged. Granted, some of them have demonstrated a real commitment to the needs of their people, but others became supporters of the welfare state because they saw that it did not
entail widespread political participation, cost them money, or
deny them the privileges of power.

The political morality of the men who have dominated the
politics of working-class white ethnic communities for most of
this century is not the principal subject of this inquiry. A far
more important consideration is the lingering influence of a
political culture which denies working people the opportunity
to use their political power more effectively. Over a decade ago
Daniel Patrick Moynihan made a revealing statement on this
score; it still has meaning today:

> The Irish (in New York City in the last quarter of the
> nineteenth and first half of the twentieth centuries) were
> immensely successful in politics. They ran the city. But
> the very parochialism and bureaucracy that enabled them
> to succeed in politics prevented them from doing much
> with government . . . They never thought of politics as
> an instrument of social change . . . their kind of politics
> involved the processes of a society that was not chang-
> ing.[6]

2. Business Unionism: *Any Self-Respecting Union Will Defend Your Right to Denounce the President of the United States. But Criticize Your Business Agent and It's at Your Own Risk,* H. W. Benson

In the last thirty years the white ethnics have entered the middle class in growing numbers. Today, the Jews are predominantly middle-class; they enjoy higher levels of education, income, and professional status than other Americans. The Irish are the most successful Catholic ethnic group, but there has been a profound increase in educational levels, income, and occupational status among all Catholic ethnic groups. The Lithuanians have demonstrated a unique ability to move rapidly from the working class into the middle class in the span of a generation. Italian-American median income is higher than that of the American population, and a larger number of Catholics hold white-collar jobs than Protestant Americans.

Nonetheless, a majority of Eastern and Southern European Catholics remain in the working class. The Poles have almost one year less education than the national average, and the Slavs a half-year. Only 17 per cent of Italians 25 years and older have earned college degrees compared to 52.2 per cent for Russian Jews, 13.9 per cent for Irish Catholics, and 5.3 per cent for Hispanic-Americans. Among the Poles, 5 per cent have earned college degrees. In New York City, where the largest congregation of Italians in the United States resides, only 5 per cent of those who are native-born have graduated from college. These educational disadvantages, however, are not translated into income disadvantages; for while Jews and Irish and German Catholics have the highest ethnic incomes, the Italian, Polish, and French Catholics are all above the national average. In fact, the Poles and Italians have higher incomes than any Protestant group except the British. From the 1950s to the 1960s there was a huge shift into the managerial and professional levels among German, Irish, and Italian Catholics, though not among the Poles. The stereotype of the blue-collar ethnic still holds true for those over forty, where the Poles and Italians are both 10 per cent below the national mean for white-collar jobs. For those under forty though, the figures are vastly different; in that group the Poles are only 2 per cent below the national average and the Italians 4 per cent. Still, according to the Census Bureau, about two-thirds of all Italian- and Polish-Americans hold blue-collar jobs. Notwithstanding the significant gains the Italians and Poles have made in recent years, a majority of them still belong to the working class.

However, unlike their parents and grandparents, they have reached the higher rungs of the industrial work force. This conclusion is supported by the fact that they are more likely to be employed in highly unionized industries than other American workers. While approximately 25 per cent of the non-agricultural labor force is unionized, an estimated four out of every ten Polish- and Italian-American workers belong to unions.[7] The Irish and Jews continue to be well situated in labor's hierarchy—George Meany and Frank Fitzsimmons or Jerry Wurf and Albert Shanker, for example—but Italians and East Europeans also are highly visible in craft and industrial labor organizations as presidents of local, city, state, and international unions; many are full-time union professionals and countless numbers of them are business agents and shop stewards. In a very significant way the labor movement is more closely associated with the white ethnics than any other major institution in the United States.

Union membership is critically important to the worker's political sophistication; electoral studies and attitudinal surveys bear this out. It enables working people to secure pertinent political information, to evaluate issues in terms of self-interest, and to develop skills necessary for effective participation in electoral politics—conducting meetings, distributing campaign literature, manning phone banks, and employing other techniques to "get out the vote." The political education and experiences acquired have made it possible for Teamster and UAW rank and filers and their families to wield influence in primaries and general elections. Polls show that union members and their kin are more inclined than unorganized workers to vote on election day, to cast their ballots for Democratic candidates, and to support progressive legislation. Many working people have successfully run for elective office because they acquired politically relevant skills through their unions. Trade unions, in short, provide pipe fitters and production workers with information and skills that educated Americans derive from a college education, business activities, and membership in professional associations.

The labor union has replaced the political machine as the most important institution serving working-class ethnics, linking them to important centers of political and economic power. In many areas unions have functioned like local party organizations; they advance issues, gather groups behind a specific program, evaluate the performance of public officials, provide relevant political information, and recruit candidates, providing money, manpower, and the organization to elect them. But in spite of the contribution they have made to white ethnic political development, many unions have perpetuated a political ethos marked by paternalism and a restricted view of collective action.

In the early years the CIO instilled workers with a new appreciation for grass-roots democracy and the potential for collective action to eliminate social and economic injustices. But in the aftermath of the Second World War, trade unionists who perceived unions as vehicles for social change were expelled or were relegated to positions of little influence. The Cold War was manipulated by right-wing enemies and conservative labor leaders in much the same fashion that the red scare was exploited to eliminate radical unionists after the First World War, although the number of card-carrying communists in the labor movement was small. This was true of the CIO as well as the AFL; for example, the United Steel Workers, after Philip Murray's death, fell into the hands of David McDonald, one of the crassest business unionists in the labor movement. Because men like McDonald secured power in other industrial unions, while many CIO affiliates suffered membership losses, Walter Reuther was forced to federate with the craft-dominated AFL on George Meany's terms. In contrast to the CIO president, Meany believed the Federation had no right to interfere with the internal operations of unions affiliated with the Federation, much less bother itself with the internal affairs of those outside the AFL-CIO.

Because of this precept, men were thrust into leadership positions who used their offices to enrich themselves at the expense of their members. The United Mine Workers Union,
one of the oldest industrial unions in the United States, was
until several years ago an instructive though exaggerated example of a union dominated by such leadership. What is
critically important about the UMW is that the gangster
regime of Tony Boyle was an inevitable outcome of the persistence of boss rule which characterized John L. Lewis's stew-
ardship of the union for close to half a century.

On December 30, 1969, three men, under cover of dark-
ness, entered a small town on the outskirts of Pittsburgh, drove
up to a house they had previously cased, broke into it and shot
its three occupants to death—Jock Yablonski, his wife, and
their daughter. The Yablonskis were murdered at the direction of W. A. "Tony" Boyle, the president of the United
Mine Workers of America. Boyle had been the head of a
UMW local in Montana before John L. Lewis brought him to
Washington in 1947 to serve as his administrative assistant.
After Lewis retired, Boyle functioned as the power behind the
throne of ailing Tom Kennedy, who replaced Lewis in 1960,
serving in that capacity until Kennedy died in 1963. That year
Boyle took office and, with a boldness which left many of his
colleagues breathless, he led a raid on the union's treasury,
callously turned his back on the union's rank and file, and
played ball with the mineowners, making himself and his
friends very wealthy men.

The kickbacks to which UMW leaders were privy alone
were a comfortable source of income. In a six-year period the
union spent $200,000 for pictures of its leaders. During the
1964 national convention, the cost of the several bands hired
to serenade the delegates amounted to over $300,000.[8] Boyle's
brother was appointed president of UMW Local 27 in Montana and his daughter Antoinette served as a counsel for the
union there; she earned an annual salary of $40,000 which was
as much as the union's general counsel in Washington made.
Boyle and his secretary-treasurer transferred $650,000 of the
union's treasury into a special account to finance their lifelong
pensions. Millions of dollars were deposited in a checking ac-

count—accruing not a penny of interest—in a Washington, D.C., bank owned by the UMW.

At the time Boyle became president, paid vacations were not yet a part of the mineworkers' contract; miners afflicted by black lung were not being compensated. Boyle did not press for safer mines; and any miner who questioned his administration was in real danger of losing his life for his trouble. For years Jock Yablonski, the head of the union's District 5 local in Pittsburgh and director of the union's political action arm—Labor's Non-Partisan League—had enjoyed a good salary, a generous expense account, and job security, turning his back on the corruption which made all these things possible. But in the mid-1960s, conscience-struck by the horrible truth that the union which had been so good to him was in the deathgrip of a gangster administration, he had a change of heart. So in 1969, with the assistance of Joseph Rauh, a liberal Washington, D.C., lawyer, and the grass-roots help of the dissident Miners for Democracy, he sought to oust Boyle from the UMW presidency.

Boyle's cronies strove to keep Yablonski's name off the ticket by rigging local elections, assaulting Yablonski's campaign workers, and intimidating miners in local delegate selection elections. But the miners had become so fed up with Boyle they overcame their fear of his goons and placed Yablonski on the ticket. Boyle then proceeded to adopt tactics he had employed in the past to maintain his tight hold over the union. He bribed important union leaders with high-paying posts; he lent locals favoring him money and denied it to those who supported Yablonski; and labor officials were paid exorbitant fees for undertaking nonexistent union duties. To insure victory, Boyle's cronies stuffed ballot boxes and used force to scare away Yablonski voters. With so much going for him, Boyle easily won the election.

Rauh had petitioned the Labor Department to intervene to guarantee an honest election. After Boyle won, Rauh demanded that the Department declare the election null and void. He was ignored. Yablonski stated publicly that he would be killed for challenging Boyle. And it was only after he lost his life that the Labor Department intervened and subsequently declared the election null and void due to flagrant and gross election violations. In a happy coda to an otherwise tragic drama, Arnold Miller defeated Boyle in 1973 and for the first time in almost a half century the men who risk their lives to extract coal from the bowels of the earth breathe the sweet air of union democracy once again.

The corruption, nepotism, and autocracy which marked Boyle's reign was the logical conclusion of the legacy John L. Lewis left upon retiring. Lewis was a giant; he was without question the most important labor leader in American history. He not only resurrected the UMW, he was the pivotal force in organizing the CIO. Under his tutelage labor leaders and organizers spearheaded industrial unionism in the steel, textile, auto, and rubber industries. Unfortunately, many of the men he tutored adopted the pattern of leadership Lewis had institutionalized in the UMW. He was intolerant of dissent, judged his colleagues on the sole basis of their loyalty to him, practiced nepotism, and ignored grass-roots participation in union affairs. Joe Finley, in *The Corrupt Kingdom*, writes that Boyle

> . . . knew how John L. Lewis had dominated the organi-
> zation, how the decisions of Lewis were never to be ques-
> tioned; how virtually every officer and representative, ex-
> cept for the isolated few who were elected, owed his job
> to the president; how the membership was accustomed to
> adulation of its leader . . .

Boyle also noted with satisfaction the "controls, the checks and balances, the restraints of rules and law that men have learned to place over their institutions were simply absent."[9]

The evolution of the UMW under Lewis's leadership was shaped by a hostile political climate, an industry dominated by ruthless mineowners, and a rank and file fragmented by race, ethnicity, and religion. At a time when labor leaders lived in a violent world, physical courage was a prerequisite to labor leadership. Only courageous men prepared to face up to club-swinging policemen or company goons could maintain their office. They, in turn, relied upon lieutenants whose physical courage took priority over the ability to write clear prose or to keep the union's books. It took strong men whose leadership was unquestioned to lead the hardy souls who joined labor unions at a time when one had to have a great deal of guts to do so. Men like Jimmy Hoffa, who were as quick to use their fists as their brains, possessed the necessary prerequisites for leadership. When it became necessary for labor unions to hire thugs of their own to protect themselves against those who were in the employ of management, criminal elements gained access to labor unions.

In addition to the American value system, which celebrates materialism and measures self-worth in terms of money, labor historians cite the above-mentioned factors to explain how boss rule, nepotism, and the use of union office for private gain became such important features of American trade unionism. Like urban political machines, labor unions adapted to the prevailing value system and social, economic, and political realities of American society. So today, there are many labor leaders, men—neither evil nor insensitive to the needs of their members—who cling to a restricted view of labor unions which evolved during an earlier era in our history. Consider in this respect the labor philosophy of George Meany, who has said, "The one word that best describes the day-to-day operations of the labor movement is 'practical.' We avoid preconceived notions, and we do not try to fit our program into some theoretical, all-embracing structure."[10]

Following the logic of his pragmatism, Meany was among the first AFL leaders to scrap Gompers' outmoded principle that unions should remain aloof from politics. Today, contrary to conventional wisdom, the AFL-CIO does not function only like an economic interest group, but also like a major faction of the Democratic Party—in a fashion similar to the role European unions play in socialist parties. The association is less formal in the United States than in Europe, but labor leaders hold important policy-making posts in the Democratic Party and the only national electoral network the Democratic Party has (at least until 1972) is comprised of unions. Labor's contribution to the electoral fortunes of liberal Democrats is common knowledge. According to Theodore White, in his narrative of the 1968 Presidential election:

The dimension of the AFL/CIO effort, unprecedented
in American history, can be caught only by its final sum-
mary figures; the ultimate registration, by labor's efforts,
of 4.6 million voters; the printing and distribution of 55
million pamphlets and leaflets out of Washington and 60
million more from local unions; telephone banks in 638
localities using 8,500 telephones, manned by 24,611
union men and women and their families; some 72,225
house-to-house canvassers; and, on election day, 94,457
volunteers serving as car-poolers, materials-distributers,
baby-sitters, poll-watchers, telephoners.[11]

In areas of the country where conservative business interests
monopolize politics, unions are often the only political force
around which progressives can rally and compete for public
office. The labor movement has supported progressive legislation contributing to the welfare of all needy Americans and
not just trade unionists; medicare, aid to education, civil rights
laws, reapportionment, and many other laws have been enacted because labor spearheaded campaigns in their behalf.

This record represents a marked departure from Gompers'
rigid business unionist philosophy; nonetheless George Meany
has run the AFL-CIO much like Gompers presided over the
AFL. Meany believes in top-down decision-making; he is not
comfortable with people who openly challenge his policies.
Nelson Cruikshank, a long-time friend and colleague, has observed, ". . . Mr. Meany doesn't know there is such a thing as
a staff meeting, where there's give and take and an exchange
of ideas. It isn't the way he was brought up."[12] Few of
Meany's critics accuse him of being dishonest and there is no
evidence that he is opposed to union democracy by conviction,
but he has not employed his considerable power and influence
to challenge union leaders who violate it either. The AFL-
CIO expelled the Teamsters when the exploits of Dave Beck
and Jimmy Hoffa became public knowledge. Meany led the
fight to oust the racketeers from the infamous International
Longshoremen's Association in the early 1950s but the Federation was silent in 1965 when Dow Wilson and Lloyd Green,
two reformers in the AFL-CIO-affiliated Painters Union, were
murdered. And when the Miners for Democracy asked him for

help in their struggle with Boyle, they were turned away. Meany contends that it is the government's and the law enforcement agencies' job to prosecute "labor racketeers." Bankers and industrialists are not held responsible for their colleagues who commit criminal acts—why should labor unions be asked to police their house?

Although he is not a racist, Meany has defended the Federation against charges that certain unions have discriminated against blacks by citing the doctrine of union autonomy; that is, as long as the affiliated unions observe the by-laws of the Federation, it has no power over their operations. During the 1972 Presidential race, however, when he sought to punish the AFL-CIO in Colorado for its support of McGovern, Meany demonstrated that he does not always adhere to this principle. The concept of union autonomy was a guiding tenet of the AFL at the turn of the century when conservatives in the Federation opposed socialist claims that unions were meant to operate as social movements in the interests of all workers whether or not they belonged to unions. The persistence of this philosophy is the basis for the contradiction that, while most business unionists are honest and concerned about their members, they feel under no obligation to assist unorganized workers or those who are being exploited or are denied their rights by autocratic union officials.

In their defense, it should be stressed that bureaucracy is a necessary evil of any large institution; that collective bargaining is a delicate art involving complex and highly technical subjects beyond the grasp of ordinary workers; that dissidents seeking to unseat incumbents are at a disadvantage; and that all of these things are true of other public and private institutions. Finally, the labor leadership is often far more progressive than the membership and some of the causes the leaders champion, like civil rights, might not receive the same level of support from the rank and file where grass-roots democracy is more widely practiced.

H. W. Benson, a crusader for union democracy, responding to such observations, has written: ". . . the labor movement is the most effective single force for liberalism (in our society). It can exist only in a democracy; it utilizes all the mecha-

nisms of democracy; it is almost always on the side of those
who seek progressive social legislation." However,

> . . . the same labor movement that insists so ardently on
> democratic rights for itself and for others in society too
> often denies those same rights to its own membership.
> Any self-respecting union will defend your right to de-
> nounce the President of the United States. But criticize
> your business agent and it's at your own risk![13]

It is sad but true that many labor leaders who reject reactionary claims that the people are "uninformed," "apathetic,"
and "easily swayed" curiously make similar arguments to account for their paternalistic treatment of the rank and file.

Whether or not a worker's union leaders adhere to democratic principles may have a profound impact upon his perception of the political universe. Because many workers have
found that they have as little say in their union as they have in
their government, they have given up on political action as a
means to treat their problems or they have turned to demagogues like George Wallace for help. The frustration which
caused some workers to vote for Wallace in the 1968 election
was not unrelated to the conviction that their unions were not
paying proper attention to them and their problems.

In spite of its defects, the labor movement has played an
important part in the passage of federal legislation reducing
racial, social, and economic inequality. Unions have played
a similar role on the state level. In highly unionized states
neither politicians nor big business callously ignore the plight
of the workingman as is customary in areas of the country
where unions are weak. Thus, health and safety laws, workmen's compensation benefits, and welfare programs are more
generously funded in New Jersey and Rhode Island than in
Virginia and Arizona. Unorganized workers have reaped benefits from labor lobbying just as they have when employers
who wish to keep unions at bay are compelled to match the
pay, wages, working conditions, and benefits which unionized
workers enjoy. It is because the white ethnic worker is dependent upon unions that labor's problems and its failure to
respond adequately to unmet rank and file needs is of special

interest to the people who are the subject of this book. The persistence of an outmoded labor philosophy is responsible for both difficulties.

The American labor movement's problems today can be conveniently separated into four categories: slow growth; jurisdictional disputes; the public's perception of the labor movement; and growing rank and file dissatisfaction.

a) The Problem of Growth

The absolute number of organized workers is the highest in history but the proportion of workers belonging to unions is down. An estimated 24.2 million Americans belong to labor organizations or public and professional employee associations which perform union functions. That is an impressive figure, yet over 60 million working Americans are not organized.[14] Granted that many in this category are unorganizable—doctors, dentists, lawyers, elected officials, small businessmen, managers, and other self-employed persons—but in 1972 26.7 per cent of the nonfarm labor force was unionized while in 1945 the comparable figure was 35.5.[15] The crux of the problem is that expanding industries, occupations, and regions of the country are those where labor unions have been weak or nonexistent.

The blue-collar unions which emerged from the CIO drive are growing slowly, not at all, or are declining in membership. The United Steel Workers of America had 1.3 million members in 1959; since then its growth has been halting, for presently it is home for about 1.4 million workers. Only about one half of its membership works in the steel industry; automation and foreign competition have taken their toll here. The picture is much the same for the UAW which today has approximately 1.4 million members—the industrial membership it had in 1959.

The changing composition of the corporate structure—conglomerates and multinational firms in particular—represents a real threat to the capacity of unions to negotiate with big business. Conglomerates can afford to outwait strikers because they can maintain profit-making activities through their subsidiaries. When a conglomerate's cosmetic affiliate is struck, it can continue to glean earnings from subsidiaries producing bread, bras, or aluminum siding. The strikers have limited savings and union strike funds are slim, so neither can afford to outwait management.

Multinational corporations are a new and ominous threat to trade unions; hovering over them like the sword of Damocles is the fear that management will use the strike or their wage demands as an excuse to shift production abroad. Under these circumstances the workers' jobs and not just their salaries or benefits are at stake. Even large unions like the UAW cannot ignore threats of this kind, but they are uncertain about how to deal with the growing number of companies relocating outside the United States, thereby robbing workers of jobs and unions of dues-paying members. One of the best examples of how the exodus of industry abroad has affected American unions is manifested in the declining membership of the International Electrical, Radio, and Machine Workers Union because General Electric, Motorola, and Singer have built plants abroad.

The craft unions, traditionally the bulwark of the AFL, are also experiencing serious difficulty maintaining their membership. The Bureau of Labor Statistics reports that 45 per cent of the carpenters in America are unionized, while 55 per cent of those in other building crafts belong to unions. These figures represent a much higher percentage than in other industries, but the trend is toward nonunion construction which in Baltimore—a "labor city"—has outpaced jobs performed by union labor. This trend is visible in other parts of the country as well.

Unions, which have functioned effectively among blue-collar workers, have fared poorly in efforts to organize white-collar employees. This is a serious failing because "in 1950 there was one nonproduction 'white collar' employee for every five production workers." In 1972 the ratio was one to three. According to Jerry Wurf, "the numbers tell a story of a labor movement that is not holding its own as the work force swells and reflects the heavy service and professional character of post-industrial society."[16]

Finally, the fastest growing areas of the country are in the South and Southwest where many industries have relocated to escape unions. The business community and power structures in these areas are hostile to labor organizations and they have used their economic and political influence to discourage unionization of their workers. If the labor movement is going to deal with problems which are national in scope, it must organize nationally. But approximately 75 per cent of the labor movement's membership works in the ten largest industrial states. There are more unionized workers in New York State than in the eleven states of the Old Confederacy, including Texas.

In spite of these dismal statistics, the old guard in the AFL-CIO is seemingly unconcerned about organized labor's inability to grow with the labor force. George Meany, in response to this problem, answered: "To me, it doesn't mean a thing. I have no concern about it."[17] Perhaps Meany's response should be taken with a grain of salt since he is not one to admit weaknesses publicly. But it is clear that many business unionists are unconcerned about labor's growth problems because as long as they can maintain their membership and enjoy the prerogatives of union office, the "problem" is someone else's, not theirs.

b) Jurisdictional Disputes

The ability of the labor movement to grow and adapt to a changing economy depends to a large extent upon union solidarity. One of the principal reasons for the 1955 AFL and CIO merger was to eliminate jurisdictional battles costing enormous sums of money and precious man hours. Pirate raids on other union's memberships were not confined to struggles between the opposing labor federations; in a three-year period prior to the merger, AFL affiliates spent $1,685,000 to combat raids from hungry competitors—all of which belonged to the AFL, not the rival CIO. The late Joseph Beirne, president of the Communications Workers of America, said in this connection, "I don't think there's any statistic anybody could compile that would give an actual picture of the time and energy and everything else that's wasted and lost in these jurisdictional fights between unions."[18]

Jurisdictional disputes have prompted bloody pitched battles where hammer-wielding hard hats have dented the skulls of fellow craft unionists, not scabs or strikebreakers. The fail-

ure of these unions to reach an accommodation is a reflection
of a labor philosophy which celebrates a no-holds-barred
contest for dues-paying members. Unions are not human
collectivities to forge cooperation among like-minded people,
but instruments for the self-aggrandizement of the "guild's"
membership. Meany has criticized the Teamsters for engaging
in union-busting because of their battle with Cesar Chavez's
AFL-CIO-affiliated United Farm Workers Union—ignoring
the fact that the Teamsters' action was a logical outcome of a
labor ethos which portrays unions as business organizations
competing for the same "market" and beholden to no one but
their "stockholders."

c) The Public Perception of Labor

A third problem confronting the labor movement is its
public image. The American people favor labor unions in
theory and believe they serve a useful purpose; but their praise
is qualified. In 1961, when a cross section of respondents were
asked whether they approved or disapproved of unions, 70 per
cent said they approved; this held true for all parts of the
country with the exception of the South. But even in Dixie 59
per cent as opposed to 24 per cent said they approved of
unions. In 1967 there was a slight decline in the number of
Americans who said they approved of unions—66 per cent said
so. The percentages for the 1970s on this score are pretty
much the same as they were in the 1960s.[19]

However, the polls show that, while the average American
approves of labor organizations, he believes they are too powerful. The Gallup organization asked a cross section of Americans in 1968: "Which of the following will be the biggest
threat to the United States in the future?" The responses were
as follows:

	All	Republicans	Democrats	Independents
Big Govt.	46%	48%	41%	54%
Big Labor	26%	32%	23%	23%
Big Business	12%	9%	14%	10%
No Opinion	16%	11%	22%	13%

These findings should give labor leaders some pause, especially
since "big unions" are deemed more threatening to the na-

tion's welfare than "big business." There is a growing number of people reporting they fear big business wields too much power in our society, but they have not changed their minds about labor unions either.

Polls demonstrate also that the American people may accept unions per se but they do not approve of their tactics. During the 1967 United Auto Workers strike with Ford Motors, 40 per cent of the American public said they favored the company and 26 per cent the union. Here is additional evidence that the public is more inclined to support big business than organized labor in industrial disputes. In this connection, when asked whether they believe "labor unions are monopolies and should come under antitrust laws," 45 per cent of the American people said they agreed while only 25 per cent disagreed. In 1966, 42 per cent to 49 per cent answered yes and no respectively to the question "Should persons be required to join unions if they work in unionized factories or businesses?" Throughout this period polls indicated that the public perceived union leaders as having the courage of their convictions, of being able to get things done for their members, but also said they were likely to be dishonest, arrogant, domineering, and out for personal gain. In 1966 respondents were asked whether they had confidence in the people running unions; 22 per cent said they had a great deal of confidence, 42 per cent had only some, and 28 per cent had hardly any at all, while 8 per cent were not sure. But five years later the American people indicated growing displeasure with labor leaders, for in 1971 only 14 per cent said they had a great deal of confidence in them and the number who said they had hardly any confidence increased from 28 per cent to 35 per cent.

Labor's tarnished public image is a cause for concern, for its right-wing enemies have used it as a weapon on numerous occasions. The Nixon Administration in its disputes with the labor movement, for example, skillfully manipulated the public's mistrust of union leaders at the expense of organized labor. A revealing incident in this regard occurred in November 1971.

On August 15 of that year, after a time of indecision, the White House had announced the adoption of its New Eco-

nomic Policy. But NEP failed to reduce inflation or
unemployment and Mr. Meany was unhappy with it. Wages
were frozen but not profits, and as prices outpaced the
worker's income, the banks and large corporations were reaping magnificent profits. The détente which characterized
Nixon/Meany relations during much of the President's first
term broke on the anvil of the Administration's adoption
of "Keynesian economics." As Meany's attacks became more
vigorous, the White House hit upon a strategy which would
both place the blame for the Administration's fitful progress
in the war against inflation on the AFL-CIO and massage the
public's fear of "big labor" to discredit George Meany and
thereby take the steam out of his charges that Richard Nixon
was to blame for the nation's economic troubles. The setting
for this counterattack was to be Bal Harbor, Florida, where
the AFL-CIO was to hold its annual convention.

It was customary to invite the President to the annual AFL-
CIO convention, but the White House did not immediately
respond to the tendered invitation. Some Washington savants
wondered whether Nixon would attend; he would not receive
a very warm welcome. His aides assumed that the reception
would be downright hostile—the delegates might boo him, in-
sult him, or respond to his defense of NEP with derisive
laughter. The thin-skinned President did not look upon the
engagement with great anticipation, but his advisers did. They
hoped the AFL-CIO delegates would vocally deride Mr.
Nixon and sent a White House operative, Pasquale Juliano, to
make sure they did just that.

The President received polite applause when he entered the
convention site. Reporters, delegates, and Nixon aides were all
noticeably on edge, anxiously awaiting the confrontation. All
knew that Mr. Nixon's speech was directed at the American
people who would tune in his Bal Harbor appearance that
night via the major networks' news programs, not the audience sitting before him. The President said he was going to
"tell it like it is." Seeking the viewers' sympathy and demonstrating his courage, he said, "Some of my advisers in the
White House" counseled him against the visit because most of
the delegates were not political friends. But he came anyway
because "when the chips are down, organized labor is for

America." Milking the patriotism of the delegates and the rank and file workers who would watch him later in the day, he talked about labor's support for a strong national defense and he voiced his appreciation for its supporting his "hard decisions" on Cambodia "to protect American fighting men." The audience applauded and Mr. Nixon's confidence began to climb, but the mood changed when he defended his economic policies. "Now, I understand there's been some disagreement about (how well the) freeze worked," but "it was a remarkable success . . ." That prompted the audience to ooh and aah in disbelief and as he continued in this vein, the audience grew more restive and broke out in laughter when he said, "And if you don't think so, go home and ask your wives who go to the grocery store."[20]

Upon finishing his speech, Meany thanked him and the President then proceeded to shake hands among the audience, at one point throwing his hands up in his customary greeting to the crowd. A White House cameraman recorded the event as he moved through the throng. George Meany, clearly upset that the whole thing had been staged, finally rapped his gavel and said, "Will the delegates and guests kindly take their seats? We will now proceed with act two." This had an electrifying effect upon the audience, which bolted upright and cheered and applauded Meany for three minutes. Immediately after the President's speech De Van Shumway and Alvin Snyder, aides to Herb Klein who masterminded public relations for the White House, called newspaper editors, friendly columnists, and network chiefs pointing out the discourtesies to the President—the failure of the labor bosses to provide a band to play "Ruffles and Flourishes," the "laughter of the delegates," and "Meany's ill-considered, mean-spirited quips."

Meany won the skirmish of Bal Harbor but Nixon won the public relations campaign by mustering the support of the media and the public. The press roasted Meany for his "rudeness," his "coolness," and his "arrogance," and editorialists peppered the delegates for being "discourteous" and "hostile" toward Nixon and his office. William Saxbe, then a senator from Ohio, said, "George Meany is a crotchety and rude old man"; Senator Barry Goldwater claimed that Meany attempted to "intimidate the President . . . with the force of

union power." Cabinet heads and White House staffers welcomed questions about the "disgraceful incident" at Bal Harbor. Their answers hit similar themes—the "arrogance" of
labor leaders, their "awesome power," their "indifference" to
the nation's welfare, and the implication that due to their
"greed" old folks, poor people, and others living on fixed incomes were severely hurt by an inflation fueled by excessive
wage demands.

Labor's poor public image has not concerned many old
guard leaders because they have done rather well in spite of
attempts by their enemies to undermine the influence of the
labor movement. But their attitude is also another manifestation of a labor philosophy which is static and indifferent to the
possible damage that organized labor will suffer unless it at-
tracts public support for programs which are critical to its future.

d) Rank and File Dissatisfaction

There is growing rank and file dissatisfaction with labor
leadership. Leaving aside complaints about the real decline in
their annual incomes and other monetary grievances, consider
the following noneconomic complaints of workers today. They
testify to the rising expectations of a new generation of
workers that labor leaders cannot ignore.

American management, through massive public relations
programs, has convinced the public that the working conditions and safety standards American workers enjoy are
unrivaled. That's simply not true. Frank Wallick, in his book
The American Worker: An Endangered Species, provides a
seemingly endless series of grim facts about the blue-collar
workplace which obliterates any self-satisfaction we may have
about the safety and health of America's labor force. Wallick
considers "safety" and "health" hazards as two equally dangerous but separate problems. The first, involving unsafe
machines, the danger of crushing accidents, explosions, and
severe burns, is well known but until recently estimates of
such accidents have been grossly underestimated.

Wallick indicates that health hazards have received even
less attention than safety hazards, yet the problem may be
even more detrimental to the worker's welfare. Traditional oc-

cupation-related diseases like black lung continue to cripple and kill hundreds of thousands of coal miners and an estimated 819,000 workers in textile mills are exposed to the hazards of cotton dust, contributing to their being afflicted with "brown lung." In other industries workers suffer eye strain and headaches from poor lighting, the air they breathe is polluted, and noise is excessive as are heat and cold. Many of these hazards are also well known, but the effects they have upon the human body have not been well documented until recently.

In some cases the use of new chemical compounds, radiation, and high speed machinery has made work environments even more dangerous. The subtlety with which some chemical substances attack the body makes them especially ominous. Wallick claims, for example, that there are some 500,000 people directly exposed to beryllium and that it reaches many, many more by an indirect route. Beryllium, an insidious metal, can be stored in a person's bone marrow for as long as fifteen and even twenty years before it suddenly kills him. It can be shaken out of work clothes to expose whole families or can blow from a factory to the surrounding community, implanting its death-dealing particles in those who live or work within approximately a mile radius of the factory. Recent press reports detail similar effects from other chemicals such as vinyl chloride and inorganic arsenic and radiation.

Some technological innovations have increased production at the expense of the workers' health. Respiratory diseases are on the rise today because high speed machinery "pulverize(s) coal and cotton dust into invisible particles that go far deeper into the lungs than dust did during an earlier and simpler technical age."[21] Production line workers like those at Lordstown, Ohio, claim that new technology compels them to build cars at a rapid pace causing greater physical strain and mental anxiety than older assembly lines.

Bob Kassen, a former Teamster who specializes in health and safety hazards, says that labor officialdom has been negligent in calling public attention to these matters and fighting for their elimination. In many instances they have acted only after rank and file complaints became so voluminous and intense that the leadership could no longer ignore them. Tony Massocchi of the Oil, Chemical, and Atomic

Workers Union also criticizes the labor movement for not lobbying for more stringent legislation protecting the worker against health hazards and for not compelling government to enforce laws already on the books. The evidence is plentiful and categorical; organized labor has not fought hard enough to make workplaces safer and healthier for its members.

Lewis Carliner, formerly of the UAW, has identified another kind of grievance about which younger workers are concerned; it might best be described as civil rights on the job. The notion that a man is innocent until proven guilty has been honored in the breach in most firms, but having internalized such "democratic ideas," younger workers are demanding that before they are fired or punished for wrongdoing, management must provide them with the right to defend themselves through procedures which honor the worker's "constitutional rights."[22] Younger workers complain about shift assignments and changes in work procedures ignoring their desires or violating their job descriptions. Prior to the present recession, one of the most volatile issues in the auto industry, prompting wildcat strikes, was forced overtime. And there are growing reports of whites—taking a leaf from the book of black civil rights activists—who have protested being cursed at by foremen or being lashed with ethnic slurs. One Polish-American steelworker brought his foreman to court, claiming that his civil rights had been violated when the foreman called him a Polack. He won!

Young blue-collar workers in particular complain that their unions are not going to bat for them on these issues and others related to job satisfaction. According to Jerry Wurf, older union officials "tend to talk to the workers with a dialogue that was created during the Depression, or created by the generation that immediately followed the Depression and was seriously affected by it." The young worker "doesn't know what the hell we're talking about and has given up trying to understand. He doesn't relate to us and we don't relate to him, and we've got to be very careful about this."[23]

Although the scope of worker discontent is in dispute, it is a mistake to conclude as some liberals and labor leaders have that the "blue-collar blues" is merely fools gold manufactured by old left alchemists who long for the reappearance of a new

militant proletariat. Clearly management and the union hierarchy can expect more energetic rank and file demands for
a say in decisions affecting them in the plant and those which
are made in the union hall. Consider, for example, that wildcat strikes not sanctioned by union officials jumped 50 per
cent in the period 1965–70 and that strikes in the summer
of 1974 forced more workers to the streets than at any time
since the post-World War II era. We should bear in mind
also that only about a quarter of the labor force is organized;
the plight of the unorganized worker is even graver than his
brother who belongs to a union. Were the unorganized worker
given a vehicle to project his discontent, perhaps social critics
would take the blue-collar blues more seriously than many
of them have.

Along with criticism attending neglect of health and safety
issues and other job-rated grievances is anger about labor's indifference to the worker's powerlessness as a consumer and
citizen. The dollar-an-hour raise a worker receives through collective bargaining is often picked from his pocket because as
a consumer he is vulnerable to the monopolistic practices of
large corporations. Because of business-controlled legislatures
and city councils, he may be stuck with shoddy merchandise
or be compelled to keep up mortgages on a house which does
not meet building codes. While the AFL-CIO may fight for
a more equitable tax system in Washington, the failure of
his union to muster its full strength to fight for fairer taxes
on the state or county level may compel him to pay proportionately more taxes than the executives who run his company.
Given the considerable power and resources which many
unions have in the industrial states, labor has the leverage
to fight on behalf of a neighborhood destined to be bulldozed
simply because the residents are working people who lack the
power to fight back. However the United Auto Workers is
one of the few labor organizations which for years has sponsored community action programs to treat such neighborhood
problems.

The sad truth is that in many places labor leaders are affiliated with machine politicians who vigorously oppose organizational activities independent of the machine or union. A
case in point is the reaction of the leadership of the United

Steel Workers local District 31 serving the Chicago-Gary area. In the late 1960s Alinsky-trained organizers put together a federation of neighborhood, church, civic, environmental, and consumer groups (the Calumet Community Congress or CCC) to fight air and water pollution, unjust taxes, and other issues involving them in confrontations with the Lake County Democratic organization and the steel corporations. Officials in District 31, under the leadership of Joe Germano, collaborated with John Krupa, the head of the local Democratic machine to destroy CCC. Community organizers and local residents active in CCC were red-baited and intimidated and steelworkers belonging to the Congress were under heavy pressure to withdraw from it. Some officials in District 31 claimed that they opposed the Congress only because the environmental reforms it advocated threatened its members' jobs. There were, however, more compelling reasons for the union's opposition. Its principal leaders were on friendly terms with Krupa and they perceived attacks against him as representing a challenge to them too. Of larger importance, some CCC leaders asserted that Germano feared that if steelworkers organized an effective community organization, it might one day represent the basis for a challenge to his rule of District 31.[24]

The foregoing lends credence to claims that ethnic machine politicians and "labor bosses" are the principal exponents of the Old Politics, but the fact is that political power is employed to achieve economic advantages at all levels of our political system, in all regions of the country, among all segments of society. It is the American way. To imply, as generations of social scientists have, that the white ethnics adhere to a private-regarding political ethos which conflicts with that of the rest of American society is simply not true. Mention already has been made of those features of the white ethnic political culture which are unique, but like the population at large—including many people who claim to be exponents of a New Politics—the white ethnics have accepted two myths about our society which get to the heart of our nation's present difficulties: our alleged free enterprise economy and pluralistic political system. Both notions are widely accepted by Americans from all walks of life but they are a distortion of the real world. As long as the electorate believes that they accurately describe our economic and political systems, it will be well nigh impossible to deal with many of our most pressing problems.

B. The Myth of Free Enterprise: *It Would Come as a Great Shock to Many Americans Were They to Learn the Truth—That the Major Corporations Are Dead Set Against Capitalism*

In many sectors of our economy competition, the defining feature of free enterprise, does not exist. Yet, many Americans believe in this myth and others act as if it is descriptive of the real world. This accounts for widescale public ignorance about the root causes of our most pressing economic and political problems—inflation, recession, poverty among plenty, the abuse of corporate power, the inability of public officials to work effectively for the commonweal, and the electorate's growing estrangement from the political process.

To strip away the half-truths, misinformation, and illusions giving credence to the myth of free enterprise, let us return to the origins of this great ruse. It was midwifed in Glasgow by a Scottish professor of moral philosophy in 1776. That year Adam Smith published his *Wealth of Nations*; it was to become the bible of nineteenth-century liberals who proclaimed—in contrast to their twentieth-century namesakes —that state interference in social and economic affairs was a blunder of the first order, disrupting natural economic processes and fomenting political autocracy. Smith's disciples today call themselves conservatives—people like *National Review* editor William Buckley, the guru of the literate right, and Milton Friedman, the much quoted University of Chicago economist.

According to Smith, abstruse economic laws regulated production and consumption, wages and profits, booms and busts. Smith spoke of this process in terms of an "invisible hand" which, if left alone, worked as deftly as a Swiss watch. Government's role in Smith's economy schema was a limited one of providing for matters the private sector could not treat —the construction of roads and canals, overseeing the public health, and other critical enterprises not the proper function

of the free economy. But that was it! Smith warned that government tampering with the process could seriously short-
circuit it and wreak havoc in society. Those misguided souls
who sought to employ government power to spare the poor
pain and the needy anxiety would only complicate matters and
prolong their suffering.

The laws governing the economy were harsh but they also
were benign. Periodically the solemnity of the market would
be shattered by recessions hurting worker and employer alike,
but such dislocations were a necessary part of the inevitable
movement toward equilibrium; for soon after a period of
decline, economic activity would begin to hum once again.
Unlike other practitioners of the gloomy science, Smith was
optimistic about the future and felt that, if left alone, the free
market would afford every member of society, the highest and
the lowest, the opportunity to prosper.

During the Gilded Age—which thrived from the aftermath
of the Civil War until the crash of 1929—the Robber Barons
found Smith's theory congenial to their self-interest. Armed
with the laws of classical economics, these laissez-faire capitalists opposed government regulation of their activities, warning
populists and progressives alike that interference with the
market would curb the economy's natural growth and thus the
bleeding hearts would kill "the goose which laid the golden
egg." By wedding Smith's notion about a self-regulating
economy to the theories of social Darwinists (who proclaimed
it was as shortsighted and suicidal to tamper with the social
order as it was to regulate the economy), the privileged
classes could cite pseudoscientific "laws" to rationalize their
indifference to the industrial workers' plight and the destruction of the yeoman farmer and small entrepreneur. Bloated
with power, the Robber Barons ran the United States like a
company town, manipulating the Constitution to emasculate
legislation designed to ameliorate the social disruption and
economic dislocation wrought by industrialization and urbanization.

The Supreme Court circumvented attempts to pass child
labor laws, to set minimum wages and maximum hours, and
to protect the worker against hazardous conditions by citing
the Fifth and Fourteenth Amendments' protections of due

process and equal protection of the laws. And what appeared to be setbacks for the exponents of laissez-faire capitalism—antitrust laws—actually proved to be weapons they could employ in their behalf. Thus antitrust legislation enacted to fight monopoly was used to sabotage trade unions and to suppress labor protest. While trumpeting the glories of free enterprise, the Robber Barons employed state power to eliminate competition and reduce risk-taking. Legislation written to regulate the railway industry, for example, was twisted to provide cartel-like arrangements with the government's blessing.

The Great Crash of 1929 caused the laissez-faire capitalists to formally scrap Adam Smith's innocent prescriptions glorifying competition; they contended that competition was disruptive, a source of uncertainty, and a costly luxury. They had, of course, reached this conclusion years earlier, forming trusts and other economic combinations in the last quarter of the nineteenth century to avoid the pitfalls of competition. These economic concentrations enabled them to wield awesome political power to fight trust-busters who wished to return to a "purer form" of capitalism and socialists who argued "if economic power is going to be concentrated, why not place it under the control of the people and make certain it's used in the public interest?"

The Depression offered the laissez-faire capitalists the opportunity to be blunt about readjustments they had made earlier in a de facto if not in a de jure fashion in the name of the public interest. They proclaimed that competition was responsible for the Depression and that monopolies were a natural part of a mature capitalist economy; it made good sense then to give monopolistic enterprises the same legal status that cartels in Europe enjoyed. So after initially resisting FDR's National Industrial Recovery Act—abolishing antitrust laws and promulgating trade associations establishing industrial codes and production quotas—the captains of finance and industry changed their minds and pressed for even more extensive collusion between government and business. Gerald Swope, General Electric's president, wrote about such an arrangement in terms of a "business commonwealth," and American businessmen cited Italian fascism as a model for an industrial order that might work well in the United States. In Rome,

Benito Mussolini spoke eloquently about collusion between
industry and government in terms of a "corporate state." Ignoring the philosophical accouterments of Italian fascism, the
American "corporativists" welcomed a marriage between the
government and industry legitimizing monopoly and allowing
the cartels, for all intents and purposes, to manage the
economy.[25]

But after NIRA was declared unconstitutional, the New
Dealers lost interest in corporativism; the ardor of the business
community also cooled because it did not trust FDR. It was
he after all who had become a traitor to his class when he gave
his blessing to the Wagner Act, enabling trade unions to organize millions of workers. To demonstrate their displeasure,
some of the nation's largest business tycoons formed the Liberty Lobby to work toward FDR's political demise.

Today most big businessmen recognize that the New Deal
has worked to their advantage; and many left-wing radicals,
agreeing with this assessment, have been unsparing in their
criticism of it. They argue that the New Deal, in the name of
the welfare state, legitimized a marriage of state and corporate
power and that, through the Wagner Act, FDR solidified a
labor/corporate alliance, which Samuel Gompers had always
sought, with the Federal government serving as the mediator
in this "corporativist" troika.[26]

To describe our present political economy in terms of corporativism is perhaps stretching a point, but John Kenneth
Galbraith has mustered evidence demonstrating that our
economy is bifurcated between a "market system" and a
"planning system." In the first instance, small entrepreneurs,
unorganized workers, and consumers operate in a more or less
competitive environment; here the free market prevails. But
the planning system operates much like a corporativist system.
Big business and big labor use state power to make certain
that whatever ill fortune befalls the people in the market system, those who belong to the planning system can be assured
their interests are served. Thus, the oil companies operate monopolistically and the AFL-CIO's members are allowed, during a wage freeze, to achieve wage rate increases denied other
workers.[27] Galbraith's analysis may be a bit too pat, and he
exaggerates the power of organized labor, but his remarks per-

taining to the fiction of competition in the planning system are by no means groundless. To label the activities of the auto, oil, and drug industries as "free enterprise" is an absurdity; but it serves the interests of the industrial Leviathans as is evidenced in their public celebration of the free market via television commercials, newspaper advertisements, and the pronouncements of their executives. Few if any of our largest and most powerful corporations operate capitalistically, but they sustain the hoax of free enterprise because it functions like a tranquilizing gas, destroying the critical faculties of the American people and confusing them as to the truth about our economy.

The free enterprise notion—and related norms like individualism and materialism—is woven into the warp and woof of the American political culture and it is one our people value highly. Because of our unique national birth and social development, Americans are more inclined to oppose state intervention in the private sector than Europeans.

> Probably business' biggest political asset lies in the extent to which the average American shares the businessmen's values and attitudes. Americans are convinced that the private enterprise system has brought them unparalleled prosperity; believe the profit system "works"; regard wide income differentials to be normal and proper; want business to be as "free" as possible; and are wary of Big Government, bureaucracy, centralized political power and high taxes. These attitudes powerfully undergird business interests; they severely limit the scope of potential legislation affecting business.[28]

It would come as a great shock to many Americans were they to learn the truth—that the major corporations are dead set against capitalism and prefer instead to work with government to manage the economy because that arrangement has proven profitable to them. Take, for example, the case of the oil industry.

In 1926 Congress awarded the oil industry a 27 per cent oil depletion allowance under the guise of encouraging oil exploration. Robert Taft, the conservative senator from Ohio, properly labeled this a giveaway, because in capitalist theory profits are the rewards businessmen receive for risk-taking; indeed, risk-taking is the only legitimate reason for an entrepreneur making a profit. Most of Senator Taft's Republican colleagues and Democratic friends who canonized him as a true conservative conveniently ignored his warning that such legislation gave some enterprises a club to beat the competition into submission. In 1959 President Eisenhower placed import quotas on foreign oil for "national security" reasons; this cost the American people billions of dollars annually. Not until 1973, the year of the energy crisis, were the import quotas lifted. Meanwhile the eight major oil companies had developed a vise-like grip over the oil industry, prompting the FTC to charge that they were operating monopolistically and illegally.

In a response to the 1973 energy crisis, President Nixon appointed several oil executives to a "crisis task force," and adopted measures enabling the major oil companies to lease public lands for oil shale production. Liberal opponents cited Nixon's action as further proof that the GOP is the party of big business, ignoring the fact that Democratic and Republican administrations alike invite corporate executives to Washington to give government their sage advice in "national emergencies." During time of war or economic hard times, representatives from the business community do their patriotic duty and help government make policy for us. Under these circumstances elected officials and executive administrators are often pushed aside by corporate agents who operate like a private government. Is it any wonder that the legislation they help write and the rulings they conceive result in windfalls for themselves and their friends?

While the consumer and working man and woman are asked to operate within capitalist guidelines, the large corporations are allowed to write their own rules. And on those occasions when economic controls are instituted, big business is treated as an exception. In 1971, President Nixon announced the imposition of wage and price controls to fight what his critics called Nixonomics—galloping inflation with high unemployment. Nixon's New Economic Policy (NEP) froze wages, but not profits or interest; consequently, lending institutions and the auto industry announced record-breaking profits in 1971 and 1972. Moreover, when profits soured for the auto industry in 1974, it announced price increases, clearly demonstrating that the free market was "inoperative." In a competitive market prices drop with demand, but just the opposite took place, proving that prices in many sectors of our economy—drugs, food, medicine, etc.—are a function of industry-wide agreements and not market forces. There is no question but that the inflation whiplashing the United States in the 1970s is related to the capacity of our nation's largest industries to manipulate government regulations to eliminate competition and manage prices.

In conjunction with the profound economic implications of this condition, there are numerous political problems which become intelligible once the political economy is placed in proper perspective. We noted earlier that the private sector has a virtual veto over urban programs. It is also apparent that the future of America's suburbs is in the hands of the same powerful interests—lending institutions, insurance companies, real estate speculators, and large corporations—responsible for the destruction of our cities and the modest progress we have achieved in rebuilding them. Moreover, there is a host of problems—the environmental crisis, the fuel shortage, the plight of the worker, the disgraceful treatment of old folks, etc.—which also are attributable to the abuse of private power. Yet neither the Republicans nor the Democrats have deemed it necessary to acknowledge the source of the malaise gripping our national life—that is, the public's inability to hold powerful private interests accountable for their actions.

In the public sector accountability is a function of the electoral process. We "vote the rascal out" when we catch a public official with his hands in the till or when it comes to our attention that he has violated the public trust if not the law; or we may end his career because his bad judgment involves us in an ill-advised war. But when we turn to private elites who make decisions having a profound public impact, we encounter an awesome accountability problem. Here, Adam Smith's notion about a self-regulating economy once again is relevant, for under a capitalist system it has been assumed that consumers, through the market, can hold GW, Standard Oil, and other large corporations accountable for their actions; but this notion is cousin to the myth that competition is a principal feature of American capitalism. As Galbraith has demonstrated, in concentrated sectors of our economy competition does not exist; and large corporations in the food, auto, and drug industries engage in price collusion to minimize the risk of competition and to insure high profits. In other words, the public cannot hold private elites accountable if the free market—the instrument of accountability—is largely an invention of corporate publicists.

C. The Myth of Political Pluralism: *The Rich and Powerful Largely Establish the Public Agenda and Frequently Prevent Issues They Disapprove of from Becoming Matters of Public Debate*

In the same way that the myth of capitalism is the basis for prevailing beliefs about our economy, the notion of political pluralism is widely believed to describe the American political system. Among its principal precepts are the following:

The pluralists reject the crude Marxist notion, best exemplified by the radical sociologist C. Wright Mills, that a single power elite dominates the principal centers of power in the United States. They agree that elites, not the masses, dominate all critical areas of American life; but the elites do not represent a single interest or group.[29] They support the prevailing economic and political order but they often bitterly disagree about how society's resources are to be allocated, who pays the bill for government support of the welfare state, etc. The ordinary citizen does not have the same capacity to influence policy that elites do, but when critical issues emerge and the public is mobilized around an issue, the elites listen and act upon mass discontent. They do so because they believe in majority rule and/or because they know if they ignore the wishes of their constituents on important matters, other spokesmen (counter-elites) will manipulate mass discontent to remove them from office or positions of influence. The pluralists contend that very few people are really interested in politics—after all, they must take care of their businesses, pursue their careers, and concern themselves with mundane matters germane to their lives. As long as the elites are accountable to the masses, mass political apathy should not cause much concern. The man on the street may not have a direct impact on public or private decision-making critical to his welfare, but he does wield indirect influence through the elites— for example, his union leader, the president of his business or farming association, the head of his religious or civil rights organization, and his elected officials.

Groups play an important part in pluralist theory for they mediate between the masses and the elites, preventing irresponsible demands on the former's part and the abuse of power on the part of the latter. Every American belongs to one or more of them—labor, business, civic, ethnic, racial, religious, and so on. It is through interest groups that he registers his preference for or against abortion, busing, minimum wages, and civil rights legislation. This description of popular participation in public affairs does not conform with that of classical democratic theory, but we all know that in a large, complicated society representatives must act on our behalf.

The pluralists contend that one of the greatest achievements of the United States has been its capacity to accommodate conflicting group demands in a relatively peaceful and equitable fashion. On this score we have done better than most other nations. Group differences are ameliorated because Americans belong to more than one of them; these ties and conflicting loyalties foster tolerance and encourage peaceful solutions to intergroup conflict. Perhaps of larger importance, an overwhelming number of Americans share a common political culture and have faith in the system's fairness. Minorities need not fear that they will be crushed by majorities. The pluralists admit that some groups are more powerful than other ones, but the dominant interests recognize that to ignore the needs of minority groups is socially disruptive and detrimental to their own interests as well as to the welfare of society at large. Moreover, as a consequence of belonging to more than one group, all of us may find ourselves in a majority on one occasion—Protestants, who belong to a religious majority—or in a minority on another occasion—as Republicans, for example. The multiplicity of different groups and interests serves as a check upon the dominance of a single interest. And policies are made as a consequence of shifting alliances. Bankers and educators may work together on one issue, for example, but take opposing positions on other ones. In a third case both may remain neutral in a struggle involving a second coalition of interest groups.

It is because the pluralists have faith in the responsiveness of the political system that they are not greatly concerned about the problem of holding economic elites accountable for their actions. According to the pluralists, the Great Depression demonstrated that something was seriously wrong with the free market and that a new self-regulating mechanism was needed. Once again, a resident of the British Isles, John Maynard Keynes, provided the answer. Keynes argued that government, through its fiscal, monetary, and taxing powers, could pump-prime a sagging economy and, through judicious use of its capacity to shape economic behavior, prevent or at the very least soften those economic collapses traditionally plaguing capitalist societies. The New Deal, in effect, demonstrated that Keynes was right and as a result of FDR's economic policies the nation—admittedly with the help of Adolf Hitler—came to grips with its economic problems without embracing obnoxious socialist bromides. The welfare state fostered a more equitable distribution of the nation's wealth than had been the case prior to the New Deal, and through the Wagner Act workers were encouraged to organize unions enabling them to countervail the power of big business. Henceforth, where the free market was inoperative it was through the political system that economic elites were held accountable for their actions.

For all intents and purposes liberal Democrats who belong to the regular wing of the party and Meanyites in the labor movement adhere to this view of our political system. Like Ben Wattenberg, the co-founder of the Coalition for a Democratic Majority—which serves as a think tank for the party's regulars—they respond to criticism from the left by trotting out the aforementioned pluralistic apologia. But the accuracy with which the pluralist model describes our political system has been criticized on the following grounds:

The pluralists underestimate the ability of powerful economic interests to use their wealth to influence public officials and legislators at all levels of government. Even the man on the street now realizes that the oil companies have great power and manipulate the U. S. Congress and the White House itself to gain tax advantages and other preferential treatment at the expense of the consumer.

It is not only the large national corporations which use their economic resources to accomplish their political objectives. The business community on the state and local level wields decisive power in matters related to zoning, planning, taxes, and other critical matters; the people one is most likely to find on planning commissions and zoning boards are realtors, contractors, and bankers. And the guardians of the public interest on state corporation and tax commissions display a probusiness bias or make policy on the erroneous assumption that our economy is capitalistic.[30]

Many matters troubling the ordinary citizen never surface and become issues. The rich and powerful largely establish the public agenda and frequently prevent issues they disapprove of from becoming matters of public debate.

The pluralists' faith in the ability of the masses to hold their leaders accountable is a bit too sanguine. Many rank and file union members do not have very much say in their unions, nor does the ordinary doctor wield much influence in the American Medical Association. And just how much power does the average Baptist or Catholic or farmer or employee have in affecting decisions in his church, farm organization, or place of employment? Questions of this kind are critical because the pluralists claim that while the "masses" do not wield direct political power, they do shape public policy indirectly through their group and associational representatives. But this statement is meaningless if the membership cannot hold its leaders accountable for their actions.

The pluralist contention that the views of all groups in society get a fair hearing and that the needs of the weaker are anticipated by the stronger is a fiction—or at the very least a sometimes thing.

While the pluralists claim to be describing the real world, they have formulated a model which opposes change and implies that popular participation in the political system is inimical to public order. For the last twenty years high school and college students have been exposed to textbooks which

allege that the common man is a bitter opponent of civil liberties for dissenters and civil rights for racial minorities.[31] This
"evidence" supports the notion that the elites and not the
masses are the real guardians of the democratic process. It is a
good thing, therefore, that the ordinary citizen does not take a
greater interest in politics. It is clear, is it not, that when he
does he turns to demagogues like Joe McCarthy and George
Wallace?

We observed earlier that the data allegedly supporting this
conclusion by no means compel us to accept it; for it is often
based on research designs discriminating against working-class
Americans or it unfairly singles them out for embracing issues
and beliefs which powerful interests in our society have manipulated for their own self-interest. Nonetheless, the widespread acceptance of the pluralist model accounts for the
anomaly that, while many New Politics reformers speak
favorably of "people power," they harbor deep-seated fears
and mistrust of the American people.

Practical politicians may not accept the academic pluralists'
model of our political system in toto, but the regulars in the
Democratic Party are inclined to be Pollyanna-ish about the
Old Politics and the state of the nation, accusing democratic
radicals and reformers of being utopian. In defending the
status quo, some have cited President Kennedy who warned
"do-gooders" a generation ago that "life is unfair." It is indeed
foolhardy to quarrel with Ben Wattenberg who chides his
New Politics opponents for ignoring the great progress we
have made in the last quarter century in the war on poverty,
racism, and ignorance.[32] Yet, Mr. Wattenberg and his colleagues ignore a host of pertinent questions.

In the richest nation in the history of mankind, should anyone suffer from inadequate medical care, or be denied decent
shelter, or look toward his old age with anxiety because we do
not have a universal medical program or pension system?
Should anyone go hungry or suffer malnutrition in the
world's most prolific food-producing economy? Why should
workers dig coal in dangerous mines yet be denied medical
protection from job-related diseases? Why should minority
Americans and other needy citizens be denied the opportunity
to actualize their human potential and look expectantly to-

ward a bright future for their children? It is possible to go on asking such questions for many pages, and what is most appalling about the shameful conditions we have ticked off is that we have the resources and know-how to deal with all of them. We have made progress to be sure, but given our enormous wealth, it is unconscionable that we have not moved with greater haste to eliminate social and economic injustice in our midst. Nor have we taken sufficient measures to meet rising demands on the part of our people for a greater voice in decisions which shape their lives.

CHAPTER VIII

The New Populism
and the White Ethnics

A. The New Populism: *A Political School Based upon Two Old and Simple Goals: the More Equal Distribution of Wealth and Income and the Decentralization of Power to Ensure More Citizen Participation in Making Decisions*, Jack Newfeld

The preceding analysis of our "free enterprise" economy and "pluralistic" political system represents a New Populist critique of American society. The people involved may not fancy the label or support a single coherent agenda for reform, but most would find themselves agreeing with Jack Newfeld's New Populist orientation. "I think of myself as part of a political school based on two old and simple goals: the more equal distribution of wealth and income, and the decentralization of power to ensure more citizen participation in making decisions."[1] In contrast to the practitioners of the Old Politics, the New Populists contend that economic concentrations inevitably lead to the abuse of political power, so in designing an agenda for change, unresponsive economic and political power must be dealt with in tandem. Toward this end, a plethora of reforms has been suggested: nationalization of the oil industry and public utilities; the formation of publicly owned enterprises to force private ones to operate competitively; breaking up concentrated industries to foster competition and corporate responsibility; adopting a progressive tax system which includes all wealth-producing sources; a national health and pension system covering every American; the decentralization of government institutions and other reforms facilitating wider citizen participation; the adoption of measures promoting industrial democracy; and the passage of legislation facilitating widespread unionization of the labor force.

These reforms are technically feasible and consistent with the principles of a democratic society; they are the basis for a New Populist program carrying us a long way toward the solution to our present difficulties, yet there is no organized political force behind them to transform these "paper plans" into public policy. A discussion of the problems to be encountered on this score is beyond the purview of this book, but there is little doubt that the New Populists can build a formal organization, select leaders, and formulate a political strategy. The new organization would be affiliated with the Democratic Party but it would operate like an independent caucus mobilizing supporters within the party and allies outside it behind a New Populist program. Presumably the people involved would include social unionists, progressive politicians, members of the congressional black caucus, civil rights leaders, new breed ethnic activists, consumer crusaders, and democratic radicals.

It will take a great deal of skill to integrate these people and the groups they represent into a viable political force, but the task is by no means insurmountable. During the 1960s many of them worked together, although on an ad hoc basis, to fight racism, poverty, and American involvement in the Vietnam war. Since then they and others like them have gained access to positions of importance in their communities, the political system, and the labor movement. They have demonstrated that the regulars in the Democratic Party who thought of them as an aberration were badly mistaken. Whether or not they can elect a President who favors their reforms, however, is open to question. Their success on this score and their ultimate impact on society depends on whether or not they can attract widespread support for their cause. If they can demonstrate that their programs are appealing to traditional Democratic voters, many regulars—albeit reluctantly—will support them. For many regular Democrats have always favored bread and butter liberalism although they have shied away from efforts to cope with corporate power because they thought it politically unpopular. These "closet populists" in the ranks of the old guard will "come out" if it can be shown that the electorate is ready for change. Conversely, it would be a mistake to infer that all the so-called New Politics Democrats are potential supporters of the New Populism. Some have favored the reformist label only because in areas where large numbers of middle-class, issue-oriented voters reside, it is politically suicidal not to be identified as a reformer. And far too many Democratic reformers and Common Cause Republicans are insensitive to the problems of working people; like many middle-class progressives early in the century, they are more interested in "clean and efficient government"—commendable goals—than in economic justice. Finally, it was noted earlier that the politics of interest can degenerate into a politics of sheer opportunism where, behind the façade of pragmatism (a word which enthralls many hard-nosed commentators), old guard politicos use influence to promote their self-interest at the expense of their constituents. The New Populists should not forget that the politics of conscience taken to an extreme can produce similar results. For throughout this century, radicals have adopted political programs which ignore the needs of the common man or further set back progressive causes because the former are victims of an affliction which may be called secular millenarianism. The New Populists must strike a balance between the Old and New Politics. This means the adoption of a political agenda involving a protracted political struggle and fundamental institutional changes to promote social and economic justice and greater citizen involvement in the political process. If a New Populist Movement is to become politically viable, this also means that dogmatic political formulas are to be avoided, that a coalition of diverse elements must be built, and that this may necessitate compromise with political adversaries and accommodation with potential allies.

Some McGovernites have learned that the new majority McGovern spoke of in 1972 does not exist and that attracting working-class Democratic voters is a prerequisite to the formation of a progressive electoral majority. They realize that it is a liability to use a label (New Politics) which in the minds of many voters is associated with elitism and indifference toward the problems of working people. Instead they prefer the New Populist label, but until they demonstrate their appeal to people they often described as "part of the problem" in the past, they will not be deserving of it.

To make a significant impact upon our society, they must attract white ethnic voters who, since the 1930s, have been the keystone in the Democratic coalition. Before they can hope to do that, they must provide answers to a host of pertinent questions: Does it make sense to talk of the white ethnics as a distinct group in light of their socioeconomic mobility and geographic dispersion? What is the source of the so-called New Ethnicity and is it relevant to the white ethnics' future political behavior? What are the prospects that the labor movement will adopt social unionist objectives in the immediate future? Does ethnicity still influence the political behavior of Catholic and Jewish ethnics and to what degree? What is the basis for the white ethnics' affinity for the Democratic Party and what lessons should the New Populists draw from it? And what issues should the New Populists keep in mind in their quest to attract white ethnic support?

B. White Ethnicity Old and New: *Millions of White Ethnics Have Begun to Assert Themselves as They Enter the Middle Class and Gain Access to Centers of Economic and Political Power*

W. Lloyd Warner wrote in 1945 that "the future of American ethnic groups seems to be limited; it is likely that they will be quickly absorbed."[2] This view gained a growing number of adherents after the war and social scientists of various political persuasions supported it. In modern society people would sever their "tribal ties" for new ones based upon self-interest and the common bond of social status. In *The Urban Villagers* Herbert Gans discounted ethnicity as a shaping influence in the lives of the Italian-Americans he studied in Boston; he attributed their tight-knit families and love of neighborhood to a shared working-class value system. Other writers predicted rising levels of education and income would relegate ethnic communalism to a shrinking circle of Americans; still others claimed suburbanization would expedite the decline of lingering ethnic values and social structures, contributing to the homogenization of the nation's population. Will Herberg presented convincing evidence that religious and not ethnic factors better explained white ethnic social and political behavior.[3] And in the early 1960s Glazer and Moynihan, in *Beyond the Melting Pot*, challenged the assumption that ethnicity had been superceded by class only to predict the ultimate victory of religion and race at the expense of ethnicity.

Today popular writers and academics alike admit that predictions about the imminent demise of ethnicity were unwarranted. According to Michael Parenti, the Melting Pot myth was a consequence of confusing acculturation with assimilation; that is, widespread acceptance of cultural values with the integration of a group through intermarriage into the social life of the larger society.[4] In most cases the white ethnics have embraced the core values of American society: egalitarianism and individualism, the Protestant "work ethic"— stressing the inherent value of labor and a reverence for self-denial—and materialism, which measures personal worth in terms of the capacity to make money. Consequently second- and third-generation Poles and Italians have more in common with Wasp Americans than residents of Warsaw or Rome. Nonetheless, there is reason to believe that a white ethnic subculture still exists in the United States; for example, the Catholic and Jewish ethnics' concept of God, human nature, family, etc. may not square with that of other Americans. This subculture may be less distinctive than it was years ago but it persists. Lingering ethnic influences shape one's personality and belief system and the way one reacts to death, stresses achievement, or values family life. But having said this, it is as unwise to exaggerate the cultural distinctiveness of the white ethnics as it is to believe in the myth of the Melting Pot.

Turning to assimilation, sociologists indicate that while the rates of ethnic intermarriage are on the rise, Poles, Greeks, Italians, and Jews do not randomly intermarry with other Americans because ethnic affinities influence their selection of friends and places of residence. This condition is likely to persist throughout this decade and well into the 1980s and perhaps beyond. Because the Census Bureau does not count third-generation Italian- or Polish-Americans in our nation's Italian or Polish stock, the marriage of a third-generation Italian-American boy to a second-generation Italian-American girl is considered an inter-ethnic marriage. This practice exaggerates assimilation. Moreover, sociologists have overlooked the fact that many, perhaps most, inter-ethnic marriages (Polish-Italian, Irish-Ukrainian, etc.) involve persons who are part of the larger white ethnic community. Such marriages contribute to assimilationist statistics, but both parties are products of a white ethnic subculture.

White ethnics spend more time socializing with their families and close friends than other Americans do. These social patterns sustain ethnically distinctive church, community, and even professional organizations.[5] And in spite of rising socioeconomic and residential mobility, there is still evidence of ethnic segregation in the North. Although the number of old inner-city ethnic enclaves is on the decline, millions of urbanites still live in them. Even in those instances where members of several different ethnic groups live together, certain areas or blocks in these neighborhoods are ethnically distinctive. And, contrary to popular wisdom, suburbanization has not destroyed ethnic communal ties. It is not uncommon to find suburbs housing a single ethnic group—Polish, Italian, or Russian Jewish. The inner-city Polish or Italian church often has been relocated and so have some of the businesses and fraternal associations; and many of the residents come from the old neighborhood. The elements which gave impetus to the formation of ethnic neighborhoods a half century ago have disappeared, but the persistent tug of ethnic communalism thrives in suburbia.

Furthermore, in the metropolitan regions of New York, Detroit, Chicago, Providence, or Boston, etc. one finds ethnically mixed communities comprised primarily of transplanted urban Italians, Poles, Jews, or Irishmen. Ethnic and religious differences aside, the people who live here have a great deal in common. Many of them have left the working-class behind, but still view the world through the prism of the immigrant/

working-class legacy of their forefathers and the urban milieu in which they were born and raised. This suburban white ethnic subculture in turn may be subdivided into Catholic and Jewish communities. Catholic social life is encapsulated in parochial schools, the Knights of Columbus, and the Ladies' Sodality. The same holds true for Jews living in suburbia; because of business ties, interaction through the synagogue, or the Hadassah, the people you are most intimate with and prefer to spend time with are other Jews.

The existence of religious suburban settlements lends credence to the Triple Melting Pot thesis of Ruby Jo Kennedy and Will Herberg, but this theory does not take into account Catholic and Jewish communities subdivided by ethnicity. In New York, Russian and German Jews still have their own organizations and social networks. And this holds true for Catholic ethnics as well. There are even discernible differences within an ethnic group; for example, Lithuanians who trace their ancestry to the second wave of European immigration do not customarily belong to the same Lithuanian organizations that newer Lithuanian immigrants do.

One additional observation is in order. Most of us talk about a community in terms of geography; a "community" is a distinct geographical setting promoting a worldview common to its members. But a "sense of community" may thrive even where the members do not live among, or even close to, one another. In many parts of America, there are communities held together by virtue of an ethnic social network or state of mind common to people spread out over a wide area; because the members have been exposed to the same values, they think alike and this common bond is the reason why they prefer to socialize with one another, even if they may have to travel considerable distances to do so. Ethnic identity has survived increasing education, economic achievements, and geographical dispersion because it is an important part of an individual's personality and social life.

To recapitulate, in the 1970s it still makes sense to talk about a white ethnic subculture comprised of Eastern and Southern European Catholics, Jews, and those of the Orthodox faith, as well as Irish Catholics who arrived at the turn of the century. The white ethnic subculture can be subdivided

along religious lines, and within each religious community nationality subdivisions are in order—Italian, Polish, Russian-
Jewish, etc. Moreover, within specific nationality groups there
is a division between the DPs and those people whose ancestors arrived with the second wave of European immigration.

An anomaly of Catholic white ethnic communities is that
while they appear to be highly organized—fraternal, social,
civic, and religious organizations abound—mass-based community organizations committed to collective action are a rarity.
The ethnic organizations are often closely affiliated with regular party organizations and the leaders use power to achieve
gains for a favored few while the majority are placated through
the distribution of symbolic rewards. The ethnic fraternals
sponsor worthy cultural and social events but the entrenched
leadership is opposed to programs treating community-wide
problems. Several years ago the ethnic fraternals stirred from a
deep sleep and complained about government neglect of
"their people" after they were embarrassed into doing so by
the example of young activists. As a result of their complaints,
the Nixon Administration appointed several ethnic leaders to
"important" posts, and this apparently satisfied them. In spite
of impressive membership figures and insurance funds suggesting that they are forces to be reckoned with, most ethnic fraternals are paper tigers, run by people who do not enjoy much
influence with those they purport to represent. They have not
attracted young people, who believe they are relics of an earlier era—unobjectionable perhaps, but hardly relevant to the
present generation and its problems.

Gene Pasymowski, the director of Action in Pennsylvania
who is active in Polish-American affairs on the East Coast, like
many of his peers, condemns the Polish-American Congress
(PAC) for turning its back on the plight of needy Poles.
"While PAC was preoccupied with the Cold War, Polish
neighborhoods and parishes were devastated. There was no
way it could affect affairs in Poland, but it's conceivable it
could have helped Polonians in the United States. The
Congress represents Poles in name only."[6] Young people from
other ethnic groups feel much the same way about the Czech,
Italian, and Lithuanian fraternal leadership.

The Catholic church is a significant force in most white ethnic areas, but it has ignored the neighborhood-related problems of its parishioners. The traditional ethnic clergy claim that the church's role is exclusively a religious and cultural one; the church is not meant to provide leadership, money, or expertise in secular enterprises. Those among the clergy and faithful who wish to use the church in the latter fashion are deemed troublemakers. Church-sponsored community action projects have been discouraged by traditionalists in the church hierarchy, who fear powerful lay community groups will turn their attention to the church power structure and cause problems for it. The Irish, who dominate the church, are not the only ones who think in these terms; many Italian and Polish prelates feel the same way.

New Leftist priests, nuns, and lay Catholic radicals are no more responsive to the plight of the Catholic working class than their ideological adversaries on the right. They have alienated Catholics of modest means and education who resent being spoken of as "part of the problem." The issues, tactics, and rhetoric which are associated with the brothers Berrigan and their friends are often marginal to working people, violate their sense of decency, or denigrate their system of values. Even worse, the publicity generated by Catholic radicals has been adroitly manipulated by conservative prelates to undermine the activities of Catholic progressives who believe the church has a vital role to play in the lives of Catholics at work and in their neighborhoods. To many Catholics the radicals are as rigid, self-righteous, and contemptuous of the faithful as the church's autocratic reactionaries.

During the 1960s liberals gained ascendancy in the church and they played an important part in the success of the Civil Rights and Anti-War Movements. Catholic liberals, lay and clerical, compelled the church to fund urban task forces in metropolitan areas throughout the country, even where Catholics were in a minority. But until the media publicized the work of Monsignor Geno Baroni, few urban development programs funded by the church were located in white ethnic neighborhoods. The people who ran these programs, like liberal urban experts elsewhere, perceived America's urban malaise exclusively in terms of the unmet needs of black and brown Americans. Even today, many liberal Italian priests and Polish nuns display the same fear, distrust, and hostility toward their blue-collar parishioners that many cosmopolitan reformers do.

This otherwise grim picture of white ethnic community leadership, however, has been brightened by the appearance of new, progressive leaders whose activities have been conveyed to the American public via the publicity surrounding the New Ethnicity.

Drive along the New Jersey Turnpike and you are bound to spot cars adorned with the green, white, and red striped Italian flag. In Midwestern industrial towns, bumper stickers proclaiming "Polish power" are a common sight; have a beer in a bar in Brooklyn and you are likely to see someone with a button inviting you to "Kiss Me, I'm Irish." There are social critics who deem these public displays of white ethnic pride as meaningless symbols, claiming the blacks made it fashionable to talk about ethnic pride, but that they have cause to do so. The flags, buttons, and other accouterments of white ethnic self-awareness are as socially significant as the hula hoop. These skeptics believe that self-styled "ethnic" spokesmen are seeking to interest fellow ethnics in the New Ethnicity to put flesh on the sparse bones of organizations desperately searching for dues-paying members; in addition to the monetary advantages accrued, they will be able to project an image of "grass-roots" support for their activities, or to secure votes to fulfill personal political ambitions.

Ethnicity has been manipulated by politicians to serve their own selfish ends, but it cannot be ignored as an authentic source of human behavior. Yet even sympathetic writers are not quite sure whether it is legitimate to talk about a New Ethnicity or not and many others who are receptive to the idea are confused about its origins.

One school of thought already alluded to stresses the catalystic influence of rising black self-awareness beginning in the late 1950s on an ethnic reawakening among Poles, Italians, and Jews at the close of the 1960s. Commentators who take this tack are inclined to question the authenticity of the New Ethnicity.[7] A second, more sympathetic view is that people in a large complex industrial society are looking for some crutch to lean on to maintain their mental equilibrium in a rapidly changing world. Even if the New Ethnicity is somewhat contrived, it is a benign indulgence and insofar as it is an antidote to the crass individualism of our society, it is a good thing. A third school of thought proclaims that there is nothing new about the persistent influence of ethnic communal values and ties; they have merely been overshadowed by the simple-minded notion that economics is the basis for human behavior. Rising levels of education and income may dampen the influence of ethnicity, but it never really disappears as a psychological and social factor in people's lives. The profound interest in Judaism among young Jews is often mentioned in this connection; individuals from various social backgrounds and political persuasions are involved in this passionate search for meaning through Judaism. This includes onetime New Leftists who took to the streets during the 1960s to protest "Amerikan Imperialism" at home and abroad. Arthur Waskow, of the Institute for Policy Studies (a radical think tank), wrote a "Freedom Seder" which was first published by *Ramparts* magazine, and young Jewish radicals are publishing other materials in an attempt to relate the Jewish experience to radical change. Some commentators explain this return to ethnic communalism as a despairing response to the demise of the New Left, the separatist policies of the Black Power movement which gave legitimacy to ethnicity, and growing pride in and later fear for the state of Israel.[8] Whatever its sources, the resurrection of Jewish communalism deserves serious and sober attention.

A fourth explanation of the New Ethnicity (not necessarily in conflict with the others) is related to the factor which social scientists predicted would spell its doom—middle-class status. Stated in the simplest form, millions of white ethnics have begun to enter the middle class and gain access to centers of economic and political power. This is especially significant in the case of Catholics. A college degree, professional status, and the self-esteem they have derived from "making it" enable them to voice truths about the old ethnic neighborhood and the blue-collar world their working-class parents were unable to articulate. They possess the self-esteem to face head-on the immigrant/working-class legacy of their grandparents, a confrontation their parents feared and avoided.

This accounts for a phenomenon which has become quite prevalent; people are salvaging names their parents scrapped in desperation to "pass" as native Americans. Dr. Williams goes to City Hall to change his name back to the one his grandfather carried with him from Italy—Guglielmi. In terms of tastes, values, and the unstated assumptions shaping his behavior, the doctor is less "ethnic" than his father, but unlike him, he is not ashamed of being Italian. At the same time, he is more, not less, inclined to be sensitive to existing anti-Italian prejudices and stereotypes. He's outraged that many otherwise enlightened people still believe that most prominent Italians somehow or other are in tight with the Mafia, and he becomes incensed when columnists imply that all Italian politicians are racists and reactionaries. Education and middle-class status, therefore, have enabled white ethnic Americans to strip away the scar tissue which their grandparents first acquired when they were physically and psychologically assaulted by native bigots decades ago. It is not surprising, then, that the most articulate exponents of Italian power are educated professionals, not restauranteurs or truck drivers, who are still numbed by the burden of inferiority often characteristic of the less educated American of Italian descent.

Ralph Perrotta, with a Harvard law degree, is better able to articulate, through the Op-Ed section of the New York *Times*, the social and economic problems plaguing lower-middle-class Italian-Americans than his immigrant tailor father. Newspaper readers and television viewers now learn about the problems of New York's Italians and Chicago's Poles—much the same ones which existed in the 1950s and 1960s—because educated men and women from these communities possess the communications skills, ego strength, and contacts to force the media to pay attention to them. The things they speak about like self-hate are derivative of an immigrant legacy but problems related to blue-collar life are also the subject of their commentary.

In the 1960s the Poverty Program, the Civil Rights Movement, and the Vietnam war radicalized many Catholic ethnics who came from communities where dissent was a stranger.

They were often the first in their family to attend college, to enter the professions, and to acquire expertise and information that led them to critically evaluate our society. Many had to leave the "old neighborhood"—as much a state of mind as a geographical setting—to gain the perspective which was a precondition to their "returning home."

The war on poverty enabled Italian youngsters from Long Island to return to East Harlem where their grandparents had once lived to work with blacks and Puerto Ricans who reside there today. It relocated Polish youngsters from suburban Detroit to Appalachia where they found raw proof that there was "another America"—a world where forty-year-old men sit on the front porches of their shacks gasping for air because their lungs are coated with lethal coal dust. Crippled laboring in the coal mines, they cannot earn a living to care for their families or derive the pride attendant upon that undertaking. The "hard times" that Grandma used to talk about in broken English gained clarity in the mind's eye of young people who had thought poverty was a phenomenon of the past. They wondered why the richest society in the history of mankind had so much deprivation and why otherwise decent middle-class Americans were so indifferent to such appalling conditions.

The Catholic ethnic youngsters who reached maturity in the 1960s were among the first in their communities to recognize the folly of U.S. involvement in Vietnam. But unlike the radicals from Berkeley who were bent on mobilizing the "proletariat" to "fight Amerikan Imperialism," they knew that mountain folk in the hollows, like the autoworker in Detroit, were deeply patriotic and that love of country was a solid part of their worldview. Having been weaned on a diet of superpatriotism, they understood why poor whites in the heartland of America drew back when a bright-eyed coed fresh out of college lectured them on American war crimes in Southeast Asia. Unlike their "cosmopolitan" friends who spoke about the "people" as a revolutionary abstraction, many thought about their friends and relatives who still carried lunch pails to the plant and lived in neighborhoods where people get emotional about the flag and the national anthem. Over time they noticed too that exponents of "people politics" were often contemptuous of the average working American—especially those "pawns of the establishment who belonged to racist unions and beat up on peace demonstrators."

Never having failed to get what they wanted, those sons and daughters of the establishment became demoralized when the war dragged on and the struggle against poverty and racism produced modest gains. Some turned their backs on politics and copped out by joining the drug culture or the Jesus Movement or disregarded notions about change altogether and joined the straight world of the affluent middle class from whence most of them came. At that point it became clear that many otherwise perceptive, decent people in the Movement, by virtue of their own ethnic and class backgrounds, were disinclined to deal with the day-to-day problems with which millions of working Americans were grappling.

It was by way of this circuitous route that many liberated white ethnics returned to their "old neighborhoods." They found what they had left behind—working people caught in an economic bind, school systems that failed white as well as black youngsters, local political institutions few people could effectively work with, and business interests which, in collusion with government, destroyed once stable, crime-free neighborhoods. "While I was marching with Doctor King, they were tearing down my old neighborhood," Peter Mollo, a South Brooklyn youth worker, told a gathering of community organizers in 1970.[9]

Sponsored by the National Center for Urban Ethnic Affairs, the participants had gathered in Washington to discuss "Ethnic and Working-Class Priorities." Activists who sought to organize people around a "working-class" agenda like the Alinsky-trained organizers from Gary, Indiana, and people like Steve Adubato of Newark who sought to mobilize his community around the common bond of ethnicity attended. So did Barbara Mikulski, who was fighting for a seat on the Baltimore City Council. A second-generation Polish-American who was a sparkplug behind the Southeast Baltimore Community Organization (SECO), she was a social worker before entering the political arena. Ms. Mikulski bucked machine resistance to win the election. The old pols in Baltimore had told her friends that Mikulski should not bother to run because they were going all out to defeat her.

Like Steve Adubato, she won because she mobilized young activists in her neighborhood and developed an effective political network. Most of the voters in her district are white ethnics; the Poles are the single largest group but her campaign revolved around issues germane to the blacks and other white working people who live in South Baltimore—poor schools, an unwanted expressway, and regressive taxes. While she did not overtly exploit ethnic loyalties, she was aware that to ignore the ethnic factor would have jeopardized her campaign. Had she not been a long-time resident of the district and had she been insensitive to the values and life-style of the constituents, she would have been defeated. Since then Ms. Mikulski has gained national notoriety; during the 1972 campaign she served as an adviser to Sargent Shriver, traveling with him and his wife Eunice on the campaign trail; after the election she was appointed chairperson of the Democratic Party's Delegate Selection Committee, and in 1974 she lost a bid for the Senate to the Republican incumbent Charles McC. Mathias.

The National Center for Urban Ethnic Affairs has helped organize community groups in over thirty cities in the mid-Atlantic states and Great Lakes region since 1970. Through provision of community organizers and community development assistance, it has enabled white ethnic neighborhoods to plug into urban programs from which they had previously been excluded. Through its ethnic clergy program it has been training Catholic priests and nuns to use community resources to deal with housing, educational, youth, and senior citizens problems. All of these activities have attracted local residents—many of whom are potential leaders—to community action programs. Baroni and his colleagues have shown young professionals, academics, and student activists how they can apply their talents in the development of worthwhile community programs and help working people project their grievances.

These new breed ethnic activists may not always see the world in the same light, but they are all intimately acquainted with the problems afflicting ordinary Americans in their neighborhoods and places of employment. In contrast to Catholic "radicals" like the brothers Berrigan or "liberated" Catholic intellectuals who are ashamed of their heritage, they do not adhere to a cultural life-style and political ethos which is anathema to many working-class Catholics. But unlike the ethnic politicians who are captives of the Old Politics, they espouse a new style of politics stressing the collective needs of the community. They are not utopian but pragmatic and prepared to work with all factions to achieve objectives redounding to the benefit of the entire community.

However, having recognized the need for organizing people at the neighborhood level and stressing the importance of community issues, a word of caution is in order. Proponents of community action have been inclined to make exaggerated claims about citizen power and participation. Working Americans throughout the country are in desperate need of community organizations to compel institutions to serve people they have been neglecting, and to demonstrate the power of collective action; but many, if not most, of our pressing domestic problems—housing, education, unemployment, inflation, medical care, etc.—require a national political thrust. This means the New Populists must reassemble the coalition which made the New Deal politically viable. Since the labor movement is the most important institution in the lives of many working people, it is bound to play a profound part in this endeavor.

C. Organized Labor and the New Populism: *Forces Are at Work Within the Labor Movement and Outside It Which Suggest a Shifting Balance of Power in Favor of Social Unionism*

There are striking similarities between the problems presently facing the labor movement and those threatening the AFL fifty years ago. In the late 1920s the proportion of organized workers was steadily declining, the forces responsible for the Great Depression were gathering steam, and the old men in the Federation ignored those who counseled them to adopt a new labor strategy. The way in which the labor movement today treats its internal problems, responds to a changing labor force, and adapts to harsh new economic realities will have a profound impact upon the New Populists' success. Some of labor's friends fear the old guard will dig in its heels and resist reform and perhaps turn toward the right rather than make changes which may jeopardize their domination of the labor movement.

In left-wing circles there is much talk about the possibility that in the face of stormy economic seas organized labor and big business may seek the safe harbor of collusion to protect their own interests at the public's expense. For years the Teamsters have fought as hard as the trucking industry for highways at the expense of mass transit; the United Steel Workers of America have lobbied with corporate management to reduce the importation of foreign steel; and defense workers, like their employers, have resisted cuts in military spending. But economic developments at home and abroad—the declining importance of highly unionized sectors of the economy, multinational corporations, foreign competition, and cartels—are compelling a growing number of labor leaders to seek even closer cooperation with management. Some of these new areas of cooperation have ominous implications for workers and society—for example, labor/management agreements in the steel and railway industry prohibiting strikes in favor of binding arbitration. Denied the right to strike, the worker is defenseless in the face of corporate power. The abolition of strikes also denies labor dissidents the means to protest their grievances when labor leaders are unresponsive to rank and file demands. A labor/management alliance cemented by narrow self-interest constitutes a threat to the consumer, small businessman, and unorganized worker and it is as detrimental to society as the polar alternative of unrelenting industrial warfare. Some radicals fear that these arrangements presage a de facto drive toward corporativism.

Another less pessimistic view envisages the resurrection of the labor strategy the Nixon Administration pursued to deny the Democrats the support of unified union allies. In spite of widespread disenchantment with President Ford's economic policies, we should not forget that the GOP's most successful labor strategist is Vice-President Nelson Rockefeller, who as governor consistently received the support of craft unions in the Empire State. His multibillion-dollar construction program in Albany is cited as an example of Rockefeller's labor strategy: undermine labor solidarity by bribing the craft unions through provision of public funding. This ploy has worked well in other industrial states and it is not unreasonable to conclude that it, or something similar to it, will be a principal component of the GOP's future labor strategy.

The foregoing presupposes the persistent domination of business unionists in the American labor movement. This is by no means implausible, but forces are at work which suggest a shifting balance of power in the labor movement favoring social unionism; they include the changing complexion of the rank and file and the rising expectations of workers, changes in the economic and political system necessitating the reorganization of unions and their political thrust, and the appearance of new, progressive labor leaders.

1. The Changing Complexion of the Rank and File

Today's young truck driver, autoworker, and secretary expect more out of life than their parents. They are challenging values—the work ethic and deference to authority—and beliefs —"those who work hard make it!"—which the older generation accepts as gospel truth. This new mindset should not be exaggerated but it is significant and it accounts for younger workers leading wildcat strikes and making demands for civil rights at work; it also explains why many of them reject the two major parties and applaud the anti-establishment rhetoric of a George Wallace or the rap of those rare Democratic radicals who have established rapport with them. Of course, in the mid-1970s traditional economic concerns have superseded workers' non-economic grievances (although issues like job satisfaction, health and safety, and industrial democracy will continue to trouble workers, especially after the economy once again picks up and unemployment declines), but this is not necessarily good news for the union leadership. The economic troubles of the 1970s have shaken rank and file confidence in their leadership and many workers are prepared to consider alternatives they previously ignored. Social unionists can undermine grass-roots business unionist support by demonstrating that it is no longer in the workers' self-interest to support leaders who adhere to an outmoded labor philosophy; that the labor movement must adapt to change; and that the people who have the vision to do so are not the old guard business unionists.

Black and Hispanic Americans in the next decade are destined to play much the same role that the white ethnics did in the 1930s through the labor movement and the Democratic Party. The mobilization of millions of persons who have not yet actualized their full economic and political potential will have a profound impact upon American society. Black and brown Americans are replacing whites in factories, mills, plants, and other industrial enterprises across the United States. Minority representation is growing in relative and absolute terms and by the end of the decade minority unionists will exert growing influence upon the labor movement.

Many of the occupational sectors which are virgin territory for union organizing are dominated by minority employees. Take the case of garbagemen, custodians, and hospital workers whom unions have previously ignored. The American Federation of State, County, and Municipal Employees (AFSCME), the fastest growing union in the United States, has organized low-income black municipal workers North and South. AFSCME doubled its membership from 1965 to 1972 and it is gathering in 1,000 dues-paying members weekly. Presently it has a total membership of well over 700,000. The union has organized hospital workers in New York and garbagemen in Memphis, and one of its vice-presidents, William Lucey, is black as are many of its members.

Rising self-awareness will facilitate unionization of black and Chicanos who do not hold union cards. The racial homogeneity of the work force, usually a by-product of past discrimination, will deny management the opportunity to play off black against white, Anglo against Chicano. In 1973, after a long and bitter strike, Willie Farah, the Texas pants tycoon, was forced to recognize the Amalgamated Clothing Workers Union. The solidarity of the predominantly Chicano work force contributed to the strike's success. A year later, one of the largest textile employers in the United States, the J. P. Stevens Company of North Carolina, gave in and recognized the demands of its employees for union recognition. The failure of the company to intimidate its labor force, a traditional ploy, was attributed by John Herling, the labor reporter, to the solidarity of the predominantly black work force.

Technological changes are destined to foster the unionization of minority workers too. The housing industry is a case in point; the United States cannot build sufficient homes and apartments to shelter its growing population—even middle-class Americans are priced out of the housing market. High interest rates, the soaring cost of land and material all account for this situation. Another contributing factor is the high cost of labor which is related to the construction industry's reluctance to adopt new technology and innovations necessary to build more quickly and at lower costs.

At the turn of this century, technological change set the stage for organizing industrial unions as applied science made it economically impossible to make products by hand. As the construction industry adopts new factory methods in the 1970s, jobs for semiskilled and unskilled workers will escalate dramatically. No doubt a large number of nonwhite workers will fill these job slots and unions which today are organized along craft lines will become "industrial organizations." Although the skilled white carpenter will earn a lower per hour wage, his annual salary will not suffer because he will be guaranteed a full work year.

As minority Americans take their proper place in the labor movement, it will become a stronger institution, better able to treat problems plaguing working Americans in general and nonwhites in particular. The growing presence of minority unionists will give new impetus to social unionism. This prophecy stems from the fact that the needs of most blacks cannot be met through collective bargaining alone. One of the reasons for the CIO's energetic involvement in politics was simply that the men and women it organized were low-paid factory operatives, not highly paid skilled workers, and social security, workmen's compensation, and other things critical to their welfare could only be obtained through government action—which meant cooperating with other progressive groups in coalition politics.

Minority unionists are much more likely to support militant tactics than their white workmates because they are disinclined to swallow whole the myths and half-truths accounting for the naïve trust of many whites in the good will of the "system." Blacks and Chicanos have learned that the system does not treat every citizen equally, and younger minority workers in many industries have "radicalized" whites with whom they work.

The growing importance of white-collar and women workers is also changing the complexion of the labor force. White-collar unions are growing much faster than blue-collar ones. In addition to the AFSCME, which has made great strides in organizing white-collar workers, the National Education Association, with a membership of 1.3 million, and the AFL-CIO's American Federation of Teachers, with 380,000 members, are the fastest growing unions in the country.[10] White-collar employees, who snubbed labor organizations in the past, are seeking union charters. "Labor bosses," who were formerly perceived by intellectuals with some disdain, are now being considered in a more positive light. In faculty coffee klatches across the country, college professors talk openly about "bringing in the Teamsters" to fight the administration and tight-fisted state legislatures which are increasing teaching work loads while dampening wage increases. High-priced technocrats in the aerospace industry were among the first to learn that without the protection of labor organizations even the elite of the labor force cannot be sure of job security or unending paychecks. An aggressive campaign to organize white-collar workers is certain to make great strides in the years ahead, and as they become a proportionately larger percentage of the labor movement, they will strengthen the hand of reformers. Many middle-class unionists, to the dismay of the old leadership, have shown a greater interest in internal union affairs than their blue-collar counterparts and they have advocated union involvement in matters which the business unionists deem beyond the purview of labor organizations. Like other middle-class Americans, they are issue-oriented and many are practitioners of the New Politics. As their influence grows and they learn to appreciate the problems of the rank and file blue-collar worker and his leadership, they will be in a position to play an important part in forging a labor/ New Populist alliance.

Women represent a vast untapped pool for unionization.

They comprise 43 per cent of the labor force today, more than double the female percentage 50 years ago. There are well over 30 million women in the labor force; 6 million belonged to unions in 1974 and that represents about 25 per cent of all union membership in the United States.[11] Labor leaders account for the small percentage of unionized women by alluding to the practice of women popping in and out of the labor force, to their being "part-time" employees, and to the fact that they work for small firms or cluster in white-collar occupations, both of which are difficult and expensive to organize. These explanations are not entirely groundless, but one of the major reasons why such a small percentage of women belong to unions is that men dominate the union movement. This prompted two hundred female trade unionists, representing twenty national and international unions, to meet in Chicago in 1973 to design a national strategy to organize workers of the "opposite sex." The meeting was the basis for the March 1974 founding of the Coalition of Labor Union Women (CLUW) in Chicago. Three thousand two hundred delegates, all of whom held union cards, representing blue- and white-collar unions, attended. Olga Madar of the UAW was elected president. CLUW represents the most meaningful step taken since the 1930s to adopt an aggressive campaign to organize the more than 30 million working women in the United States. The potential for success here is great, for every year growing numbers of women are entering the labor force and most of them plan to work for the rest of their lives. Rising family incomes since the end of World War II are directly attributable to the wife's joining the husband in the labor force. In 1940 about 16 per cent of married women worked full-time but by 1969 the percentage was 39.6. Economic necessity and the desire to fulfill themselves outside the home have contributed to an even larger percentage of wives seeking full-time jobs. A growing number of women, due to divorce, separation, or desertion, are becoming heads of households and working full-time; and smaller families are enabling women to break free of the home earlier than at any time in our history. The arguments that have traditionally been offered to explain the small percentage of women in the labor movement no longer hold water.[12]

2. Coming to Grips with a Changing Political Economy

The second set of factors shattering labor's complacency is related to union/management relations and the expanding role of government in American life. The emergence of conglomerates and the growth of multinational companies, competition from abroad, the declining importance of collective bargaining in the face of greater government intervention in the economy, and growing recognition on the part of the rank and file that as consumers and citizens they are powerless at the hands of big business and government—all require the American labor movement to adopt a new modus operandi to grapple with these changes.

Changes in the American economy account for heated discussion in labor circles about union consolidation; the combined power of several small unions is greater than the clout of each one alone, and even larger, healthier unions are considering merging in the face of conglomerate employers. Unions organized along craft lines and union autonomy itself are likely victims of conglomerate power. Increasingly it makes more sense to incorporate workers in a single plant (or industry) into one union than to have them belong to a host of labor organizations which cannot operate as a unified collective force. In the face of large conglomerates, several small unions may discover their merging is the only guarantee they have that they can bargain equally with management.

The looming presence of multinational corporations represents a profound challenge to the labor movement. The AFL-CIO claims that over one million American workers have lost jobs because American firms have relocated abroad. Today, while the AFL-CIO favors tariffs to reduce the importation of foreign goods, it is less certain about coping with the growing number of companies who are building plants abroad, depriving American workers of jobs and unions of dues-paying members. Multinational companies have sidestepped the need to bargain with unions by shifting the scene of action overseas and one of the ways unions are going to have to deal with this development is through political action of some kind.

Changes in the international market, including the changing economic position of so-called Third World countries

have provided added incentive for intensive government intervention in our domestic economy. Management, labor, the
farmer, and the consumer all must look to Washington for answers to their problems: the imposition of wage and price controls to fight inflation; the adoption of new monetary measures
to meet economic dislocations; tighter government regulation
of economic output; etc. The labor movement will be compelled to become more, not less, active in political matters as
jobs, wages, and prices become the province of Presidential
and congressional action, not the subject of collective bargaining.

Many labor leaders are not happy with the declining importance of collective bargaining, but matters formerly the subject of labor/management negotiations increasingly have become the subject of legislation. There is no doubt that this
trend will gather strength in the next decade. This means that
the labor movement must reach out and secure the support of
progressive allies to achieve gains, through the political
process, formerly obtained through collective bargaining. That
support in turn should be given on the condition that unions
stop discriminating against minority workers, that they adopt
a more aggressive strategy to organize those segments of the
work force not belonging to unions, that they take measures to
foster wider grass-roots democracy and clear their house of dis-
reputable union officials, and finally that they join a new
progressive coalition to eliminate existing social, economic,
and political injustices.

3. The Appearance of New Social Unionist Leaders

The CIO emerged during the 1930s because the AFL's
leadership lacked the vision, nerve, or interest to organize
workers into industrial unions. The CIO succeeded because
industrial unionists within the Federation, with the assistance
of labor radicals and middle-class progressives, provided the
leadership necessary to forge industrial workers into a mighty
collective force for economic and political action. Contrary to
the proclamations of leftist critics, there are numerous labor
leaders who have never surrendered their commitment to
social unionism. Jerry Wurf of AFSCME, Leonard Woodcock
of the UAW, and the Teamsters' Harold Gibbons represent a

sample of union leaders who best exemplify social unionism. Gibbons, the former president of the Teamsters' Midwest Conference, who played an active role in poverty and community programs in the greater St. Louis metropolitan area for years and supported McGovern in 1972, is proof that even unions which have a reputation for racketeering and union autocracy have many forward-looking men and women in their ranks. Arnold Miller and the brave men who organized the Miners for Democracy to oust Tony Boyle belie the charge that the rank and file are apathetic and indifferent to corrupt leadership. Miller and the dissidents who supported him put their lives on the line in opposing Boyle. Today District 31 of the United Steel Workers of America is presided over by Ed Sadlowski, a young labor radical whose dissident slate defeated Joe Germano's hand-picked candidates. Many observers believe that prospects of Sadlowski's eventually becoming president of the International Union are good. Within the ranks of labor leadership today, there are men and women who can play the same role that Lewis, Hillman, and their colleagues did in the 1930s to spearhead a new organizational drive in the South and among minority workers, women, and white-collar employees. The changing composition of the labor force and the challenges which are buffeting the labor movement suggest that profound readjustments within it are inevitable.

Since 1972 progressive trade unionists have signified that they will no longer accept the leadership of George Meany and the old men in the Executive Council of the AFL-CIO. Al Barkan and his colleagues at COPE discovered in December 1974 at the midterm convention of the Democratic Party that the Federation's old guard cannot ignore the coalition of middle-class reformers and progressive labor leaders which dominated the convention. During the 1960s liberal reformers, minority activists, and young Americans who earned their spurs in the poverty and antiwar movements developed a national network which proved most effective during the Democratic primaries in 1972. Consequently the Democratic Party now has two electoral networks, enhancing the prospects of liberal Democratic candidates. Many labor leaders in the AFL-CIO do not like this idea but others who have long identified with the old guard now recognize that the labor movement needs the middle-class reformers and their black allies as much as the latter groups need the support of organized labor. It may not happen for several years but social unionists, with the help of middle-class reformers and the support of minority workers and rank and file dissidents, will in the near future have a greater impact upon the labor movement than at any time since the rise of the CIO.

D. The Democratic Party and the White Ethnics: *The Group-Anchored White Ethnic Attachment to the Democratic Party Remains Firmly Fixed*

Some activists deserving the New Populist label are toying with the idea of forming a third party, citing the failure of the Old Politics, the growing incidence of ticket-splitting, the propensity of an increasing number of voters to identify themselves as Independents, and the disintegration of the two major parties as the basis for doing so. If a significant number of them choose this option, they will strengthen the status quo elements within the Democratic Party and perhaps even enable the Republicans to secure a new lease on the White House in 1976. Since the mid-nineteenth century the vast majority of Americans have perceived the two major parties as the only legitimate political organizations in our polity. Third parties have rarely enjoyed a long life-span or attracted a large popular following. Most have been single issue movements, regionally based, or they have championed reforms ultimately adopted by the GOP and its rival.

There are fundamental structural reasons for the weakness of the two major parties and the failure of third parties in the United States. Ours is a federal system comprised of fifty states, fostering decentralized political organizations. Regional, ethnic, racial, religious, and class differences have further weakened them, although none of these cleavages has been serious enough to produce highly disciplined ideological movements. Since U.S. senators and governors can extract funds from their own state organizations and from private sources, the "national party" cannot use the club of money to discipline them. The same goes for U.S. congressmen and local candidates who can thumb their noses at state organizations and get away with their apostasy because they possess an independent power base. In many places there are no state party organizations to speak of but rather loose political alliances comprised of a multiplicity of factions. The truth is that many "state parties" only function like authentic political organizations during election time. And it makes little sense to talk about the "national" Republican or Democratic Party either, especially if we mean by this centralized political organizations making policy for state and local affiliates.

All of these factors accounting for the weaknesses of the two major parties pertain to third parties too. Moreover, ours is a Presidential and not a Parliamentary system and we elect candidates by majority vote and not proportional representation, so minority party candidates have little incentive to remain independent from the major parties; for even if they receive 15 per cent of the vote, they cannot hope to secure 15 per cent of the seats as they would in a Parliamentary system with proportional representation.

In addition to the foregoing observations, the New Populists must keep the following in mind: in spite of the decline of the regular party organizations, suburbanization, socioeconomic mobility, and disenchantment with the New Politics reformers, the white ethnic's group-anchored attachment to the Democratic Party remains firmly fixed.

The most influential formulation of ethnic politics developed after the Second World War was the work of Robert Dahl, the prominent Yale political scientist. He contended that there were three stages to ethnic politics. The first found the ethnic group socioeconomically homogeneous; since most members belong to the working class, they adopt a common pattern of political behavior. In the second stage, socioeconomic mobility changes the group's configuration, for now some of its members have entered the middle class as white-collar workers, businessmen, and professionals. The group is no longer politically homogeneous as it was during the first stage, yet its middle-class members still favor candidates who belong to their ethnic community. The third stage finds the group highly heterogeneous with large segments of it belonging to the middle and upper middle classes. "To these people, ethnic politics is often embarrassing or meaningless. Political attitudes and loyalties have become a function of socioeconomic characteristics."[13] At this point the tug of ethnicity has lost its pull. Dahl's "assimilationist" theory prevailed for many years until political scientists criticized it for not adequately explaining the persistence of ethnic voting, especially among middle-class voters. Raymond Wolfinger formulated what he called a "mobilization" theory of ethnic politics to provide an answer.

> Middle-class status is a virtual prerequisite for candidacy for major office; an ethnic group's development of sufficient political skills and influence to secure such a nomination also requires the development of a middle class. Therefore ethnic voting will be greatest when the ethnic group has produced a middle class, in the second and third generation, not in the first.[14]

The middle class, in other words, possesses the skills and resources to mobilize an ethnic community behind one of their own candidates. Wolfinger claims that the ethnic factor will continue to influence political behavior although he concedes that "continuing education, regional migration, intermarriage, and assorted intergroup contact are all likely to hasten assimilation."[15] Wolfinger's theory is a necessary readjustment to Dahl's, although it fails to tell us precisely when ethnicity will disappear as a shaping influence.

Political scientists have conducted a great deal of research on ethnic voting behavior and the following observations can be made with some measure of confidence.

The principal cause of ethnic politics anywhere in the world is discrimination, real or imagined, suffered by an ethnic minority. The New Immigrants, denied equal access to economic, social, and political prerogatives white Protestants enjoyed, formed their own political organizations and (until they became affixed to the machine) judged candidates, issues, and parties on the basis of who were truly sensitive to the "folk," what legislation was critical to the community, and which political party would best serve its interest. Even after the discriminatory practices giving rise to ethnic solidarity declined, voters who were subject to past acts of discrimination did not easily forget them. This explains why rates of political participation in some places have been higher among white ethnics than among similarly situated native Americans. It also explains why, during primaries or when other cues like party affiliation or prior knowledge about either candidate does not exist, voters favor candidates belonging to their own ethnic group.

In many places electoral data support Wolfinger's contention that ethnicity may figure most prominently in the politics of an ethnic minority when its members enter the middle class in large numbers, providing a cadre for mobilizing the community into a powerful voting bloc. The ethnic factor may also come into play the first time a member of that group runs for high office; many Irish Catholics who realigned with the Republican Party after World War II voted for John F. Kennedy for President in his race against Richard Nixon in 1960. On the other hand, a fellow ethnic may be discouraged from running for office if his candidacy is deemed detrimental to the group's welfare; a Jewish candidate who is judged to be unqualified by his co-religionists may not receive their votes because, if elected, he would be a source of embarrassment to them.

Lingering ethnic affinities may become manifest where an ethnic group makes a bid for political power giving rise to heightened ethnic self-consciousness on the part of the entire electorate. The conflict between the blacks and Italians in Newark is descriptive of this situation and the prominence of Jews among the reformist wing of the Democratic Party in New York may account for many Catholics aggregating together in reaction to "Jewish political power."

The dialectic of ethnic conflict may also help explain why Catholic ethnics in New York City are more inclined to vote for Republicans and conservatives than their co-religionists in Chicago and Buffalo. Unlike New York, where the Jews have become a dominant force in the Democratic Party, the Democratic political organizations in the last two cities are controlled by Catholics. Yet it would be a grave error to attribute Catholic enmity toward the reformers solely in terms of bigotry. Anti-Semitism has caused some Catholics to turn toward the GOP; others have done so because they perceive "Jewish power" as a threat to the Catholic interest, but we should not ignore a class-related explanation either. The New York reformers are predominantly middle-class persons who advocate changes which low income Catholics (and many Jews) cannot abide. The confluence of religious, ethnic, and class factors coming together has caused political pundits who entertain a single motive for political behavior to wring their hands in frustration.

Voters who may not feel ethnic or speak of themselves as ethnics cannot forget their ethnicity because other Americans refuse to. Two enterprising political scientists found in California that Americans continue to cling to ethnic prejudices in their voting preferences.

> In California, if a candidate has a Scandinavian surname, he has a 24 per cent advantage of candidates with other ethnic names. If he has an English surname, he will enjoy a slight advantage. An Irish or Greek surname gives him neither an advantage nor a disadvantage. However, with a Spanish surname he suffers an 11 per cent disadvantage; with a Jewish last name, a 14 per cent disadvantage; and Italians, by far the worst off, have a 30 per cent disadvantage.[16]

In other parts of the country voters may not feel the same way that the California electorate does about the importance of ethnicity but the data testify to the fact that Americans do think it is an important consideration in casting their ballots.

Because ethnicity is deemed divisive, politicians have been reluctant to make overt ethnic appeals. During the 1964 senatorial campaign between incumbent Kenneth Keating and Robert F. Kennedy, *Newsweek* reported, "From the stump, New York politicians righteously deplore any suggestions that their red-blooded American constituents might be influenced by bloc voting patterns; off the stump they find it hard to discuss strategy in any other terms."[17] Politicians take ethnicity seriously, in many cases because it is a shorthand way of categorizing the electorate, not only in terms of their religion and nationality, but also in terms of social class and issue orientation. Of course, many politicians manipulate ethnic affiliations to promote their political fortunes. It is difficult to determine how important this practice is to the persistence of the ethnic factor, but it certainly encourages voters to look at the political universe through the prism of ethnicity.

These data by no means suggest that ethnicity is more important than social class in determining voting preferences. Ethnicity continues to shape political behavior but its influence is variable and not constant. In New York, Irish Catholics have rejected Irish candidates whom they perceive as too liberal for their tastes. In the 1965 Democratic mayoralty primary, Congressmen William Fitts Ryan and Paul O'Dwyer only received 11 and 7 per cent of the votes cast by Irish Catholics, while "City Council President Paul Screvane and City Comptroller Abraham Beame together won almost five out of every six votes cast in Irish precincts."[18] And while John F. Kennedy captured Irish Republican votes in 1960, he did best among low income Irish Catholics and not those who resided in middle-class districts. In Illinois, moreover, urban Poles are more inclined to vote for a Polish candidate than rural Poles are; here is evidence that geographical dispersion as well as middle-class status may dampen ethnicity in voting behavior.[19]

When truly vital issues are at stake, ethnic appeals may fail to produce desired results and no matter how salient a voter's ethnic identification may be, it will prove politically irrelevant barring a perceived connection between this identity and the election. These factors probably explain the failure of Senator Muskie to monopolize the Polish-American vote during the 1972 Presidential primaries. Moreover, where social class and ethnicity conflict, the voter may forget his ethnic affiliation and vote his pocketbook. This does not mean that social class is a better predictor of political behavior than ethnicity; it all depends upon the circumstances, the existing issues and political climate, the ethnic electorate's sensitivity, its perception of the candidate, etc. Finally, some studies show that, taken together, ethnicity and social class more accurately predict voting preferences than either one standing alone.[20]

This brings us back to the matter of the white ethnics' affinity for the Democratic Party. The evidence is overwhelming; it shows that Catholics and Jews, whatever their

economic status, are far more inclined to vote for a Democratic than a Republican candidate. In 1952, 70 per cent of
the Irish Catholics, 62 per cent of the Italian Catholics, and
76 per cent of the Polish Catholics voted for Democratic
congressmen. The comparable figures for 1970 were 73 per
cent, 62 per cent, and 73 per cent respectively. The Irish percentage increased, the Italian remained the same, and the
Polish dropped only three points. During this period the Poles
were 21 percentage points more likely to vote for Democrats
in congressional races than the national average, the Irish 15
percentage points, and the Italians 7 percentage points.[21]

The white ethnics rebuffed George McGovern in 1972, but
looking at the Democratic Party's voting constituencies—the
poor, the blacks, union members, Catholics, Southerners, and
Americans living in center-city—we find the poor's contribution to McGovern amounted to 10 per cent, the blacks 22 per
cent, unionists 32 per cent, Catholics 34 per cent, the South
25 per cent, and center-city voters 14 per cent.[22] (Because of
overlapping, the total is more than 100 per cent.) The
Catholics' contribution was clearly the largest and in congressional, local, and statewide races that year, Catholics generally
turned their backs on Republican candidates. One third of the
nation's Democrats are Catholics and that figure approaches
two fifths outside the South.

In 1972, when white ethnic dissatisfaction with the Democratic Party was acute, most Catholics and Jews told pollsters
that they identified with the Democratic Party. From 1963 to
1972 the Democratic Party's popularity with the white ethnics
slipped, but in every case the slippage was relatively slight.

DEMOCRATIC PARTY IDENTIFICATION, 1963 AND 1972[23]

	Irish	Italian	Polish	Jewish
1972	61%	63%	72%	69%
1963	70%	67%	77%	65%

Party identification is critically important; political scientists have found that it is the best single predictor of voting
behavior. Among political consultants and reform-minded politicians, however, it has become fashionable to debunk the importance of party identification; for example, if party i.d. is so

important, how can one account for widespread ticket-splitting and the noticeable decline in partisanship among many traditional Democratic voters? The answer is that when many traditional Democratic voters proclaim that they identify with the Democratic Party, they are thinking about local or state Democratic politicians with whom they share a common issue orientation, ethnic affiliation, or political culture, not about the "national Democratic politicians" who adhere to a political ethos which is alien to them. In other words, the confusion which exists among academics and political practitioners alike regarding the importance of party identification is explained by political culture.

To a significant degree, ethnicity explains why Catholics and Jews identify with the Democratic Party while white Protestants favor the GOP. The nexus between ethnicity and party affiliation is also the basis for an enigma troubling political writers for years—namely, that the so-called "conservative Republican Party" is home for liberals like Clifford Case while the allegedly "liberal Democratic Party" embraces reactionaries like James Eastland. Why? A partial answer is that historical ethnic factors accounting for this conundrum are at work in both New Jersey and Mississippi. In New Jersey the Catholic ethnic influence in the Democratic Party has compelled many otherwise liberal Wasps to affiliate with the GOP, while in Mississippi no loyal (or pragmatic) son of the Confederacy would have anything to do with the "nigger-loving" Republican Party. It was only after Southern whites began to perceive the GOP in the second half of the twentieth century as the "white man's party," that millions of them began to vote for Republican candidates.

Today ethnicity explains why a Wasp farmer in Michigan faithfully votes for Republicans while his Polish neighbor would not think of casting his ballot for any candidate other than a Democrat even though they are both men of the soil and earn identical yearly incomes. This discrepancy may be a contemporary manifestation of Protestant/Catholic feuding in times past. Here the ethnic factor cuts both ways: the Polish-American votes for the Democratic Party because he identifies it with the welfare of American Polonians while his Wasp neighbor opposes Democrats for precisely that reason.

Middle-class status has caused some white ethnics to bolt
the Democratic Party for economic interests. Nonetheless,
Jewish businessmen, Irish attorneys, and Polish M.D.s, for example, are still more likely to vote for Democrats than their
Wasp colleagues and to support economic reforms critical to
working Americans. Like their relatives who drive trucks or old
high school friends who walk a policeman's beat, they believe
the Democratic Party is "their party" and best represents them.

Many white ethnics still labor at blue-collar jobs and most
of them still think of themselves as working people. If anything, their group-anchored attachment to the Democratic
Party is bound to be strengthened by the economic trouble
which has hounded the United States in the 1970s. Their
confidence may be misplaced, but they will not break with the
past and consistently give the bulk of their votes to the Republican Party in the foreseeable future.

E. Reaching Out to the White Ethnics: *The New Populists Must Develop a Political Strategy Which Is Both Stylistically and Substantively People Oriented*

The New Populists can attract traditional Democratic
voters to a left of center agenda if they develop a political
strategy which is both stylistically and substantively people
oriented. To do so they must demonstrate a real appreciation
for what makes the white ethnics tick, what concerns them,
what their dreams and fears are, how they perceive the world,
what symbols, values, and words turn them on and which ones
turn them off. In this connection, four areas of concern
deserve to be considered: preserving a way of life; ethnic
issues; the economic issue; and wider participation in decision-
making.

1. Preserving a Way of Life

On the eve of the 1970 elections, Richard Scammon and
Ben Wattenberg's *The Real Majority* was published. The authors warned that the turmoil of the 1960s had given impetus
to a host of non-economic concerns, which they spoke of in
terms of "the social issue"—racial strife, widespread social
unrest, the counterculture, and other activities which threat-

ened the ordinary American's way of life. If candidates ignored the social issue, they did so at great political risk. McGovernites cited the book's findings as further evidence of middle-America's conservatism. The inference was that a voter's orientation toward social issues was something of a litmus test to determine his conservatism or liberalism. Someone who voiced concern about pot or busing was labeled conservative, while a swinging businessman who smoked grass on weekends was labeled liberal even if his positions on bread and butter issues were unknown.

The National Opinion Research Center (NORC) conducted a survey in 1971 to determine ethnic attitudes on a range of issues including many of those which fit Scammon and Wattenberg's description of the "social issue." The survey revealed that Italians, Poles, and Anglo-Saxon Protestants all agreed that the "most serious issues" were war, marijuana, inflation, crime, and pollution. War was everyone's first choice, but the Poles and Italians, like the Anglo-Saxons, placed marijuana second. These three groups, along with the other two surveyed—the Irish and German Catholics—overwhelmingly disliked "hippies" and "radical students."

The Catholic ethnics were more liberal on issues like pollution, gun control, poverty, neighborhood and school integration, and civil liberties than white Protestants. But they were more inclined to take a hard (conservative) line on the punishment of criminals, rioters, and radicals, favor capital punishment, and oppose busing and the legalization of marijuana. The Poles were most unfavorable to welfare recipients and the Italians were most inclined to dislike liberals. As we observed earlier in an evaluation of racial attitudes, the ethnics are more liberal than other Americans on some social matters and more conservative on others. Thus, it is questionable whether they deserve the conservative label even if non-economic issues are the basis for comparison.[24]

Ethnic opposition to busing, however, is disquieting since it is potentially a national issue and it sets them off against blacks who are also a vital component of the New Populists' coalition. Perhaps there is no way that this issue can be treated without displeasing one or both parties to the dispute. Nevertheless, it is a grave error to attribute white op-

position to busing exclusively to racial prejudice as many liberal and black writers have done.

There are white residents of South Boston who oppose busing because they are racially prejudiced, but others oppose it
for nonracial reasons. One of the most prevalent is race-
related, but not a matter of prejudice per se, and that is fear of
violence. Parents who are asked to send their children to Roxbury know that most inner-city black schools and neighborhoods are dangerous places for whites to be. Blacks in
many Northern cities have a reputation for being tougher than
whites and, products of a ghetto street culture, they are more
inclined to use a weapon in a street fight. This widespread fear
of black violence has not received proper attention from the
media or from interracial experts, but it is uppermost in the
minds of whites throughout the metropolitan North who con-
template sending their children to predominantly black
schools.

In addition to their fears of black violence, inner-city whites
have reacted emotionally to busing schemes because their inability to resist them—like the vulnerability of their communities to bulldozers—is vivid proof that they lack power, that
they cannot protect the things which mean most to them—
their children and neighborhoods. In many areas busing is
seen as a device favored by affluent suburbanites who are
remote from the problem to force white working people to
sacrifice their kids in the name of racial justice. It has not been
widely publicized, but the Coleman Report—which undergirds
the need for busing—noted that lower-class children of all
races suffer educational deprivation. So sending low income
whites to attend school with low income blacks may harm
both groups. And is it unreasonable to compare white demands for neighborhood schools with black pleas for community control? Racial strife is a serious social problem in
America; it cannot be avoided, but it is a grave mistake to
place the burden of dealing with it on society's lower class
alone. To many working-class whites who cannot afford to
send their children to private schools, this is what busing
means.

The propensity to interpret our urban malaise primarily
from a racial perspective accounts for the failure to focus on

problems common to white and black urbanites alike. "Contrary to liberal opinion, many of the things the ethnics complain about have nothing to do with blacks, but with the inability of working people to protect the things which mean most to them—their families, homes, and neighborhoods."[25] Even where public and private grants have been made available to ethnic neighborhoods, it is usually in racially troubled areas, not in cities, small towns, or blue-collar suburbs where few blacks live or work.

The problems encountered in these communities may not attract the attention of the media, but they are of paramount importance to people who fear their neighborhood is to be bulldozed, their church destroyed, and they will have to leave their homes, friends, and relatives. Marc Fried, a psychiatrist who studied the impact of urban renewal upon an Italian community in the West End of Boston, found that relocation produced profound psychological and social deprivation among the people involved. "Since most notably in the working class effective relationships with others are dependent upon a continuing sense of common group identity, the experience of loss and disruption of these affiliations is intense and frequently irrevocable."[26]

Highly mobile members of the middle class do not appreciate how important the neighborhood is to working-class white ethnics, especially those who have lived in a single community for many years. Even persons who have left the old neighborhood for the suburbs have brought their old value system with them. New alien influences like drugs, sexual license, and other forms of permissive behavior threatening the integrity of the family are perceived as socially destructive. People will fight as hard to preserve a way of life as they will struggle to protect their children or property and the New Populists should never forget it.

The working American's resistance to change is not merely a product of a rigid value system, but a pragmatic posture stemming from circumstances. Unlike the supermarket clerk or truck driver, the affluent exponent of change enjoys good connections, a college degree, and the self-confidence which comes from being one of society's "winners." He is confident about his ability to cope with change and is certain he will not become one of its victims. The American of modest means and education, however, is a product of a different culture; it is one marked by the reality that ordinary people at best have a marginal impact upon their environment and none upon powerful people who make important decisions.

Due to rising levels of education, exposure to the mass media, and greater economic security, however, working people have become more receptive to certain changes than was the case one or two generations ago. For example, in contrast to the 1960s, polls now show that women from all social strata have begun to demonstrate an interest in the new roles for women about which their well-educated sisters talk. But predominantly middle-class organizations like NOW have failed to develop programs germane to lower-middle-class women whose support is critical to the ultimate success of the women's movement. Consciousness raising sessions and seminars treating the works of Germaine Greer, Simone de Beauvoir, or Jill Johnston are not very relevant to the average American woman and much of what she is likely to hear at these sessions is bound to turn her off. Those middle-class women's libbers who have bothered to interact with women working in factories or typing pools have found that they are keenly interested in issues like equal pay for equal work, equitable promotions, and other matters which affect their economic well-being and job prospects.

The New Populists can gain rapport with working people by demonstrating a real concern for their problems at work and at home, and in many instances they can help solve some of them. Tony Massocchi of the Oil, Chemical, and Atomic Workers Union has praised highly those physicians, public health workers, and medical researchers who have provided technical assistance to his union in its campaign to publicize and fight occupational health hazards. Pro bono lawyers, urban experts, academics, and other professionals can play a similar critical role in helping working people come to grips with the problems they encounter in their communities. It is through concrete action that the New Populists must bridge the gap of distrust which separates them from the working people of the United States. When it can be demonstrated to the ordinary person that he can cope with mundane problems through collaboration with his peers, larger ones previously deemed nearly impossible to treat will be considered in a new, more positive manner. To develop the average American's political consciousness, it is necessary to help him through a slow, step-by-step process, moving from smaller to larger actions. Middle-class radicals often avoid such political work because it is tedious and because they are inclined to confuse intellectually elegant conceptual schemes with the real world.

2. Ethnic Issues

In spite of the persistence of the ethnic factor and the growing influence of the New Ethnicity, there are few national "ethnic issues"—that is, issues which attract an overwhelming number of people from a specific ethnic group regardless of their residency, education, income, occupation, social status, religious beliefs, or political preferences. One of the rare national ethnic issues (among whites) is the profound concern of American Jews about the fate of Israel. The Yom Kippur War had a galvanizing effect upon Jews in the United States when it became apparent that the Israelis no longer enjoy a decisive military advantage, that the Arabs can manipulate their oil to blackmail Israel's friends, and that time is on the Arabs' side. This profound power shift in the Middle East has caused Jews from all walks of life—New Leftists and Republicans, those who are orthodox in their faith and those who belong to reform synagogues, left-wing writers and Wall Street brokers, "Germans" and "Russians"—to band together to collect money and lobby to protect Israel from its enemies and lukewarm friends.

The Greek-American community's concern about the plight of Greeks in Cyprus due to the 1974 Turkish invasion of the island is another example of a national ethnic issue. In the aftermath of the Greek-Turkish conflict on Cyprus, Greeks from all parts of the United States lobbied hard and prompted Congress to withhold military aid from Turkey. Throughout this century ethnic minorities in the United States often have demonstrated that in the case of foreign policy issues affecting their former homeland, they can achieve a level of solidarity that they have been unable or unwilling to produce vis-à-vis domestic issues.

Among Catholic ethnic groups there is no issue which has drawn an overwhelming number of Catholics together. A majority of Catholics oppose abortion, but the difference between them and Protestant Americans is not great; Gallup found that 41 per cent of the Catholic population favored abortion "through the third month of pregnancy" while 50 per cent disapproved. The comparable figures among Protestants were 52 per cent and 48 per cent respectively. An even larger percentage of Catholics favor federal aid to parochial schools—73 per cent—but neither abortion nor parochial school aid has had a profound emotional impact upon Catholics equivalent to Jewish concern about the fate of Israel.[27] A clash between the women's liberation movement and the Catholic church, however, appears to be in the offing, although it is too early to predict the scope of that confrontation. But the Catholic church and the American Catholic community are not identical and even if the church's hierarchy took a united stand against the women's movement (an unlikely prospect), the nation's Catholics would not.

It is even more apparent that there is no single Irish, Ukrainian, or Polish issue. Not many Irish-Americans have demonstrated concern about the communal slaughter in Ulster and only a small minority of Lithuanians or Ukrainians talk about the plight of the "captive peoples" living behind the Iron Curtain. The same goes for Americans whose former homelands are now ruled by indigenous communist governments like those in Poland and Czechoslovakia. In Polish-American papers like the *Post-Eagle*—published in New Jersey but circulated to Polonians throughout the United States—it is not uncommon to read favorable comments about the Polish government. The publisher and his readers are not leftists, but people who take great pride in their heritage and in the accomplishments of the Polish nation in the last quarter century.

Rising ethnic self-awareness may give impetus to the mobilization of ethnic voters behind issues which presently do not receive their support, for example concern among Lithuanian-Americans about religious and ethnic persecution against

Lithuanians in the USSR. But to imply, as Michael Novak does in *The Rise of the Unmeltable Ethnics*, that there are issues around which the white ethnics can be organized nationally is to misread the importance of the ethnic factor in our political process. In many areas there are numerous issues germane to a specific ethnic group associated with real or imagined acts of discrimination, the destruction of a neighborhood or parish, etc. There are also numerous instances of ethnic groups at odds, for example conflict between the blacks and Italians in Newark, the Catholics and Jews in New York, or those which involve Polish and Irish antagonists in the Catholic church, but these are local in character. To the people concerned, these issues are important and they deserve to be taken seriously, but they are local ones.

While it is dangerous to misconstrue the nature and scope of ethnicity in the American political process, the day of the ethnically balanced ticket is by no means over. In places, heightened ethnic self-awareness may necessitate progressives, who otherwise view such arrangements as reprehensible, to pay homage to deep-seated ethnic affinities. This does not mean that hacks must be appointed to office or be selected as community representatives; fortunately there is an ample number of well-qualified people in every ethnic community to meet the requirements of ethnic representation where necessary.

It should be emphasized that the ethnic issues mentioned above are qualitatively different than the stated goals of ethnic minorities in other multi-ethnic societies. In the United States there is no ethnic group which is demanding corporate status as is the case of the French separatists in Canada or the Basque separatists in Spain. It is very unlikely that any ethnic group in the United States in the future will make a serious effort to achieve such separatist goals.

3. The Economic Issue

The economy will be the principal issue in 1976 and for the rest of this decade. Double digit rates of inflation and unemployment figures which are the highest since the Great Depression have had a profound impact upon the American people. There is rising public concern about our declining standard of living and the fear that a major depression equivalent to the crash of the 1930s is no longer as unthinkable as it was once. In the early part of the 1970s inflation was the number one concern of the American people. From 1972 to 1973 there was a fifteen point jump from 57 per cent to 72 per cent in the number of Americans who reported that inflation was their principal economic worry. It hit those living on fixed incomes and the poor the hardest but the real income of the American worker shrank and even middle-class Americans had to make economic sacrifices.

Since late 1974 the fear of recession has begun to compete with inflation as the nation's number one issue. Against the backdrop of predictions that the unemployment rate will reach 9 or 10 per cent, people who had previously assumed their standard of living would consistently soar upward were forced to face the harsh truth that they would have to accept a lower living standard, that their jobs were no longer secure, and that government could not guarantee against an even more precipitous downturn in the economy. In assessing the political implications of the electorate's preoccupation with economic hard times, it is fair to expect the Republicans, who were in power during the worst recession since the 1930s, to suffer for it. But ironically, the legislation the Democratic Party championed during the New Deal—unemployment insurance, social security, and other welfare schemes Republicans have traditionally opposed—may help ameliorate the political repercussions stemming from the economic difficulties wracking the country in the 1970s. Nevertheless, the nation's economic problems in the 1970s have prompted the electorate to look more closely at the distribution of wealth in the United States and to ask questions pertaining to the awesome power of big business. Thus, in contrast to polls taken in the 1960s, those today show there has been a significant rise in the proportion of Americans who believe that "the rich get richer and the poor get poorer" and that "big business has too much power in our society."[28]

The energy crisis has demonstrated that the concentration of power in the hands of a few large corporations represents a real threat to society and that the power of big business cannot be ignored. Even prior to the recession, polls conducted by NORC indicated that the white ethnics were more concerned about the power of big business than white Protestants. Whereas 76 per cent of the Wasps responded that they liked big business, the respective percentages for the Catholic ethnic groups were 42 per cent for the Irish, 31 per cent for the Germans, 57 per cent for the Italians, and 33 per cent for the Poles. The Catholics, moreover, were more inclined to express a dislike for business than the Protestants, of whom only 14 per cent admitted to this bias. These findings show that one of the significant differences between the political orientation of the white ethnics and white Protestants is the former's rather well developed mistrust of corporate power.[29]

Furthermore, while they may hold big government suspect too, they are more inclined to favor government intervention in the economy than their fellow Americans. Andrew Greeley has found evidence refuting the proposition that the Catholic ethnics are more private regarding than other Americans—that is most opposed to government programs which treat collective problems. He discovered that Southern and Eastern Europeans are more likely than Jews to support the service and welfare orientation of government; and while 43 per cent of the Anglo-Saxons sampled said that the government should use "all of its resources" to eliminate poverty, 66 per cent of the Irish, 62 per cent of the Italians, and 74 per cent of the Poles said so. The Jews in turn continue to score higher on these matters than white Protestants do and Catholic blue-collar workers are more likely than other white workers to favor a guaranteed minimum wage. If economic criteria are used to determine liberal or conservative attitudes, the white ethnics are clearly deserving of the liberal label. Here is further evidence that the white ethnics are more inclined to accept the kinds of reforms that the New Populists talk about than other white Americans.[30]

But in formulating their economic programs the New Populists will be making a serious mistake if they ignore the American economic creed, which holds that private property is linked to political liberty, that the profit motive is a vital and proper way to reward productive members of society, and that competition is the basis for a free economy and serves as a check upon the concentration of economic and political power. In developing a substantive assault on corporate power, they might well ponder the failure of American socialists to attract popular support for their cause. One of the fatal socialist errors is to cling to the sectarian view that the ordinary citizen is a victim of "false consciousness"—that the values, symbols, and beliefs which give purpose to his life are all derivative of a capitalist con job. Because the socialists refuse to accept this commitment to the American economic creed as authentic or voluntary, they have ignored the far-reaching implications of demonstrating to the electorate that our "free enterprise" system in reality does not fully measure up to the ideals of the American economic creed. Big business, for example, uses its economic leverage to dominate governmental decisions, reducing competition—the single most important element in any free economy.

Consider also the socialists' tendency to blithely ignore fears about the concentration of resources in the hands of the state; this cavalier attitude has been adroitly manipulated by corporate publicists to undermine important public programs. Opinion surveys show that the public in the 1970s has lost confidence in government's capacity to solve many of their problems—the federal government in particular. Reforms eliciting greater government intervention in the economy, therefore, may not be easy to sell to the American people. Of course, they do not understand that many things they do not like about "big government" are often attributable to the ability of powerful groups in the private sector to manipulate the state to achieve economic gains at the expense of the consumer and taxpayer. This should be one of the principal public education goals of the New Populists.

The New Populists must be careful in their choice of rhetoric. It is unfortunate that many democratic radicals persist in using the word "socialism" to describe their program for change; the word connotes to the American people—even though unfairly—a specter of totalitarian rule and a drab life which is hardly attractive to the poor, the working class, or the middle class in the United States. The socialists have presented the most incisive analysis of the structural basis of our economic, social and political malaise—inherent in capitalism is the tendency to concentrate economic power and to use it to manipulate the political system against competition, labor, and the consumer. But they have not convinced the American electorate that their alternatives are economically viable and politically benign. It is especially important that the New Populists not follow the example of the socialists and reject modest reforms in favor of comprehensive societal read-justments which the people are unprepared to accept because they fear such changes will deny them their political liberties and/or consign them to a lower living standard. Reforms some socialists might deem modest are not only more likely to be politically viable but they can serve as prototypes demon-strating that greater public planning and other notions run-ning counter to the American political culture are not to be feared but welcomed. The success of such incremental reforms will help dispel the fears of Mr. and Mrs. America about the socialist cure being more lethal than the capitalist sickness.

It can be demonstrated in fact that the medicine is not all that harsh, that the corporate interests are violating the Amer-ican economic creed while the changes the New Populists propose are supportive of it. For example, in breaking up con-centrated industries competition may be reaffirmed and, con-trary to the myth of bigness, production will rise. This action will help us in our war on inflation and deny the corporate Leviathans the means to circumvent our political system to vi-olate the laws of the market and undermine public regulation of big business.

Because of widespread fears attending our economic trou-bles, fundamental readjustments in our economy which five or ten years ago were politically implausible are now feasible. The energy crisis, for example, has caused Americans from all walks of life, including U.S. congressmen, George Meany, and the Teamsters, to talk openly about the nationalization of the oil industry and public utilities. Such talk would have been unthinkable in 1972. During the 1960s, although the streets were aflow with protesters and the tranquility of academia was shattered by radicals denouncing Amerikan Imperialism, no savvy political analyst paid much attention to New Leftists who called for the nationalization of our nation's major indus-tries or even those liberals who spoke about greater corpo-rate responsibility. Few Americans favor widespread nation-alization of basic industries, but now the American people have begun to stir and they only await the leadership to move against those powerful economic interests which control so many areas of our lives.

It is uncertain how fast a majority of the electorate is prepared to move to fight corporate power and to support other necessary readjustments in our economic and political institutions. The New Populists can help voters focus upon the source of our problems and mobilize them into a powerful collective force, but first they must demonstrate that they are fighting for changes which are supportive of our political culture and are of real concern to the "little guy."

4. Participating in Decision-Making

Pollsters report a significant rise in the number of Americans who claim that "what we say doesn't count much anymore," that "the people running the country don't really care what happens to us," and that "we feel left out of things going on around us." These feelings, taken together with dwindling confidence in our institutions, explain why the turnout rate has declined in the last several Presidential elections. When reports to this effect first circulated, the initial reaction was one of gloom, but upon further reflection it is apparent that there is a more positive aspect to this behavior—namely, that the American people expect more from government than their forebearers did and they will employ higher standards of performance to judge their leaders.

One feature of white ethnic discontent which has received little attention is that the grandsons and granddaughters of poor immigrants now demand a greater voice in decisions that affect their lives at home, at work, or in society at large. The New Populists must respond to such sentiments in a concrete fashion. On the community level, this means that representatives from white ethnic neighborhood organizations must be welcomed in those urban-oriented programs and political coalitions which presently are dominated by black and middle-class activists. Funds, technical expertise, and avenues of influence must be opened up to community organizations that have begun to burgeon in many white ethnic neighborhoods. There are numerous progressive leaders in these neighborhoods and they can play a pivotal role in breaking down the barrier of distrust which separates middle-class progressives and working people. They in turn need the kind of help that professional middle-class progressives possess and it is through such meaningful interaction that a New Populist coalition can be forged.

Professionals sensitive to the needs of workers at their place of employment can also help facilitate this objective. For example, they might follow the lead of Joe Rauh and lend their support to labor dissidents who are fighting autocratic or criminally controlled union leaders. In addition to his contribution to Arnold Miller's victory, Rauh has worked on behalf of Ed Sadlowski who broke the Germano machine control of District 31 in the Chicago/Gary area. The assistance Tony Massocchi received from progressive medical workers and doctors is another example of how middle-class professionals can play a critical role in workers' lives. Despite mutual distrust and past failures, the time has come for the resurrection of the alliance between workers and intellectuals which contributed to the success of the CIO.

In their activities, formal or ad hoc, the New Populists must make certain that representatives from the groups which they wish to aggregate into a coalition participate in policy-making matters from the outset. Thus, several years ago when consumer activists sponsored a tax action day in cities across the United States, they sought to include community representatives—many people who had never protested or marched before—in the planning of that event. This should be pro forma for the New Populists. One of the failures of the Movement in the 1960s was that middle-class activists planned events that were bound to fail because they never sought counsel from the people they purportedly sought to reach. The participation of people who represent various groups in the coalition is consistent with the premium which the New Populists place upon citizen action. It also is insurance against the use of rhetoric and tactics attractive to cosmopolitan activists but anathema to voters who represent an electoral majority.

The success of the New Populists then will largely depend upon their attracting in the 1970s voters who in many cases were on the "other side" during the 1960s, or at least were depicted as such. The prospects for recruiting white ethnic voters will increase immeasurably because of the presence of new breed ethnic leaders who know that the people they repre- sent and speak for are concerned about economic matters but also about the viability of values giving meaning and purpose to their lives. Not far removed from a working-class past, they know that the average working American is not entrenched in the middle class and that the blue-collar blues among young workers are real and not illusory. They also know that millions of people are frustrated because they cannot influence govern- ment or big business, and that it is not just a matter of meet- ing legitimate demands for economic security, better schools, protection against fast-buck realtors or remote government of- ficials—it is also a question of participating in decisions which are crucial to them. Working people everywhere want to have some voice in determining the values which the schools and the mass media convey to their children and some say in the future of their country. The New Populists must give them that chance.

Notes and Sources

CHAPTER ONE

1. Kevin P. Phillips, *The Emerging Republican Majority* (New Rochelle, N.Y.: Arlington House, 1969), pp. 39 and 44.

2. Ernest R. May and Janet Fraser, eds., *Campaign 1972* (Cambridge: Harvard University Press, 1973), p. 267.

3. William Raspberry, "Busing in Boston: Mr. Ford's Higher Responsibility," Washington *Post*, Oct. 11, 1964.

4. Kevin P. Phillips, *Mediacracy* (Garden City, N.Y.: Doubleday & Co., 1975), p. 74.

5. Arthur Schlesinger, Jr., "The 1969 Election," *Vital Speeches*, Dec. 15, 1968, p. 149.

6. New York *Times*, May 26, 1968.

7. Frederick G. Dutton, *Changing Sources of Power* (New York: McGraw-Hill, 1971), p. 4.

8. *Ibid.*, p. 118.

9. Seymour Martin Lipset, *Political Man* (Garden City, N.Y.: Doubleday & Co., 1963), p. 114.

10. *The Age of Reform* (New York: Vintage Books, 1955); *City Politics* (Cambridge: Harvard University Press, 1965).

11. Ben Wattenberg, *The Real America* (Garden City, N.Y.: Doubleday & Co., 1974).

12. Richard J. Krickus, "Organizing Neighborhoods: Gary and Newark," *The World of the Blue-Collar Worker*, ed. Irving Howe (New York: Quadrangle Books, 1972), pp. 72–88.

13. Gabriel Almond and Sidney Verba, *The Civic Culture*

(Princeton: Princeton University Press, 1963); Donald J. Devine, *The Political Culture of the United States* (Boston: Little, Brown & Co., 1972); Robert D. Hess and Judith V. Torney, *The Development of Political Attitudes in Children* (Garden City, N.Y.: Doubleday Anchor Books, 1968); Roberta S. Sigel, *Learning About Politics* (New York: Random House, 1970).

Chapter Two

1. John Higham, *Strangers in the Land* (New York: Atheneum, 1971), p. 324.

2. William V. Shannon, *The American Irish* (New York: Macmillan, 1964), pp. 28–29.

3. Seymour Martin Lipset and Earl Raab, *The Politics of Unreason* (New York: Harper and Row, 1970), p. 73.

4. *Ibid.*, p. 79.

5. Joseph G. Rayback, *A History of American Labor* (New York: The Free Press, 1966), pp. 156–57.

6. Edward G. Hartmann, *The Movement to Americanize the Immigrants* (New York: Columbia University Press, 1948), p. 66.

7. Philip Taylor, *The Distant Magnet* (London: Eyre & Spottiswoode, 1971), p. 239.

8. Madison Grant, *The Passing of the Great Race* (New York: Charles Scribner's Sons, 1916), pp. 89–90.

9. Higham, *op. cit.*, pp. 275–76.

10. *Ibid.*, p. 273.

11. Taylor, *op. cit.*, p. 16.

12. Gerald Rosemblum, *Immigrant Workers* (New York: Basic Books, 1973), p. 71.

13. *Ibid.*, p. 72.

14. Theodore Saloutos, *They Remember America* (Berkeley: University of California Press, 1956), p. 30.

15. Rosemblum, *op. cit.*, p. 33.

16. Humbert S. Nelli, *Italians in Chicago: 1880–1930* (New York: Oxford University Press, 1970), pp. 58–59.

17. *Ibid.*, p. 61.

18. Howard Morley Sachar, *The Course of Modern Jewish*

History (New York: Dell Publications, 1958), pp. 240–60. In this book the term "Russian Jews" will often be used to include Jews from all parts of Eastern Europe. This is in line with the practice of many writers at the turn of the century to distinguish the West European Jews from those who came from Poland, Lithuania, and other nations which were part of the Russian Empire.

19. Saloutos, *op. cit.*, p. 12.

20. Taylor, *op. cit.*, pp. 171–82.

21. Emily Dinwiddie, "Some Aspects of Italian History and Social Conditions in Philadelphia," ed. Lydio Tomasi, *The Italians in America* (New York: The Center for Migration Studies, 1972), p. 121.

22. Thorsten Sellin, "Crime and the Second Generation Immigrant," ed. Wayne Moquin, *Makers of America*, Vol. 8 (Chicago: Encyclopaedia Britannica Educational Corporation, 1971), pp. 135–38.

23. Luciano J. Iorizzo, "The Padrone and Immigrant Distribution," eds. S. M. Tomasi and M. H. Engel, *The Italian Experience in the United States* (Staten Island, N.Y.: Center for Migration Studies, 1970), pp. 50–51.

24. Alvin Toffler, *Future Shock* (New York: Bantam Books, 1972), pp. 11–12.

25. Caroline Golab, "The Impact of the Industrial Experience on the Immigrant Family," unpublished paper, pp. 31 and 29.

26. Herbert Gans, *The Urban Villagers* (New York: The Free Press, 1962), and Harold J. Abramson, *Ethnic Diversity in Catholic America* (New York: John Wiley & Sons, 1973).

27. Oscar Handlin, *The Uprooted* (New York: Grosset and Dunlap, 1951), p. 203.

28. Richard Gambino, *Blood of My Blood* (Garden City, N.Y.: Doubleday & Co., 1974), p. 301.

29. Robert E. Park and Herbert A. Miller, *Old World Traits Transplanted* (New York: Harper & Row, 1921), p. 211.

30. Joseph Lopreato, *Italian Americans* (New York: Random House, 1970), p. 88.

31. Nelli, *op. cit.*, pp. 181–82.

32. Andrew M. Greeley, *That Most Distressful Nation* (Chicago: Quadrangle Books, 1972), p. 93.

33. Joseph A. Wytrwal, *Poles in American History and Tradition* (Detroit: Endurance Press, 1969), pp. 262–63.

34. Marc Karson, *American Labor Unions and Politics* (Carbondale: Southern Illinois University Press, 1958), pp. 215 and 217.

35. John T. Ellis, *American Catholicism* (Chicago: University of Chicago Press, 1956), p. 136.

36. Robert E. Park, *The Immigrant Press and Its Control* (New York: Harper and Brothers, 1922), p. 93.

37. *Makers of America, op. cit.*, Vol. 4, pp. 65 and 67.

38. John Higham, "Introduction," Abraham Cahan, *The Rise of David Levinsky* (New York: Harper, 1966), p. v.

39. Park and Miller, *op. cit.*, pp. 106–7.

40. Park, *op. cit.*, p. 88.

41. Park and Miller, *op. cit.*, p. 228.

42. Park and Miller, *ibid.*, p. 239. While the ethnic benevolent associations left a lot to be desired, Edgar Litt suggests that they were to have a profound impact upon the white ethnics' perception of "welfare politics." ". . . the politics of reciprocal benevolence had its roots in the fraternal societies and welfare agencies constructed by successive ethnic groups, for the fundamental concept of the ethnic association was private welfare and it is but a small step to perceiving politics itself as a device for the trading of favors." *Ethnic Politics in America* (Glenville, Ill.: Scott Foresman & Co., 1970), p. 44.

43. John Fante, "The Odyssey of a Wop," ed. Oscar Handlin, *Children of the Uprooted* (New York: George Braziller, 1966), pp. 394–98.

44. Jane Addams, *Twenty Years at Hull House* (New York: A Signet Classic, 1961).

45. Higham, *op. cit.*, p. 245.

46. Colin Greer, *The Great School Legend* (New York: Basic Books, 1972), p. 108.

47. *Ibid.*, p. 84.

48. Charles E. Silberman, *Crisis in the Classroom* (New York: Vintage Books, 1970), p. 58.

49. Fante, *op. cit.*, p. 394.

CHAPTER THREE

1. Melvyn Dubofsky, *We Shall Be All* (Chicago: Quadrangle Books, 1969), p. 6.

2. Rosenblum, *op. cit.*, p. 75.

3. David Brody, *Steelworkers in America* (Cambridge: Harvard University Press, 1960), p. 141.

4. Nathan Glazer and Daniel P. Moynihan, *Beyond the Melting Pot* (Cambridge: M.I.T. Press, 1971), p. 192.

5. Dubofsky, *op. cit.*, p. 87.

6. Victor Greene, *The Slavic Community on Strike* (Notre Dame: Notre Dame University Press, 1972), p. 80.

7. *Ibid.*, p. 102.

8. *Ibid.*, pp. 108–9.

9. *Ibid.*, pp. 131–32.

10. *Ibid.*, p. 139.

11. *Ibid.*, p. 151.

12. *Ibid.*, p. 193.

13. *Ibid.*, p. 199.

14. William Cahn, *Mill Town* (New York: Camberon & Kahn, 1954), pp. 80–81.

15. Dubofsky, *op. cit.*, p. 228.

16. *Ibid.*

17. Patrick Renshaw, *The Wobblies* (New York: Anchor Books, 1968), pp. 103–4.

18. Dubofsky, *op. cit.*, p. 242.

19. *Ibid.*, p. 253.

20. David Brody, *Labor in Crisis* (Philadelphia: J. B. Lippincott Co., 1965), pp. 30–31.

21. Commission of Inquiry Interchurch World Movement, *Report on the Steel Strike of 1919* (New York: Harcourt, Brace and Howe, 1920), p. 85.

22. Brody, *Steelworkers in America, op. cit.*, pp. 100–1.

23. Commission of Inquiry, *op. cit.*, p. 104.

24. *Ibid.*, p. 15.

25. Brody, *Labor in Crisis, op. cit.*, pp. 132–33.

26. Commission of Inquiry, *op. cit.*, p. 43.

27. Brody, *Labor in Crisis, op. cit.,* p. 155.

28. *Ibid.,* p. 157.

29. *Ibid.,* p. 42.

30. Commission of Inquiry, *op. cit.,* p. 162.

31. Brody, *Labor in Crisis, op. cit.,* p. 157.

32. Philip S. Foner, *History of the Labor Movement in the United States,* Vol. 3 (New York: International Publishers, 1964), pp. 258–59.

33. Carroll Wright, "The Influences of Trade Unions Upon Immigrants," *Makers of America, op. cit.,* Vol. 6, p. 94.

34. *Ibid.*

35. *Ibid.,* p. 98.

36. *Ibid.,* p. 99.

<h3 style="text-align:center">CHAPTER FOUR</h3>

1. Park and Miller, *op. cit.,* p. 146.

2. Nathan Glazer, "Ethnic Groups in America," eds. Morroe Berger, Theodore Abel, and Charles H. Page, *Freedom and Control in Modern Society* (New York: D. Van Nostrand Co., 1954), p. 166.

3. Park and Miller, *op. cit.,* p. 136.

4. Park, *op. cit.,* p. 297; the data on the immigrant press in this chapter is all taken from this book.

5. Joseph S. Roucek, *American Lithuanians* (New York: Lithuanian Alliance of America, 1940).

6. Park and Miller, *op. cit.,* pp. 137–38.

7. James Weinstein, *The Decline of Socialism in America* (New York: Vintage Books, 1969), p. 183.

8. Park, *op. cit.,* p. 68.

9. Edgar Litt, *op. cit.,* p. 96.

10. James Q. Wilson and Edward Banfield, *op. cit.,* p. 125.

11. Richard Hofstadter, *op. cit.,* p. 9.

12. Fred I. Greenstein, "The Changing Pattern of Urban Party Politics," ed. Alan Shank, *Political Power and the Urban Crisis* (Boston: Holbrook Press, Inc., 1969), p. 157.

13. *Ibid.,* p. 158.

14. Shannon, *op. cit.,* pp. 69–70.

15. Elmer E. Cornwell, Jr., "Bosses, Machines and Ethnic Politics," eds. Harry H. Bailey, Jr., and Ellis Katz, *Ethnic Group Politics* (Columbus, Ohio: Charles E. Merrill Co., 1969), pp. 194–95.

16. Alex Gottfried, *Boss Cermak of Chicago* (Seattle: University of Washington Press, 1962).

17. Martin Meyerson and Edward C. Banfield, "A Machine at Work," ed. Edward C. Banfield, *Urban Government* (New York: The Free Press, 1969), pp. 169–70.

18. Mike Royko, *Boss* (New York: New American Library, 1971), pp. 62–63.

19. *Ibid.*, p. 84.

20. Litt, *op. cit.*

21. Louis L. Gerson, *The Hyphenate in Recent American Politics and Diplomacy* (Lawrence, Kansas: The University of Kansas Press, 1964), p. 62.

22. *Ibid.*, p. 104.

23. Everett Carll Ladd, Jr., *American Political Parties* (New York: W. W. Norton & Co., 1970), p. 162.

24. *Ibid.*, p. 165.

25. Samuel Lubell, *The Future of American Politics* (New York: Doubleday Anchor Books, 1956), p. 53.

26. *Ibid.*, p. 83.

27. Daniel Bell, *The End of Ideology* (New York: The Free Press, 1962), p. 145. Historically, ethnic gangs in America have sprung from an environment of economic deprivation fertilized by the premium our society places on money. The Irish, Jewish, and Italian gangsters embraced the ethics the Wasp tycoons favored, but, lacking the right connections, they resorted to tactics which brought widespread attention to their exploits. Prohibition afforded the ethnic gangs the opportunity to expand their gambling and white slavery activities, and it enabled criminal elements to bribe city officials to win contracts and participate in a host of legitimate enterprises—trucking, construction, etc. The ethnic hoods occasionally were generous, passing out money to needy members of the community, donating funds to build churches, or making it possible for one of their landsmen to go into business. But these men were hardly Robin Hoods as some writers would have us believe.

Criminals from every ethnic group have begun their careers among their own people, who become their first victims. Typically, the Italian grocer was compelled to purchase overpriced olive oil from thugs who had formerly lived in the same Sicilian village that he did. The kosher butcher paid protection money to extortionists who had fled Russian persecution just as he had. And the Irish longshoreman who had to pay for the right to labor on the docks often divvied up his paycheck with a loyal son of County Cork. In each case the majority of honest, hard-working people in the community suffered grievously from the presence of mobsters in their midst.

28. Peter Roberts, "The New Pittsburghers," *Makers of America*, Vol. 6, *op. cit.*, p. 126.

29. C. Wright Mills, *New Men of Power* (New York: Harcourt, Brace & World, 1948), p. 87.

30. Bernard Karsh and Phillips L. Garman, "The Impact of the Political Left," eds. Milton Derber and Edwin Young, *Labor and the New Deal* (Madison: University of Wisconsin Press, 1957), p. 83.

31. Seymour Martin Lipset, *The First New Nation* (Garden City, N.Y.: Anchor Books, 1967), p. 193.

32. Donald J. Devine, *op. cit.*, pp. 118–19.

33. Saul D. Alinsky, *John L. Lewis* (New York: Vintage Books, 1970), p. 184.

34. J. David Greenstone, *Labor in American Politics* (New York: Vintage Books, 1969), p. 67.

Chapter Five

1. Irving Howe, "Stevenson and the Intellectuals," *Dissent*, Winter 1954, p. 15.

2. Peter R. Rosenblatt, "The New Politics: A Cautionary Tale," Washington *Post*, Sept. 3, 1972.

3. Glazer and Moynihan, *op. cit.*, p. lix.

4. Bernard Rosenberg and Irving Howe, "American Jews: Are They Turning Right?" *Dissent*, Winter 1974, p. 32.

5. Andrew M. Greeley, *Why Can't They Be Like Us?* (New York: The American Jewish Committee, 1969), p. 73.

6. New York *Times*, Nov. 2, 1969.

7. Rosenblatt, *op. cit.*

8. Glazer and Moynihan, *op. cit.*, p. lxv.

9. Dutton, *op. cit.*, p. 207.

10. Haynes B. Johnson and George C. Wilson, *Army in Anguish* (New York: Pocket Books, 1972).

11. Charles A. Reich, *The Greening of America* (New York: Bantam Books, 1971), pp. 376 and 373.

12. Richard Scammon and Ben Wattenberg, *The Real Majority* (New York: Coward-McCann, Inc., 1970), pp. 48–54.

13. Dutton, *op. cit.*, p. 16.

14. Philip Converse et al., "Continuity and Change in American Politics: Parties and Issues in the 1968 Election," *American Political Science Review*, Dec. 1969, pp. 1106–19.

15. Richard Barnet, *Roots of War* (Baltimore: Penguin Books, Inc., 1972), p. 324.

16. *Ibid.*

17. *Ibid.*, p. 305.

18. "White Paper" distributed by AFL-CIO, "The McGovern Record."

19. Richard Hamilton, *Class and Politics in the United States* (New York: John Wiley & Sons, 1972), pp. 449–50.

20. *Ibid.*, p. 450.

21. *Ibid.*, p. 454.

22. The poll data cited here comes from the following sources: Patricia Cayo Sexton and Brendan Sexton, *Blue Collars and Hard Hats* (New York: Random House, 1971), p. 102; George Gallup, ed. *Gallup Poll* (New York: Random House, 1972), Vol. III, p. 2028; Gallup Index, Aug. 1972, p. 4; Gallup Index, Aug. 1972, p. 26; Gallup Index, Nov. 1973, p. 16; Gallup Index, Dec. 1973, p. 12.

23. Andrew Greeley, *Building Coalitions* (New York: Franklin Watts, 1974), p. 362.

24. Louis Harris, *The Anguish of Change* (New York: W. W. Norton, Inc., 1973), pp. 66–67.

25. Sextons, *op. cit.*, p. 99.

26. The Twadorski, Adubato, and Gaby references and others not footnoted are taken from personal interviews.

27. Mike Royko, "A Hard Look at Singer 59," Chicago *Daily News*, July 6, 1972.

28. Jack Newfeld, "Of Reform Hacks and Guideline Junkies," *Village Voice*, July 20, 1972.

29. Richard J. Krickus, "Why McGovern Turns Off the Ethnics," Washington *Post (Outlook)*, Nov. 5, 1972.

CHAPTER SIX

1. New York *Times*, July 27, 1972, and *Time*, May 12, 1975, p. 74.

2. "God May Be a Democrat But the Vote Is for Nixon," *Time*, Oct. 30, 1972.

3. Kevin P. Phillips, "The New Majority," Washington *Post*, Aug. 30, 1972. Phillips at a later date criticized Nixon for making a deal with congressional Democrats, costing Republicans running for the House and Senate dearly. See his *Mediacracy*.

4. Frederick K. Wirt et al., *On the City's Rim: Politics and Policy in Suburbia* (Lexington, Mass.: D. C. Heath & Co., 1972), pp. 49–81.

5. Perry L. Weed, *The White Ethnic Movement and Ethnic Politics* (New York: Praeger, 1973), pp. 156–88.

6. Mark R. Levy and Michael S. Kramer, *The Ethnic Factor* (New York: A Touchstone Book, 1973), p. 226. In assessing white ethnic voting data, it should be kept in mind that, in contrast to large religio-ethnic groups like the Irish Catholics, the Italian Catholics, and the Polish Catholics, precise data for smaller ethnic groups like the Lithuanians and Hungarians is not customarily available. Consequently, voting analysts in the United States subsume Lithuanians under the Slavic rubric. The Lithuanians are not Slavs but they and other small Eastern European ethnic groups in the United States are so designated because of data limitations.

7. Washington *Post*, Nov. 29, 1972.

8. Steve Adubato and Richard J. Krickus, "Stabilizing White Ethnic Neighborhoods," ed. Joseph A. Ryan, *White Ethnics: Life in Working-Class America* (Englewood Cliffs, N.J.: Prentice-Hall, Inc., 1973), pp. 82–93.

9. S. M. Miller, "Sharing the Burden of Change," ed. Louise Kapp Howe, *The White Majority* (New York: Vintage Books, 1970), pp. 279–93.

10. Richard Harwood, Washington *Post*, Sept. 29, 1969.

11. Adubato and Krickus, *op. cit.*, p. 86.

12. New York *Times*, Oct. 17, 1973.

13. Gans, *op. cit.*, pp. 281–335.

14. Harold Kaplan, *Urban Renewal Politics* (New York: Columbia University Press, 1963), p. 16.

15. Washington *Post*, June 20, 1973.

16. Robert C. Wood, "Small Town in a Great Society," *The Bemis Lecture Series*, Lincoln, Mass. (unpublished lecture, Dec. 8, 1967).

17. The quotations in this section are derivative of interviews the author conducted in the early 1970s.

18. For a more detailed discussion of these matters, see Richard J. Krickus, "The White Ethnics," *City* Magazine, May–June, 1971, pp. 23–33.

19. Theodore H. White, "The Making of the President, 1964" (New York: Atheneum Publishers, 1965), p. 234.

20. Levy and Kramer, *op. cit.*, pp. 225 and 240, and Gary R. Orren and William Schneider, "Ideological and Coalition Politics: The 1972 Presidential Primaries," unpublished manuscript.

21. Lipset and Raab, *op. cit.*, pp. 338–73.

22. Henry Cohen and Gary Sandrow, *Philadelphia Chooses a Mayor, 1971* (New York: American Jewish Committee, 1972) and Thomas F. Pettigrew, "When a Black Man Runs for Mayor," Harlan Hahn, *People and Politics in Urban Society* (Beverly Hills: Sage Publications, 1972), pp. 95–118.

23. Levy and Kramer, *op. cit.*, 109–17.

24. Glazer and Moynihan, *op. cit.*, pp. xxiii–iv and p. lxxiv.

25. In this section unnumbered quotations represent interviews the author conducted in Newark in the early 1970s.

26. Krickus, "Organizing Neighborhoods," *op. cit.*

27. *Whitetown, USA* (New York: Vintage Books, 1970).

28. Hamilton, *op. cit.*, pp. 405–506.

29. Press release, Urban League, Aug. 19, 1970.

30. Hamilton, *op. cit.*, p. 407.

31. Greeley, *Building Coalitions, op. cit.*, pp. 366–68.

32. *Ibid.*, p. 368.

33. Nathan Glazer, "The Issue of Cultural Pluralism Today," *Pluralism Beyond the Frontiers* (San Francisco: The American Jewish Committee, 1971), p. 5.

34. Greeley, *Building Coalitions, op. cit.*, p. 366.

35. Gambino, *op. cit.*, p. 300.

36. *Ibid.*, pp. 309 and 308.

37. Washington *Post*, Sept. 3, 1972.

CHAPTER SEVEN

1. Interview. While scholars and journalists have dwelt upon corruption associated with urban ethnic machines, they have failed to pay proper attention to political corruption in America. Our political science textbooks imply that political corruption is an aberration in our society, but it exists at all levels of government, in all parts of the United States, and involves every ethnic group.

2. "Notes Toward a Blue-Collar Reform Movement," Michael Wink, S. M. Tomasi, and Geno Baroni, *Pieces of a Dream* (New York: Center for Migration Studies, 1972), pp. 154–55.

3. Interview with Councilman Anthony Garafoli.

4. Raymond E. Wolfinger, *The Politics of Progress* (Englewood Cliffs, N.J.: Prentice-Hall, 1974), p. 63.

5. John Esposito and John Fiorillo, "Who's Left on the Block?" unpublished paper (New York Center for Ethnic Affairs, 1975), p. 50.

6. Glazer and Moynihan, *op. cit.*, p. 229.

7. Gambino, *op. cit.*, pp. 223–24; Andrew Greeley, *Ethnicity in the United States: A Preliminary Reconnaissance* (New York: John Wiley & Sons, 1974), pp. 64–87; and Levy and Kramer, *op. cit.*, pp. 143 and 166.

8. Joseph E. Finley, *The Corrupt Kingdom* (New York: Simon and Schuster, 1972), pp. 236–42.

9. *Ibid.*, p. 237.

10. Joseph C. Goulden, *Meany* (New York: Atheneum, 1972), p. 466.

11. Theodore H. White, *The Making of the President, 1968* (New York: Pocket Books, 1969), pp. 453–54.

12. Goulden, *op. cit.*, p. 230.

13. H. W. Benson, "Apathy and Other Axioms," Howe, *op. cit.*, p. 211.

14. Washington *Post*, August 13, 1975.

15. Unless otherwise indicated, the labor-related data in this section are derived from Jerry Wurf, "Labor Battles with Itself," Washington *Post*, Oct. 14, 1973.

16. *Ibid.*

17. Haynes Johnson and Nick Kotz, *The Unions* (New York: Pocket Books, 1972), p. 14.

18. *Ibid.*

19. The poll data below come from the following sources: George Gallup, *op. cit.*, Vol. III, p. 1706; *ibid.*, p. 2085; *ibid.*, p. 2154; *ibid.*, p. 2085; *ibid.*, p. 1992; Johnson and Kotz, *op. cit.*, p. 68; *ibid.*

20. Goulden, *op. cit.*, pp. 443–50.

21. *The American Worker: An Endangered Species* (New York: Ballantine Books, 1972), p. 6.

22. Interview.

23. Johnson and Kotz, *op. cit.*, p. 53.

24. Krickus, "Organizing Neighborhoods," *op. cit.*

25. Ellis W. Hawley, *The New Deal and the Problem of Monopoly* (Princeton: Princeton University Press, 1966).

26. Roland Radosh, *American Labor and United States Foreign Policy* (New York: Vintage Books, 1969).

27. John K. Galbraith, *Economics and the Public Purpose* (Boston: Houghton Mifflin, 1973).

28. Reo M. Christenson et al., *Ideologies and Modern Politics* (New York: Dodd, Mead & Co., 1971), p. 243.

29. For the classic exposition of pluralism, see Robert Dahl, *Who Governs?*, *op. cit.*

30. For empirical findings which clash with the pluralistic model of community power, see Edward C. Hayes, *Power Structure and Urban Policy* (New York: McGraw-Hill, 1972), and Michael Parenti, "Power and Pluralism: A View from the Bottom," *Journal of Politics* (August 1970), pp. 501–30.

31. For example, S. M. Lipset's *Political Man*, *op. cit.*, Thomas R. Dye and L. Harmon Zeigler, *The Irony of De-*

mocracy (Belmont, Calif.: Duxbury Press, second edition, 1972), and Almond and Verba's *The Civic Culture, op. cit.*

32. *The Real America* (Garden City, N.Y.: Doubleday & Co., 1974).

CHAPTER EIGHT

1. Jack Newfeld, "A Populist Manifesto," *New York* Magazine, July 19, 1971, p. 39.

2. Rudolph J. Vecoli, "Ethnicity: A Neglected Dimension of American History," ed. Murray Friedman, *Overcoming Middle Class Rage* (Philadelphia: The Westminster Press, 1971), p. 160.

3. Will Herberg, *Protestant, Catholic, Jew* (Garden City, N.Y.: Anchor Doubleday, 1960).

4. Michael Parenti, "Ethnic Politics and the Persistence of Ethnic Identification," *American Political Science Review*, Sept. 19, 1967, pp. 717–26.

5. Abramson, *Ethnic Diversity in Catholic America, op. cit.*

6. Gene Pasymowski, interview.

7. For a skeptical interpretation of rising white ethnic self-awareness, see Martin Kilson, "Blacks and Neo-Ethnicity in American Political Life," Nathan Glazer and Daniel P. Moynihan, *Ethnicity* (Cambridge: Harvard University Press, 1975), pp. 236–66.

8. Peter Dreier and Jack Nusan Porter, "Jewish Radicalism in Transition," *Society*, Jan./Feb. 1975, pp. 34–43.

9. Interview.

10. These figures were gathered in 1973. In August 1975 the United States Labor Department reported that 2.6 million workers belonged to public and professional employee associations. About four fifths of this group was associated with the National Education Association. As of 1974 white-collar membership in union and employee associations amounted to 5.9 million. This segment of the labor force that year accounted for 24.3 per cent of all union and employee association membership, Washington *Post*, August 13, 1975.

11. Washington *Post, ibid.*

12. Patricia Cayo Sexton, "Workers (Female) Arise!" *Dissent*, Summer 1974, pp. 380–95.

13. Dahl, *op. cit.*, p. 35.

14. Wolfinger, *op. cit.*, p. 49.

15. *Ibid.*, p. 55.

16. Gary C. Byrne and J. Kristian Pueschel, "But Who Should I Vote for County Coroner?" *Journal of Politics*, August 1974, p. 382.

17. Wolfinger, *op. cit.*, p. 35.

18. Levy and Kramer, *op. cit.*, p. 132.

19. Robert A. Lorinskas, Brett W. Hawkins, and Stephen D. Edwards, "The Persistence of Ethnic Voting in Urban and Rural Areas," Brett Hawkins and Robert A. Lorinskas, *The Ethnic Factor in American Politics* (Columbus, Ohio: Charles E. Merrill Co., 1970), pp. 124–33.

20. Abraham H. Miller, "Ethnicity and Party Identification," *Western Political Quarterly*, Sept. 1974, pp. 479–90.

21. Greeley, *Building Coalitions*, *op. cit.*, p. 356.

22. Robert Axelrod, "Communication to Editor," *American Political Science Review*, June 1974, pp. 717–20.

23. Levy and Kramer, *op. cit.*, p. 237.

24. Greeley, *Building Coalitions*, *op. cit.*

25. Pasymowski, interview.

26. Marc Fried, "Grieving for a Lost Home: Psychological Costs of Relocation," James Q. Wilson, *Urban Renewal* (Cambridge: M.I.T. Press, 1967), p. 366.

27. Gallup Poll, Index, Nov. 1974.

28. Poll data collected for U. S. Senate subcommittee on governmental relations, circulated by United Auto Workers, Community Action Department, 1974.

29. Greeley, *Building Coalitions*, *op. cit.*, p. 360.

30. *Ibid.*, p. 363.

Index

418   *Index*

DATE DUE

MAR 3 0 '87			
MAR 1 2 '91			
FEB 09 '95			
FEB 21 '95			
JAN 02 '96			
NOV 0 4 2005			
	261-2500		Printed in USA